Serverless Architectures on AWS

PETER SBARSKI

with Forewords by Patrick Debois
and Donald F. Ferguson

MANNING

SHELTER ISLAND

For online information and ordering of this and other Manning books, please visit
www.manning.com. The publisher offers discounts on this book when ordered in quantity.
For more information, please contact

> Special Sales Department
> Manning Publications Co.
> 20 Baldwin Road
> PO Box 761
> Shelter Island, NY 11964
> Email: orders@manning.com

Manning Publications Co.
20 Baldwin Road
PO Box 761
Shelter Island, NY 11964

Development editor:	Toni Arritola
Technical development editor:	Kostas Passadis
Project editors:	Kevin Sullivan and Janet Vail
Copyeditor:	Linda Recktenwald
Proofreader:	Melody Dolab
Technical proofreader:	David Fombella Pombal
Typesetter:	Dottie Marsico
Cover designer:	Marija Tudor

ISBN 9781617293825
Printed in the United States of America
2 3 4 5 6 7 8 9 10 – EBM – 22 21 20 19 18

To my mum and dad,
who always supported and encouraged my passion
for computing

contents

foreword

By Patrick Debois, DevOps Jedi
Founder of DevOpsDays
CTO, Small Town Heroes

Write programs that do one thing and do it well. Write programs designed to work together. These are the core ideas of the Unix philosophy, first articulated by Unix designer Ken Thompson. In recent years, companies like Google, Netflix, Uber, and Airbnb have proven that in modern distributed systems you can easily replace the word programs with the word services. The latest twist on this idea, serverless computing, is a manifestation of how the intelligent combination of hosted services and self-managing infrastructure can result in significant improvements in development time and operating cost.

Serverless Architectures on AWS balances emerging serverless design patterns with a set of practical, down-to-earth case studies, making it ideal for both beginners and advanced practitioners. Serverless is a new discipline, and this author succeeds in covering a wide spectrum of topics without losing depth and focus. He writes with clear passion, an eye for detail, and a treasure trove of knowledge to share.

Serverless computing requires a shift in how you build software architectures, and as with many paradigm shifts, you have to unlearn some of your habits. While being enthusiastic about the new technology, the author goes to great lengths to point out the benefits and limits of these new types of architectures. As a bonus, he gives insight into his own journey running a real-life serverless-based architecture. His "put your money where your mouth is" attitude shows the ultimate payoff of serverless, helping your business to focus and succeed.

foreword

By Dr. Donald F. Ferguson
CTO and Cofounder, Seeka TV
Adjunct professor,
Department of Computer Science,
Columbia University

Many technologies have profoundly transformed application development, testing, and delivery. Cloud computing and various forms of "as-a-service" are examples of technologies that are redefining application development and delivery. Many teams and projects struggle and sometimes fail when attempting to exploit new technology. The primary reason for failure is applying the current application architecture and programming model to a radically different technology. Well-designed, -implemented, and -delivered cloud-spanning applications are radically different from traditional applications. *Serverless Architectures on AWS* does an excellent job of explaining the new application architecture and provides detailed, practical guidance on how to succeed.

Infrastructure as a Service (IaaS), Software as a Service (SaaS) and Platform as a Service (PaaS) are cloud versions of the on-premise application and infrastructure architecture. The models deliver value but can never fully exploit the potential of the cloud. SaaS provides semi-standard solutions to business problems but doesn't enable rapid development and deployment of more targeted applications. IaaS and PaaS deliver resource usage efficiency but don't eliminate the cost to configure and manage software server infrastructure. None of these models enable exploitation of the explosion in web-callable APIs that form the API economy. *Serverless architectures* are the only architectures that eliminate the cost of server software and deliver the flexibility to rapidly develop, deploy, and manage targeted, focused cloud applications.

Part I—First Steps of this book provides the foundation for building serverless architecture. The section explains the new architecture's essential features and benefits. This includes a clear explanation of the technology's pros and cons and guidance for selection. Equally important, the section introduces *architecture design patterns*. Realizing best practices through applying design patterns is the single most important factor in the successful adoption of transformational computing technology. The section explains the patterns within the context of a real solution that the author implemented using serverless architectures: "Code rules and slides drool." The author's practical experience and success are a primary reason for my recommending this book.

People often mistakenly equate serverless with a specific technology; for example, AWS Lambda functions. Serverless architecture is much broader and includes UI design, publish/subscribe infrastructure, workflows/orchestration, active databases, API gateways and management, and data services. In aggregate, these technologies can be overwhelming. *Serverless Architectures on AWS* explains the contributing technologies' roles and uses. The book also provides a detailed walkthrough on how to use Amazon Web Services' implementation of the technology through building a working application. The initial cookbook and tutorial are core to being able to repeatably and reliably use the technology.

The data layer and security are two of the hardest architecture areas of any application. *Serverless Architectures on AWS* has detailed sections on both topics. The material explains the concepts (for example, authentication and authorization), positions the concepts within application scenarios (for example, web applications), and provides concrete, detailed examples of how to design and implement security and the data layer. The details include examples using non-AWS technology like Auth0 and Google Firebase.

My company is building its solution using AWS and serverless architecture. In this endeavor I've found this book and the author's other material to be essential to our progress. I teach advanced topics in computer science at Columbia University, where the classes focus on internet applications and cloud-spanning applications. This book's material is a foundation for much of what I teach. My experience demonstrates that *Serverless Architectures on AWS* is a pivotal book that's crucial to exploitation of cloud computing. The detailed information about AWS within the context of a real application is priceless, and the concepts and patterns apply to any serverless solution using any technology.

preface

The first time I heard about AWS Lambda was from Sam Kroonenburg. Lambda had just been released, but Sam was already excited by its prospects. He told me about execution of functions in the cloud, the potential for automation within AWS, and development of event-driven workflows. It was fascinating and full of endless potential. The thought of being able to run my code without having to provision or look after infrastructure seemed very cool and not a moment too soon. As a software engineer, I always wanted to focus on architecture and code rather than infrastructure, operations, and system management. Here was my opportunity to do so with Amazon Web Services.

After some months, the API Gateway came out and solved one of the biggest problems with Lambda at the time. It became possible to invoke Lambda functions using standard HTTP requests. The dream of creating fast, scalable back ends for applications without having to touch a server was happening right in front of us. The first major serverless project I worked on, started by Sam Kroonenburg, was A Cloud Guru, which grew into a large learning-management system. This platform, entirely serverless, cost very little to run and allowed for quick iteration cycles. It was a lot of fun to work on because we could focus on adding business value and new features without having to worry about infrastructure management or complex operations, and the platform could scale like crazy.

While building A Cloud Guru, we also realized that being serverless wasn't just about running code in Lambda. It was also about using third-party services and products. We used a managed authentication service and a managed database that saved us weeks, if not months, of development time. We identified aspects of our system that were important but that we didn't need to build, like payment processing and customer messaging. We found great third-party services that worked brilliantly with our serverless back end and integrated them with the rest of our system.

The third key component was, of course, selecting the right patterns and architectures. We recognized that event-driven architectures were natural to serverless applications, and we worked to make our entire system event-driven. We thought about security, reliability, and scalability, and how functions and back end services needed to be composed to make the most of them.

Having helped to build one of the first large-scale serverless applications and having reviewed other serverless systems since then, one thing is clear to me: the combination of scalable cloud functions, reliable third-party services, and serverless architectures and patterns is the next step in the evolution of cloud computing. Over the next few years, we'll see startups and established enterprises adopt the serverless approach. It will help them innovate and move more quickly than their competition. This book is a glimpse of what this future holds and an instruction manual for how to get started today. I hope that you enjoy *Serverless Architectures on AWS* and join me on this serverless journey.

acknowledgments

This book wouldn't have been written without the encouragement, feedback, and support of my colleagues, peers, family, and friends. I'm lucky to have been surrounded by talented people who lent me their ear and gave invaluable advice and opinion.

I'm grateful to many people for helping me, but there are a few I'd like to mention by name. First and foremost, I would like to thank my editor, Toni Arritola, who made the writing of this book a great experience. Toni's thoughtful feedback on the book's structure, language, and narrative was extraordinarily helpful. Her attention to detail, ability to respond at all times of the day, and enthusiasm were—and remain—second to none.

Austen Collins, the creator of the Serverless Framework, made a major contribution to the book in the form of a section on the Serverless Framework. There's no one better to write about a framework than its creator, so I'm thankful to Austen for volunteering his time and effort. I hope that everyone who reads this book—and, in particular, reads Austen's excellent treatise—spends time learning, understanding, and adopting the Serverless Framework.

I'd also like to thank Sam Kroonenburg, who introduced me to the serverless way and helped with thoughtful feedback and review throughout the writing of this book. Sam's enthusiasm for AWS Lambda and ideas on architecture and design inspired me to put pen to paper in the first place. Another special thank-you goes to Ryan Brown, who read the book and gave detailed, blow-by-blow commentary and critique. This book is far better for Ryan's reading and careful and considered feedback.

Additional thanks must go out to Donald Ferguson and Patrick Debois for writing two very special forewords. Donald and Patrick have done a lot for software engineering and for the serverless community especially. I'm in awe of their accomplishments and very thankful for their time and involvement.

I'd like to thank a few others who gave me feedback and encouragement. These people include Ryan Kroonenburg, Mike Chambers, John McKim, Adrian Cantrill, Daniel Parker, Allan Brown, Nick Triantafillou, Drew Firment, Neil Walker, Alex Mackey, and Ilia Mogilevsky. I'd like to thank Mike Stephens of Manning, Kostas Passadis, and David Fombella Pombal for helping to bring this book to fruition. In addition, these acknowledgments wouldn't be complete if I didn't thank the Manning reviewers who generously read and commented on the text during its development, including Alain Couniot, Andy Wiesendanger, Colin Joyce, Craig Smith, Daniel Vásquez, Diego Santiviago, John Huffman, Josiah Dykstra, Kent R. Spillner, Markus Breuer, Saioa Picado Fernández, Sau Fai Fong, Sean Hull, and Vijaykumar Borkar.

Finally, I'd like to thank my family, including my dad and brother, and all my other relatives, for finding the inner strength to listen to me talk about the book at every gathering. And I'd like to thank Durdana Masud, who helped me greatly throughout my writing, starting with positive cheer and inspiration to looking at umpteen color palettes in an effort to help me select colors for the original images used in the manuscript. Thank you.

about this book

Whether you are a beginner or an expert, just starting out in IT or have years of experience, this book will take you on a journey through serverless architectures. You'll learn about key patterns, find out about the pros and cons of applying serverless methodologies, and build your own serverless video-sharing website using AWS Lambda, API Gateway, Elastic Transcoder, S3, Auth0, and Firebase. You'll also learn a lot about AWS and recommended frameworks for organizing and deploying your serverless applications.

This book is organized into three parts. The first takes you through basic serverless principles and discusses key architectures and patterns. You begin building your first event-driven pipeline using AWS Lambda and learn about key AWS services, like the omnipresent and all-powerful Identity and Access Management service.

The second part focuses on authentication and authorization, AWS Lambda, and the API Gateway. All chapters in this part are important to understanding and building serverless applications. After you read and work through them, you'll have a thorough grasp of the key technologies needed for serverless applications.

The third part addresses those additional services and architectures needed to build real-world applications. A key focus is file and data storage using S3 and Google's Firebase, respectively. The final chapter adds more information about some of the techniques and services that you can apply to grow your serverless applications.

At the end of the book, you'll find seven appendixes that give you additional information on various topics. The last appendix, for example, covers the Serverless Framework and the Serverless Application Mode (SAM); you should definitely read through and try the steps in this appendix.

AWS and other services like Auth0 and Firebase evolve quickly, so don't be surprised if some of the screenshots or instructions are different by the time you read this book. The fundamentals of serverless event-driven architectures remain the same, but some of the minor things, such as button positioning or labels, may change over time. This book is suitable for developers and solution architects who are new to AWS and cloud computing, as well as for those who are veterans. My hope is that you'll discover a new way to build applications that is cheaper, more scalable, and heaps more fun!

Code conventions

This book provides many examples of code. These appear throughout the text and as separate code listings. Code appears in a `fixed-width font just like this`, so you'll know when you see it.

Getting the source code

All of the source code used in the book is available on the Manning website (https://manning.com/books/serverless-architectures-on-aws) or in my GitHub repository (https://github.com/sbarski/serverless-architectures-aws). I love GitHub, so if you'd like to contribute to the source code, please open a pull request. If you see a problem, please file an issue.

Author online

Purchase of *Serverless Architectures on AWS* includes free access to a private web forum run by Manning Publications where you can make comments about the book, ask technical questions, and receive help from the lead author and from other users. To access the forum and subscribe to it, point your web browser to www.manning.com/books/serverless-architectures-on-aws. This page provides information on how to get on the forum once you are registered, what kind of help is available, and the rules of conduct on the forum.

Manning's commitment to our readers is to provide a venue where a meaningful dialog between individual readers and between readers and the author can take place. It is not a commitment to any specific amount of participation on the part of the author, whose contribution to the forum remains voluntary (and unpaid). We suggest you try asking the author some challenging questions lest his interest stray! The Author Online forum and the archives of previous discussions will be accessible from the publisher's website as long as the book is in print.

about the author

 PETER SBARSKI is Vice President of Engineering at A Cloud Guru and the organizer of Serverlessconf, the world's first conference dedicated entirely to serverless architectures and technologies. He enjoys running in-person workshops and writing an occasional blog post on serverless architectures. Peter has an extensive career working in IT and has led teams across large enterprise solutions with a focus on web and AWS cloud technologies. His specialties include back end architecture, microservices, and orchestration of systems.

Peter holds a PhD in computer science from Monash University, Australia, and can be followed on Twitter (@sbarski) and GitHub (https://github.com/sbarski).

about the cover

The figure on the cover of *Serverless Architectures on AWS* is captioned "Man from Stupno/Sisak, Croatia." The illustration is taken from a reproduction of an album of Croatian traditional costumes from the mid-nineteenth century by Nikola Arsenović, published by the Ethnographic Museum in Split, Croatia, in 2003. The illustrations were obtained from a helpful librarian at the Ethnographic Museum in Split, itself situated in the Roman core of the medieval center of the town: the ruins of Emperor Diocletian's retirement palace from around AD 304. The book includes finely colored illustrations of figures from different regions of Croatia, accompanied by descriptions of the costumes and of everyday life.

Dress codes and lifestyles have changed over the last 200 years, and the diversity by region, so rich at the time, has faded away. It's now hard to tell apart the inhabitants of different continents, let alone of different hamlets or towns separated by only a few miles. Perhaps we have traded cultural diversity for a more varied personal life—certainly for a more varied and fast-paced technological life. Manning celebrates the inventiveness and initiative of the computer business with book covers based on the rich diversity of regional life of two centuries ago, brought back to life by illustrations from old books and collections like this one.

Part 1

First steps

You're now taking the first steps toward mastery of serverless architectures. The first part of this book takes you through the concepts and introduces you to the five principles of serverless architectures. You'll learn about several useful designs and architectures, and you'll begin building your own media-transcoding pipeline using Lambda, S3, and the Elastic Transcoder. Beginning with the third chapter and continuing thereafter, you'll find fun exercises to try in your spare time. These exercises are optional but highly recommended, because they'll reinforce your knowledge and understanding of serverless technologies and architectures.

Going serverless

This chapter covers

- Traditional system and application architectures
- Key characteristics of serverless architectures and their benefits
- How serverless architectures and microservices fit into the picture
- Considerations when transitioning from server to serverless

If you ask software developers what software architecture is, you might get answers ranging from "it's a blueprint or a plan" to "a conceptual model" to "the big picture." It's undoubtedly true that architecture, or lack thereof, can make or break software. Good architecture may help to scale a web or mobile application, and poor architecture may cause serious issues that necessitate a costly rewrite. Understanding the implication of choice regarding architecture and being able to plan ahead is paramount to creating effective, high-performing, and ultimately successful software systems.

This book is about how to go beyond traditional back-end architectures that require you to interact with a server in some shape or form. It describes how to create *serverless* back ends that rely entirely on a compute service such as Amazon Web Services (AWS) Lambda and an assortment of useful third-party APIs, services, and products. It shows how to build the next generation of systems that can scale and handle demanding computational requirements without having to provision or manage a single server. Importantly, this book describes techniques that can help developers quickly deliver products to market while maintaining a high level of quality and performance by using services and architectures that today's cloud has to offer.

The first chapter of this book is about why we think serverless is a game changer for software developers and solution architects. This chapter introduces key services such as AWS Lambda and describes the principles of serverless architecture to help you understand what makes a true serverless system.

What's in a name?

Before we start, we should mention that the word *serverless* is a bit of a misnomer. Whether you use a compute service such as AWS Lambda to execute your code, or interact with an API, there are still servers running in the background. The difference is that these servers are hidden from you. There's no infrastructure for you to think about and no way to tweak the underlying operating system. Someone else takes care of the nitty-gritty details of infrastructure management, freeing your time for other things. Serverless is about running code in a compute service and interacting with services and APIs to get the job done.

1.1   How we got to where we are

If you look at systems powering most of today's web-enabled software, you'll see back-end servers performing various forms of computation and client-side front ends providing an interface for users to operate via their browser, mobile, or desktop device.

In a typical web application, the server accepts HTTP requests from the front end and processes requests. Data might travel through numerous application layers before being saved to a database. The back end, finally, generates a response—it could be in the form of JSON or fully rendered markup—which is sent back to the client (figure 1.1). Naturally, most systems are more complex once elements such as load balancing, transactions, clustering, caching, messaging, and data redundancy are taken into account. Most of this software requires servers running in data centers or in the cloud that need to be managed, maintained, patched, and backed up.

Provisioning, managing, and patching of servers is a time-consuming task that often requires dedicated operations people. A non-trivial environment is hard to set up and operate effectively. Infrastructure and hardware are necessary components of any IT system, but they're often also a distraction from what should be the core focus—solving the business problem.

Over the past few years, technologies such as platform as a service (PaaS) and containers have appeared as potential solutions to the headache of inconsistent infrastructure

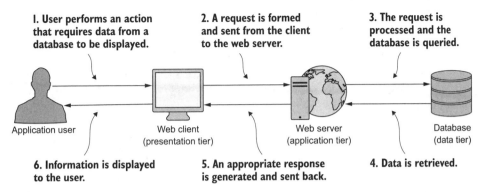

1. User performs an action that requires data from a database to be displayed.

2. A request is formed and sent from the client to the web server.

3. The request is processed and the database is queried.

Application user

Web client (presentation tier)

Web server (application tier)

Database (data tier)

6. Information is displayed to the user.

5. An appropriate response is generated and sent back.

4. Data is retrieved.

Figure 1.1 This is a basic request-response (client-server) message exchange pattern that most developers are familiar with. There's only one web server and one database in this figure. Most systems are much more complex.

environments, conflicts, and server management overheard. PaaS is a form of cloud computing that provides a platform for users to run their software while hiding some of the underlying infrastructure. To make effective use of PaaS, developers need to write software that targets the features and capabilities of the platform. Moving a legacy application designed to run on a standalone server to a PaaS service often leads to additional development effort because of the ephemeral nature of most PaaS implementations. Still, given a choice, many developers would understandably choose to use PaaS rather than more traditional, more manual solutions thanks to reduced maintenance and platform support requirements.

Containerization is a way of isolating an application with its own environment. It's a lightweight alternative to full-blown virtualization. Containers are isolated and lightweight but they need to be deployed to a server—whether in a public or private cloud or onsite. They're an excellent solution when dependencies are in play, but they have their own housekeeping challenges and complexities. They're not as easy as being able to run code directly in the cloud.

Finally, we make our way to Lambda, which is a compute service from Amazon Web Services. Lambda can execute code in a massively parallelized way in response to events. Lambda takes your code and runs it without any need to provision servers, install software, deploy containers, or worry about low-level detail. AWS takes care of provisioning and management of their Elastic Compute Cloud (EC2) servers that run the actual code and provides a high-availability compute infrastructure—including capacity provisioning and automated scaling—that the developer doesn't need to think about. The words *serverless architectures* refer to these new kinds of software architectures that don't rely on direct access to a server to work. By taking Lambda and making use of various powerful single-purpose APIs and web services, developers can build loosely coupled, scalable, and efficient architectures quickly. *Moving away from servers and infrastructure concerns, as well as allowing the developer to primarily focus on code, is the ultimate goal behind serverless.*

1.1.1 *Service-oriented architecture and microservices*

Among system and application architectures, service-oriented architecture (SOA) has a lot of name recognition among software developers. It's an architecture that clearly conceptualized the idea that a system can be composed of many independent services. Much has been written about SOA, but it remains controversial and misunderstood because developers often confuse design philosophy with specific implementation and attributes.

SOA doesn't dictate the use of any particular technology. Instead, it encourages an architectural approach in which developers create autonomous services that communicate via message passing and often have a schema or a contract that defines how messages are created or exchanged. Service reusability and autonomy, composability, granularity, and discoverability are all important principles associated with SOA.

Microservices and serverless architectures are spiritual descendants of service-oriented architecture. They retain many of the aforementioned principles and ideas while attempting to address the complexity of old-fashioned service-oriented architectures.

ON MICROSERVICES

There has been a recent trend to implement systems with microservices. Developers tend to think of microservices as small, standalone, fully independent services built around a particular business purpose or capability.

Ideally, microservices should be easy to replace, with each service written in an appropriate framework and language. The mere fact that microservices can be written in different general-purpose or domain-specific languages (DSL) is a drawing card for many developers. Benefits can be gained from using the right language or a specialized set of libraries for the job. Nevertheless, it can often be a trap, too. Having a mix of languages and frameworks can be hard to support, and, without strict discipline, can lead to confusion down the road.

Each microservice can maintain state and store data. And if microservices are correctly decoupled, development teams can work and deploy microservices independently of one another. On the other hand, eventual consistency, transaction management, and complex error recovery can make things more difficult (especially without a sound plan).

It can be argued that serverless architecture embodies many principles from microservices too. After all, depending on how you design the system, every compute function could be considered to be its own standalone service. But you don't need to fully embrace the microservices mantra if you don't want to.

Serverless architectures give you the freedom to apply as few or as many microservice principles as you would like without forcing you down a single path. This book shows examples of architectures where parts of a monolithic system are re-implemented as serverless architecture without applying all of the microservices tenets. It's then up to you to decide how far to take your architecture based on your requirements and preference (chapter 10 has more to say on the issue of microservices and design).

1.1.2 *Software design*

Software design has evolved from the days of code running on a mainframe to multi-tier systems where the presentation, data, and application/logic tiers feature prominently in many designs. Within each tier there may be multiple logical layers that deal with particular aspects of functionality or domain. There are also cross-cutting components, such as logging or exception-handling systems, that can span numerous layers. The preference for layering is understandable. Layering allows developers to decouple concerns and have more maintainable applications.

But the converse can also be true. Having too many layers can lead to inefficiencies. A small change can often cascade and cause the developer to modify every layer throughout the system, costing considerable time and energy in implementation and testing. The more layers there are, the more complex and unwieldy the system might become over time. Figure 1.2 shows an example of a tiered architecture with multiple layers.

Serverless architectures can help with the problem of layering and having to update too many things. There's room for developers to remove or minimize layering by breaking the system into functions and allowing the front end to securely communicate with services and even the database directly, as shown in figure 1.3. All of this can be done in an organized way to prevent spaghetti implementations and dependency nightmares by clearly defining service boundaries, allowing Lambda functions to be autonomous, and planning how functions and services will interact.

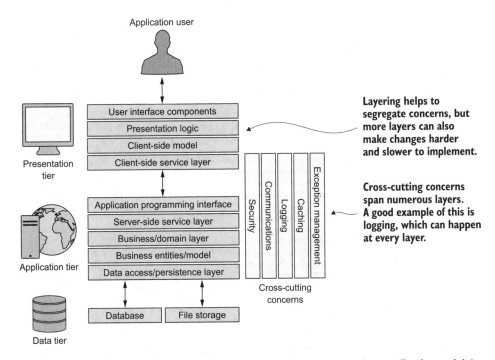

Figure 1.2 A typical three-tier application is usually made up of presentation, application, and data tiers. A tier may have multiple layers with specific responsibilities.

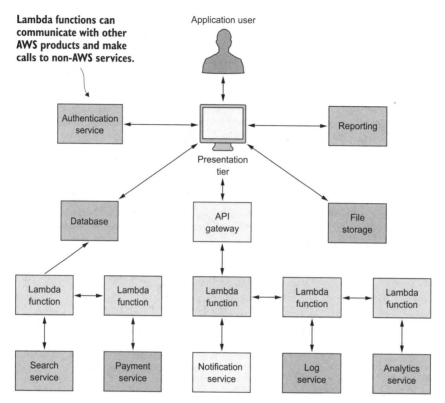

Figure 1.3   In a serverless architecture there's no single traditional back end. The front end of the application communicates directly with services, the database, or compute functions via an API gateway. Some services, however, must be hidden behind compute service functions, where additional security measures and validation can take place.

A serverless approach doesn't solve all problems, nor does it remove the underlying intricacies of the system. But when implemented correctly it can provide opportunities to reduce, organize, and manage complexity. A well-planned serverless architecture can make future changes easier, which is an important factor for any long-term application. The next section and later chapters discuss the organization and orchestration of services in more detail.

Tiers vs. layers

There is confusion among some developers about the difference between layers and tiers. A *tier* is a module boundary that exists to provide isolation between major components of a system. A presentation tier that's visible to the user is separate from the application tier, which encompasses business logic. In turn, the data tier is another separate system that can manage, persist, and provide access to data. Components grouped in a tier can physically reside on different infrastructures.

Layers are logical slices that carry out specific responsibilities in an application. Each tier can have multiple layers within it that are responsible for different elements of functionality such as domain services.

1.2 Principles of serverless architectures

Here we define five principles of serverless architectures that describe how an ideal serverless system should be built. Use these principles to help guide your decisions when building serverless applications:

1. Use a compute service to execute code on demand (no servers).
2. Write single-purpose stateless functions.
3. Design push-based, event-driven pipelines.
4. Create thicker, more powerful front ends.
5. Embrace third-party services.

Let's look at each of these principles in more detail.

1.2.1 Use a compute service to execute code on demand

Serverless architectures are a natural extension of ideas raised in SOA. In serverless architecture all custom code is written and executed as isolated, independent, and often granular functions that are run in a stateless compute service such as AWS Lambda. Developers can write functions to carry out almost any common task, such as reading and writing to a data source, calling out to other functions, and performing a calculation. In more complex cases, developers can set up more elaborate pipelines and orchestrate invocations of multiple functions. There might be scenarios where a server is still needed to do something. These cases, however, may be far and few between, and as a developer you should avoid running and interacting with a server if possible.

So, what is Lambda exactly?

AWS Lambda is a compute service that executes code written in JavaScript (node.js), Python, C#, or Java on AWS infrastructure. Source code (JARs or DLLs in case of Java or C#) is zipped up and deployed to an isolated container that has an allocation of memory, disk space, and CPU. The combination of code, configuration, and dependencies is typically referred to as a *Lambda function*. The Lambda runtime can invoke a function multiple times in parallel. Lambda supports push and pull event models of operation and integrates with a large number of AWS services. Chapter 6 covers Lambda in more detail, including its event model, methods of invocation, and best practice with regard to design. Note that Lambda isn't the only game in town. Microsoft Azure Functions, IBM Bluemix, OpenWhisk, and Google Cloud Functions are other compute services you might want to look at.

1.2.2 *Write single-purpose stateless functions*

As a software engineer, you should try to design your functions with the single responsibility principle (SRP) in mind. A function that does just one thing is more testable and robust and leads to fewer bugs and unexpected side effects. By composing and combining functions and services in a loose orchestration, you can build complex back-end systems that are still understandable and easy to manage. A granular function with a well-defined interface is also more likely to be reused within a serverless architecture.

Code written for a compute service such as Lambda should be created in a *stateless* style. It must not assume that local resources or processes will survive beyond the immediate session (chapter 6 has more to say on this). Statelessness is powerful because it allows the platform to quickly scale to handle an ever-changing number of incoming events or requests.

1.2.3 *Design push-based, event-driven pipelines*

Serverless architectures can be built to serve any purpose. Systems can be built serverless from scratch, or existing monolithic applications can be gradually reengineered to take advantage of this architecture. The most flexible and powerful serverless designs are event-driven. In chapter 3, for example, you'll build an event-driven, push-based pipeline to see how quickly you can put together a system to encode video to different bitrates and formats. You'll achieve this by connecting Amazon's Simple Storage Service (S3), Lambda, and Elastic Transcoder together (figure 1.4).

Building event-driven, push-based systems will often reduce cost and complexity (you won't need to run extra code to poll for changes) and potentially make the overall user experience smoother. It goes without saying that although event-driven, push-based models are a good goal, they might not be appropriate or achievable in all circumstances. Sometimes you'll have to implement a Lambda function that polls the event source or runs on a schedule. We'll cover different event models and you'll work through examples in later chapters.

1.2.4 *Create thicker, more powerful front ends*

It's important to remember that custom code running in Lambda should be quick to execute. Functions that terminate sooner are cheaper because Lambda pricing is based on the number of requests, the duration of execution, and the amount of allocated memory. Having less to do in Lambda is cheaper. Moreover, building a rich front end (in lieu of a complex back end) that can talk to third-party services directly can be conducive to a better user experience. Fewer hops between online resources and reduced latency will result in a better perception of performance and usability of the application. In other words, you don't have to route everything through a compute service. Your front end may be able to communicate directly with a search provider, a database, or another useful API.

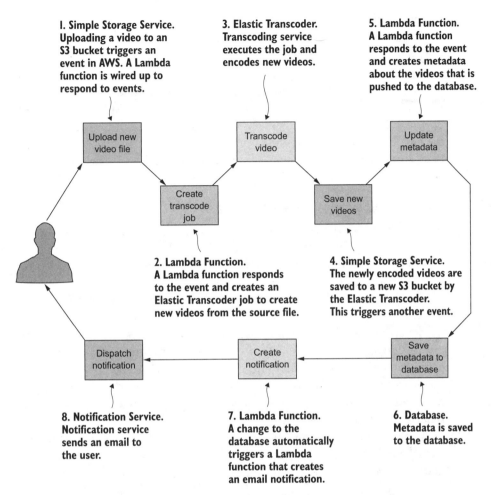

Figure 1.4 A push-based pipeline style of design works well with serverless architectures. In this example a user uploads a video, which is transcoded to a different format.

Digitally signed tokens can allow front ends to talk to disparate services, including databases, in a secure manner. This is in contrast to traditional systems where all communication flows through the back-end server.

Not everything, however, can or should be done in the front end. There are secrets that cannot be trusted to the client device. Processing a credit card or sending emails to subscribers must be done only by a service that runs outside the end user's control. In this case, a compute service must be used to coordinate action, validate data, and enforce security.

The other important point to consider is consistency. If the front end is responsible for writing to multiple services and fails midway through, it can leave the system in an inconsistent state. In this scenario, a Lambda function should be used because it can be designed to gracefully handle errors and retry failed operations.

1.2.5   *Embrace third-party services*

Third-party services are welcome to join the show if they can provide value and reduce custom code. It goes without saying, however, that when a third-party service is considered, factors such as price, capability, availability, documentation, and support must be assessed. It's far more useful for developers to spend time solving a problem unique to their domain than re-creating functionality already implemented by someone else. Don't build for the sake of building if viable third-party services and APIs are available. Stand on the shoulders of giants to reach new heights. Appendix A has a short list of Amazon Web Services and non-Amazon Web Services we've found useful. We'll look at most of those services in more detail as we move through the book.

1.3   *Transitioning from a server to services*

One advantage of the serverless approach is that existing applications can be gradually converted to serverless architecture. If a developer is faced with a monolithic code base, they can gradually tease it apart and create Lambda functions that the application can communicate with.

The best approach is to initially create a prototype to test developer assumptions about how the system would function if it was going to be partly or fully serverless. Legacy systems tend to have interesting constraints that require creative solutions; and as with any architectural refactors at a large scale, there are inevitably going to be compromises. The system may end up being a hybrid—see figure 1.5—but it may be better to have some of its components use Lambda and third-party services rather than remain with an unchanged legacy architecture that no longer scales or that requires expensive infrastructure to run.

The transition from a legacy, server-based application to a scalable serverless architecture may take time to get right. It needs to be approached carefully and slowly, and developers need to have a good test plan and a great DevOps strategy in place before they begin.

1.4   *Serverless pros and cons*

There are advantages to implementing a system as fully or partially serverless, including reduced cost and accelerated time to market. But you need to carefully consider the road to serverless architecture in the context of the application being created.

1.4.1   *Decision drivers*

Serverless is not a silver bullet in all circumstances. It may not be appropriate for latency-sensitive applications or software with specific service-level agreements (SLA). Vendor lock-in can be an issue for enterprise and government clients, and decentralization of services can be a challenge.

NOT FOR EVERYONE

Lambda runs in a public cloud, so mission-critical applications shouldn't necessarily be based on it. A banking system that performs high-volume transactions or a patient

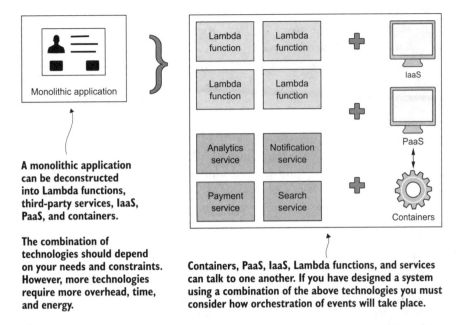

A monolithic application can be deconstructed into Lambda functions, third-party services, IaaS, PaaS, and containers.

The combination of technologies should depend on your needs and constraints. However, more technologies require more overhead, time, and energy.

Containers, PaaS, IaaS, Lambda functions, and services can talk to one another. If you have designed a system using a combination of the above technologies you must consider how orchestration of events will take place.

Figure 1.5　Serverless architecture is not an all-or-nothing proposition. If you currently have a monolithic application running on servers, you can begin to gradually extract components and run them in isolated services or compute functions. You can decouple a monolithic application into an assortment of infrastructure as a service (IaaS), PaaS, containers, Lambda functions, and third-party services if it helps.

life-support system requires a higher level of performance and reliability than a public cloud system can provide. It's possible that organizations could employ dedicated hardware or run private or hybrid clouds with their own compute services that might meet serviceability and reliability requirements. In that case, these architectures could be adopted.

SERVICE LEVELS

AWS has an SLA for some services but not for others, so that may be a factor in your decision. For most systems, the reliability offered by AWS is sufficient, but some enterprise use cases may require additional guarantees. Non-AWS third-party services are in the same boat. Some may have strong SLAs, whereas others may not have one at all.

CUSTOMIZATION

When it comes to Lambda, the efficiencies gained from having Amazon look after the platform and scale functions come at the expense of being able to customize the operating system or tweak the underlying instance. You can modify the amount of RAM allocated to a function and change timeouts, but that's about it (see chapter 6 for more information). Similarly, different third-party services will have varying levels of customization and flexibility.

VENDOR LOCK-IN

Vendor lock-in is another issue. If a developer decides to use third-party APIs and services, including AWS, there's a chance that architecture could become strongly coupled to the platform being used. The implications of vendor lock-in and the risk of using third-party services—including company viability, data sovereignty and privacy, cost, support, documentation, and available feature set—need to be thoroughly considered.

DECENTRALIZATION

Moving from a monolithic approach to a more decentralized serverless approach doesn't automatically reduce the complexity of the underlying system either. The distributed nature of the solution can introduce its own challenges because of the need to make remote rather than in-process calls and the need to handle failures and latency across a network.

1.4.2 When to use serverless

Serverless architecture allows developers to focus on software design and code rather than infrastructure. Scalability and high availability are easier to achieve, and the pricing is often fairer because you pay only for what you use. Importantly with serverless, you have a potential to reduce some of the complexity of the system by minimizing the number of layers and amount of code you need.

NO MORE SERVERS

Tasks such as server configuration and management, patching, and maintenance are taken care of by the vendor, which saves time and money. Amazon looks after the health of its fleet of servers that power Lambda. If you don't have specific requirements to manage or modify compute resources, then having Amazon or another vendor look after them is a great solution. You're responsible only for your own code, leaving operational and administrative tasks to a different set of capable hands.

MANY USES

The statelessness and scalability of compute can be used to solve problems that benefit from parallel processing. Back ends for CRUD applications, e-commerce, back-office systems, complex web apps, and all kinds of mobile and desktop software can be built quickly using serverless architectures. Tasks that used to take weeks can be done in days or hours as long as the right combination of technologies is chosen. A serverless approach can work exceptionally well for startups that want to innovate and move quickly.

LOW COST

The traditional server-based architecture requires servers that don't necessarily run at full capacity all of the time. Scaling, even with automated systems, involves a new server, which is often wasted until there's a temporary upsurge in traffic or new data. Serverless systems are much more granular with regard to scaling and are cost-effective, especially when peak loads are uneven or unexpected. With Lambda you only pay for what you use (chapter 4 shows how to calculate cost for Lambda and the API Gateway).

LESS CODE

We mentioned at the start of the chapter that serverless architecture provides an opportunity to reduce some of the complexity and code in comparison to more traditional systems. There's less need to have a multilayered back-end system, especially if you allow the front end to do more work and talk to services (and the database) directly.

SCALABLE AND FLEXIBLE

As a developer you don't need to use serverless architecture to replace your entire back end if you don't want to or are unable to do so. You can use Lambda to solve specific problems, especially if they stand to benefit from parallelization. It goes without saying that serverless systems can scale more easily than traditional systems. For example, consider the following solutions:

- ConnectWise, an IT services company, uses Lambda to process inbound logs, which has reduced their server maintenance needs from weeks to hours (https://aws.amazon.com/solutions/case-studies/connectwise/).
- Netflix uses Lambda to automate validation of backup completions and automate the encoding process of media files (https://aws.amazon.com/solutions/case-studies/netflix-and-aws-lambda/).

You can use Lambda for extract, transform, and load (ETL) jobs, real-time file processing, and virtually anything else without having to touch your existing codebase. Just write a function and run it.

1.5   *Summary*

The cloud has been and continues to be a game changer for IT infrastructure and software development. Software developers need to think about the ways they can maximize use of cloud platforms to gain a competitive advantage.

Serverless architectures are the latest advance for developers and organizations to think about, study, and adopt. This exciting new shift in architecture will grow quickly as software developers embrace compute services such as AWS Lambda. And, in many cases, serverless applications will be cheaper to run and faster to implement.

There's also a need to reduce complexity and costs associated with running infrastructure and carrying out development of traditional software systems. The reduction in cost and time spent on infrastructure maintenance and the benefits of scalability are good reasons for organizations and developers to consider serverless architectures.

In this chapter you learned what serverless architecture is, looked at its principles, and saw how it compares to traditional architectures. In the next chapter, we'll explore important architectures and patterns, and we'll discuss specific use cases where serverless architectures were used to solve a problem.

Architectures and patterns

This chapter covers

- Use cases for serverless architectures
- Examples of patterns and architectures

What are the use cases for serverless architectures, and what kinds of architectures and patterns are useful? We're often asked about use cases as people learn about a serverless approach to the design of systems. We find that it's helpful to look at how others have applied technology and what kinds of use cases, designs, and architectures they've produced. Our discussion will center on these use cases and sample architectures. This chapter will give you a solid understanding of where serverless architectures are a good fit and how to think about design of serverless systems.

2.1   Use cases

Serverless technologies and architectures can be used to build entire systems, create isolated components, or implement specific, granular tasks. The scope for use of serverless design is large, and one of its advantages is that it's possible to use it for small and large tasks alike. We've designed serverless systems that power web and mobile applications for tens of thousands of users, and we've built simple systems to solve specific, minute problems. It's worth remembering that serverless is not just about running code in a compute service such as Lambda. It's also about using third-party services and APIs to cut down on the amount of work you must do.

2.1.1   *Application back end*

In this book you're going to build a back end for a media-sharing, YouTube-like application. It will allow users to upload video files, transcode these files to different playable formats, and then allow other users to view them. You'll construct an entirely serverless back end for a fully featured web application with a database and a RESTful API. And we're going to show that serverless technologies are appropriate for building scalable back ends for all kinds of web, mobile, and desktop applications.

Technologies such as AWS Lambda are relatively new, but we've already seen large serverless back ends that power entire businesses. Our serverless platform, called A Cloud Guru (http://acloud.guru), supports many thousands of users collaborating in real time and streaming hundreds of gigabytes of video. Another example is Instant (http://instant.cm), which is a serverless content management system for static websites. And yet another example is a hybrid-serverless system built by EPX Labs. We'll discuss all of these systems later in the chapter.

Apart from web and mobile applications, serverless is a great fit for IoT applications. Amazon Web Services (AWS) has an IoT platform (https://aws.amazon.com/iot-platform/how-it-works/) that combines the following:

- Authentication and authorization
- Communications gateway
- Registry (a way to assign a unique identity to each device)
- Device shadowing (persistent device state)
- A rules engine (a service to transform and route device messages to AWS services)

The rules engine, for example, can save files to Amazon's Simple Storage Service (S3), push data to an Amazon Simple Queue Service (SQS) queue, and invoke AWS Lambda functions. Amazon's IoT platform makes it easy to build scalable IoT back ends for devices without having to run a server.

A serverless application back end is appealing because it removes a lot of infrastructure management, has granular and predictable billing (especially when a serverless compute service such as Lambda is used), and can scale well to meet uneven demand.

2.1.2   *Data processing and manipulation*

A common use for serverless technologies is data processing, conversion, manipulation, and transcoding. We've seen Lambda functions built by other developers for processing of CSV, JSON, and XML files; collation and aggregation of data; image resizing; and format conversion. Lambda and AWS services are well suited for building event-driven pipelines for data-processing tasks.

In chapter 3, you'll build the first part of your application, which is a powerful pipeline for converting videos from one format to another. This pipeline will set file permissions and generate metadata files. It will run only when a new video file is added to a designated S3 bucket, meaning that you'll pay only for execution of Lambda when there's something to do and not while the system is idling. More broadly, however, we find data processing to be an excellent use case for serverless technologies, especially when we use a Lambda function in concert with other services.

2.1.3 *Real-time analytics*

Ingestion of data—such as logs, system events, transactions, or user clicks—can be accomplished using services such as Amazon Kinesis Streams (see appendix A for more information on Kinesis). Lambda functions can react to new records in a stream, and can process, save, or discard data quickly. A Lambda function can be configured to run when a specific number (batch size) of records is available for processing, so that it doesn't have to execute for every individual record added to the stream.

Kinesis streams and Lambda functions are a good fit for applications that generate a lot of data that needs to be analyzed, aggregated, and stored. When it comes to Kinesis, the number of functions spawned to process messages off a stream is the same as the number of shards (therefore, there's one Lambda function per shard). Furthermore, if a Lambda function fails to process a batch, it will retry. This can keep going for up to 24 hours (which is how long Kinesis will keep data around before it expires) if processing fails each time. But even with these little gotchas (which you now know), the combination of Kinesis streams and Lambda is really powerful if you want to do real-time processing and analytics.

2.1.4 *Legacy API proxy*

One innovative use case of the Amazon API Gateway and Lambda (which we've seen a few times) is what we refer to as the legacy API proxy. Here, developers use API Gateway and Lambda to create a new API layer over legacy APIs and services to make them easier to use. The API Gateway is used to create a RESTful interface, and Lambda functions are used to transpose request/response and marshal data to formats that legacy services understand. This approach makes legacy services easier to consume for modern clients that may not support older protocols and data formats.

2.1.5 *Scheduled services*

Lambda functions can run on a schedule, which makes them effective for repetitive tasks like data backups, imports and exports, reminders, and alerts. We've seen developers use Lambda functions on a schedule to periodically ping their websites to see if they're online and send an email or a text message if they're not. There are Lambda blueprints available for this (a *blueprint* is a template with sample code that can be selected when creating a new Lambda function). And we've seen developers write Lambda functions to perform nightly downloads of files off their servers and send daily account statements to users. Repetitive tasks such as file backup and file validation can also be done easily with Lambda thanks to the scheduling capability that you can set and forget.

2.1.6 *Bots and skills*

Another popular use of Lambda functions and serverless technologies is to build bots (a *bot* is an app or a script that runs automated tasks) for services such as Slack (a popular chat system—https://slack.com). A bot made for Slack can respond to commands, carry out small tasks, and send reports and notifications. We, for example, built a Slack bot in Lambda to report on the number of online sales made each day via our education platform. And we've seen developers build bots for Telegram, Skype, and Facebook's messenger platform.

Similarly, developers write Lambda functions to power Amazon Echo skills. Amazon Echo is a hands-free speaker that responds to voice commands. Developers can implement *skills* to extend Echo's capabilities even further (a skill is essentially an app that can respond to a person's voice; for more information, see http://amzn.to/2b5NMFj). You can write a skill to order a pizza or quiz yourself on geography. Amazon Echo is driven entirely by voice, and *skills* are powered by Lambda.

2.2 *Architectures*

The two overarching architectures that we'll discuss in this book are *compute as back end* (that is, back ends for web and mobile applications) and *compute as glue* (pipelines built to carry out workflows). These two architectures are complementary. It's highly likely that you'll build and combine these architectures if you end up working on any kind of real-world serverless system. Most of the architectures and patterns described in this chapter are specializations and variations of these two to some extent.

2.2.1 *Compute as back end*

The compute-as-back-end architecture describes an approach where a serverless compute service such as Lambda and third-party services are used to build a back end for web, mobile, and desktop applications. You may note in figure 2.1 that the front end links directly to the database and an authentication service. This is because there's no need to put every service behind an API Gateway if the front end can communicate with them in a secure manner (for example, using delegation tokens; chapters 5 and 9 discuss this in more detail). One of the aims of this architecture is to allow the front end to communicate with services, encompass custom logic in Lambda functions, and provide uniform access to functions via a RESTful interface.

In chapter 1, we described our principles of serverless architectures. Among them we mentioned thicker front ends (principle 4) and encouraged the use of third-party services (principle 5). These two principles are particularly relevant if you're building a serverless back end rather than event-driven pipelines. We find that good serverless systems try to minimize the scope and the footprint of Lambda functions so that these functions do only the bare minimum (call them *nano functions*, if you will) and primarily focus on the tasks that must not be done in the front end because of privacy or security concerns. Nevertheless, finding the right level of granularity for a function

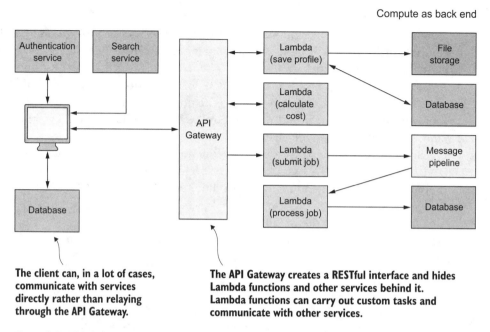

The client can, in a lot of cases, communicate with services directly rather than relaying through the API Gateway.

The API Gateway creates a RESTful interface and hides Lambda functions and other services behind it. Lambda functions can carry out custom tasks and communicate with other services.

Figure 2.1   This is a rather simple back-end architecture for storing, calculating, and retrieving data. The front end can read directly from the database and securely communicate with different services. It can also invoke Lambda functions through the API Gateway.

can be a challenging task. Make functions too granular and you'll end up with a sprawling back end, which can be painful to debug and maintain after a long time. Ignore granularity and you'll risk building mini-monoliths that nobody wants (one helpful lesson we've learned is to try to minimize the number of data transformations in a Lambda function to keep complexity under control).

A CLOUD GURU

A Cloud Guru (https://acloud.guru) is an online education platform for solution architects, system administrators, and developers wanting to learn Amazon Web Services. The core features of the platform include (streaming) video courses, practice exams and quizzes, and real-time discussion forums. A Cloud Guru is also an e-commerce platform that allows students to buy courses and watch them at their leisure. Instructors who create courses for A Cloud Guru can upload videos directly to an S3 bucket, which are immediately transcoded to a number of different formats (1080p, 720p, HLS, WebM, and so on) and are made available for students to view. The Cloud Guru platform uses Firebase as its primary client-facing database, which allows clients to receive updates in near real time without refreshing or polling (Firebase uses web sockets to push updates to all connected devices at the same time). Figure 2.2 shows a cut down version of the architecture used by A Cloud Guru.

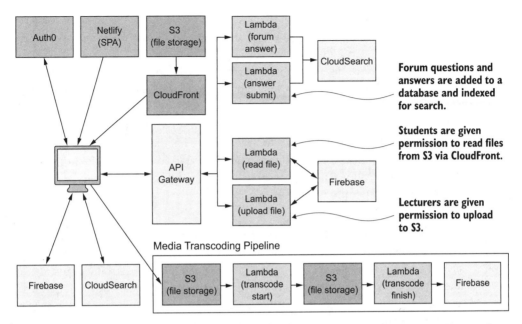

Figure 2.2 illustrates the following labeled elements: Auth0, Netlify (SPA), S3 (file storage), Lambda (forum answer), CloudSearch, CloudFront, Lambda (answer submit), API Gateway, Lambda (read file), Firebase, Lambda (upload file), Firebase, CloudSearch, Media Transcoding Pipeline, S3 (file storage), Lambda (transcode start), S3 (file storage), Lambda (transcode finish), Firebase.

Forum questions and answers are added to a database and indexed for search.

Students are given permission to read files from S3 via CloudFront.

Lecturers are given permission to upload to S3.

Figure 2.2 This is a simplified version of the Cloud Guru architecture. Current production architecture has additional Lambda functions and services for performing payments, managing administration, gamification, reporting, and analytics.

Note the following about the Cloud Guru architecture given in figure 2.2:

- The front end is built using AngularJS and is hosted by Netlify (https://netlify.com). You could use S3 and CloudFront (CloudFront is a global content delivery network provided by AWS) instead of Netlify if you wanted to.
- Auth0 is used to provide registration and authentication facilities. It creates delegation tokens that allow the front end to directly and securely communicate with other services such as Firebase.
- Firebase is the real-time database used by A Cloud Guru. Every client creates a connection to Firebase using web sockets and receives updates from it in near real time. This means that clients receive updates as they happen without having to poll.
- Lecturers who create content for the platform can upload files (usually videos, but they could be other types) straight to S3 buckets via their browser. For this to work, the web application invokes a Lambda function (via the API Gateway) to request the necessary upload credentials first. As soon as credentials are retrieved, the client web application begins a file upload to S3 via HTTP. All of this happens behind the scenes and is opaque to the user.
- Once a file is uploaded to S3, it automatically kicks off a chain of events (our event-driven pipeline) that transcodes the video, saves new files in another

bucket, updates the database, and immediately makes transcoded videos available to other users. Throughout this book you'll write a similar system and see how it works in detail.

- To view videos, users are given permission by another Lambda function. Permissions are valid for 24 hours, after which they must be renewed. Files are accessed via CloudFront.

- Users can submit questions and answers to the forums. Questions, answers, and comments are recorded in the database. This data is then sent for indexing to AWS CloudSearch, which is a managed searching and indexing service from AWS. This allows users to search and view questions, answers, and comments that other people have written.

INSTANT

Instant (http://instant.cm) is a startup that helps website owners add content management facilities—including inline text editing and localization—to their static websites. The founders, Marcel Panse and Sander Nagtegaal, describe it as instant content management system. Instant works by adding a small JavaScript library to a website and making a minor change to HTML. This allows developers and administrators to edit text elements directly via the website's user interface. Draft edits made to the text are stored in DynamoDB (see appendix A on DynamoDB). The final, production version of the text (that the end user sees) is served as a JSON file from an S3 bucket via Amazon CloudFront (figure 2.3).

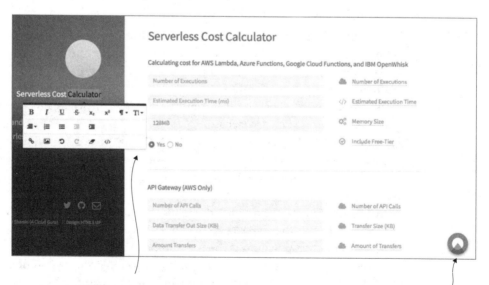

With Instant you can edit the text of your website and then have it published for everyone else to see.

The JavaScript widget provided by Instant allows you to log in to your account, discard the current edit, or make it live.

Figure 2.3   You can use Instant to add support for multiple languages, which makes it a powerful service if you need to localize your website and don't have a content management system.

A simplified version of the Instant architecture is shown in figure 2.4. Note the following about the Instant architecture:

- (This is not shown in the diagram.) A JavaScript library must be added to a website that wants to use Instant. Authentication is done via Google (with the user's own Google account) by clicking a widget that appears in the website at a special URL (for example, yourwebsite.com/#edit). After successful authentication with Google, the Instant JavaScript widget authenticates with AWS Cognito, which provisions temporary AWS IAM credentials (see appendix A for information on AWS Cognito).
- Route 53, Amazon's Domain Name System (DNS) web service, is used to route requests either to CloudFront or to the API Gateway. (See appendix A for more information on Route 53.)
- As a user edits text on their website, the Instant widget sends changes to the API Gateway, which invokes a Lambda function. This Lambda function saves drafts to DynamoDB, along with relevant metadata.
- When the user decides to publish their edit (by selecting an option in the Instant widget), data from DynamoDB is read and saved in S3 as a static JSON file. This file is served from S3 via CloudFront. The Instant widget parses the JSON file received from CloudFront and updates the text on the website for the end user to see.

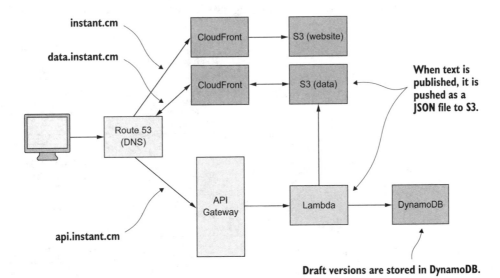

Figure 2.4   The Instant system uses AWS Lambda, API Gateway, DynamoDB, S3, CloudFront, and Amazon Route 53 as its main components. The system scales to support many clients.

Marcel and Sander make a few points about their system:

> *The use of Lambda functions leads to an architecture of microservices quite naturally. Every function is completely shielded from the rest of the code. It gets better: the same Lambda function can fire in parallel in almost infinite numbers—and this is all done completely automated.*

In terms of cost, Marcel and Sander share the following:

> *With our serverless setup, we primarily pay for data transfer through CloudFront, a tiny bit for storage and for each millisecond that our Lambda functions run. Since we know on average what a new customer uses, we can calculate the costs per customer exactly. That's something we couldn't do in the past, when multiple users were shared across the same infrastructure.*

Overall, Marcel and Sander find that adopting an entirely serverless approach has been a winner for them primarily from the perspectives of operations, performance, and cost.

2.2.2 *Legacy API proxy*

The legacy API proxy architecture is an innovative example of how serverless technologies can solve problems. As we mentioned in section 2.1.4, systems with outdated services and APIs can be difficult to use in modern environments. They might not conform to modern protocols or standards, which might make interoperability with current systems harder. One way to alleviate this problem is to use the API Gateway and Lambda in front of those legacy services. The API Gateway and Lambda functions can transform requests made by clients and invoke legacy services directly, as shown in figure 2.5.

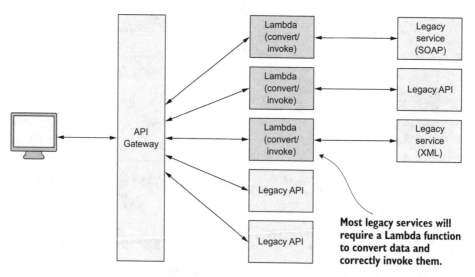

Figure 2.5   The API proxy architecture is used to build a modern API interface over old services and APIs.

The API Gateway can transform requests (to an extent) and issue requests against other HTTP endpoints (see chapter 7). But it works only in a number of fairly basic (and limited) use cases where only JSON transformation is needed. In more complex scenarios, however, a Lambda function is needed to convert data, issue requests, and process responses. Take a Simple Object Access Protocol (SOAP) service as an example. You'd need to write a Lambda function to connect to a SOAP service and then map responses to JSON. Thankfully, there are libraries that can take care of much of the heavy lifting in a Lambda function (for example, there are SOAP clients that can be downloaded from the npm registry for this purpose; see https://www.npmjs.com/package/soap).

2.2.3 *Hybrid*

As we mentioned in chapter 1, serverless technologies and architectures are not an all-or-nothing proposition. They can be adopted and used alongside traditional systems. The hybrid approach may work especially well if a part of the existing infrastructure is already in AWS. We've also seen adoption of serverless technologies and architectures in organizations with developers initially creating standalone components (often to do additional data processing, database backups, and basic alerting) and over time integrating these components into their main systems; see figure 2.6.

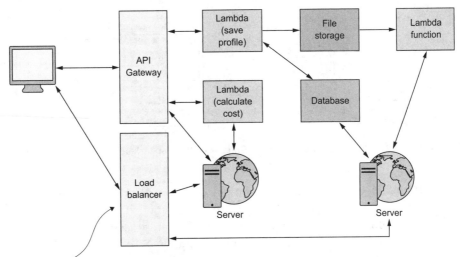

Any legacy system can use functions and services. This can allow you to slowly introduce serverless technologies without disturbing too much of the world order.

Figure 2.6   The hybrid approach is useful if you have a legacy system that uses servers.

EFFICIENT HYBRID-SERVERLESS JOB-PROCESSING SYSTEM

EPX Labs (http://epxlabs.com) proudly state that the "future of IT Operations and Application Development is less about servers and more about services." They specialize in serverless architectures, with one of their recent solutions being a hybrid serverless system designed to carry out maintenance and management jobs on a distributed server-based infrastructure running on Amazon's Elastic Compute Cloud (EC2) (figure 2.7).

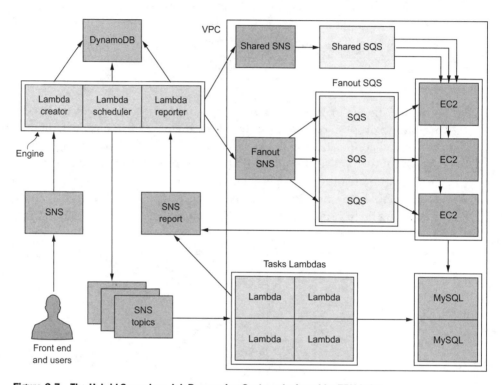

Figure 2.7   The Hybrid-Serverless Job-Processing System designed by EPX Labs

Evan Sinicin and Prachetas Prabhu of EPX Labs describe the system they had to work with as a "multi-tenant Magento (https://magento.com) application running on multiple frontend servers. Magento requires certain processes to run on the servers such as cache clearing and maintenance operations. Additionally, all site management operations such as build, delete, and modify require a mix of on-server operations (building out directory structures, modifying configuration files, etc.) as well as database operations (creating new database, modifying data in database, and so on)." Evan and Prachetas created a scalable serverless system to assist with these tasks. Here's how they describe how the system is built and the way it works:

- The system is broken into two parts: the engine, which is responsible for creating, dispatching, and managing jobs, and the task processors.

- The engine consists of several Lambda functions fronted by the Simple Notification Service (SNS—see appendix A for more information). Task processors are a mix of Lambda and Python processes.

- A job is created by sending JSON data to the creator (part of the engine) via an SNS topic. Each job is broken down into a set of discrete tasks. Tasks fall into three categories:
  - Individual server tasks—must be executed on all servers.
  - Shared server tasks—must be executed by one server.
  - Lambda tasks—executed by a Lambda function.

- Once created in DynamoDB, the job is sent to the scheduler, which identifies the next task to be run and dispatches it. The scheduler dispatches the task based on the type of task, either pinging a task Lambda via SNS or placing messages onto the shared or fan-out Simple Queue Service (SQS) queues (see section 2.3 for more information on these patterns).

- Task execution on the servers is handled by custom-written Python services. Two services run on each server; one polls the shared SQS queue for shared server tasks and the other polls the individual server queue (specific to an EC2 instance). These services continually poll the SQS queues for incoming task messages and execute them based on the contained information. To keep this service stateless, all data required for processing is encapsulated in the encrypted message.

- Each Lambda task corresponds to a discrete Lambda function fronted by an SNS topic. Typically, Lambda tasks operate on the MySQL databases backing Magento; therefore, they run in the virtual private cloud (VPC). To keep these Lambda functions stateless, all data required for processing is encapsulated in the encrypted message itself.

- Upon completion or failure, the task processors will report the success or failure to the engine by invoking the reporter Lambda via SNS. The reporter Lambda will update the job in DynamoDB and invoke the scheduler to do any cleanup (in the case of a failure) or dispatch the next task.

2.2.4 GraphQL

GraphQL (http://graphql.org) is a popular data query language developed by Facebook in 2012 and released publicly in 2015. It was designed as an alternative to REST (Representational State Transfer) because of REST's perceived weaknesses (multiple round-trips, over-fetching, and problems with versioning). GraphQL attempts to solve these problems by providing a hierarchical, declarative way of performing queries from a single end point (for example, api/graphql); see figure 2.8.

GraphQL gives power to the client. Instead of specifying the structure of the response on the server, it's defined on the client (http://bit.ly/2aTjlh5). The client can specify what properties and relationships to return. GraphQL aggregates data

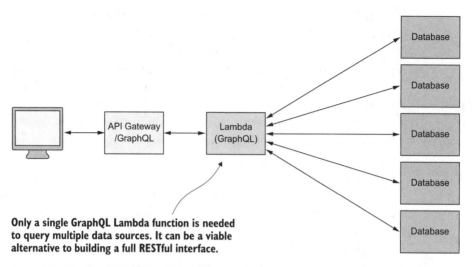

Only a single GraphQL Lambda function is needed to query multiple data sources. It can be a viable alternative to building a full RESTful interface.

Figure 2.8   The GraphQL and Lambda architecture has become popular in the serverless community.

from multiple sources and returns it to the client in a single round trip, which makes it an efficient system for retrieving data. According to Facebook, GraphQL serves millions of requests per second from nearly 1,000 different versions of its application.

In serverless architectures, GraphQL is usually hosted and run from a single Lambda function, which can be connected to an API Gateway (there are also hosted solutions of GraphQL like scaphold.io). GraphQL can query and write to multiple data sources, such as DynamoDB tables, and assemble a response that matches the request. A serverless GraphQL is a rather interesting approach you might want to look at next time you need to design an interface for your API and query data. Check out the following articles if you want to implement GraphQL in a serverless architecture:

- "A Serverless Blog leveraging GraphQL to offer a REST API with only 1 end-point" (https://github.com/serverless/serverless-graphql-blog)
- "Serverless GraphQL" (http://bit.ly/2aN7Pc2)
- "Pokémon Go and GraphQL with AWS Lambda" (http://bit.ly/2aIhCud)

2.2.5 *Compute as glue*

The compute-as-glue architecture shown in figure 2.9 describes the idea that we can use Lambda functions to create powerful execution pipelines and workflows. This often involves using Lambda as *glue* between different services, coordinating and invoking them. With this style of architecture, the focus of the developer is on the design of their pipeline, coordination, and flow of data. The parallelism of serverless compute services like Lambda helps to make these architectures appealing. The example you're going to build in this book uses this pattern to create an event-driven pipeline that transcodes videos (chapter 3, in particular, focuses on creating pipelines and applying this pattern to solve a complex task rather easily).

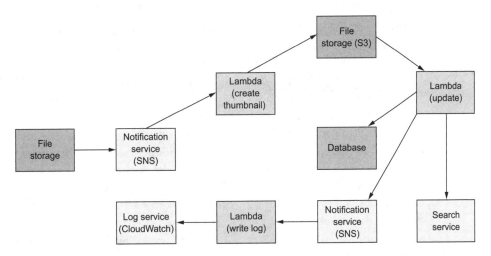

Figure 2.9 **The compute-as-glue architecture uses Lambda functions to connect different services and APIs to achieve a task. In this pipeline, a simple image transformation results in a new file, an update to a database, an update to a search service, and a new entry to a log service.**

LISTHUB PROCESSING ENGINE

EPX Labs has built a system to process large real estate XML feeds (figure 2.10). Evan Sinicin and Prachetas Prabhu say that the goal of their system is "to pull the feed, separate the large file into single XML documents, and process them in parallel. Processing includes parsing, validation, hydration, and storing."

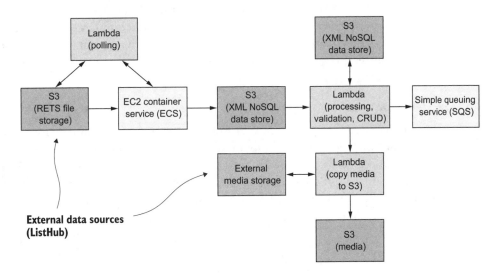

Figure 2.10 **EPX Labs has built a system to effortlessly process large (10 GB+) XML documents.**

They go on to describe how the system works in more detail:

- The system was designed to process a real estate listing XML feed. The feed is provided by ListHub as a massive (10 GB+) XML document with millions of nested listings. This file is provided via S3 for direct download and processing. The listings conform to the Real Estate Standards Organization (RETS) standard.
- ListHub does not have any sort of push capabilities, so the polling Lambda checks the last-modified metadata of the S3 object to see if a new feed has been posted. This usually occurs every 12 hours or so.
- Once a new feed has been published, the polling Lambda spins up an EC2 Container Service (ECS) container to carry out the parsing of the massive file. ECS is used because this process can take a long time (Lambda can run for a maximum of 5 minutes). The ECS container has a Clojure program that asynchronously processes the feed file and places the parsed information into S3.
- EPX Labs uses S3 as a NoSQL store. Using an S3 PutObject event trigger, each new XML listing placed into S3 triggers a Lambda that carries out the validation and hydration processes. Another S3 bucket stores processed listing IDs (as object keys). The validation Lambda can quickly verify that the listing hasn't been processed on a previous run by checking whether the ID/key already exists.
- The validation Lambda also triggers the hydration Lambda ("Copy Media to S3 Lambda"). This Lambda copies assets such as pictures and videos to an S3 bucket so they can be displayed on the front end.
- The final step is to save the relevant, normalized listing data into the final data store that serves the front end and other systems. To avoid overwhelming the data store with writes, the listing data is put onto an SQS queue so it can be processed at a rate the final data store can handle.
- Evan and Prachetas say that their approach yields a number of benefits, including that they can use S3 as a cheap, high-performance, and scalable NoSQL data store and that they can use Lambda to undertake massively concurrent processing.

2.2.6 *Real-time processing*

As discussed in section 2.1.3, Amazon Kinesis Streams is a technology that can help process and analyze large amounts of streaming data. This data can include logs, events, transactions, social media feeds—virtually anything you can think of—as shown in figure 2.11. It's a good way to continuously collect data that may change over time. Lambda is a perfect tool for Kinesis Streams because it scales automatically in response to how much data there is to process.

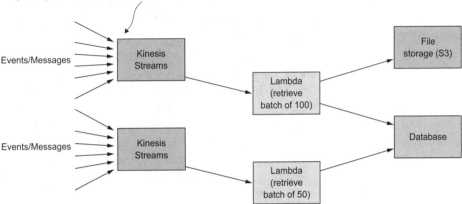

Kinesis Streams can ingest a lot of messages that can be processed with Lambda functions. Data-intensive applications that perform real-time reporting and analytics can benefit from this architecture.

Figure 2.11   Lambda is a perfect tool to process data in near real time.

With Kinesis Streams you can accomplish the following:

- Control how much data is passed into a Kinesis stream before a Lambda function is invoked and how data gets to Kinesis in the first place
- Put a Kinesis stream behind an API Gateway
- Push data to the stream directly from a client or have a Lambda function add records to it

2.3 *Patterns*

Patterns are architectural solutions to problems in software design. They're designed to address common problems found in software development. They're also an excellent communications tool for developers working together on a solution. It's far easier to find an answer to a problem if everyone in the room understands which patterns are applicable, how they work, their advantages, and their disadvantages. The patterns presented in this section are useful for solving design problems in serverless architectures. But these patterns aren't exclusive to serverless. They were used in distributed systems long before serverless technologies became viable. Apart from the patterns presented in this chapter, we recommend that you become familiar with patterns relating to authentication (see chapter 4 for a discussion of the federated identity pattern), data management (CQRS, event sourcing, materialized views, sharding), and error handling (retry pattern). Learning and applying these patterns will make you a better software engineer, regardless of the platform you choose to use.

2.3.1   *Command pattern*

With the GraphQL architecture (section 2.2.4), we discussed the fact that a single end point can be used to cater to different requests with different data (a single GraphQL endpoint can accept any combination of fields from a client and create a response that matches the request). The same idea can be applied more generally. You can design a system in which a specific Lambda function controls and invokes other functions. You can connect it to an API Gateway or invoke it manually and pass messages to it to invoke other Lambda functions.

In software engineering, the command pattern (figure 2.12) is used to "encapsulate a request as an object, thereby letting you parameterize clients with different requests, queue or log requests, and support undoable operations" because of the "need to issue requests to objects without knowing anything about the operation being requested or the receiver of the request" (http://bit.ly/29ZaoWt). The command pattern allows you to decouple the caller of the operation from the entity that carries out the required processing.

In practice, this pattern can simplify the API Gateway implementation, because you may not want or need to create a RESTful URI for every type of request. It can also make versioning simpler. The command Lambda function could work with different versions of your clients and invoke the right Lambda function that's needed by the client.

WHEN TO USE THIS

This pattern is useful if you want to decouple the caller and the receiver. Having a way to pass arguments as an object, and allowing clients to be parametrized with different requests, can reduce coupling between components and help make the system more extensible. Be aware of using this approach if you need to return a response to the API Gateway. Adding another function will increase latency.

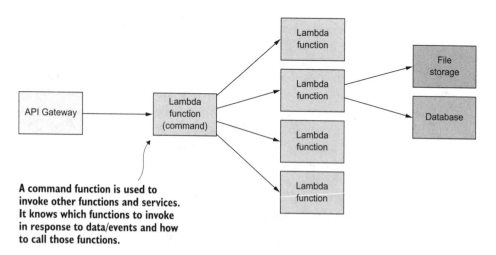

A command function is used to invoke other functions and services. It knows which functions to invoke in response to data/events and how to call those functions.

Figure 2.12   The command pattern is used to invoke and control functions and services from a single function.

2.3.2   *Messaging pattern*

Messaging patterns, shown in figure 2.13, are popular in distributed systems because they allow developers to build scalable and robust systems by decoupling functions and services from direct dependence on one another and allowing storage of events/records/requests in a queue. The reliability comes from the fact that if the consuming service goes offline, messages are retained in the queue and can still be processed at a later time.

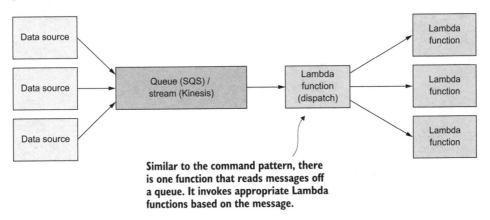

Similar to the command pattern, there is one function that reads messages off a queue. It invokes appropriate Lambda functions based on the message.

Figure 2.13   The messaging pattern, and its many variations, are popular in distributed environments.

This pattern features a message queue with a sender that can post to the queue and a receiver that can retrieve messages from the queue. In terms of implementation in AWS, you can build this pattern on top of the Simple Queue Service. Unfortunately, at the moment Lambda doesn't integrate directly with SQS, so one approach to addressing this problem is to run a Lambda function on a schedule and let it check the queue every so often.

Depending on how the system is designed, a message queue can have a single sender/receiver or multiple senders/receivers. SQS queues typically have one receiver per queue. If you needed to have multiple consumers, a straightforward way to do it is to introduce multiple queues into the system (figure 2.14). A strategy you could apply is to combine SQS with Amazon SNS. SQS queues could subscribe to an SNS topic; pushing a message to the topic would automatically push the message to all of the subscribed queues.

Kinesis Streams is an alternative to SQS, although it doesn't have some features, such as dead lettering of messages (http://amzn.to/2a3HJzH). Kinesis Streams integrates with Lambda, provides an ordered sequence of records, and supports multiple consumers.

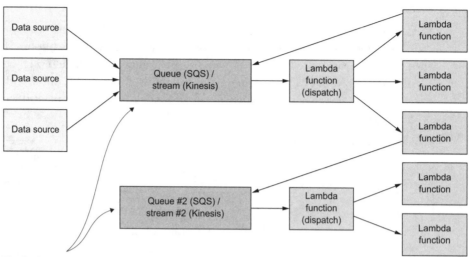

Use multiple queues/streams to decouple
multiple components in your system.

**Figure 2.14 Your system may have multiple queues/streams and Lambda functions to process all
incoming data.**

WHEN TO USE THIS

This is a popular pattern used to handle workloads and data processing. The queue
serves as a buffer, so if the consuming service crashes, data isn't lost. It remains in the
queue until the service can restart and begin processing it again. A message queue can
make future changes easier, too, because there's less coupling between functions. In
an environment that has a lot of data processing, messages, and requests, try to minimize the number of functions that are directly dependent on other functions and use
the messaging pattern instead.

2.3.3   *Priority queue pattern*

A great benefit of using a platform such as AWS and serverless architectures is that
capacity planning and scalability are more of a concern for Amazon's engineers than
for you. But in some cases, you may want to control how and when messages get dealt
with by your system. This is where you might need to have different queues, topics, or
streams to feed messages to your functions. Your system might go one step further and
have entirely different workflows for messages of different priority. Messages that need
immediate attention might go through a flow that expedites the process by using
more expensive services and APIs with more capacity. Messages that don't need to be
processed quickly can go through a different workflow, as shown in figure 2.15.

This pattern might involve the creation and use of entirely different SNS topics,
Kinesis Streams, SQS queues, Lambda functions, and even third-party services. Try to

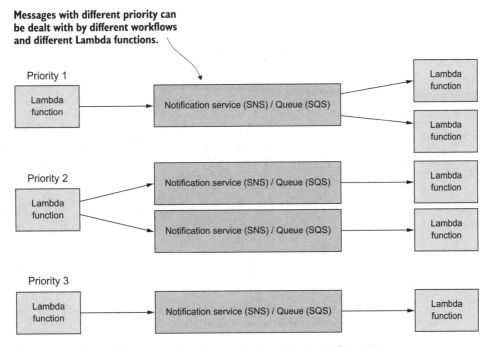

Figure 2.15 The priority queue pattern is an evolution of the messaging pattern.

use this pattern sparingly, because additional components, dependencies, and work-flows will result in more complexity.

WHEN TO USE THIS

This pattern works when you need to have a different priority on processing of messages. Your system can implement workflows and use different services and APIs to cater to many types of needs and users (for example, paying versus nonpaying users).

2.3.4 Fan-out pattern

Fan-out is a type of messaging pattern that's familiar to many users of AWS. Generally, the fan-out pattern is used to push a message out to all listening/subscribed clients of a particular queue or a message pipeline. In AWS, this pattern is usually implemented using SNS topics that allow multiple subscribers to be invoked when a new message is added to a topic. Take S3 as an example. When a new file is added to a bucket, S3 can invoke a single Lambda function with information about the file. But what if you need to invoke two, three, or more Lambda functions at the same time? The original function could be modified to invoke other functions (like the command pattern), but that's a lot of work if all you need is to run functions in parallel. The answer is to use the fan-out pattern using SNS; see figure 2.16.

**A message added to an SNS topic can force invocation
of multiple Lambda functions in parallel.**

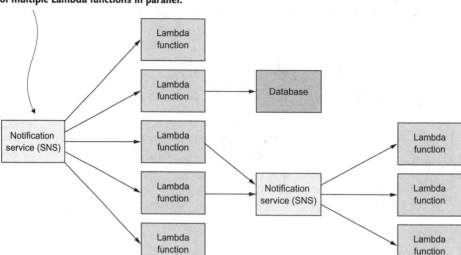

**Figure 2.16   The fan-out pattern is useful because many AWS services (such as S3) can't invoke
more than one Lambda function when an event takes place.**

SNS topics are communications/messaging channels that can have multiple publishers and subscribers (including Lambda functions). When a new message is added to a topic, it forces invocation of all subscribers in parallel, thus causing the event to *fan out*. Going back to the S3 example discussed earlier, instead of invoking a single-message Lambda function, you can configure S3 to push a message onto an SNS topic to invoke all subscribed functions at the same time. It's an effective way to create event-driven architectures and perform operations in parallel. You'll implement this yourself in chapter 3.

WHEN TO USE THIS

This pattern is useful if you need to invoke multiple Lambda functions at the same time. An SNS topic will try and retry to invoke your Lambda functions if it fails to deliver the message or if the function fails to execute. Furthermore, the fan-out pattern can be used for more than just invocation of multiple Lambda functions. SNS topics support other subscribers such as email and SQS queues. Adding a new message to a topic can invoke Lambda functions, send an email, or push a message on to an SQS queue, all at the same time.

2.3.5   *Pipes and filters pattern*

The purpose of the pipes and filters pattern is to decompose a complex processing task into a series of manageable, discrete services organized in a pipeline (figure 2.17). Components designed to transform data are traditionally referred to as *filters*, whereas

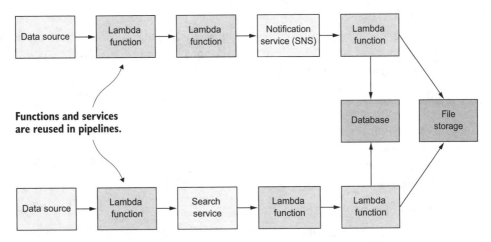

Figure 2.17 This pattern encourages the construction of pipelines to pass and transform data from its destination (sink).

connectors that pass data from one component to the next component are referred to as *pipes*. Serverless architecture lends itself well to this kind of pattern. This is useful for all kinds of tasks where multiple steps are required to achieve a result.

We recommend that every Lambda function be written as a granular service or a task with the single-responsibility principle in mind. Inputs and outputs should be clearly defined (that is, there should be a clear interface) and any side effects minimized. Following this advice will allow you to create functions that can be reused in pipelines and more broadly within your serverless system. You might notice that this pattern is similar to the compute-as-glue architecture we described previously. The compute-as-glue architecture is closely inspired by this pattern.

WHEN TO USE THIS

Whenever you have a complex task, try to break it down into a series of functions (a pipeline) and apply the following rules:

- Make sure your function follows the single-responsibility principle.
- Make the function idempotent; that is, your function should always produce the same output for given input.
- Clearly define an interface for the function. Make sure inputs and outputs are clearly stated.
- Create a black box. The consumer of the function shouldn't have to know how it works, but it must know to use it and what kind of output to expect every time.

2.4   *Summary*

This chapter focused on use cases, architectures, and patterns. These are critical to understand and consider before embarking on a journey to build your system. The architectures we discussing include the following:

- Compute as back end
- Compute as glue
- Legacy API wrapper
- Hybrid
- GraphQL
- Real-time processing

In terms of patterns, we covered these:

- Command pattern
- Messaging pattern
- Priority queue pattern
- Fan-out pattern
- Pipes and filters pattern

Throughout the rest of this book, we're going to apply elements we explored in this chapter, with a particular focus on creating compute-as-back-end and compute-as-glue architectures. In the next chapter, you'll begin building your serverless applications by implementing the compute-as-glue architecture and trying the fan-out pattern.

Building a
serverless application

This chapter covers

- Writing, testing, and deploying Lambda functions
- Creating a basic event-driven system for transcoding videos
- Using AWS services such as Simple Storage Service, Simple Notification Service, and the Elastic Transcoder

---

To give you a thorough understanding of serverless architectures, you're going to build a serverless application. Specifically, you'll build a video-sharing website, a YouTube mini clone, which we'll call *24-Hour Video*. This application will have a website with user registration and authentication capabilities. Your users will be able to watch and upload videos. Any videos uploaded to the system will be transcoded to different resolutions and bitrates so that people on different connections and devices will be able to watch them. You'll use a number of AWS services to build your application, including AWS Lambda, S3, Elastic Transcoder, SNS, and non-AWS services such as Auth0 and Firebase. In this chapter, we'll focus on building your serverless pipeline for transcoding uploaded videos.

3.1   *24-Hour Video*

Before we jump in to the nitty-gritty of the chapter, let's step ahead and look at what you're going to accomplish by the time you get to the final chapter. Figure 3.1 shows a 10,000-foot view of the major components you're going to develop. These include a transcoding pipeline, a website, and a custom API. At the end, you'll also have a full-fledged system with a database and a user system.

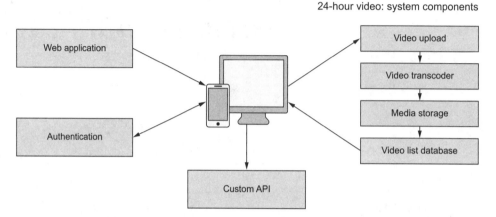

Figure 3.1   **These are the major components you'll create as you work through the book.**

The website you're going to build will look like figure 3.2. Videos uploaded by your users will be shown on the main page. Your users will be able to click any video and play it.

Figure 3.2   **The website you'll build for 24-Hour Video**

The overall purpose of building 24-Hour Video throughout the book is threefold:

- To demonstrate how easy it is to create a serverless back end using AWS Lambda and other services. Each chapter will add new functionality to 24-Hour Video.
- To implement and explore different serverless architectures and patterns. We'll also show you useful tips and tricks.
- To allow you to try exercises found at the end of every chapter. Several exercises will assume that you've built 24-Hour Video and ask you to implement additional features or make changes. These exercises are great to test whether you understand new concepts. They're fun, too!

Before you begin, however, you need to set up your machine, install the necessary tooling, and configure a few services in AWS. Details for that process are in appendix B, "Installation and setup." Go through appendix B first, and then come back here to begin your adventure!

3.1.1 General requirements

You're going to build an important part of your system in this chapter: an event-driven pipeline that will take uploaded videos and encode them to different formats and bitrates. 24-Hour Video will be an event-driven, push-based system where the workflow to encode videos will be triggered automatically by an upload to an S3 bucket. Figure 3.3 shows the two main components you're going to work on.

A quick note about AWS costs: most of AWS services have a free tier. By following the 24-Hour Video example, you should stay within the free tier of most services. Elastic Transcoder, however, is likely to be the one that costs a little. Its free tier includes 20 minutes of SD output and 10 minutes of HD (720p or above) output per month (a minute refers to the length of the source video, not transcoder execution time). As usual, costs are dependent on the region where Elastic Transcoder is used. In the eastern part of the United States, for example, the price for 1 minute of HD output per

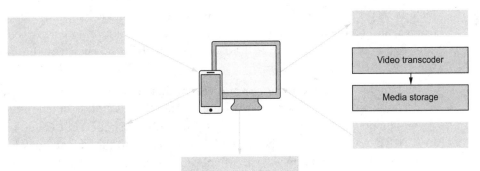

Figure 3.3 The serverless transcoding pipeline will be your first challenge.

month is $.03. This makes a 10-minute source file cost 30 cents to encode. Elastic Transcoder pricing for other regions can be found at https://aws.amazon.com/elastictranscoder/pricing/.

The S3 free tier allows users to store 5 GB of data with standard storage, issue 20,000 GET requests and 2,000 PUT requests, and transfer 15 GB of data out each month. Lambda provides a free tier with 1M free requests and 400,000 GB-seconds of compute time. You should be well within the free tiers of those services with your basic system.

The following are the high-level requirements for 24-Hour Video:

- The transcoding process will convert uploaded source videos to three different resolutions and bitrates: generic 720p, generic 1080p, and a web/YouTube/ Facebook–friendly 720p with a lower bitrate.
- There will be two S3 buckets. Source files will go into the upload bucket. Newly transcoded files will be saved to the transcoded videos S3 bucket.
- The permissions of each transcoded file will be modified to make them publicly viewable and downloadable.
- After each successful transcoding, you'll be sent an email notification with information about the file. This will be done using SNS.
- A small JSON file with video metadata will be created and placed alongside each transcoded video. This metadata will contain basic information about the file, such as its size, number of streams, and duration.

To make things simpler to manage, you'll set up a build and deployment system using the Node Package Manager (npm). You'll want to do it as early as possible to have an automated process for testing, packaging Lambda functions, and deploying them to AWS. You will, however, temporarily set aside other developmental and operational aspects such as versioning or deployment and come back to them later.

3.1.2 Amazon Web Services

To create your serverless back end, you'll use several services provided by AWS. These include S3 for storage of files, Elastic Transcoder for video conversion, SNS for notifications, and Lambda for running custom code and orchestrating key parts of the system. Refer to appendix A for a short overview of these services. For the most part, you'll use the following AWS services:

- Lambda will handle parts of the system that require coordination or can't be done directly by other services. You'll create three Lambda functions:
- The first Lambda function will create and submit Elastic Transcoder jobs. It will trigger automatically whenever a file is uploaded to the upload bucket.
- The second function will run whenever a new, transcoded video appears in the `transcoded videos` bucket. This function will change the file's permissions so that it becomes publicly accessible. This will allow your users to view and download the new file.

- The third function will also run in response to the creation of a new, transcoded file. It will analyze the video, create a metadata file, and save it in S3.
- Elastic Transcoder will encode videos to different resolutions and bitrates. Default encoding presets will alleviate the need to create custom profiles for the transcoder.
- SNS will issue notifications when a transcoded file is placed in the `transcoded videos` bucket. This notification will be used to send an email with information about the file and invoke the last two Lambda functions.

Figure 3.4 shows a detailed flow of the proposed approach. Note that the only point where a user needs to interact with the system is at the initial upload stage. This figure and the architecture may look complex, but we'll break the system into manageable chunks and tackle them one by one.

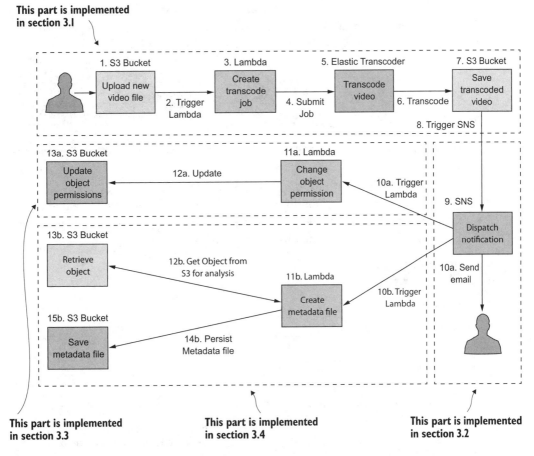

Figure 3.4 This back end is built with S3, SNS, Elastic Transcoder, and Lambda. This figure may seem complex initially, but we'll break it down, and you'll build a scalable serverless system in no time at all.

3.1.3   *Creating your first Lambda function*

Now that you've taken care of the setup and configuration details in appendix B, it's time to write the first Lambda function. In the same directory as package.json, which you created during installation, create a new file named index.js and open it in your favorite text editor. This file will contain the first function. The important thing to know is that you must define a function handler, which will be invoked by the Lambda runtime. The handler takes three parameters—event, context, and callback—and is defined as follows:

```
exports.handler = function(event, context, callback){}
```

Your Lambda function will be invoked from S3 as soon as a new file is placed in a bucket. Information about the uploaded video will be passed to the Lambda function via the event object. It will include the bucket name and the key of the file being uploaded. This function will then prepare a job for the Elastic Transcoder; it will specify the input file and all possible outputs. Finally, it will submit the job and write a message to an Amazon CloudWatch Log stream. Figure 3.5 visualizes this part of the process.

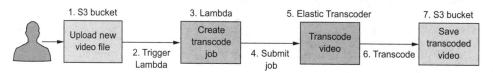

Figure 3.5   **The first Lambda function will react to an event in S3 and create an Elastic Transcoder job.**

Listing 3.1 shows this function's implementation; copy it into index.js. Don't forget to set PipelineId to the corresponding Elastic Transcoder pipeline you created earlier. You can find the Pipeline ID (figure 3.6) in the Elastic Transcoder console by clicking the magnifier button next to the pipeline you created in appendix B.

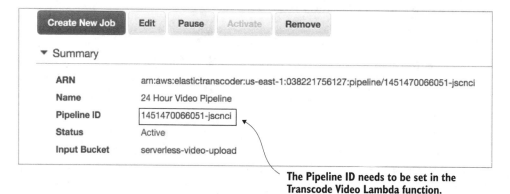

Figure 3.6   **You need to set the correct pipeline ID in the first Lambda function to create and execute jobs.**

SOURCE CODE AT YOUR FINGERTIPS   Our GitHub repository at https://github .com/sbarski/serverless-architectures-aws has all the code snippets and listings you need for this book. So you don't have to manually type anything out—unless you really want to.

Listing 3.1   Transcode video Lambda

S3 key names are URL-encoded. A filename "My Birthday Video.mp4" is represented as "My+Birthday+ Video.mp4." You need to decode the key name to get the original filename with spaces.

The Output Key Prefix creates a logical hierarchy (folder) for your file in the transcoded videos bucket.

The key uniquely identifies an object in the bucket. It's made up of the original filename and any additional key name prefixes. This code isn't particularly safe. It doesn't handle errors or unexpected issues gracefully. Can you improve it?

Remember to change the PipelineId to match the pipeline ID of your Elastic Transcoder pipeline.

The extension of the original key isn't needed for new transcodings. The key name can still be used in the naming of your output videos.

```
'use strict';

var AWS = require('aws-sdk');

var elasticTranscoder = new AWS.ElasticTranscoder({
region: 'us-east-1'
});

exports.handler = function(event, context, callback){
    var key = event.Records[0].s3.object.key;

    var sourceKey = decodeURIComponent(key.replace(/\+/g, " "));

    var outputKey = sourceKey.split('.')[0];

    console.log('key:', key, sourceKey, outputKey);

    var params = {
        PipelineId: '1451470066051-jscnci',
        OutputKeyPrefix: outputKey + '/',
        Input: {
            Key: sourceKey
        },
        Outputs: [
        {
            Key: outputKey + '-1080p' + '.mp4',
            PresetId: '1351620000001-000001'
        },
        {
            Key: outputKey + '-720p' + '.mp4',
            PresetId: '1351620000001-000010'
        },
        {
            Key: outputKey + '-web-720p' + '.mp4',
            PresetId: '1351620000001-100070'
        }
        ]};
```

System presets are used to specify the output of the Elastic Transcoder. You can create your own or select other premade presets. To see a list of all available premade presets go to https://docs.aws.amazon.com/ elastictranscoder/latest/developerguide/ system-presets.html.

Generic 1080p Elastic Transcoder preset

Generic 720p Elastic Transcoder preset

Web-friendly 720p Elastic Transcoder preset

```
elasticTranscoder.createJob(params, function(error, data){
    if (error){
        callback(error);        ◁
    }
});
};
```

If Elastic Transcoder fails to create a job, write the error to CloudWatch via the callback function.

3.1.4   *Naming your Lambda*

You can name the file containing your Lambda function something other than index.js. If you do that, you'll have to modify the handler value in Lambda's configuration panel in AWS to reflect the new name of the file. For example, if you decide to name your file TranscodeVideo.js rather than index.js, you'll have to modify the handler to be TranscodeVideo.handler in the AWS console (figure 3.7).

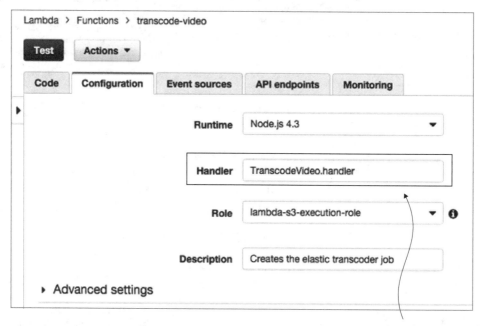

Remember to update the handler if you rename your files at a later date.

Figure 3.7   The Lambda runtime needs to know the handler function to execute your code.

3.1.5   *Testing locally*

Having copied the function from listing 3.1 into index.js, you can think about how to test it locally on your machine. A way to do that is to simulate events and have the function react to them. This means you have to invoke the function and pass three parameters representing the context, event, and callback objects. The function will execute as if it was running in Lambda, and you'll see a result without having to deploy it.

You can run Lambda functions locally using an npm module called run-local-lambda. To install this module, execute the following command from a terminal window (make sure you're in the function's directory): `npm install run-local-lambda --save-dev`.

> **NOTE** This module allows you to invoke your Lambda function but it doesn't emulate Lambda's environment. It doesn't respect memory size or the CPU, ephemeral local disk storage, or the operating system of real Lambda in AWS.

Modify package.json, as in the next listing, to change the test script. The test script will invoke the function and pass the contents of event.json, a file you're about to create, as the event object. For more information about this npm module, including additional parameters and examples, see https://www.npmjs.com/package/run-local-lambda.

Listing 3.2   Test script

```
"scripts": {
    "test": "run-local-lambda --file index.js --event tests/event.json"   ◁─┐
}
```

**The test script uses the run-local-lambda npm module to run the Lambda function.
There are four optional parameters: --file, --event, --handler, and --timeout.**

The test script requires an event.json file to function. This file must contain the specification of the event object that run-local-lambda will pass in to the Lambda function. In the same directory as index.js, create a subdirectory called tests and then create a file called event.json in it. Copy the next listing into event.json and save it.

Listing 3.3   Simulating the event object

```
{
  "Records":[
    {
      "eventVersion":"2.0",
      "eventSource":"aws:s3",
      "awsRegion":"us-east-1",
      "eventTime":"2016-12-11T00:00:00.000Z",
      "eventName":"ObjectCreated:Put",
      "userIdentity":{
        "principalId":"A3MCB9FEJCFJSY"
      },
      "requestParameters":{
        "sourceIPAddress":"127.0.0.1"
      },
      "responseElements":{
        "x-amz-request-id":"3966C864F562A6A0",
        "x-amz-id-2":"2radsa8X4nKpba7KbgVurmc7rwe/"
      },
      "s3":{
```

**The S3 declaration is the most
important part of this file. This
is what the event object
structure looks like when S3
triggers a Lambda function.**

```
      "s3SchemaVersion":"1.0",
      "configurationId":"Video Upload",
      "bucket":{
        "name":"serverless-video-upload",          ◁────
        "ownerIdentity":{
           "principalId":"A3MCB9FEJCFJSY"
        },
        "arn":"arn:aws:s3:::serverless-video-upload"
      },
      "object":{
        "key":"my video.mp4",                       ◁────────
        "size":2236480,
        "eTag":"ddb7a52094d2079a27ac44f83ca669e9",
        "sequencer": "005686091F4FFF1565"
      }
    }
  }
 }
]
}
```

In AWS these parameters would be your bucket name and the key of the uploaded object. For the purposes of your local test, you can set these parameters to anything you want.

The key is the name of the file. For your test you can set this to anything you want.

To execute the test, run npm test from a terminal window in the directory of the function. If it works, you should see the values of key, sourceKey, and outputKey print to the terminal.

Having run the test script, you might see an error message with an AccessDenied-Exception. That's normal, because your user lambda-upload doesn't have permissions to create new Elastic Transcoder jobs. Once uploaded to AWS, your function will run correctly because it will assume the identity and access management (IAM) role defined in appendix B. One of the exercises at the end of this chapter will be to add a policy to the IAM user (lambda-upload) to create Elastic Transcoder jobs from your local system.

3.1.6   *Deploying to AWS*

You're now ready to deploy the function to AWS. To do that, you need to modify package .json to create predeploy and deploy scripts. The predeploy script creates a zip file of the function. The deploy script then deploys the zip file to AWS. Note that if you're a Windows user, you won't have the zip file, which is needed by the predeploy script, installed by default. Please refer to appendix B and the sidebar "Zip and Windows" for further information. Update package.json to include deploy and predeploy scripts, as shown in the following listing.

Listing 3.4   Predeploy and deploy scripts

```
"scripts": {
    "test": "run-local-lambda --file index.js --event tests/event.json",
    "deploy": "aws lambda update-function-code --function-name
 ⇨arn:aws:lambda:us-east-1:038221756127:function:transcode-video
 ⇨--zip-file fileb://Lambda-Deployment.zip",
    "predeploy": "zip -r Lambda-Deployment.zip * -x *.zip *.json *.log"  ◁
}
```

The AWS CLI deploys your function code. There are two main parameters. The --function-name parameter requires the name of the function or its ARN (it is bolded). The --zip-file parameter requires the name of the zip file that contains the function. The zip file is created by the predeploy script.

npm runs predeploy before it runs the deploy script. The predeploy script creates a zip of the function, local node modules, and any other files in the current directory. You're specifically excluding zip, json, and log files from being zipped into the deployment file because they're not needed.

For deployment to work, the `--function-name` parameter must match the name or the ARN of the function. If you wish to use the ARN, follow these steps:

- In the AWS console click Lambda.
- Click `transcode-video` and copy the ARN of the function (figure 3.8).
- Open package.json and change the ARN value in the deploy script to the value copied from the AWS console.

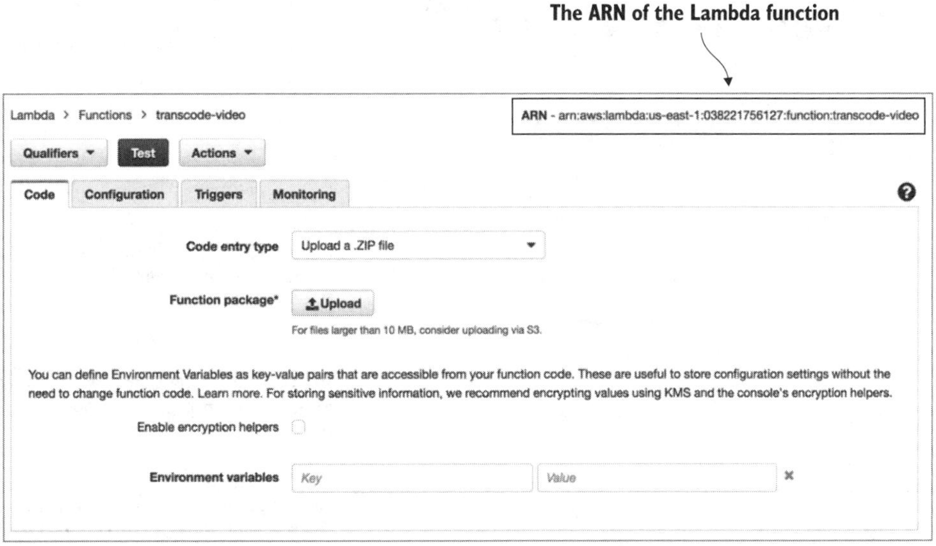

The ARN of the Lambda function

Figure 3.8   You need to copy the ARN of your Lambda function to package.json for the deployment to work.

Having updated the ARN value in the deploy script, execute `npm run deploy` from the terminal. This will zip up the function and deploy it to AWS. If the deployment was successful, you'll see the current function configuration, including timeout and memory size, printed to the terminal (chapter 6 goes into more detail on function configuration options and what all of this represents).

3.1.7   *Connecting S3 to Lambda*

The last step before you can test the function in AWS is to connect S3 to Lambda. You need to configure S3 to raise an event and invoke a Lambda function whenever a new file is added to the upload bucket (figure 3.9).

Figure 3.9   S3 will trigger Lambda when you add a new file to the bucket.

To configure S3, follow these steps:

1   Open the upload bucket (`serverless-video-upload`) in the AWS console, select Properties, click Events, and click Add Notification.

2   Give your event a name, such as Video Upload, and then under Events select ObjectCreate (All).

3   Select Lambda Function from the Send To drop-down. Finally, from the Lambda drop-down select your `transcode-video` function and click Save (figure 3.10).

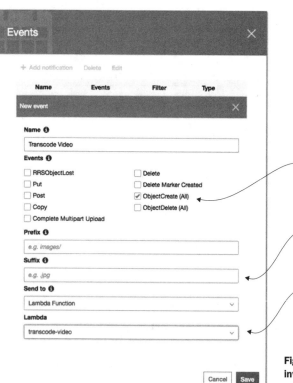

ObjectCreated(All) is the event needed to trigger your Lambda function.

You can optionally scope event invocations for a single suffix such as mp4.

Set the Lambda function to invoke when a new object is placed in the bucket.

Figure 3.10   You need to configure S3 to invoke the right Lambda function when you add a new object to the bucket.

Permissions error

If this is your first time connecting S3 to Lambda, you may see a permissions error. If that happens, you'll need to use Lambda's console to set up the event instead:

- In the AWS console click Lambda.
- Select the transcode-video function.
- Select the Triggers tab.
- Select Add trigger.
- Click on the box in the popup and select S3.
- Select the upload bucket and set event type as *Object Created (All)*.
- Select Submit to finish.

3.1.8   *Testing in AWS*

To test the function in AWS, upload a video to the upload bucket. Follow these steps:

1   Click into the video upload bucket, and then select Upload (figure 3.11).
2   You'll see an upload dialog appear on your screen. Click Add Files, select a file from your computer, and click the Upload button. All other settings can be left as they are.

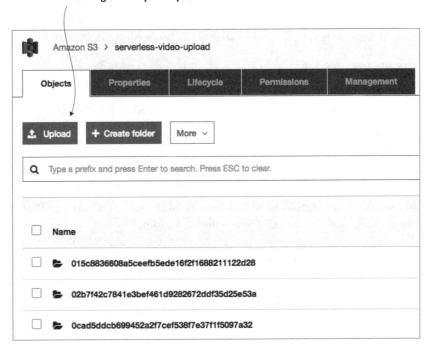

Figure 3.11   It's better to upload a small file initially because it makes the upload and transcoding a lot quicker.

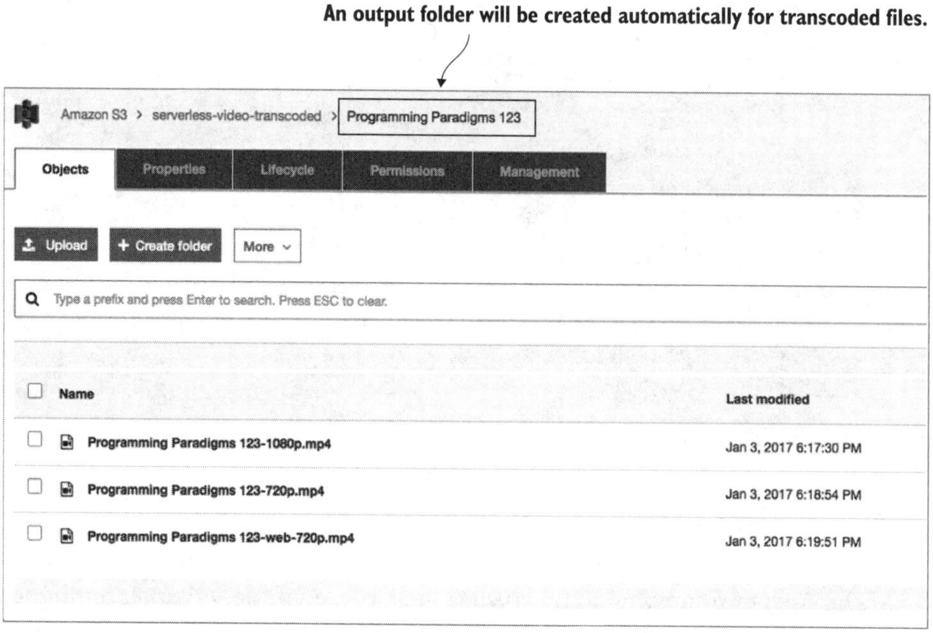

An output folder will be created automatically for transcoded files.

Figure 3.12 Elastic Transcoder will generate three new files and place them in a folder in the transcoded videos S3 bucket.

After a time, you should see three new videos in the `transcoded videos` bucket. These files should appear in a folder rather than in the root of the bucket (figure 3.12).

3.1.9 Looking at logs

Having performed a test in the previous section, you should see three new files in the `transcoded videos` bucket. But things may not always go as smoothly. In case of problems, such as new files not appearing, you can check two logs for errors. The first is a Lambda log in CloudWatch. To see the log, do the following:

1 Choose Lambda in the AWS console and then click the function name.
2 Choose the Monitoring tab and then click View Logs in CloudWatch (figure 3.13).

The latest log stream should be at the top, but if it's not, you can sort log streams by date by clicking the Last Event Time column header. If you click into a log stream, you'll see log entries with more detail. Often, if you make an error, these logs will reveal what happened. See chapter 4 for more information about CloudWatch and logging.

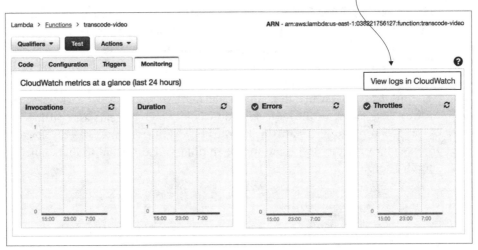

Click the link to view logs. You can also navigate to these logs via CloudWatch.

Figure 3.13 Logs and metrics are accessible from the Monitoring tab of each function in the Lambda console.

If Lambda logs reveal nothing out of the ordinary, take a look at the Elastic Transcoder logs:

1 Click Elastic Transcoder in the AWS console, then click Jobs, and select your pipeline.

2 Click Search to see a recent list of jobs (figure 3.14). The Status column shows whether the job was (successfully) completed or if there was an error. Click the job to see more information about it.

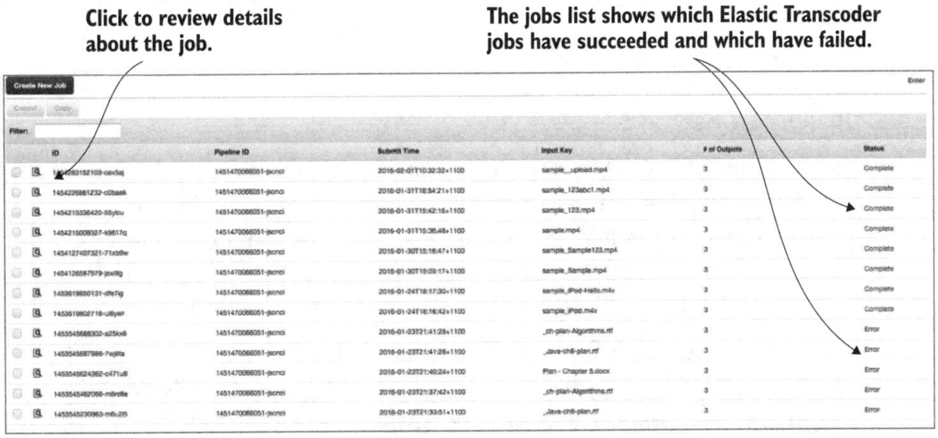

Click to review details about the job.

The jobs list shows which Elastic Transcoder jobs have succeeded and which have failed.

Figure 3.14 The Elastic Transcoder job list can reveal if a job has failed. Failures can occur for a variety of reasons, including the source file being deleted before the job started or a file with the same name already present in the target bucket.

3.2   Configuring Simple Notification Service

The next part of the job is to connect Simple Notification Service to your `transcoded` `videos` bucket. After Elastic Transcoder saves a new file to this bucket, you need to send an email and invoke two other Lambda functions to make the new file publicly accessible and to create a JSON file with metadata.

You'll create an SNS topic and three subscriptions. One subscription will be used for email and the other two will trigger Lambda functions (you're implementing the fan-out pattern described in chapter 2). The `transcoded videos` bucket will automatically create event notifications as soon as new video appears and push a notification to an SNS topic to kick-start this bit of the workflow. Figure 3.15 displays this part of the system with the SNS topic in the middle and three subscribers consuming new notifications.

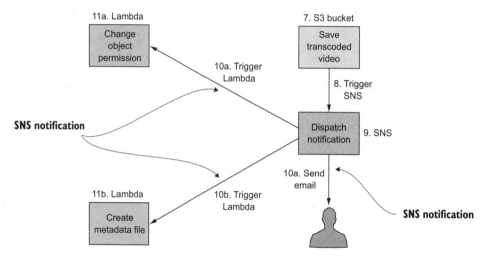

Figure 3.15   To create multiple notifications, you need to use SNS. You can add multiple subscribers and perform operations in parallel.

3.2.1   Connecting SNS to S3

Create a new SNS topic by clicking SNS in the AWS console and then selecting Create Topic. Give your topic a name such as transcoded-video-notifications.

You need to connect S3 to SNS so that when a new object is added to the `transcoded videos` bucket, an event is pushed to SNS. To achieve this, the SNS security policy must be modified to allow communication with S3:

1 In the SNS console, click Topics and then click the ARN of your topic (`transcoded-video-notifications`). The Topic Details view will appear.
2 Click the Other Topic Actions drop-down, select Edit Topic Policy, and then click the Advanced View tab.

3 Scroll to the bottom of the policy until you see the Condition declaration. Replace it with a new condition, as shown in listing 3.5. Click Update Policy to save.

Figure 3.16 shows what the updated policy looks like. Make sure to modify the SourceArn to reflect the name of your bucket. It should be in the following form: arn:aws:s3:*:*:<your bucket name>.

Listing 3.5   SNS condition

```
"Condition": {
  "ArnLike": {
    "aws:SourceArn": "arn:aws:s3:*:*:serverless-video-transcoded"    ◁
  }
}
```

Change serverless-video-transcoded to the name of your transcoded videos bucket for the access policy to work correctly.

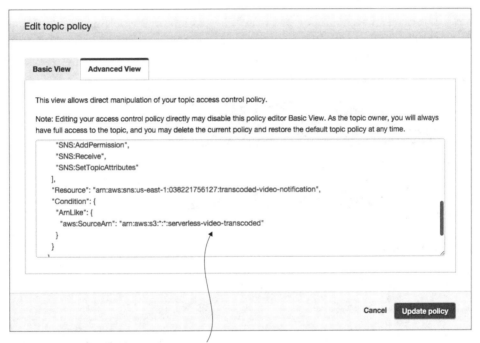

This condition allows an S3 bucket (serverless-video-transcoded) to interact with this SNS topic.

Figure 3.16   The resource policy for the SNS topic needs to be updated to work with S3. See chapter 4 for more information on security, policies, and permissions.

Finally, connect S3 to SNS:

1   In the AWS console click S3 and open the `transcoded videos` bucket.
2   Click Properties and choose Events.
3   Click the Add Notification button.
4   Set a name for the event, such as "Transcoded Video."
5   Enable the ObjectCreate (All) check box.
6   From the Send To drop-down, select SNS Topic.
7   From the SNS drop-down, select the SNS topic you created (`transcoded-video-notification`).
8   You can optionally set a suffix such as `mp4`. If you do that, new event notifications will be created only for files that have an `mp4` extension. If you decide to tackle section 3.4, you'll definitely have to come back and set the suffix to `mp4` (figure 3.17).
9   Click Save.

If you get an error message such as, "Permissions on the destination topic do not allow S3 to publish notifications from this bucket" when trying to save, double-check that you copied listing 3.5 correctly. If you get stuck, have a look at http://amzn.to/1pgkl4X for more helpful information.

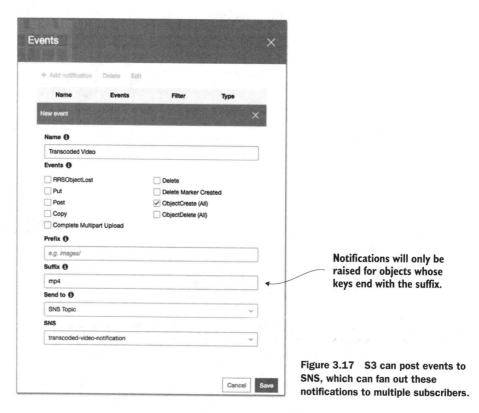

Notifications will only be raised for objects whose keys end with the suffix.

Figure 3.17   S3 can post events to SNS, which can fan out these notifications to multiple subscribers.

3.2.2 Getting email from SNS

One of your requirements is to get an email about each transcoded file. You have an SNS topic that receives events from an S3 bucket whenever a new transcoded file is saved in it. You need to create a new email subscription for the topic so that you can begin receiving emails. In the SNS console, follow these steps:

1 Click Topics and then click the name of your SNS topic (`transcoded-video-notifications`). The check box to the topic should be selected.
2 Click Actions, and select Subscribe to Topic. You should see a Create Subscription dialog appear.
3 In the dialog select Email as the protocol and enter your email address as the endpoint.
4 Click Create Subscription to save and exit the dialog.

SNS will immediately send a confirmation email, which you must activate to receive further notifications. Going forward, you'll receive an email whenever a file is added to the bucket.

3.2.3 Testing SNS

To test if SNS is working, upload a video file to the upload bucket. You can also rename an existing file in the bucket to trigger the workflow. You should receive an email for each transcoded file.

3.3 Setting video permissions

The second Lambda function you create will make your newly transcoded files publicly accessible. Figure 3.18 shows this part of the workflow. In chapter 8, we'll look at securing access to files using signed URLs, but for now your transcoded videos will be available for everyone to play and download.

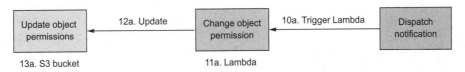

Figure 3.18 This part of the workflow modifies the access control list of the newly transcoded video file to make it publicly accessible.

3.3.1 Creating the second function

First, create the second Lambda function in AWS the way you created the first one. This time, though, name your function `set-permissions`. You can follow the instructions in appendix B again. Then, on your system, create a copy of the directory containing the first Lambda function. You'll use this copy as a basis for the second function. Open package.json and change all references of `transcode-video` to `set-permissions`.

Also, change the ARN in the deploy script to reflect the ARN of the new function created in AWS.

In the second Lambda function, you'll need to perform two tasks:

1 Extract the bucket and key of the new video from the event object.
2 Set the access control list (ACL) attribute of the video to `public-read` to make it publicly accessible.

The next listing shows a reference implementation for the second function. Copy it to index.js, replacing anything that's already there.

Listing 3.6 Changing the ACL of an S3 object

```
"use strict";

var AWS = require('aws-sdk');

var s3 = new AWS.S3();

exports.handler = function(event, context, callback){
   var message = JSON.parse(event.Records[0].Sns.Message);

   var sourceBucket = message.Records[0].s3.bucket.name;
   var sourceKey =
     ➥decodeURIComponent(message.Records[0].s3.object.key.replace(/\+/g, " "));

   var params = {
     Bucket: sourceBucket,
     Key: sourceKey,
     ACL: 'public-read'
   };

   s3.putObjectAcl(params, function(err, data){
      if (err){
        callback(err);
      }
   });
};
```

The bucket name and the key are extracted in a slightly different way than the first function because the event originates from SNS rather than directly from S3.

The goal of this function is to set the right ACL; 'public-read' will make the file publicly accessible.

3.3.2 *Configuring and securing*

Having copied over the second Lambda function to index.js, perform a deployment using `npm run deploy`. Finally, you need to connect Lambda to SNS:

1 In the AWS console click SNS, select Topics, and then click the ARN of your topic (`transcoded-video-notifications`).
2 Click the Create Subscription button and select AWS Lambda.
3 From the Endpoint drop-down, select the `set-permissions` Lambda function, and click Create Subscription.

There's still one more security issue: the role under which the Lambda function executes has permissions only to download or upload new objects to the bucket. But this role doesn't have permission to change the object ACL. You can fix this by creating a new inline policy for the role (`lambda-s3-execution-role`) you've been using:

1 In the AWS console click IAM, select Roles, and click `lambda-s3-execution-role`.

2 Expand Inline Policies, click the Click Here link, and select Policy Generator.

3 In the AWS Service drop-down, select Amazon S3 and then select PutObjectAcl in Actions.

4 In the ARN textbox, type `arn:aws:s3:::<your-bucket-name>/*`, where `<your-bucket-name>` is the name of your bucket for transcoded videos.

5 Click Add Statement, then click Next Step, and click Apply Policy to save.

SECURITY AND ROLES In a production environment, you should create separate roles for your Lambda functions, especially if they'll use different resources and require different permissions.

3.3.3 Testing the second function

Having configured role permissions, you can test the second Lambda function by uploading or renaming a video in the upload bucket. To see if the function has worked, find any newly created file in the `transcoded videos` bucket, select it, and click Permissions. You should see the second Grantee setting configured for Everyone with the Open/Download check box selected (figure 3.19). You can now copy the URL that's given just above on that same page and share it with others.

If something goes wrong with the Lambda function, look at CloudWatch logs for the function. They might reveal clues as to what happened.

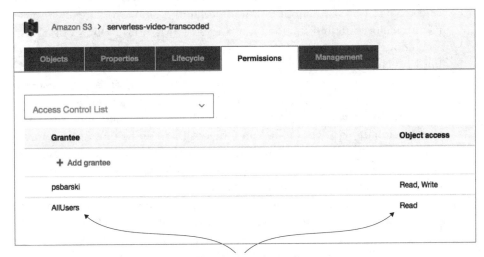

The Grantee must be set to AllUsers
and Object access set to Read.

Figure 3.19 Check if the Lambda function successfully updated the object ACL by looking at its permissions in the S3 console.

3.4   *Generating metadata*

The third Lambda function needs to create a JSON file with metadata about the video. It should also save the metadata file next to the video. This Lambda function will be invoked via SNS just like the one before it. The problem in this function is how to analyze the video and get the required metadata.

FFmpeg is a command-line utility that records and converts video and audio. It has several components, including the excellent FFprobe, which can be used to extract media information. You're going to use FFprobe to extract metadata and then save it to a file. This section is slightly more advanced than other sections, but it's also optional. You'll learn a lot by working through it, but you can skip it without affecting what you do in other chapters.

3.4.1   *Creating the third function and FFprobe*

There are two ways to acquire FFprobe. The first way is to spin up a copy of EC2 with Amazon Linux, grab the FFmpeg source code, and build FFprobe. If you do that, you'll need to create a static build of the utility. The second way is to find a static build of FFmpeg for Linux (for example, https://www.johnvansickle.com/ffmpeg/) from a reputable source or a distribution. If you decide to compile your own binaries, per the article "Running Arbitrary Executables in AWS Lambda" (http://amzn.to/29yhvpD), ensure that they're either statically linked or built for the matching version of Amazon Linux. The current version of Amazon Linux in use within AWS Lambda can always be found on the Supported Versions page (http://amzn.to/29w0c6W) of the Lambda docs.

Having acquired a static copy of FFprobe, create the third Lambda function in the AWS console, and name it `extract-metadata`. Set the role for this function to `lambda-s3-execution-role`, timeout to 2 minutes, and memory to 256 MB. You can reduce memory allocation and timeout at a later stage when everything works. On your system, copy the second function and associated files into a new directory to create the third function. Open package.json and change all occurrences of the old function name (`set-permissions`) to the new one (`extract-metadata`). Make sure to update the ARN in package.json, as well as to reflect the ARN of the new function.

In the function directory, create a new subdirectory called bin. Copy your statically built version of FFprobe into it. You'll be pushing Lambda to the max with this function, so make sure to include only FFprobe and not the other components. The maximum deployment package size for Lambda is 50 MB, so including too many unnecessary files may cause your deployment to fail.

The third Lambda function works by copying the video from S3 to a /tmp directory on its local filesystem. It then executes FFprobe and collects the required information. Finally, it creates a JSON file with the required data and saves it in the bucket next to the file (figure 3.20). Lambda has a maximum disk capacity of 512 MB, so this function won't work if your videos are larger.

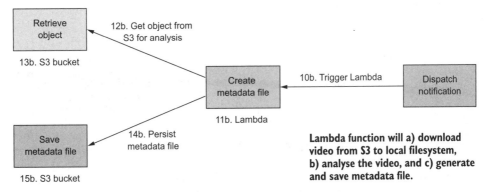

Figure 3.20 The third Lambda function will retrieve an object from S3, run FFprobe, and save metadata back to the bucket.

Listing 3.7 shows an implementation of the third Lambda function. Replace the contents of index.js with the code in the listing. Once you've finished, deploy the third function to AWS.

File permissions

Any script or program you wish to execute in Lambda must have the right (executable) file permissions. Unfortunately, you can't change file permissions directly in Lambda, so it must be done on your computer before the function is deployed. If you use Linux or Mac, it's easy. Run `chmod +x bin/ffprobe` from a terminal command line (you must be in the Lambda function's directory). You can then deploy the function, and FFprobe will work. If you're on Windows, it's trickier because it doesn't come with the `chmod` command. One way you can solve this problem is by spinning up an Amazon Linux machine in AWS, copying FFprobe over, changing permissions, and then copying the file back.

Listing 3.7 Extracting metadata

```
"use strict";

var AWS = require('aws-sdk');
var exec = require('child_process').exec;
var fs = require('fs');

process.env['PATH'] = process.env['PATH'] + ':' +
➥process.env['LAMBDA_TASK_ROOT'];

var s3 = new AWS.S3();

function saveMetadataToS3(body, bucket, key, callback){
        console.log('Saving metadata to s3');
```

```
    s3.putObject({
      Bucket: bucket,
      Key: key,
      Body: body
    }, function(error, data){
      if (error){
        callback(error);
      }
    });
}
```

> You need to copy FFprobe to the bin
> directory for the command to execute.
> Make sure that FFprobe has the right
> permissions (chmod +x) to execute.

```
function extractMetadata(sourceBucket, sourceKey, localFilename, callback){
    console.log('Extracting metadata');

    var cmd = 'bin/ffprobe -v quiet -print_format json
    ➥-show_format "/tmp/' + localFilename + '"';

      exec(cmd, function(error, stdout, stderr){
        if (error === null){
          var metadataKey = sourceKey.split('.')[0] + '.json';
          saveMetadataToS3(stdout, sourceBucket, metadataKey, callback);
        } else {
          console.log(stderr);
          callback(error);
        }
      });
}
```

> To open a read stream, the
> createReadStream method requires the
> path of the file. This stream can then be
> piped to createWriteStream and used
> to create a file on the local filesystem.

```
function saveFileToFilesystem(sourceBucket, sourceKey, callback){
    console.log('Saving to filesystem');

    var localFilename = sourceKey.split('/').pop();
    var file = fs.createWriteStream('/tmp/' + localFilename);

    var stream = s3.getObject({Bucket: sourceBucket, Key:
    ➥sourceKey}).createReadStream().pipe(file);

    stream.on('error', function(error){
      callback(error);
    });

    stream.on('close', function(){
      extractMetadata(sourceBucket, sourceKey, localFilename, callback);
    });
}

exports.handler = function(event, context, callback){
    var message = JSON.parse(event.Records[0].Sns.Message);

    var sourceBucket = message.Records[0].s3.bucket.name;
    var sourceKey =
    ➥decodeURIComponent(message.Records[0].s3.object.key.replace(/\+/g, " "));

    saveFileToFilesystem(sourceBucket, sourceKey, callback);
};
```

> This function has three steps: it copies an object from S3
> to the local filesystem (saveFileToFilesystem), extracts
> metadata from the file (extractMetadata), and saves
> metadata to a new file in S3 (saveMetadataToS3).

You may notice that the function in listing 3.7 has many callbacks. Having numerous callbacks in a function that essentially carries out sequential operations makes it harder to read and understand. Chapter 6 introduces a pattern called *async waterfall* that makes composition of asynchronous operations easier to manage.

3.5 Finishing touches

The third Lambda function needs to subscribe to the SNS topic. Create a new subscription for it just as you did for the second Lambda function:

1 In the AWS console click SNS, select Topics, and then click the ARN of your topic (`transcoded-video-notifications`).
2 Click the Create Subscription button and select AWS Lambda.
3 In the Endpoint drop-down, select the `extract-metadata` Lambda function and click Create Subscription.

Deploy the third function to AWS, and you're now ready to run the whole process end to end. Upload a video to the upload bucket; you should see JSON files created and placed next to the video files in the `transcoded videos` bucket (figure 3.21).

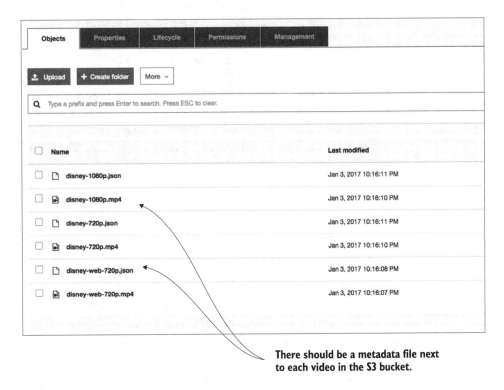

There should be a metadata file next to each video in the S3 bucket.

Figure 3.21 The full workflow should now be operational. If something doesn't work, check CloudWatch logs for clues about what went wrong.

You might also see a few errors in CloudWatch if you didn't set an mp4 suffix in the S3 event configuration back in section 3.2.1. If you didn't set the suffix, your workflow will trigger automatically whenever any new object is saved to the transcoded videos bucket. When a JSON file is saved, the workflow runs again, except the extract-metadata function doesn't know how to deal with a JSON file, which causes an error.

To fix this problem, S3 needs to create notifications only for objects that end with mp4 so that other types of files including JSON don't trigger the workflow:

1 Open the transcoded videos bucket in S3, click Properties, click Events, and edit the event notification.

2 In the Suffix textbox, type mp4, and save.

Of course, if you did this back in section 3.2.1, you don't need to do it again.

3.6 *Exercises*

At the moment, 24-Hour Video is functional, but it has a number of limitations that have been left for you to solve as an exercise. See you if you can implement a solution for the following problems:

1 A file with more than one period in its name (for example, Lecture 1.1 – Programming Paradigms.mp4) will produce transcoded files with truncated names. Implement a fix so that filenames with multiple periods work.

2 Currently, any file uploaded to the upload bucket will trigger the workflow. The Elastic Transcoder, however, will fail if it's given invalid input (for example, a file that's not a video). Modify the first Lambda function to check the extension of the uploaded file and submit only avi, mp4, or mov files to Elastic Transcoder. Any invalid files should be deleted from the bucket.

3 The functions that you've written are somewhat unsafe. They don't always gracefully handle errors or invalid input. Go through each function and modify it to do additional error checking and handling where you see fit.

4 The JSON metadata file is not publicly accessible. Modify the third Lambda function to make the file publicly viewable, similar to the videos in the bucket.

5 The current system creates three similar transcoded videos. The main difference between them is the resolution and bitrate. To make the system more varied, add support for HLS and webm formats.

6 The files in the upload bucket will remain there until you delete them. Come up with a way to clean up the bucket automatically after 24 hours. You might want to have a look at the Lifecycle options in S3 for ideas.

7 Running a Lambda function to create a metadata file for each transcoded file is unnecessary if you care only about information that's constant, such as the length of the video. Modify the system to create a metadata file off the original upload, and then save it next to the transcoded files in the transcoded videos bucket.

8 Videos uploaded to the upload bucket must have unique filenames for the system to work properly. The Elastic Transcoder won't create new files if another file with the same name already exists in the `transcoded videos` bucket. Modify the first Lambda function to create transcoded videos with unique filenames.

9 The test that you've built for the first Lambda function won't work because the IAM user (`lambda-upload`) doesn't have permissions to create Elastic Transcoder jobs. In chapter 6 we'll look at more robust ways of testing Lambda functions, but for now, add the right permissions to the IAM user so that you can create new jobs by running the test locally.

3.7 Summary

In this chapter, we covered the basics of creating a serverless back end, including the following:

- IAM users and roles
- Storage and event notifications in S3
- Configuration and usage of the Elastic Transcoder
- Implementation of custom Lambda functions
- Testing and deployments using npm
- SNS and multiple subscriber workflows

In the next chapter, we'll look at AWS security, logging, alerting, and billing in more detail. This information is important to know to create secure serverless architecture, to know where to look for answers when things go wrong, and to avoid unexpected and unwelcome surprises on the monthly bill.

Setting up your cloud

This chapter covers

- Security model and identity management in AWS
- Logging, alerting, and custom metrics
- Monitoring and estimating AWS costs

Most of the architecture described in this book is built on top of AWS. This means you need a clear understanding of AWS from the perspectives of security, logging, alerting, and costs. It doesn't matter whether you use Lambda alone or have a large mix of services. Being able to configure security correctly, knowing where to look for logs, and controlling cost are important. This chapter is designed so that you can understand these concerns and learn where to look for important information in AWS.

AWS security is a complex subject, but this chapter gives you an overview of the difference between users and roles and shows you how to create policies. This information is needed to configure a system in which services can communicate effectively and securely.

Logging and alerting are critical components of any system, serverless or traditional. They can help to surface serious events such as failing services or sudden escalation of costs. When things go bad, you'll be thankful that you have a robust logging and alerting framework in place.

Cost is an important consideration when using a platform such as AWS and implementing serverless architecture. It's essential to understand the cost calculation of the services you're going to use. This is useful not only for avoiding bill shock but also for predicting next month's costs and beyond. We look at estimating the cost of services and discuss strategies for tracking costs and keeping them under control.

This chapter is not an exhaustive guide to AWS security, logging, and costs. If you have further questions after reading this chapter, take a look at AWS documentation (https://aws.amazon.com/documentation) and books such as *Amazon Web Services in Action* by Andreas Wittig and Michael Wittig (Manning Publications, 2016).

4.1 Security model and identity management

In chapter 3 and appendix B, you created an Identity and Access Management (IAM) user and a number of roles in order to use Lambda, S3, SNS, and Elastic Transcoder and to perform deployments from your machine to AWS. You also modified a resource-based policy in SNS and changed the access control list (ACL) of an object in an S3 bucket. All of those actions are needed to meet security requirements of AWS. In this section, you'll learn about users, groups, roles, and policies in more detail.

4.1.1 Creating and managing IAM users

As you'll recall, an IAM user is an entity in AWS that identifies a human user, an application, or a service. A user normally has a set of credentials and permissions that can be used to access resources and services across AWS. In appendix B, for example, you created a user called `lambda-upload` to allow you to upload Lambda functions.

An IAM user typically has a friendly name to help you identify the user and an Amazon Resource Name (ARN) that uniquely identifies it across AWS. Figure 4.1 shows a summary page and an ARN for a fictional user named Alfred. You can get to this summary in the AWS console by clicking IAM in the AWS console, clicking Users in the navigation pane, and then clicking the name of the user you want to view.

You can create IAM users to represent human users, applications, or services. IAM users created to work on behalf of an application or a service sometimes are referred to as service accounts. These types of IAM users can access AWS service APIs using an access key. An access key for an IAM user can be generated when the user is initially created, or you can create it later by clicking Users in the IAM console, clicking the required user name, selecting Security Credentials, and then clicking the Create Access Key button.

The two components of an access key are the Access Key ID and the Secret Access Key. The Access Key ID can be shared publicly, but the Secret Access Key must be kept hidden. If the Secret Access Key is revealed, the whole key must be immediately invalidated and re-created. An IAM user can have, at most, two active access keys.

If an IAM user is created for a real person, then that user should be assigned a password. This password will allow a human user to log into the AWS console and use services and APIs directly.

The Amazon Resource Name (ARN) of user Alfred

Users > Alfred

Users: Alfred

User ARN	arn:aws:iam::038221756127:user/Alfred
Path	/
Creation time	2016-01-30 22:27 UTC+1100

Permissions   Groups (0)   Security credentials   Access Advisor

ℹ   Get started with permissions

This user doesn't have any permissions yet. Get started by adding the user to a group, copying permissions attaching a policy directly. Learn more

Add permissions

Figure 4.1   The IAM console shows metadata such as the ARN, groups, and creation time for every IAM user in your account.

The Manage Password option is available for any IAM user. Users with a password can log in to the AWS console.

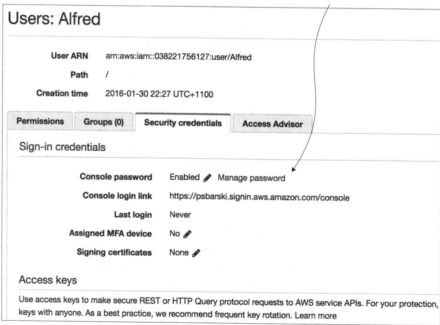

Users: Alfred

User ARN	arn:aws:iam::038221756127:user/Alfred
Path	/
Creation time	2016-01-30 22:27 UTC+1100

Permissions   Groups (0)   **Security credentials**   Access Advisor

Sign-in credentials

Console password	Enabled ✎ Manage password
Console login link	https://psbarski.signin.aws.amazon.com/console
Last login	Never
Assigned MFA device	No ✎
Signing certificates	None ✎

Access keys

Use access keys to make secure REST or HTTP Query protocol requests to AWS service APIs. For your protection, keys with anyone. As a best practice, we recommend frequent key rotation. Learn more

Figure 4.2   IAM users have a number of options, including being able to set a password, change access keys, and enable multifactor authentication.

To create a password for an IAM user, follow these steps:

1. In the IAM console, click Users in the navigation pane.
2. Click the required username to open the user's settings.
3. Click the Security Credentials tab and then click Manage Password (figure 4.2).
4. In the popup, choose whether to enable or disable console access, type in a new custom password, or let the system autogenerate one. You can also force the user to create a new password at the next sign-in (figure 4.3).

After a user is assigned a password, they can log into the AWS console by navigating to https://<Account-ID>.signin.aws.amazon.com/console. To get the account ID, click Support in the upper-right navigation bar, and then click Support Center. The account ID (or account number) is shown at the top right of the console. You may want to set up an alias for the account ID also, so that your users don't have to remember it (for more information about aliases, see http://amzn.to/1MgvWvf).

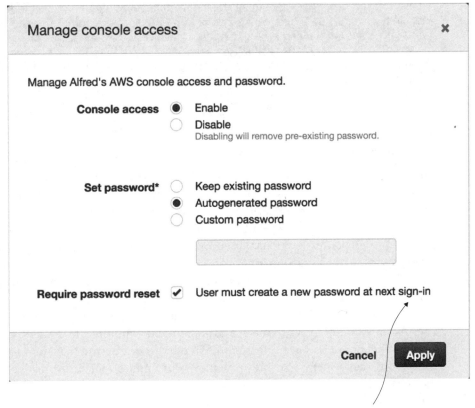

Asking the user to set a new password is good practice,
as long as a good password policy is established.

Figure 4.3　Make sure to create a good password policy with a high degree of complexity if you allow users to log into the AWS console. Password policy can be set up in Account Settings of the IAM console.

Multi-factor authentication

Multi-factor authentication (MFA) adds another layer of security by prompting users to enter an authentication code from their MFA device when they try to sign into the console (this is in addition to the usual username and password). It makes it more difficult for an attacker to compromise an account. Any modern smartphone can act as a virtual MFA appliance using an application such as Google Authenticator or AWS Virtual MFA. It's recommended that you enable MFA for any user who might use the AWS console. You'll find the option Assign MFA Device in the Security Credentials tab when you click an IAM user in the console.

Temporary security credentials

At this time, there's a limit of 5,000 users per AWS account, but you can raise the limit if needed. An alternative to increasing the number of users is to use temporary security credentials. These work similarly to IAM users but can be made to expire after a preset time and can be generated dynamically. See Amazon's online documentation at http://docs.aws.amazon.com/IAM/latest/UserGuide/id_credentials_temp.html for more information on temporary security credentials. You can find more information about IAM users at http://docs.aws.amazon.com/IAM/latest/UserGuide/id_users.html.

4.1.2 Creating groups

Groups represent a collection of IAM users. They provide an easy way to specify permissions for multiple users at once. For example, you may want to create a group for developers or testers in your organization or have a group called Lambda to allow all members of that group to execute Lambda functions. Amazon recommends using groups to assign permissions to IAM users rather than defining permissions individually.

Any user who joins a group inherits permissions assigned to the group. Similarly, if a user leaves a group, the group's permissions are removed from the user. Furthermore, groups can contain only users, not other groups or entities such as roles.

AWS doesn't provide a default group, but it's easy to create a group if you need one. As an example, you'll create a group to allow multiple IAM users to upload Lambda functions. This group may come in handy because you may want to set up a continuous deployment pipeline to deploy your application. Best practice suggests that you ought to create IAM users for different environments (staging, production, and so on). If you add them to this group, they'll have correct permissions to perform deployments.

1 Create the group in the IAM console by clicking Groups and then clicking Create New Group.

2 Give the group a name, such as `Lambda-DevOps`, and click Next Step.

3 Do not attach any policies to the group. Click Next Step and then click Create Group to save and exit.

4 Having performed the first three steps, you are returned to the Groups page.

5 Click `Lambda-DevOps`, make sure that the Permissions tab is selected, and then expand the Inline Policies section. Click the Click Here link in the Inline Policy section and select Custom Policy.

6 Set a name for the policy, such as `Lambda-Upload-Policy`, and copy the code in the next listing to the policy document body.

Listing 4.1 Lambda Upload Policy

```
{
    "Version": "2012-10-17",
    "Statement": [
        {
            "Sid": "Stmt1451465505000",
            "Effect": "Allow",
            "Action": [
                "lambda:GetFunction",
                "lambda:UpdateFunctionCode",
                "lambda:UpdateFunctionConfiguration"
            ],
            "Resource": [
                "arn:aws:lambda:*"
            ]
        }
    ]
}
```

A Statement ID (Sid) is an optional policy identifier that you can set. It should be unique within the policy but you can make it up.

Allow three actions that can get the required Lambda function, update the function code, and update its configuration.

This policy applies to all Lambda functions, as indicated by the wildcard.

7 Click Apply Policy to save and exit. If you review the group, it should be similar to figure 4.4.

8 Find the original `lambda-upload` user and remove their inline policy.

9 Click the Groups tab and then click Add User to Groups. Select the `lambda-upload` user from the list and click Add to Groups.

10 Click the Permissions tab. You should see a new inline policy called `Lambda-Upload-Policy`, which you can view. If you decide to remove the policy later, you'll need to remove the user from the group. Figure 4.5 shows how you can do that from the Groups tab.

11 Test the deployment of one of your functions as you learned to do in chapter 3.

IAM > Groups > **Lambda-DevOps**

▾ Summary

Group ARN:	arn:aws:iam::038221756127:group/Lambda-DevOps
Users (in this group):	0
Path:	/
Creation Time:	2016-03-25 15:37 UTC+1100

Users	**Permissions**	Access Advisor

Managed Policies

There are no managed policies attached to this group.

Attach Policy

Inline Policies

This view shows all inline policies that are embedded in this group.

Create Group Policy

Policy Name	Actions
Lambda-Upload-Policy	Show Policy | Edit Policy | Remove Policy | Simulate Policy

A group's policy can be managed as if it were any regular user or role. Managed and inline policies are allowed.

Figure 4.4   There should be one inline policy attached to this group. You can add additional managed or inline policies to this group later.

Users > lambda-upload

Users: lambda-upload

User ARN	arn:aws:iam::038221756127:user/lambda-upload
Path	/
Creation time	2015-12-30 14:49 UTC+1100

Permissions	**Groups (1)**	Security credentials	Access Advisor

Add user to groups

Group name ▾	Attached permissions	
Lambda-DevOps	Lambda-Upload-Policy	✖

Remove user from group

Figure 4.5   This user doesn't have an inline or managed policy. One group policy applies, however.

4.1.3 Creating roles

A *role* is a set of permissions that a user, application, or a service can assume for a period of time. A role is not uniquely coupled to a specific user, nor does it have associated credentials such as passwords or access keys. It's designed to grant permissions to a user or a service that typically doesn't have access to the required resource. In chapter 3, you created a role to allow Lambda functions to access S3. This is a common use case within AWS.

Delegation is an important concept associated with roles. Put simply, delegation is concerned with the granting of permissions to a third party to allow access to a particular resource. It involves establishing a trust relationship between a trusting account that owns the resource and a trusted account that contains the users or applications that need to access the resource. Figure 4.6 shows a role with a trust relationship established for a service called CloudCheckr, which you can read more about in section 4.3.2.

Federation is another concept that's discussed often in the context of roles. Federation is the process of creating a trust relationship between an external identity provider such as Facebook, Google, or an enterprise identity system that supports Security Assertion Markup Language (SAML) 2.0, and AWS. It enables users to log in via one of those external identity providers and assume an IAM role with temporary credentials.

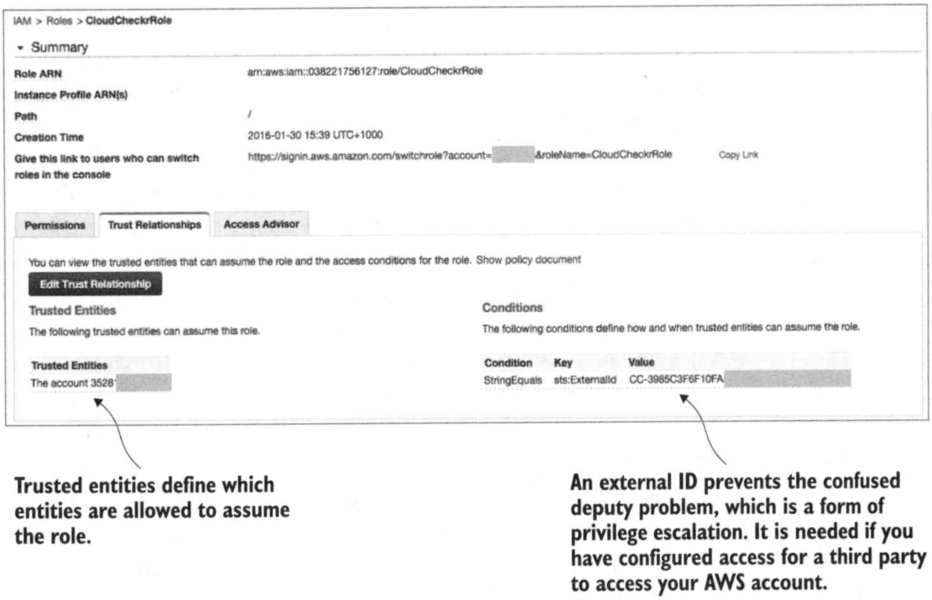

Trusted entities define which entities are allowed to assume the role.

An external ID prevents the confused deputy problem, which is a form of privilege escalation. It is needed if you have configured access for a third party to access your AWS account.

Figure 4.6   This role grants CloudCheckr access to the AWS account to perform analysis of costs and recommend improvements.

4.1.4 Resources

Permissions in AWS are either identity-based or resource-based. Identity-based permissions specify what an IAM user or a role may do. Resource-based permissions specify what an AWS resource, such as an S3 bucket or an SNS topic, is allowed to do or who can have access to it. In chapter 3, you modified the policy of an SNS topic to allow it to communicate with S3. That was an example of a resource-based policy that you had to change to meet your requirements.

A resource-based policy often specifies who has access to the given resource. This allows trusted users to access the resource without having to assume a role. The AWS user guide states: "cross-account access with a resource-based policy has an advantage over a role. With a resource that is accessed through a resource-based policy, the user still works in the trusted account and does not have to give up his or her user permissions in place of the role permissions. In other words, the user continues to have access to resources in the trusted account at the same time as he or she has access to the resource in the trusting account" (http://docs.aws.amazon.com/IAM/latest/UserGuide/id_roles_compare-resource-policies.html). Not all AWS services support resource-based policies, however. Currently, the only services that do are S3 buckets, SNS topics, SQS queues, Glacier vaults, OpsWorks stacks, and Lambda functions.

4.1.5 Permissions and policies

When you initially create an IAM user, it's unable to access or do anything in your account. You need to grant the user permissions by creating a policy that describes what the user is allowed to do. The same goes for a new group or role. A new group or a role needs to be assigned a policy to have any effect.

The scope of any policy can vary. You can give your user or role administrator access to the whole account or specify individual actions. It's better to be granular and specify only permissions that are needed to get the job done (least privilege access). Start with a minimum set of permissions and add additional permissions only if necessary.

There are two types of policies: managed and inline. Managed policies apply to users, groups, and roles but not to resources. Managed policies are standalone. Some managed policies are created and maintained by AWS. You also can also create and maintain customer-managed policies. Managed policies are great for reusability and change management. If you use a customer-managed policy and decide to modify it, all changes are automatically applied to all IAM users, roles, and groups that the policy is attached to. Managed policies allow for easier versioning and rollbacks.

Inline policies are created and attached directly to a specific user, group, or role. When an entity is deleted, the inline policies embedded within it are deleted also. Resource-based policies are always inline. To add an inline or a managed policy, click into the required user, group, or role and then click the Permissions tab. You can attach, view, or detach a managed policy and similarly create, view, or remove an inline policy.

A policy is specified using JSON notation. The following listing shows a managed `AWSLambdaExecute` policy.

Listing 4.2 `AWSLambdaExecute` policy

Version specifies the policy language version. The current version is 2012-10-17. If you're creating a custom policy, make sure to include the version and set it to 2012-10-17.

The statement array contains one or more statements that specify the actual permissions that make up the policy.

```
{
    "Version":"2012-10-17",
    "Statement":[
        {
            "Effect":"Allow",
            "Action": "logs:*",
            "Resource":"arn:aws:logs:*:*:*"
        },
        {
            "Effect":"Allow",
            "Action":[
                "s3:GetObject",
                "s3:PutObject"
            ],
            "Resource":"arn:aws:s3:::*"
        }
    ]
}
```

The Effect element is required and specifies whether the statement allows or denies access to the resource. The only two available options are Allow and Deny.

The Action element, or an array, specifies the specific actions on the resource that should be allowed or denied. The use of a wildcard (*) character is allowed; for example, "Action": "s3:*".

The Resource element identifies the object or objects that the statement applies to. It can be specific or include a wildcard to refer to multiple entities.

Many IAM policies contain additional elements such as Principal, Sid, and Condition. The Principal element specifies an IAM user, an account, or a service that's allowed or denied access to a resource. The Principal element isn't used in policies that are attached to IAM users or groups. Instead, they're used in roles to specify who can assume the role. They're also common to resource-based policies. Statement ID (Sid) is required in policies for certain AWS services, such as SNS. A condition allows you to specify rules that dictate when a policy should apply. An example of a condition is presented in the next listing.

Listing 4.3 Policy condition

You can use a number of conditional elements. These include DateEquals, DateLessThan, DateMoreThan, StringEquals, StringLike, StringNotEquals, and ArnEquals.

```
"Condition": {
    "DateLessThan": {
            "aws:CurrentTime": "2016-10-12T12:00:00Z"
        },
        "IpAddress": {
            "aws:SourceIp": "127.0.0.1"
        }
    }
```

The condition keys represent values that come from the request issued by a user. Possible keys include SourceIp, CurrentTime, Referer, SourceArn, userid, and username. The value can be either a specific literal value such as "127.0.0.1" or a policy variable.

Multiple conditions

The AWS documentation at http://amzn.to/21UofNi states "If there are multiple condition operators, or if there are multiple keys attached to a single condition operator, the conditions are evaluated using a logical AND. If a single condition operator includes multiple values for one key, that condition operator is evaluated using a logical OR." See http://amzn.to/21UofNi for great examples you can follow and a whole heap of useful documentation.

Amazon recommends using conditions, to the extent that is practical, for security. The next listing, for example, shows an S3 bucket policy that forces content to be served only over HTTPS/SSL. This policy refuses connections over unencrypted HTTP.

Listing 4.4   Policy to enforce HTTPS/SSL

```
{
    "Version": "2012-10-17",
    "Id": "123",
    "Statement": [
        {
            "Effect": "Deny",
            "Principal": "*",                      ◁─────┐  This policy explicitly denies access
            "Action": "s3:*",                      ◁─────┘  to s3 if the condition is met.
            "Resource": "arn:aws:s3:::my-bucket/*",
            "Condition": {
                "Bool": {
                    "aws:SecureTransport": false   ◁────┐
                }
            }
        }
    ]
}
```

The condition is met when requests are not sent using SSL. This forces the policy to block access to the bucket if a user tries to access it over regular, unencrypted HTTP.

4.2   Logging and alerting

CloudWatch is an AWS component for monitoring resources and services running on AWS, setting alarms based on a wide range of metrics, and viewing statistics on the performance of your resources. When you begin to build your serverless system, you're likely to use logging more than any other feature of CloudWatch. It will help to track and debug issues in Lambda functions, and it's likely that you'll rely it on for some time. Its other features, however, will become important as your system matures and goes to production. You'll use CloudWatch to track metrics and set alarms for unexpected events.

As with most services, AWS has a different pricing model for CloudWatch depending on the region. Assuming you're using CloudWatch in the eastern United States (northern Virginia), the price is $0.50 per GB of logs ingested and $0.03 per GB for archiving logs per month. Alarms cost $0.10 per alarm per month, and custom metrics are $0.50 per metric. The free tier in CloudWatch consists of 10 custom metrics, 10 alarms, 1,000 SNS email notifications per customer, 5 GB of data ingestion, and 5 GB of archived storage per month.

CloudTrail is an AWS service that records API calls. It records information such as the identity of the API caller, the source IP address, and the event. This data is saved in a log file in an S3 bucket. CloudTrail is an effective way to generate logs and gather information about what AWS services are doing and who's invoking them. For example, you can use it to view the event that the Elastic Transcoder used to kick off a new job or find who deleted a useful S3 bucket and when. CloudTrail supports a number of AWS services including CloudSearch, DynamoDB, Kinesis, API Gateway, and Lambda, and it can be configured to push logs straight to a CloudWatch log group.

The free tier in CloudTrail allows you to create a free trail per region. For additional trails, however, the charge is $2.00 per 100,000 events recorded.

4.2.1 Setting up logging

The log section of CloudWatch can be accessed by clicking CloudWatch in the AWS console and then clicking Logs in the navigation pane. You're likely to see a set of log groups already created that correspond to the three functions that you developed in chapter 3. Click any of the log groups to see a list of log streams. Log streams contain log events, which are the raw records of events that occurred. Every log event has a timestamp and an event message. The cogwheel on the right side allows you to add more columns to the default two-column view. You can choose to show columns with creation time, the last event time, the first event time, and the ARN. Figure 4.7 shows the main log view. In traditional architectures, developers or solution architects usually install log agents on their Elastic Compute Cloud (EC2) instances and use them to log to CloudWatch. With serverless architecture, you don't need to worry about provisioning EC2 instances and installing agents. Lambda logs to CloudWatch automatically, which can work out fairly well in practice, especially if you have a good logging framework (we'll talk more about it in chapter 6).

The Actions menu has options to create and delete log groups, export data, and create subscriptions.

You can create metric filters using the Actions menu, and you can use filters to create custom alerts.

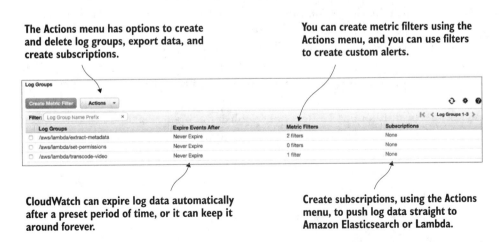

CloudWatch can expire log data automatically after a preset period of time, or it can keep it around forever.

Create subscriptions, using the Actions menu, to push log data straight to Amazon Elasticsearch or Lambda.

Figure 4.7   You should see three log groups for the three Lambda functions previously created.

4.2.2 Log retention

The CloudWatch log data is stored indefinitely. It never expires. If you want Cloud-Watch to delete logs automatically after a set period, you can configure it in the CloudWatch console:

1 Click the Log page in the CloudWatch console, and in the Expire Events After column, click Never Expires to change the retention period.
2 In the Edit Retention dialog, select the desired period. It can range from 1 day to 10 years to Never Expire.

4.2.3 *Filters, metrics, and alarms*

Metric filters specify patterns that run against incoming log events. If there's a match, a CloudWatch metric is updated, which can then be used to produce a graph or create an alarm.

A metric filter contains the following important components:

- *Pattern*—Used to specify what term or phrase to look for in a log.
- *Value*—The value to publish to a metric. It can be a count or a specific term extracted from the log.
- *Metric name*—The name of the CloudWatch metric that will contain the result as specified by the value.
- *Namespace*—A grouping for related metrics.
- *Filter name*—The name of the filter.

You're going to create a metric filter, a metric, and an alarm to help track how many times a Lambda function exits abnormally because of an error:

1 In the CloudWatch console, click Log in the navigation pane and then select the check box next to the log group called /aws/lambda/transcode-video. (This is the log group that you created for the first Lambda function in chapter 3.)
2 Click the Create Metric Filter button to continue. In the Filter Pattern text box, type Process exited before completing request.
3 You can now test the pattern if you have any log events that have shown this error message before. You can look through existing log streams by using the drop-down just below where you entered the pattern and then clicking the Test Pattern button. See figure 4.8 for an example. Note that "Filters do not retroactively filter data. Filters only publish the metric data points for events that happen after the filter was created" (http://amzn.to/1RFsxDo).

Select from available log streams from the
drop-down. Oldest log streams are at the
top, and newer ones are at the bottom.

Match log events
on terms, values,
or phrases.

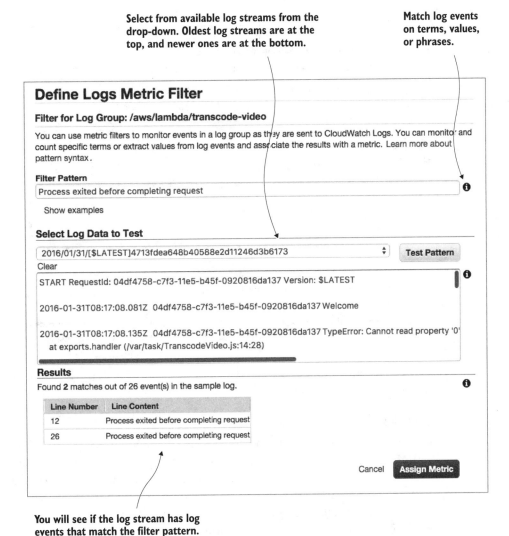

Define Logs Metric Filter

Filter for Log Group: /aws/lambda/transcode-video

You can use metric filters to monitor events in a log group as they are sent to CloudWatch Logs. You can monitor and count specific terms or extract values from log events and associate the results with a metric. Learn more about pattern syntax.

Filter Pattern

Process exited before completing request   ⓘ

Show examples

Select Log Data to Test

2016/01/31/[$LATEST]4713fdea648b40588e2d11246d3b6173   ⇕   **Test Pattern**

Clear

START RequestId: 04df4758-c7f3-11e5-b45f-0920816da137 Version: $LATEST   ⓘ

2016-01-31T08:17:08.081Z 04df4758-c7f3-11e5-b45f-0920816da137 Welcome

2016-01-31T08:17:08.135Z 04df4758-c7f3-11e5-b45f-0920816da137 TypeError: Cannot read property '0'
    at exports.handler (/var/task/TranscodeVideo.js:14:28)

Results

Found **2** matches out of 26 event(s) in the sample log.   ⓘ

Line Number	Line Content
12	Process exited before completing request
26	Process exited before completing request

Cancel   **Assign Metric**

You will see if the log stream has log
events that match the filter pattern.

Figure 4.8 Filter patterns support wildcards and conditions. See the AWS guide at http://amzn.to/1QLF8WW for more information on filter and pattern syntax.

4 Click Assign Metric and then give your filter a name and set metric details. The metric namespace allows you to group related metrics together, so use something like `LambdaErrors` and then give your new metric a name such as `Lambda-ProcessExitErrorCount` (figure 4.9).

5 Click Create Filter to create the metric filter.

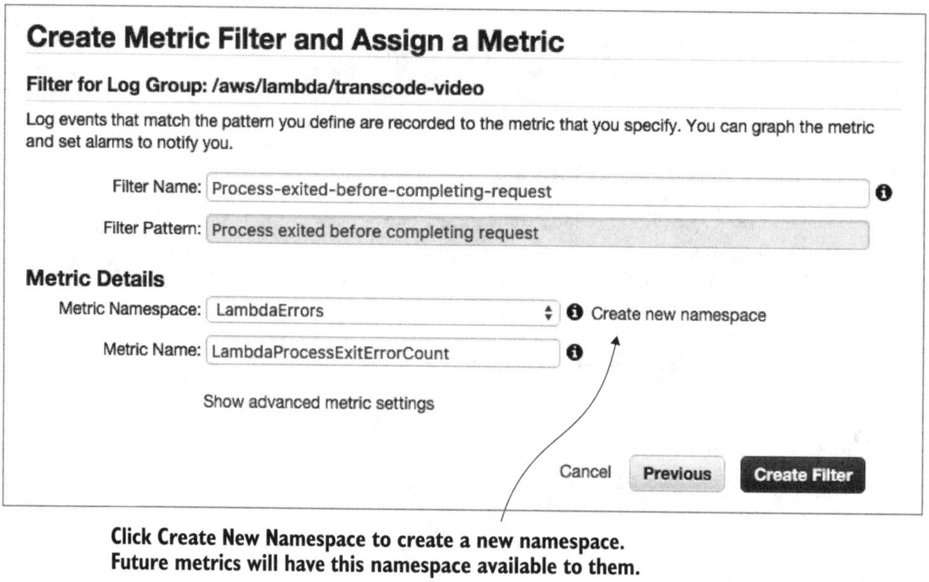

Create Metric Filter and Assign a Metric

Filter for Log Group: /aws/lambda/transcode-video

Log events that match the pattern you define are recorded to the metric that you specify. You can graph the metric and set alarms to notify you.

Filter Name: `Process-exited-before-completing-request` ❶

Filter Pattern: `Process exited before completing request`

Metric Details

Metric Namespace: `LambdaErrors` ⬍ ❶ Create new namespace

Metric Name: `LambdaProcessExitErrorCount` ❶

Show advanced metric settings

Cancel   **Previous**   **Create Filter**

**Click Create New Namespace to create a new namespace.
Future metrics will have this namespace available to them.**

Figure 4.9 Grouping metrics under a namespace makes it easy to organize groups of metrics together. You can access the namespace and view related metrics from the navigation pane in CloudWatch.

Having created your metric, you can create an alarm for it. Section 4.2.6 explains how to create alarms based on metrics.

4.2.4 *Searching log data*

You also can search log data in CloudWatch using the metric filter pattern syntax. To search through existing log data, navigate to the Logs page and click the desired log group. Click the Search Log Group button, and type a pattern in the Filter text box. Optionally, you can set a date and time to restrict the scope of the search. If you want to do a search within a particular log stream, you can click it first and then type your pattern. For more information on filter and pattern syntax, go to http://amzn.to/1miUFTd.

4.2.5 *S3 and logging*

S3 is able to track access requests and log information separately from CloudWatch. These logs are useful for auditing and attaining additional insights into who or what service is accessing your buckets. S3 logs store information such as the bucket name, request time and action, and response status.

24-Hour Video relies on S3 for storage of video files, and it's likely that many systems using serverless architecture will use S3 also. Therefore, to learn how to activate and use S3 logging, you'll need to enable it for the first bucket you created back in chapter 3:

1 In the S3 console, create a new bucket to store log files. Name this bucket `serverless-video-logs`.

2 Click the first bucket you created in chapter 3, which would be `serverless-video-upload`, and then select Properties:

3 Click Logging and enable the logging capability of the bucket.

4 From the Target Bucket drop-down, select the bucket that you created in step 1.

5 In the target prefix, type `upload/` and save. Figure 4.10 shows this example.

6 To test the system, upload or rename an object in the first bucket. Logs may take several hours to appear, so give them some time.

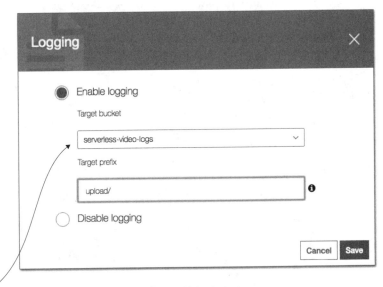

Setting the target prefix will create virtual folders in the S3 bucket. This will help to organize and store multiple logs in the same bucket.

Figure 4.10   Logging for an S3 bucket can be enabled and disabled at any time. Enabling this option will modify the ACL of the target bucket to give the Log Delivery group permission to write to the bucket.

4.2.6   *More on alarms*

CloudWatch alarms monitor metrics, such as duration, errors, invocations, or throttles, and perform an action, such as sending a message to SNS, when the number of events goes over the established threshold in a given timeframe. An alarm has three possible states:

- *OK*—The monitored metric is within the defined threshold.
- *Insufficient Data*—Not enough data available to determine state.
- *Alarm*—The metric is outside the bounds of the defined threshold and action will be taken.

Let's create an alarm that triggers a notification for Lambda errors. This alarm sends an email if three or more Lambda errors occur in a one-minute span:

1 Create an SNS topic called `lambda-error-notifications` and subscribe to it with your email address.
2 In the AWS console, click SNS. Select Topics in the navigation pane and click the Create New Topic button.
3 A dialog should appear onscreen asking for information about the topic. Set the topic and display names to `lambda-error-notifications`. Click Create Topic to save.
4 You will remain in the Topics list view after creating the topic, and your new topic will appear in the list. Select the check box next to it and click Actions.

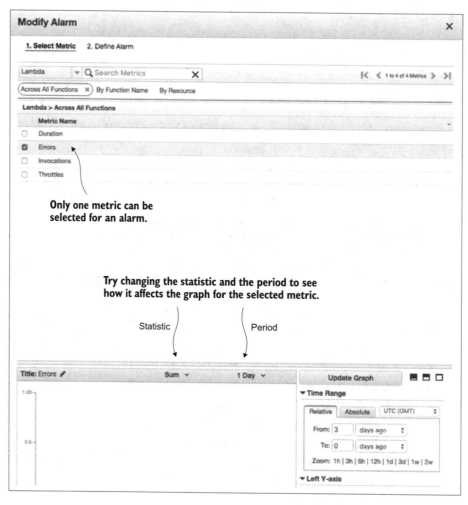

Figure 4.11   Creating an alarm is a straightforward process. You can find in-depth information at http://docs.aws.amazon.com/AmazonCloudWatch/latest/monitoring/ConsoleAlarms.html.

5 From the Actions menu select Subscribe to Topic. You'll see another dialog appear titled Create Subscription.

6 In the dialog, set Protocol to Email and type your email address in the endpoint text box.

7 Click Create Subscription to save and close the dialog.

8 Remember to check your email and confirm the subscription.

9 In the CloudWatch console click Alarms and then click Create Alarm.

10 In the Alarm dialog click Lambda Metric, and then under the heading of Lambda > Across All Functions, select the Errors check box. Figure 4.11 shows this page in detail. Click Next to go to the second page.

11 The second page of this dialog is where you configure the threshold, the period, and action (figure 4.12).

12 Type a name for the alarm, such as `lambda-errors`, and then set the threshold to 3 or more errors for one consecutive period.

13 Change Period to 1 minute and then change Statistic to Sum.

14 Under Actions, select the SNS topic you created earlier from the second drop-down.

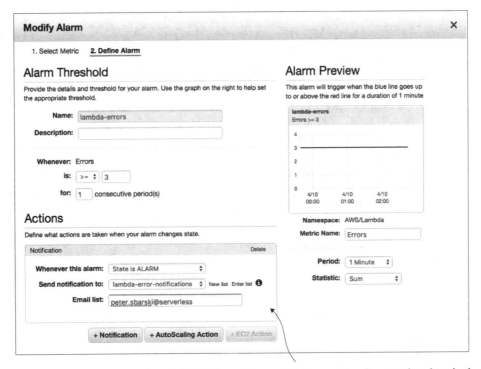

Set the SNS topic and the email list in case the alarm needs to be raised.

Figure 4.12 To complete the creation of the alarm, set the number of occurrences in a consecutive period to trigger the alarm and specify the resulting action.

15 Click Create Alarm to finalize the creation of the alarm.

16 Now you need to test the alarm to make sure it has been set up correctly:

17 Open Lambda in the AWS console and click the radio button next to any of the functions you created in chapter 3.

18 From the Actions drop-down, select Test Function (figure 4.13).

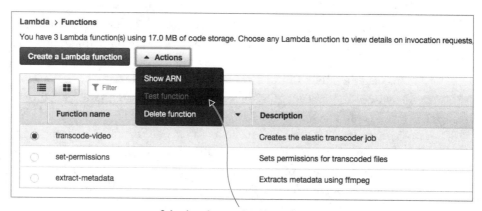

Selecting the test function will give you a
range of event templates to choose from.

Figure 4.13   You can use the Test Function feature to test your Lambda functions directly in the AWS console.

19 You'll see a list of test events to choose from. The first Hello World test is enough to cause an error, so leave it selected and click Save and Test.

20 The test should cause an immediate error. The execution result should show "Failed" and the error message should say "Process exited before completing request" (figure 4.14).

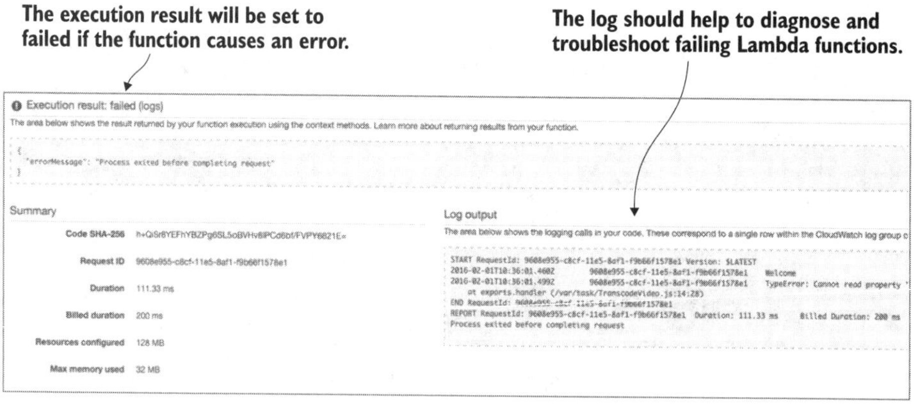

The execution result will be set to
failed if the function causes an error.

The log should help to diagnose and
troubleshoot failing Lambda functions.

Figure 4.14   The Lambda console shows whether the test succeeded or failed, the function's log output, and a useful summary of execution.

21 Click the Test button three or four more times to make sure that there's enough data for the alarm.

22 Check your email, because you should receive a notification from CloudWatch.

4.2.7 *CloudTrail*

CloudTrail records API calls made across your account by users or services on behalf of a user. It provides a convenient way to audit API calls and to help diagnose and troubleshoot issues. CloudTrail introduces the concept of trails, which are configurations that enable logging of APIs. There are two types of trails—one that applies to all regions and one that applies to a single, specific region. You should enable CloudTrail because it helps to understand what's happening within the system when things go wrong. Let's walk through the steps to create a trail for your region:

1 Click CloudTrail in the AWS console, and then click Get Started Now.

2 Give your trail a name, such as 24-Hour-Video, and set Apply Trail to All Regions to No.

3 Set Create a New S3 Bucket to No, and from the S3 Bucket drop-down list select the bucket for logs (`serverless-video-logs`) you created earlier in section 4.2.5.

4 Click Advanced to have a look at additional options. You don't need to set anything, but you can enable SNS notifications and log file validations if you want (figure 4.15).

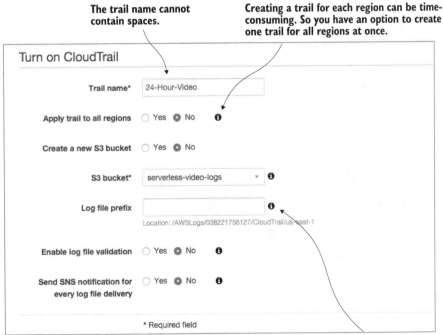

The trail name cannot contain spaces.

Creating a trail for each region can be time-consuming. So you have an option to create one trail for all regions at once.

You can add one additional log prefix.

Figure 4.15 Creating a new trail shouldn't take long. The only two mandatory fields are the name and the S3 bucket.

5 Click Turn On to save the trail and complete your configuration.

6 After the trail is created, you're taken to a table that lists all trails for your account across all regions. You created only one trail, so click it to inspect and configure its options.

7 The one thing you need to configure is integration with CloudWatch, so do it now:

8 In the Trail Configuration page, click Configure under the CloudWatch Logs section.

9 Specify a new log group or leave the default value in the text box (figure 4.16).

10 Click Continue and then click Allow. Doing this creates a new role to allow CloudTrail to issue required CloudWatch API calls.

The API Activity History page in CloudTrail shows create, modify, and delete API calls executed over the past seven days. You can expand each event and then click the View

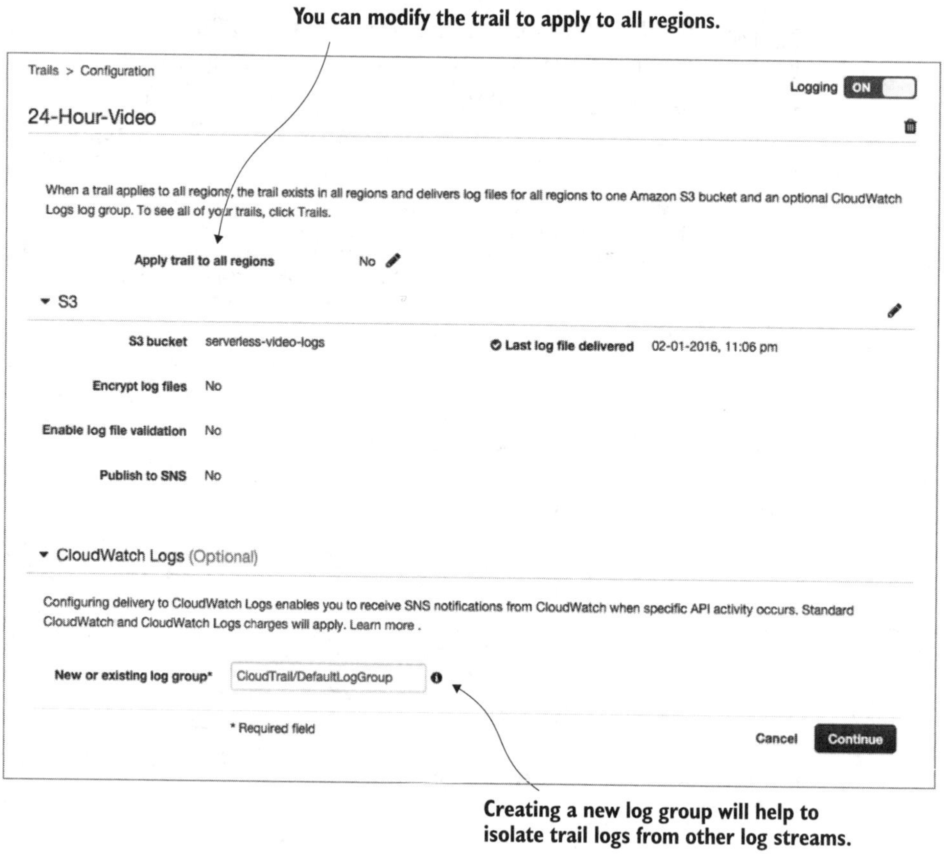

You can modify the trail to apply to all regions.

Trails > Configuration

24-Hour-Video   Logging **ON**

When a trail applies to all regions, the trail exists in all regions and delivers log files for all regions to one Amazon S3 bucket and an optional CloudWatch Logs log group. To see all of your trails, click Trails.

Apply trail to all regions   No ✎

▼ S3

S3 bucket   serverless-video-logs   ⟳ **Last log file delivered**   02-01-2016, 11:06 pm

Encrypt log files   No

Enable log file validation   No

Publish to SNS   No

▼ CloudWatch Logs (Optional)

Configuring delivery to CloudWatch Logs enables you to receive SNS notifications from CloudWatch when specific API activity occurs. Standard CloudWatch and CloudWatch Logs charges will apply. Learn more .

New or existing log group*   [CloudTrail/DefaultLogGroup] ❶

* Required field   Cancel   **Continue**

Creating a new log group will help to isolate trail logs from other log streams.

Figure 4.16 Configure CloudWatch integration with CloudTrail. This allows you to create metrics and alarms for the incoming trail log data.

Event button to see more information. Events may take up to 15 minutes to appear. Alternatively, you can inspect the S3 bucket for the full log of the API activity or look at the appropriate log group created in CloudWatch.

4.3 Costs

Receiving an unpleasant surprise in the form of a large bill at the end of the month is disappointing and stressful. CloudWatch can create billing alarms that send notifications if total charges for the month exceed a predefined threshold. This is useful not only to avoid unexpectedly large bills but also to catch potential misconfigurations of your system. For example, it's easy to misconfigure a Lambda function and inadvertently allocate 1.5 GB of RAM to it. The function might not do anything useful except wait for 15 seconds to receive a response from a database. In a very heavy-duty environment, the system might perform 2 million invocations of the function a month, costing a little over $743.00. The same function with 128 MB of RAM would cost around $56.00 per month. If you perform cost calculations up front and have a sensible billing alarm, you'll quickly realize that something is going on when billing alerts begin to come through.

4.3.1 Creating billing alerts

Follow these steps to create a billing alert:

1 Enable billing alerts in the Billing and Cost Management console (figure 4.17).
2 In the main AWS console, click your name (or the name of the IAM user that's representing you) and then click My Billing Dashboard.
3 Click Preferences in the navigation pane and then enable the check box next to Receive Billing Alerts.
4 Click Save Preferences.

Once enabled, the billing alert option cannot be disabled.

Dashboard	**Preferences**
Bills	
Cost Explorer	☐ **Receive PDF Invoice By Email**
Budgets	Turn on this feature to receive a PDF version of your invoice by email. Invoices are generally available within the first three (
Reports	
Cost Allocation Tags	☑ **Receive Billing Alerts**
Payment Methods	Turn on this feature to monitor your AWS usage charges and recurring fees automatically, making it easier to track and man receive email notifications when your charges reach a specified threshold. Once enabled, this preference cannot be disable(
Payment History	
Consolidated Billing	☐ **Receive Billing Reports**
Preferences	Turn on this feature to receive ongoing reports of your AWS charges once or more daily. AWS delivers these reports to the . For consolidated billing customers, AWS generates reports only for paying accounts. Linked accounts cannot sign up for bill
Credits	
Tax Settings	Save to S3 Bucket: [bucket name] [Verify]
DevPay	
	[Save preferences]

Figure 4.17 The Preferences page allows you to manage how invoices and billing reports are received.

5 Open the CloudWatch console and select Billing in the navigation pane.

6 Click the Create Alarm button and then click the Billing Metrics subheader.

7 Under Billing > Total Estimated Charge select the first check box (this is the Estimated Charges metric). Selecting this option captures estimated charges across all AWS services. You can, however, go granular and select specific services.

8 Click the Create Alarm button in the lower-right corner to open the Create Alarm dialog.

9 This dialog is similar to the dialog you used in section 4.2.6. Set your spending threshold and select an SNS topic for the delivery of notifications. You can, optionally, click New list and enter an email address directly (figure 4.18).

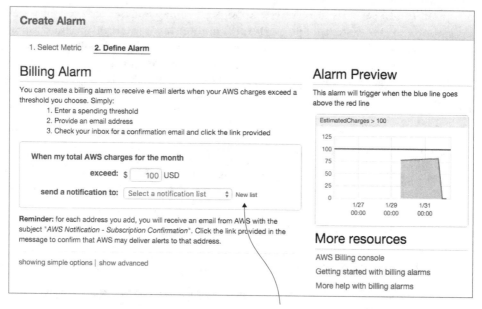

Clicking New List will allow you to enter an email address directly, without having to select an SNS topic.

Figure 4.18   It's good practice to create multiple billing alarms to keep you informed of ongoing costs.

4.3.2   *Monitoring and optimizing costs*

Services such as CloudCheckr (http://cloudcheckr.com) can help to track costs, send alerts, and even suggest savings by analyzing services and resources in use. Cloud-Checkr comprises several different AWS services, including S3, CloudSearch, SES, SNS, and DynamoDB. It's richer in features and easier to use than some of the standard AWS features. It's worth considering for its recommendations and daily notifications.

AWS also has a service called Trusted Advisor that suggests improvements to performance, fault tolerance, security, and cost optimization. Unfortunately, the free version of Trusted Advisor is limited, so if you want to explore all of the features and recommendations it has to offer, you must upgrade to a paid monthly plan or access it through an AWS enterprise account.

Cost Explorer (figure 4.19) is a useful, albeit high-level, reporting and analytics tool built into AWS. You must activate it first by clicking your name (or the IAM username) in the top-right corner of the AWS console, selecting My Billing Dashboard, then clicking Cost Explorer from the navigation pane and enabling it. Cost Explorer analyzes your costs for the current month and the past four months. It then creates a forecast for the next three months. Initially, you may not see any information, because it takes 24 hours for AWS to process data for the current month. Processing data for previous months make take even longer. More information about Cost Explorer is available at http://amzn.to/1KvN0g2.

There are four standard reports to choose from but you can create your own reports too.

The forecast allows you to guesstimate and assess possible costs well into the future.

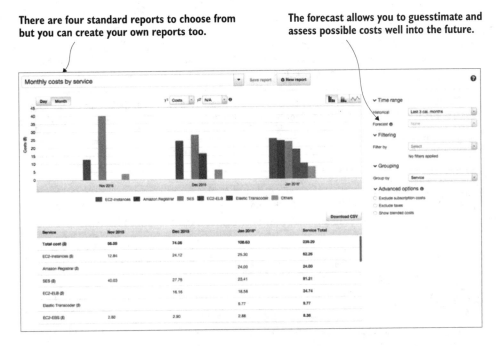

Figure 4.19 The Cost Explorer tool allows you to review historical costs and estimate what future costs may be.

4.3.3 Using the Simple Monthly Calculator

The Simple Monthly Calculator (http://calculator.s3.amazonaws.com/index.html) is a web application developed by Amazon to help model costs for many of its services. This tool allows you to select a service on the left side of the console and then enter information related to the consumption of that particular resource to get an indicative cost. Figure 4.20 shows a snippet of the Simple Monthly Calculator with an estimated monthly cost of $650.00. That estimate is mainly of costs for S3, CloudFront,

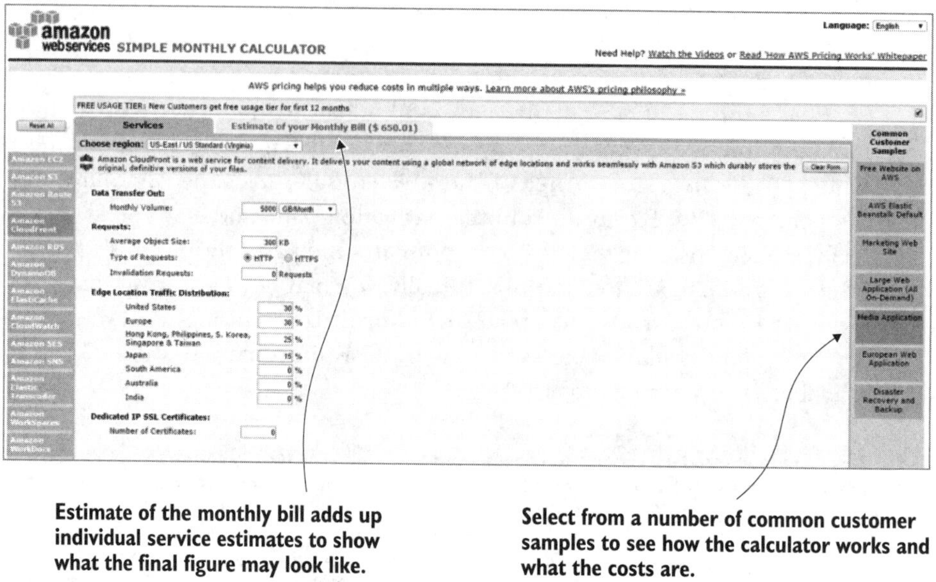

Estimate of the monthly bill adds up individual service estimates to show what the final figure may look like.

Select from a number of common customer samples to see how the calculator works and what the costs are.

Figure 4.20   The Simple Monthly Calculator is a great tool to work out the estimated costs in advance. You can use these estimates to create billing alarms at a later stage.

and the AWS support plan. It's a complex tool and it's not without usability issues, but it can help with estimates.

You can click Common Customer Samples on the right side of the console or enter your own values to see estimates. If you take the Media Application customer sample, something that could serve as a model for 24-Hour Video, it breaks down as follows:

- The S3 estimated cost is $9.01. It includes 300 GB storage, 200 PUT/COPY/POST/LIST requests, 100 GET and other requests, 2 GB/month data transfer out, and 10 GB/month data transfer in.
- The CloudFront estimated cost is $549.96. It includes 5000 GB/month data transfer out with an average object size of 300 KB. The edge location traffic distribution is 30% for the United States and Europe, 15% for Japan, and 25% for Hong Kong, Philippines, South Korea, Singapore, and Taiwan.
- The AWS business support plan is $100.00.

4.3.4   *Calculating Lambda and API Gateway costs*

The cost of running serverless architecture often can be a lot less than running traditional infrastructure. Naturally, the cost of each service you might use will be different, but you can look at what it takes to run a serverless system with Lambda and the API Gateway.

Amazon's pricing for Lambda (https://aws.amazon.com/lambda/pricing/) is based on the number of requests, duration of execution, and the amount of memory allocated to the function. The first million requests are free, with each subsequent million charged at $0.20. Duration is based on how long the function takes to execute, rounded up to the next 100 ms. Amazon charges in 100 ms increments while also taking into account the amount of memory reserved for the function.

A function created with 1 GB of memory will cost $0.000001667 per 100ms of execution time, whereas a function created with 128 MB of memory will cost $0.000000208 per 100 ms. Note that Amazon prices may differ depending on the region and that they're subject to change at any time.

Amazon provides a perpetual free tier with 1 million free requests and 400,000 GB-seconds of compute time per month. This means that a user can perform a million requests and spend an equivalent of 400,000 seconds running a function created with 1 GB of memory before they have to pay.

As an example, consider a scenario where you have to run a 256 MB function 5 million times a month. The function executes for two seconds each time. The cost calculation follows:

Monthly request charge:

- The free tier provides 1 million requests, which means that there are only 4 million billable requests (5M requests – 1M free requests = 4M requests).
- Each million is priced at $0.20, which makes the request charge $0.80 (4M requests * $0.2/M = $0.80).

Monthly compute charge:

- The compute price for a function per GB-second is $0.00001667. The free tier provides 400,000 GB-seconds free.
- In this scenario, the function runs for 10 ms (5M * 2 seconds).
- 10M seconds at 256 MB of memory equates to 2,500,000 GB-seconds (10,000,000 * 256 MB/1024 = 2,500,000).
- The total billable amount of GB-seconds for the month is 2,100,000 (2,500,000 GB-seconds – 400,000 free tier GB-seconds = 2,100,000).
- The compute charge is therefore $35.007 (2,100,000 GB-seconds * $0.00001667 = $35.007).

The total cost of running Lambda in this example is $35.807. The API Gateway pricing is based on the number of API calls received and the amount of data transferred out of AWS. In the eastern United States, Amazon charges $3.50 for each million API calls received and $0.09/GB for the first 10 TB transferred out. Given the previous example and assuming that monthly outbound data transfer is 100 GB a month, the API Gateway pricing is as follows:

Monthly API charge:

- The free tier includes one million API calls per month but is valid for only 12 months. Given that it's not a perpetual free tier, it won't be included in this calculation.
- The total API cost is $17.50 (5M requests * $3.50/M = $17.50).

Monthly data charge:

- The data charge is $9.00 (100 GB * $0.09/GB = $9).

The API Gateway cost in this example is $26.50. The total cost of Lambda and the API Gateway is $62.307 per month. It's worthwhile to attempt to model how many requests and operations you may have to handle on an ongoing basis. If you expect 2M invocations of a Lambda function that uses only 128 MB of memory and runs for a second, you'll pay approximately $0.20 month. If you expect 2M invocations of a function with 512 MB of RAM that runs for 5 seconds, you'll pay a little more than $75.00. With Lambda, you have an opportunity to assess costs, plan ahead, and pay for only what you actually use. Finally, don't forget to factor in other services such as S3 or SNS, no matter how insignificant their cost may seem to be.

Serverless calculator

The online serverless calculator (http://serverlesscalc.com) is an easy-to-use tool we built to help you model Lambda costs. All you need to do is specify the number of Lambda executions per month, the estimated execution time, and the size (in memory) of your function. The calculator will immediately show you the monthly Lambda charge, including request and compute cost breakdowns. Moreover, this tool will allow you to compare Lambda costs to other similar serverless compute technologies such as Azure Functions and IBM OpenWhisk.

4.4   *Exercises*

Having read about AWS Identity and Access Management, monitoring, logging, and alerting and having implemented 24-Hour Video in chapter 3, try to complete the following exercises:

1   Create the `Lambda-DevOps` group as described previously in this chapter. Assign the current `Lambda-Upload` IAM user to it. Then create two more users, `Lambda-Upload-Staging` and `Lambda-Upload-Production`, and assign those two users to `Lambda-DevOps`. Remember to save the access keys of the two new users in a secure place.

2   Modify the bucket policy of the second bucket in 24-Hour Video, the `video-transcoded-bucket`, to accept only SSL connections. The policy should reject all non-SSL connections. See listing 4.4 for reference.

3   In CloudWatch, set the retention period of all log groups to 6 months.

4   Set up logging for the second bucket you created in chapter 3. Change the target prefix to `transcoded/`.

5   Set up a billing alarm to notify you if you've spent more than $100 in a month and another alarm to notify if you've spent more than $500.00.

6   Create a trail in CloudTrail to monitor the account that hosts 24-Hour Video.

4.5   Summary

In this chapter, we covered a number of core concepts that you need to know to build serverless architectures with AWS effectively. Security, logging, alerting, and cost controls are not always exciting but are nearly always critical to the success of a system. You learned about the following:

- Identity and Access Management in AWS including users, groups, roles, policies, and permissions
- Using CloudWatch to review logs and create alarms based on custom metrics
- Enabling logging in S3
- Monitoring of ongoing costs using built-in alerting and services such as Cloud-Checkr and Trusted Advisor
- Setting up CloudTrail to monitor API invocations of AWS services
- Estimating costs for Lambda and the API Gateway and using the Simple Monthly Calculator

In the next chapter, you'll learn about authentication and authorization in serverless architectures. You'll use Auth0 to build this capability and create a secure user system. We'll introduce the API Gateway and you'll begin putting together a user interface for 24-Hour Video.

Part 2

Core Ideas

You've read through part 1 and now feel comfortable with some of the core concepts and principles of serverless architectures. It's time to go deeper and look at authentication and authorization principles, as well as AWS Lambda and API Gateway, in more detail. In the next few chapters, you'll write Lambda functions, configure a RESTful API, and even set up a website with user authentication. You'll learn how quickly a single developer can put together a serverless back end and how powerful serverless technologies can be.

Authentication
and authorization

This chapter covers

- Authentication and authorization in serverless architecture
- Auth0 as a central service for authentication
- JSON Web Tokens and delegation tokens
- AWS API Gateway and custom authorizers

One of the first questions we're asked is usually about authentication and authorization in a serverless environment. Without a server, how does one authenticate users and secure access to resources? To help answer these questions, we introduce an AWS service called Cognito and another (non-AWS) service called Auth0. We also introduce the AWS API Gateway and show how to use it to create an API. We show you how to secure this API using custom authorizers and connect it to Lambda functions. Lastly, we show how to extend 24-Hour Video to provide sign-in, sign-out, and user-profile facilities by combining features of Auth0, API Gateway, and Lambda.

5.1   *Authentication in a serverless environment*

In modern web and mobile applications, authentication and authorization can take a number of forms. Allowing users to directly sign up with the application or sign in via an enterprise directory is important. It can be equally important to allow users to authenticate with a third-party identity provider (IdP) such as Google, Facebook, or Twitter. You might ask how one implements and manages all the required authentication, authorization, user sign-up, and user validation concerns without a server. The answer is by using services such as AWS Cognito and Auth0 and technologies such as delegation tokens. Before we discuss these services and technologies in more detail, you may want to look at appendix C. This appendix serves as a nice refresher on the topics of authentication and authorization, OpenID, and OAuth 2.0.

5.1.1   *A serverless approach*

Authenticating a user and then authorizing access to needed services may seem like a challenge without a server, but it isn't difficult once you understand what's possible:

- You can use services such as Cognito (https://aws.amazon.com/cognito) or Auth0 (https://auth0.com) to help implement an authentication system.
- You can use tokens to exchange and verify user information between services. In this chapter, you'll use JSON Web Tokens (JWT). These tokens can encapsulate necessary information (claims) about the user. Your Lambda functions can verify that a token is legitimate and then allow execution to continue if everything is okay. You can even check the validity of a token in the API Gateway before the relevant Lambda function is run (more on that in section 5.3).
- You can create delegation tokens using a Lambda function or Auth0. Delegation tokens can be used to authorize direct access to services from the front end.

Figure 5.1 shows what a possible authentication and authorization architecture may look like in a serverless application. The process of authentication is managed using Auth0, which takes care of authentication and creation of delegation tokens needed for direct authentication with other services. As you can see in the figure, the client can access the database directly or send requests to a Lambda function that can access the database using its own credentials. You have flexibility in choosing the best approach for your system.

> **JSON Web Tokens**
>
> Throughout this chapter we'll refer to JWT, which stands for JSON Web Token. The Internet Engineering Task Force (IETF) describes JWT as a "compact, URL-safe means of representing claims to be transferred between two parties. The claims in a JWT are encoded as a JSON object that is used as the payload of a JSON Web Signature (JWS) structure or as the plaintext of a JSON Web Encryption (JWE) structure, enabling the claims to be digitally signed or integrity protected with a Message Authentication Code (MAC) and/or encrypted" (http://bit.ly/1Spxog6). See the section on JWT in appendix C to learn more.

I. User logs in using an authentication service such as Auth0.

3. Client writes to the database. It includes a delegation token (retrieved in step 2) that authorizes this action.

4. Client sends a request to the AWS API Gateway. It includes the original JWT retrieved in step 2.

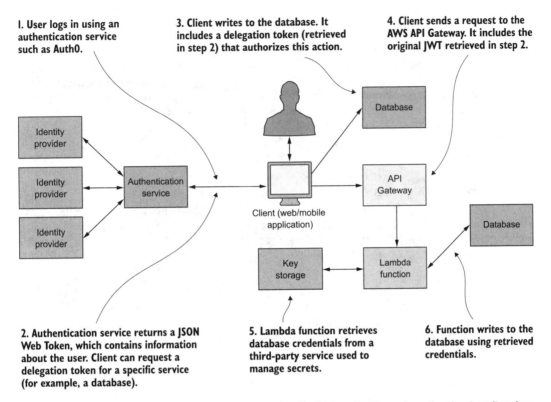

2. Authentication service returns a JSON Web Token, which contains information about the user. Client can request a delegation token for a specific service (for example, a database).

5. Lambda function retrieves database credentials from a third-party service used to manage secrets.

6. Function writes to the database using retrieved credentials.

Figure 5.1 In a serverless architecture, you should let the client interact with services directly where it makes sense.

In chapter 1, we told you that in serverless architecture "the presentation tier of the application communicates directly with services, the database, or compute functions via an API gateway. Many services can be accessed directly by the front end. Some services need to be hidden behind compute service functions where additional security measures and validation can take place." This description stands in contrast to many traditional systems where communication often flows through a back end that coordinates access to the database and services. So when designing your serverless system for authentication and authorization, remember the following points:

- Use an established, industry-supported method for authentication and authorization such as OpenID Connect and JWT.
- Make use of delegation tokens and allow the front end to communicate directly with services (and the database) when it makes sense (that is, do this only when an interruption to the client won't place the system in an inconsistent state and only if it's secure to do so).

> **Delegation tokens**
>
> Later in the book, in chapter 9, we're going to show how to use a JWT-based delegation token to authorize access to your database and to other services. JWT is great, but it's not supported by all services everywhere. There will be times when you'll have to use signatures or temporary credentials instead. In this chapter (and beyond) assume that delegation tokens are JSON Web Tokens. But if we use other ways of granting temporary access to services, we'll clearly mention it.

> **Making things easier in the long term**
>
> When building your serverless architecture, try to reduce the number of steps your system has to take to perform an action. Allow your front end to communicate with services directly if it's secure and appropriate to do so. This will reduce latency and make the system easier to manage.
>
> Furthermore, don't come up with your own way of performing authentication and authorization. Try to adopt common protocols and specifications. You're likely to integrate with multiple third-party services and APIs that implement these as well. Security is difficult, so if you follow tried-and-tested models for authentication and authorization, you're more likely to succeed.

5.1.2   *Amazon Cognito*

As a developer, you can build your own authentication and authorization system if you wish to do so. OpenID Connect and OAuth 2.0 can help you support external identity providers. Add a Lambda function, a database, and a sign-up/sign-in page, and you can begin to authenticate users. But why build when someone else might have already done it? Let's look at existing services to see if they can reduce the amount of work you would normally have to do.

Amazon Cognito (https://aws.amazon.com/cognito) is a service from Amazon that can help with authentication. You can use it to build an entire registration and login system, and it can integrate with public identity providers or your own (existing) authentication process.

Authenticated and unauthenticated users going through Cognito are assigned an IAM role/temporary credentials. This allows users to access resources and services in AWS. Cognito can also save end-user data. This data can be synced and accessed across different devices. Figure 5.2 shows how a user can authenticate with an identity provider and then get access to a database in AWS. Cognito acts as an intermediary (see http://amzn.to/1SmsmPt for more information on Cognito authentication flows).

Cognito is a great service but it has a number of limitations. Useful features such as password reset require a bit of manual implementation and don't have some of the more advanced features such as log on via TouchID. Cognito is a great system but there's another alternative we should explore: a service called Auth0.

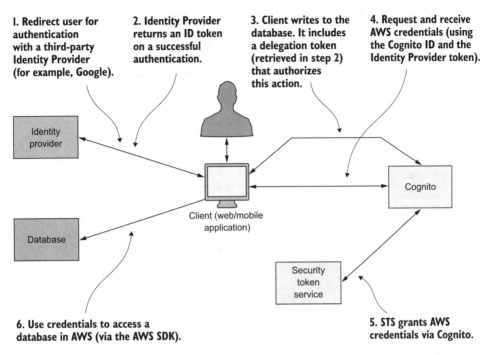

I. Redirect user for authentication with a third-party Identity Provider (for example, Google).

2. Identity Provider returns an ID token on a successful authentication.

3. Client writes to the database. It includes a delegation token (retrieved in step 2) that authorizes this action.

4. Request and receive AWS credentials (using the Cognito ID and the Identity Provider token).

6. Use credentials to access a database in AWS (via the AWS SDK).

5. STS grants AWS credentials via Cognito.

Figure 5.2 The (enhanced) authentication flow with Cognito and a security token service (STS), which grants temporary AWS credentials. Assume here that the client uses AWS SDK to invoke the resource (that is, the database in this figure) directly.

5.1.3 *Auth0*

Auth0 (https://auth0.com) can be labeled a universal identity platform. It supports custom user sign-up/sign-in with a username and a password, integrates with identity providers that use OAuth 2.0 and OAuth 1.0, and connects to enterprise directories. It also has advanced features such as multi-factor authentication and TouchID support.

When a user authenticates with Auth0, the client application receives a JSON Web Token. This token can be used in a Lambda function if it needs to identify the user, or it can be used to request a delegation token (from Auth0) for another service. Auth0 integrates well with AWS. It can obtain temporary AWS credentials to securely access AWS resources, so you don't lose anything by using Auth0 instead of Cognito (for more information about integration with AWS see https://auth0.com/docs/integrations/aws).

Cognito and Auth0 are both very capable systems. You should explore the unique features they offer and make an assessment based on the requirements of your project. In the next section, we'll explore how to handle user authentication in a serverless application using Auth0 and JWT.

5.2   Adding authentication to 24-Hour Video

In this section, you're going to add sign-in/sign-out and user-profile features to 24-Hour Video. You'll use Auth0 to handle user sign-up and authentication, and we'll show you how to secure access to Lambda functions. So far, we've focused only on building the 24-Hour Video back end and neglected the front end. You're now going to build an interface so that users can interact with the system (figure 5.3.)

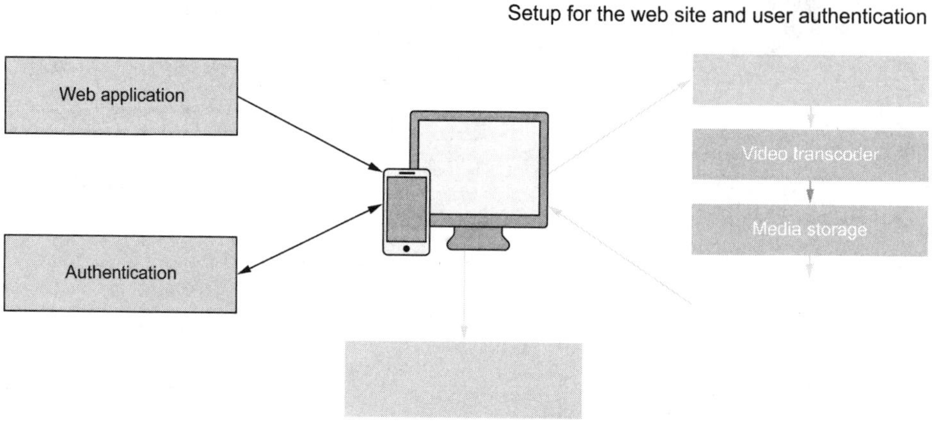

Setup for the web site and user authentication

Web application

Authentication

Video transcoder

Media storage

Figure 5.3   In this chapter you're going to add authentication and begin building your website.

Furthermore, we'll introduce the AWS API Gateway in more detail. You can use this AWS service to create an API between back-end services and the front end. The API Gateway is covered in more detail in chapter 7, so feel free to jump to it if you need further information or clarification as you follow this example.

5.2.1   The plan

The plan for adding an authentication/authorization system to 24-Hour Video is as follows:

1 Create a basic website to serve as a user interface. It will have sign-in, sign-out, and user-profile buttons. In later chapters, you'll add additional capability to this website such as video playback.

2 Register an application with Auth0 and integrate it with the website. Users should be able to log in via Auth0 and receive a JSON Web Token that identifies them.

3 Add an API Gateway to allow the website to invoke Lambda functions.

4 Create a user-profile Lambda function. This function will decode the user's JWT and invoke an Auth0 endpoint to get more information about the user. It will then return this information to the website via the API Gateway. For the moment, you don't have a database, so there isn't any additional information

you can store about the user. But after chapter 9, you'll have a database in which you can save extra user information.

5 Configure the API Gateway to invoke the `user-profile` Lambda function using an HTTP GET request.

6 Modify the API Gateway to perform JWT validation before the request hits an integration endpoint (that is, before the request reaches your Lambda function). You'll create a special Lambda function to validate your JWT and connect it to the API Gateway as a custom authorizer to run on every request.

Figure 5.4 shows the authentication/authorization architecture you're going to build in steps 1–5. Step 6 is described in more detail in section 5.3.5.

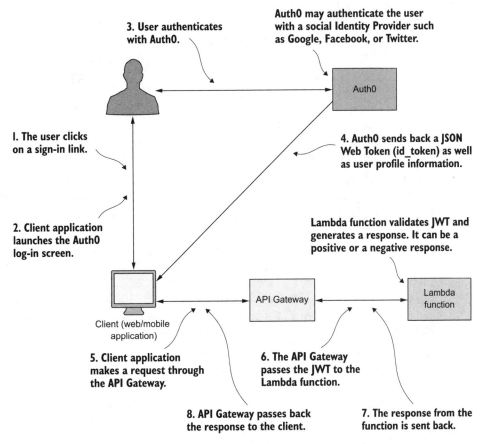

Figure 5.4 The basic authentication/authorization flow with Auth0 and JWT that you'll implement for 24-Hour Video

5.2.2   *Invoking Lambda directly*

At this stage, you might ask, why can't I get temporary AWS credentials and invoke Lambda directly from the 24-Hour Video website? Why do I need an API Gateway at all? Those are fair questions. You do have two ways of invoking Lambda functions. One way is to use the SDK; the other is to go through an interface created by the API Gateway. If you use the SDK approach, it would mean the following:

- The user would have to download a portion of the AWS SDK.
- 24-Hour Video would become coupled to specific Lambda functions. Changing these functions later could become painful and might require a redeployment of the website.
- It would be harder to prevent a rogue user from abusing the system and invoking Lambda thousands of times. With the API Gateway, you can throttle requests, authorize requests, and even cache responses.
- The API Gateway allows you to design and build a uniform RESTful interface that other clients can interact with using simple HTTP requests and standard HTTP verbs.

When it comes to Lambda and a web application, creating a RESTful interface using the API Gateway and putting your functions behind it is the way to go.

5.2.3   *24-Hour Video website*

If you're building a large web application today, you might choose one of the available single-page application (SPA) frameworks such as Angular or React. For the purposes of this example, you're going to create a website using Bootstrap and jQuery. The reason for doing so is to allow you to focus on the serverless aspects of the system rather than configuration and management of an SPA framework. If you wish to use your favorite SPA rather than vanilla JavaScript and jQuery, feel free to do so. You'll be able to follow this example with a few minor tweaks. Figure 5.5 shows what this basic website will look like initially.

A quick way to create a skeleton website is to download the Bootstrap version of the Initializr template (you can accept all default settings when downloading) from http://initializr.com. Extract the download to a new directory such as 24-hour-video. You're going to make changes to this website and install additional packages. To help manage dependencies and later to perform deployments, you'll use npm as you did for Lambda functions in chapter 3. Open a terminal window and do the following:

1 Change to the website directory and run `npm init` from it. Answer questions from npm to create a package.json file.
2 You'll need a web server to host your website. A good module you can use is local-web-server. Run the following command from the terminal to install it:

```
npm install local-web-server --save-dev
```

3 Modify package.json to look like the following listing. It will allow you to run npm `start`, which then launches the web server and hosts the website.

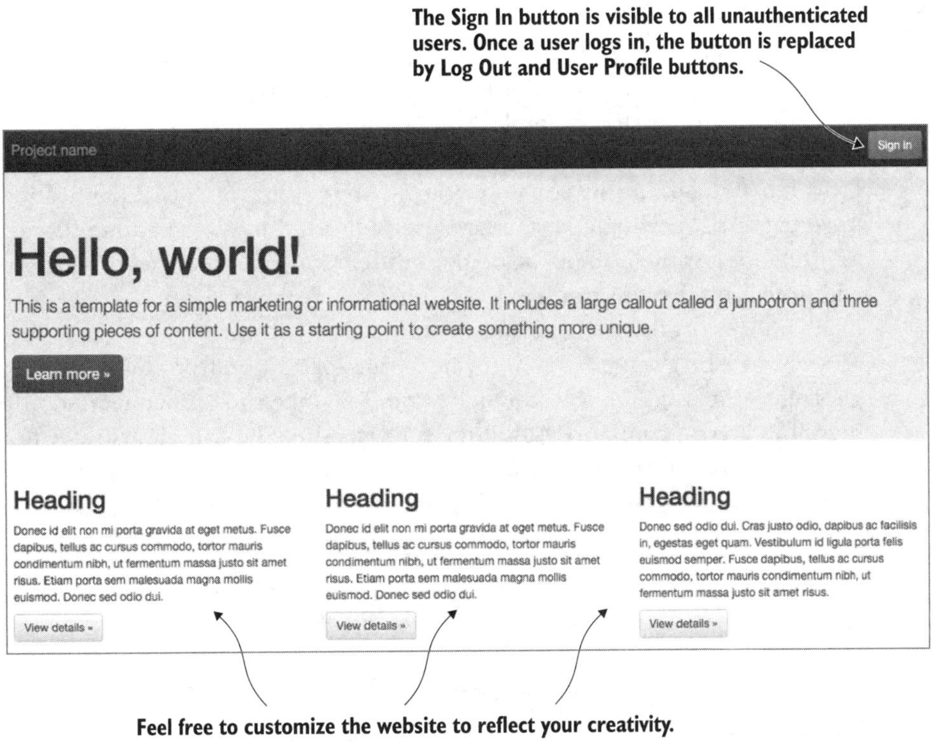

The Sign In button is visible to all unauthenticated users. Once a user logs in, the button is replaced by Log Out and User Profile buttons.

Feel free to customize the website to reflect your creativity.

Figure 5.5 The Initializr Bootstrap template looks like this with an added Sign In button.

Listing 5.1 Package.json for the website

```
{
  "name": "24-hour-video",
  "version": "1.0.0",
  "description": "The 24 Hour Video Website",
  "local-web-server": {
    "port": 8100,
    "forbid": "*.json"
  },
  "scripts": {
    "start": "ws",
    "test": "echo \"Error: no test specified\" && exit 1"
  },
  "author": "Peter Sbarski",
  "license": "BSD-2-Clause",
  "devDependencies": {
    "local-web-server": "^1.2.6"
  }
}
```

Port 8100 is unlikely to clash with other open ports on your system, but you can change it to anything you want.

Running npm start will launch the web server.

Your version number could be different but that's okay. Everything should still work.

Run npm start from the terminal and open http://127.0.0.1:8100 in your web browser to see the website.

5.2.4   *Auth0 configuration*

Now you can integrate Auth0 with the website. Register a new account at https://auth0.com. You'll need to type in a preferred Auth0 account name, which could be anything (for example, your organization or website name) and select a region (choose US West). After creating the account, you might see an Authentication Providers pop-up. In this pop-up you can choose the types of authentication to offer to your users. They include standard username and password authentication, as well as integration with Facebook, Google, Twitter, and Windows Live. You can configure additional connections or remove the ones you've chosen later.

You'll start with a default app in Auth0 that you can use as a basis for 24-Hour Video. You'll be given an option to choose an application type (figure 5.6). Select Single Page App and then select jQuery. You'll be taken to a documentation page that describes how to configure Auth0 for your website. You can always refer to this page for additional information, and you should because Auth0 documentation is excellent. For now, however, click the Settings tab that's under the Default App heading.

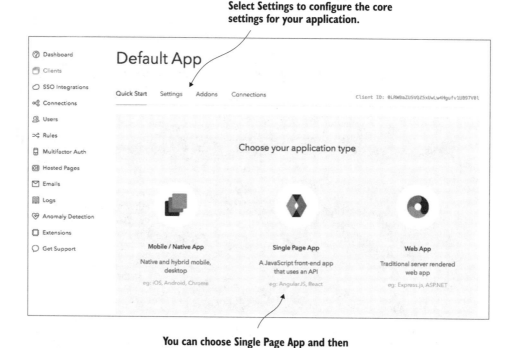

Figure 5.6   Auth0 has a sparse and easy-to-use dashboard. We love it.

In the Settings tab you'll need to configure a couple of options (figure 5.7):

1 From the Client Type drop-down select Single Page Application (if it's not already selected).
2 In Allowed Callback URLs type `http://127.0.0.1:8100`.
3 Click Save Changes at the bottom.

Auth0 will send responses to only the URLs that are specified in Allowed Callback URLs. If you forget to specify your website URL there, Auth0 will show an error during sign-in.

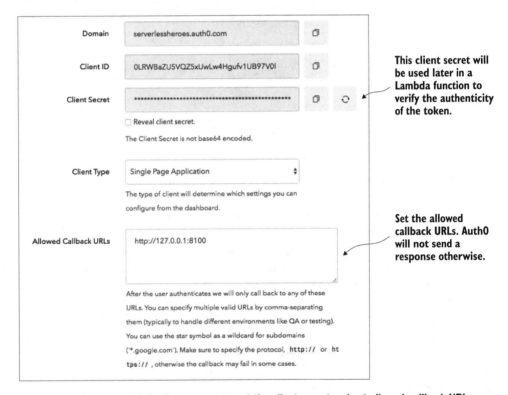

Figure 5.7   Use the Auth0 Settings screen to get the client secret and set allowed callback URLs.

You should also look at Connections (on the left menu) to see which types of integrations, such as database-driven, social, enterprise, or password-less, you could use. If you click Social under Connections, you'll see a list of third-party authentication providers that you can enable for your web application (figure 5.8).

Having two or three social connections enabled is usually enough for most applications. Users will get confused and use multiple accounts to sign in to the system. When that happens, you'll get questions from people asking why their account is different or why things are missing. It's possible to link accounts together, but that's outside the scope of this chapter; see http://bit.ly/1PRKiRe if you need more information on how

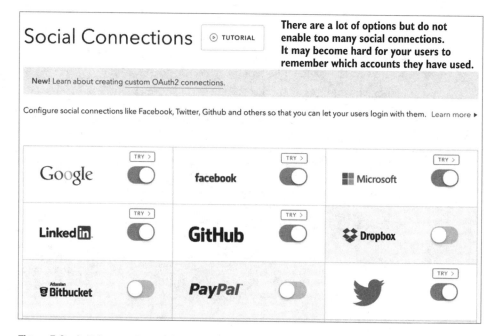

Figure 5.8   Auth0 supports social, database, and enterprise connections.

to do it. Note that the free Auth0 account supports only two social identity providers. If you want to use more, you'll have to go on a paid plan.

If you decide to enable integration with a third-party identity provider such as Google or GitHub, you'll need to do a bit of configuration. When you click an identity provider in Auth0, you'll see the information, such as an API key, that needs to be entered. Auth0 always provides a link to a page that explains how to obtain needed keys, client IDs, and secrets (figure 5.9). For 24-Hour Video, make sure to enable and configure at least one identity provider, such as Google or GitHub, to see how it works. An exercise at the end of the chapter will ask you to do this.

5.2.5   *Adding Auth0 to the website*

In this section, you'll connect the website to Auth0. The user will be able to register and sign in to Auth0 and receive their JSON Web Token. This token will be stored in the browser's local storage and included in every subsequent request to the API Gateway. The user will also be able to sign out, which will remove the token from local storage. Figure 5.10 shows this part of the workflow. Please be aware that in a real system, including this token in every request isn't a best practice. You should control where the token is sent so that third parties don't accidentally intercept it. An exercise at the end of the chapter asks you to address this problem.

Auth0 Lock is a free widget from Auth0 that provides a nice-looking sign-in/sign-up dialog box. It simplifies the authentication flow and has a few interesting features

There is a helpful page for every identity provider that shows how to get relevant configuration information.

The Clients tab allows you to select which of your clients (for example, 24-Hour Video) can use this identity provider.

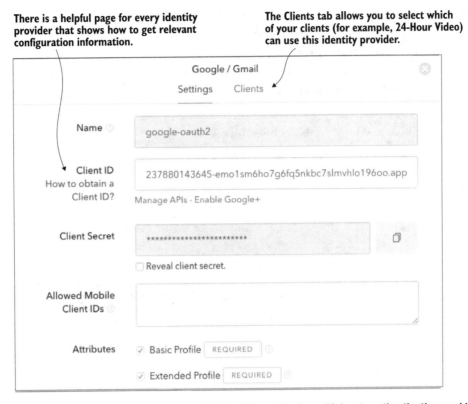

Figure 5.9 Auth0 has guides to help you find key information from third-party authentication providers.

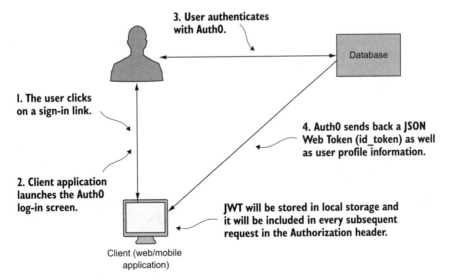

3. User authenticates with Auth0.

1. The user clicks on a sign-in link.

2. Client application launches the Auth0 log-in screen.

4. Auth0 sends back a JSON Web Token (id_token) as well as user profile information.

JWT will be stored in local storage and it will be included in every subsequent request in the Authorization header.

Figure 5.10 Now that you've completed this section, your users will be able to sign into and out of the website.

(for example, it can remember which identity provider the user used in a previous session). You're going to use this, so next we'll look at the following:

- Adding Auth0 Lock to the website
- Adding sign-in, sign-out, and user profile buttons
- Adding a sprinkle of JavaScript to show the login dialog and save the JWT token in local storage once the user authenticates

To add Auth0 Lock to the website, follow these steps:

1 Open index.html in your favorite HTML editor.
2 Add `<script src="https://cdn.auth0.com/js/lock-9.min.js"></script>` above the line that says `<script src="js/main.js"></script>` (which is at the bottom of the file).
3 To add buttons, remove the login form beginning with the line `<form class="navbar-form navbar-right" role="form">` and replace it with the code in the next listing.

Listing 5.2   Adding buttons to index.html

```
<div class="navbar-form navbar-right">
  <button id="user-profile" class="btn btn-default">
    <img id="profilepicture" /> <span id="profilename"></span>
  </button>
  <button id="auth0-login" class="btn btn-success">Sign in</button>
  <button id="auth0-logout" class="btn btn-success">Sign Out</button>
</div>
```

The profile picture will be retrieved via Auth0.

These buttons will trigger the click event in user-controller.js.

You need to add JavaScript to wire up the buttons. Create the following two files in the js directory of the website:

- user-controller.js
- config.js

Now add the following lines above `<script src="js/main.js"></script>` but below `<script src="https://cdn.auth0.com/js/lock-9.min.js"></script>` in index.html:

```
<script src="js/user-controller.js"></script>
<script src="js/config.js"></script>
```

Copy the next listing to user-controller.js. This code is responsible for initializing Auth0 Lock, wiring up click events for the buttons, storing the JWT in local storage, and then including it in every subsequent request in the Authorization header.

Listing 5.3   Contents of user-controller.js

```
var userController = {
  data: {
    auth0Lock: null,
    config: null
  },
  uiElements: {
    loginButton: null,
    logoutButton: null,
    profileButton: null,
    profileNameLabel: null,
    profileImage: null
  },
  init: function(config) {
    var that = this;

    this.uiElements.loginButton = $('#auth0-login');
    this.uiElements.logoutButton = $('#auth0-logout');
    this.uiElements.profileButton = $('#user-profile');
    this.uiElements.profileNameLabel = $('#profilename');
    this.uiElements.profileImage = $('#profilepicture');

    this.data.config = config;
    this.data.auth0Lock =
      new Auth0Lock(config.auth0.clientId, config.auth0.domain);

    var idToken = localStorage.getItem('userToken');

    if (idToken) {
      this.configureAuthenticatedRequests();
      this.data.auth0Lock.getProfile(idToken, function(err, profile) {
        if (err) {
          return alert('There was an error getting the profile: ' +
            err.message);
        }
        that.showUserAuthenticationDetails(profile);
      });
    }

    this.wireEvents();
  },
  configureAuthenticatedRequests: function() {
    $.ajaxSetup({
      'beforeSend': function(xhr) {
        xhr.setRequestHeader('Authorization',
          'Bearer ' + localStorage.getItem('userToken'));
      }
    });
  },
  showUserAuthenticationDetails: function(profile) {
    var showAuthenticationElements = !!profile;

    if (showAuthenticationElements) {
      this.uiElements.profileNameLabel.text(profile.nickname);
      this.uiElements.profileImage.attr('src', profile.picture);
    }
```

The Auth0 client ID and domain will be set in the config.js file.

If the user token already exists, you can try retrieving the profile from Auth0.

This token will be sent in the Authorization header in all future requests. Doing this may be insecure, so in section 5.5 we ask you to fix it.

```
            this.uiElements.loginButton.toggle(!showAuthenticationElements);
            this.uiElements.logoutButton.toggle(showAuthenticationElements);
            this.uiElements.profileButton.toggle(showAuthenticationElements);
        },
      wireEvents: function() {
        var that = this;

        this.uiElements.loginButton.click(function(e) {
          var params = {
            authParams: {
              scope: 'openid email user_metadata picture'
            }
          };

          that.data.auth0Lock.show(params, function(err, profile, token) {
            if (err) {
              alert('There was an error');
            } else {
              localStorage.setItem('userToken', token);
              that.configureAuthenticatedRequests();
              that.showUserAuthenticationDetails(profile);
            }
          });
        });

        this.uiElements.logoutButton.click(function(e) {
          localStorage.removeItem('userToken');

          that.uiElements.logoutButton.hide();
          that.uiElements.profileButton.hide();
          that.uiElements.loginButton.show();
        });
      }
    }
```

> **Auth0 Lock will display a dialog and allow users to register and log in.**

> **Save the JWT token to browser's local storage.**

> **Clicking Logout removes the user's token from local storage, makes the Login button visible, and hides the Profile and Logout buttons.**

Copy the code that follows to config.js. Remember to set the correct client ID and Auth0 domain.

Listing 5.4 Contents of config.js

```
var configConstants = {
    auth0: {
        domain: 'AUTH0-DOMAIN',
        clientId: 'AUTH0-CLIENTID'
    }
};
```

> **The Auth0 domain and client ID can be obtained from the Auth0 dashboard (figure 5.6).**

Copy the code in the next listing to main.js.

Listing 5.5 Contents of main.js

```
(function(){
    $(document).ready(function(){
        userController.init(configConstants);
    });
}());
```

> **Run the userController.init function to wire up events and set up Auth0.**

Finally, modify main.css (located in the css directory of the website) to have the styles given in the following listing.

Listing 5.6　Contents of main.css

```
#auth0-logout {
    display: none;
}

#user-profile {
    display: none;
}

#profilepicture {
    height: 20px;
    width: 20px;

}
```

5.2.6　Testing Auth0 integration

To test Auth0 integration, check that the web server is running in the terminal. If it isn't, then run it by executing `npm start`. Open the page in the browser and click the Sign In button. You should see the Auth0 Lock dialog (figure 5.11). Sign up right now (note that you're creating a new user for the 24-Hour Video app; this isn't the same

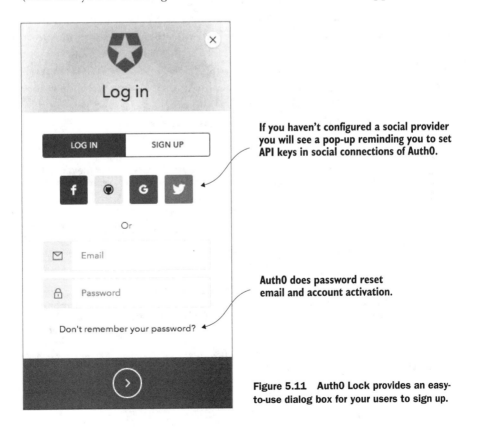

If you haven't configured a social provider you will see a pop-up reminding you to set API keys in social connections of Auth0.

Auth0 does password reset email and account activation.

Figure 5.11　Auth0 Lock provides an easy-to-use dialog box for your users to sign up.

user you used to sign up to Auth0 in the first place), and Auth0 should immediately sign you in to your website. The JWT should be transmitted and saved in the browser's local storage (if you use Chrome, you can open Developer Tools, select Storage, click Local Storage, click http://127.0.0.1:8000, and you'll see the userToken). Click the Sign Out button to log out and delete the JWT from local storage.

Go back to the Auth0 dashboard and click Users. You'll see all users registered with the site. You can contact, block, delete, view location, or even sign in as a different user. If you signed in successfully before, you should see your user details in the list.

If something didn't work and you couldn't sign in, open your browser's developer tools and inspect the Console and Network tabs for any messages from Auth0. Double-check that you set the Allowed Callback URL in Auth0 to be the URL of your website, and check that you have the correct client ID and the domain.

5.3   *Integration with AWS*

Now you're going to create a Lambda function that will accept the JWT from the website, validate it, and then request more information about the user from Auth0. You could issue a request to Auth0 straight from the browser and get information about the user that way. You don't need a Lambda function to do this, but this example is designed to show how to deal with JWT in Lambda and, a little later, some of the code will serve as a basis for your custom authorizer.

As we mentioned earlier, there are two ways to invoke a Lambda function: using the AWS SDK or via an API Gateway. We'll go with the second option, so you need to create an API Gateway. Your website will issue requests to an API Gateway resource and include JWT in the Authorization header of the request. The API Gateway will capture requests, route them to the Lambda function, and then send Lambda responses back to the client. Figure 5.12 shows this part of the workflow.

You'll now work on the custom API (figure 5.13).

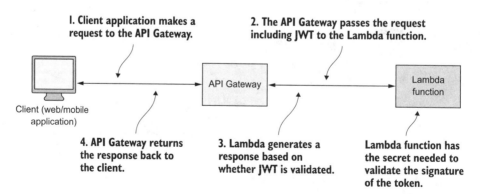

Figure 5.12   The website invokes a Lambda function via the API Gateway. The request includes JWT in the Authorization header.

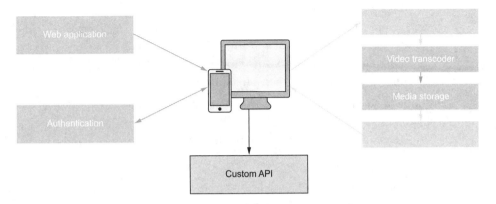

Figure 5.13 **You'll build and use your custom API throughout the next few chapters.**

5.3.1 *User profile Lambda*

Before implementing a user profile Lambda function, you should create a new IAM role for it. You could reuse the role you created earlier (`lambda-s3-execution-role`), but it has one too many permissions you don't need. So let's see how to make a new one with fewer permissions:

1 Create a new role in the IAM console.
2 Name it `api-gateway-lambda-exec-role`.
3 In step 2 of the role-creation process, select AWS Lambda.
4 From the list of policies, select `AWSLambdaBasicExecutionRole`.
5 Click Create Role to save.

Having created a new role, you can focus on the Lambda function. This function will do the following:

- Validate JSON Web Tokens.
- Invoke an Auth0 endpoint to retrieve information about the user.
- Send a response to the website.

Create the function in AWS right now:

1 Click Lambda in the AWS console.
2 Click the Create a Lambda Function button and select the Blank Function blueprint.
3 Click Next on the Triggers screen.
4 Name the function `user-profile`.
5 Select `api-gateway-lambda-exec-role` from the Existing Role drop-down.
6 Leave all other settings as they are, and then save and create the function.

On your computer, set up the function:

1 Make a copy of one of the Lambda functions you worked on in chapter 3.
2 Change the name and any relevant metadata in package.json (remember to update the function name or the ARN in the deploy script).
3 If you have the AWS SDK in the list of dependencies in package.json, you can remove it because you won't need it for this function.

You now need to add an npm module called jsonwebtoken. This module will help to verify the integrity of the token and decode it.

In a terminal window change to the directory of the function and run

```
npm install jsonwebtoken --save
```

Also, to make a request to Auth0 to retrieve user information, you're going to use a library called request. Install request by running npm install request --save from the terminal. Your package.json should look similar to the next listing.

Listing 5.7 Package.json for the `user-profile` Lambda function

```
{
  "name": "user-profile",
  "version": "1.0.0",
  "description": "This Lambda function returns the current user-profile",
  "main": "index.js",
  "scripts": {
    "deploy": "aws lambda update-function-code
 --function-name user-profile --zip-file fileb://Lambda-Deployment.zip",
    "predeploy": "zip -r Lambda-Deployment.zip * -x *.zip *.json *.log"
  },
  "dependencies": {
    "jsonwebtoken": "^5.7.0",
    "request": "^2.69.0"
  },
  "author": "Peter Sbarski",
  "license": "BSD-2-Clause",
}
```

> You can delete unused scripts (like the test script) and dependencies if they aren't needed in this function.

> Your version numbers may be different.

Open index.js and replace its contents with code in the next listing. This code is responsible for validating and decoding the token. If it succeeds, it sends a request to the tokeninfo endpoint provided by Auth0. The JWT is included in the body of the request to Auth0. The tokeninfo endpoint returns information about the user, which is then sent back to the website.

Listing 5.8 Contents of the `user-profile` Lambda function

```
'use strict';

var jwt = require('jsonwebtoken');
var request = require('request');

exports.handler = function(event, context, callback){
```

```
            if (!event.authToken) {
                callback('Could not find authToken');
                return;
            }

            var token = event.authToken.split(' ')[1];

            var secretBuffer =
            new Buffer(process.env.AUTH0_SECRET);
            jwt.verify(token, secretBuffer, function(err, decoded){
                if(err){
                    console.log('Failed jwt verification: ', err,
                        'auth: ', event.authToken);
                    callback('Authorization Failed');
                } else {
                var body = {
                    'id_token': token
                };

                var options = {
                    url: 'https://'+ process.env.DOMAIN + '/tokeninfo',
                    method: 'POST',
                    json: true,
                    body: body
                };

                request(options, function(error, response, body){
                    if (!error && response.statusCode === 200) {
                        callback(null, body);
                    } else {
                        callback(error);
                    }
                });
                }
            })
        };
```

event.authToken needs to be split because it contains the word *Bearer* before the token.

AUTH0_SECRET and DOMAIN are Lambda's environment variables. You can set and modify these in Lambda's console.

The jsonwebtoken module can verify and decode at the same time. It's a useful utility if you need to check the integrity of a token and extract claims.

The request module is an excellent utility for performing all kinds of requests. If the error object is not null, you can assume that the request succeeded and send back its body via the API Gateway.

Environment variables

Environment variables are Lambda's way of storing configuration settings, database connections strings, and other useful information without having to embed them in a function. Saving settings in environment variables is highly recommended because it allows developers to update those settings without having to redeploy the function. Environment variables can be changed independently and in isolation from the function. The AWS platform makes environment variables available to the function via process.env (for Node.js). Furthermore, environment variables can be encrypted via KMS, which provides a good way to store important secrets. Chapter 6 has more information on this useful feature.

Deploy the function to AWS by running `npm run deploy` from the terminal. Finally, you need to create two environment variables for your Lambda function to store the Auth0 domain and the Auth0 secret (figure 5.14). Listing 5.8 uses these two variables to verify the token and issue a request to Auth0. To add these two variables, do the following:

1   Open Lambda in the AWS console and click the `user-profile` function.
2   At the bottom of the Code tab, you should see a section for environment variables.
3   Add a variable called DOMAIN followed by the Auth0 domain.
4   Add another variable called AUTH0_SECRET followed by the Auth0 secret. The domain and the secret can be copied from Auth0 (figure 5.6). It's easy to mix up the Auth0 client ID and secret, so double-check that you've copied the right value.
5   Click the Save button at the top to persist your settings.

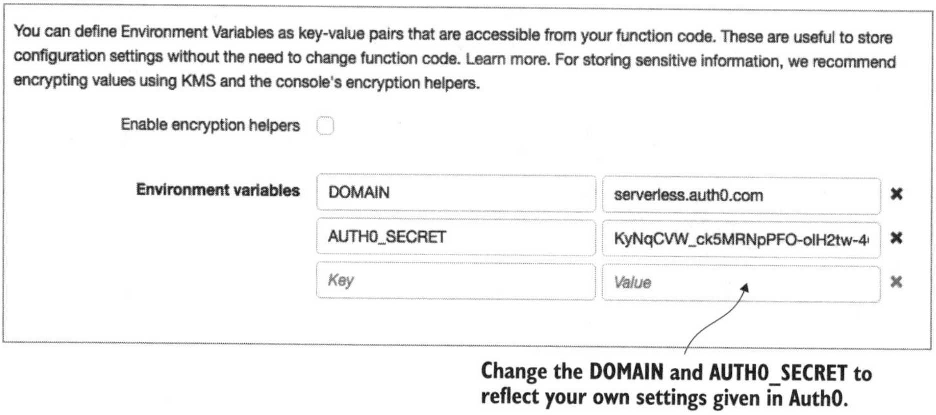

Change the **DOMAIN** and **AUTH0_SECRET** to reflect your own settings given in Auth0.

Figure 5.14   The DOMAIN and AUTH0_SECRET must be set for the Lambda function to run correctly.

5.3.2   *API Gateway*

You need to set up an API Gateway to accept requests from your website and invoke the `user-profile` Lambda function. You also need to create a resource, add support for a GET method, and enable cross-origin resource sharing (CORS):

1   In the AWS console, click API Gateway.
2   Type in a name for your API, such as `24-hour-video` and, optionally, a description.
3   Click Create API to create your first API.

APIs in the Gateway are built around resources. Every resource can be combined with an HTTP method such as HEAD, GET, POST, PUT, OPTIONS, PATCH, or DELETE. You're going to create a resource called user-profile and combine it with a GET method. In the API you just created, follow these steps:

1   Click Actions and select Create Resource.
2   Type `User Profile` in the Resource Name field. The Resource Path field should automatically fill in (figure 5.15).

New Child Resource

Use this page to create a new child resource for your resource.

Configure as ☐proxy resource ☐ ❶

Resource Name* user-profile

Resource Path* / user-profile

You can add path parameters using brackets. For example, the resource path **{username}** represents a path parameter called 'username'. Configuring /{proxy+} as a proxy resource catches all requests to its sub-resources. For example, it works for a GET request to /foo. To handle requests to /, add a new ANY method on the / resource.

Enable API Gateway CORS ☐ ❶

* Required   Cancel   **Create Resource**

We will have to enable CORS but don't do it right now. You will do it once you've created a GET method for this resource.

Figure 5.15   Creating a resource takes a few seconds in the API Gateway.

3 Click the Create Resource button to create and save the resource.
4 The left list should now show the /user-profile resource.
5 Make sure the resource is selected, and click Actions again.
6 Click Create Method to create a new GET method.
7 Under the /user-profile resource, click the drop-down and select GET (figure 5.16).
8 Click the check mark button to save.

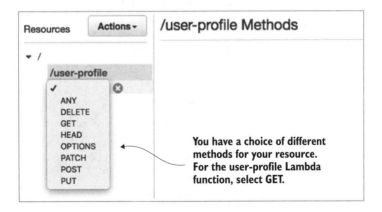

Resources Actions ▾   /user-profile Methods

▾ /
  /user-profile
  ✓   ⊗
    ANY
    DELETE
    GET
    HEAD
    OPTIONS ◄─── **You have a choice of different methods for your resource. For the user-profile Lambda function, select GET.**
    PATCH
    POST
    PUT

Figure 5.16   Select the GET method for the /user-profile resource. You'll use it to retrieve information about the user.

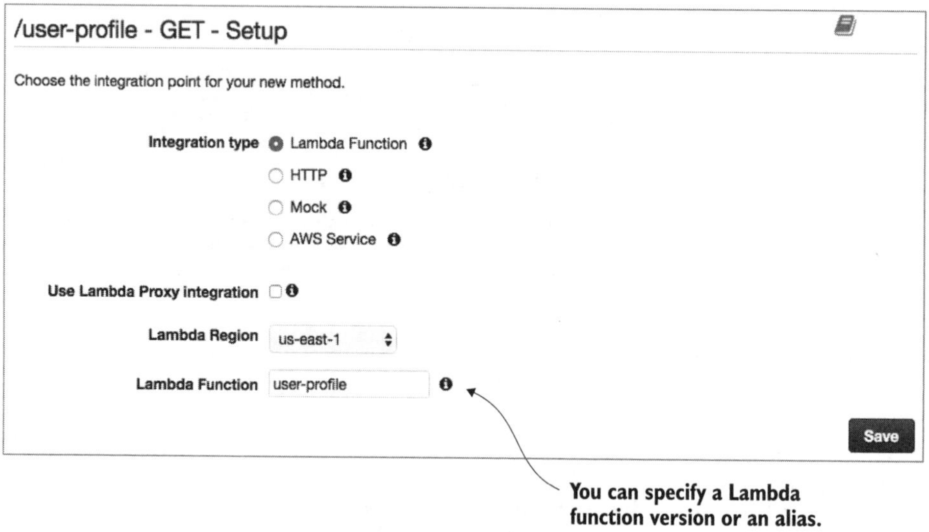

/user-profile - GET - Setup

Choose the integration point for your new method.

Integration type ● Lambda Function ❶
○ HTTP ❶
○ Mock ❶
○ AWS Service ❶

Use Lambda Proxy integration ☐ ❶

Lambda Region   us-east-1 ⬍

Lambda Function   user-profile   ❶

You can specify a Lambda
function version or an alias.

Save

Figure 5.17   You need to set up this integration request before CORS can be enabled.

Having saved the GET method, you should immediately see the Integration Request screen (figure 5.17):

1 Click the Lambda Function radio button.
2 Select your region (for example, us-east-1) from the Lambda Region drop-down menu.
3 Type user-profile in the Lambda Function text box.
4 Click Save.
5 Click OK if you're asked if it's okay to add permissions to the Lambda function.

Next, you need to enable CORS:

1 Click the /user-profile resource.
2 Click Actions.
3 Select Enable CORS.
4 The CORS configuration screen can be left with the defaults. The Access-Control-Allow-Origin field is set to a wildcard, which means that any other domain/origin can send a request to your endpoint. This is fine for now, but you'll restrict it down the road, especially as you get ready to roll out staging and production environments (figure 5.18).
5 Click Enable CORS and Replace Existing CORS Headers to save the configuration.
6 Click Yes, and replace existing values in the confirmation box that pops up.

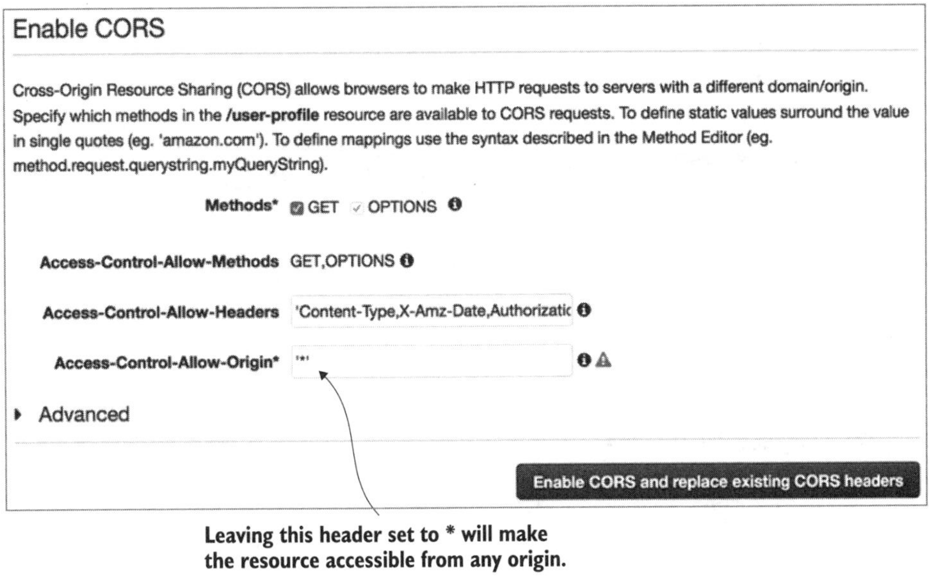

**Leaving this header set to * will make
the resource accessible from any origin.**

Figure 5.18 CORS will enable you to access this API from your website.

5.3.3 *Mappings*

If you look at listing 5.8, you'll see code that refers to event.authToken. This is the JWT token passed in via the Authorization header from the website. To make this token available in a Lambda function, you need to create a mapping in the API Gateway.

> **Mapping templates**
>
> In listing 5.9 you're creating a mapping using the Velocity Template Language (VTL). This mapping extracts a value from the HTTP (method) request and makes it available to your Lambda function (via a property called authToken on the event object). A mapping template transforms data from one format to another. See chapter 7 for more information on mapping templates.

This mapping will extract the Authorization header and add it as an authToken to the event object:

1. Click the GET method under the /user-profile resource.
2. Click Integration Request.
3. Expand Body Mapping Templates.
4. Click Add Mapping Template.
5. Type in application/json and click the check mark button.

6 Select Yes, Secure This Integration if you see a dialog box titled Change Passthrough Behavior.

7 In the Template box type in the code in the next listing.

8 Click Save once you're finished (figure 5.19).

Listing 5.9   Mapping template for the token

```
{
    "authToken" : "$input.params('Authorization')"
}
```

Mapping takes elements out of a request and makes them available as properties on the event object.

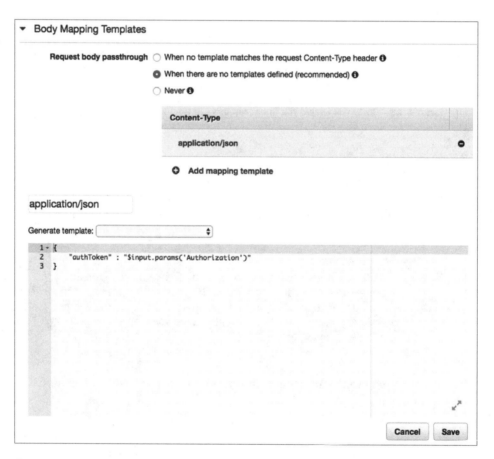

Figure 5.19   A mapping template can transform elements of a request to properties accessible via the event object in a Lambda function.

Lambda proxy integration

In figure 5.17, you might have noticed a check box labeled Use Lambda Proxy Integration. If you had enabled that check box, the incoming HTTP request—including all headers, query string parameters, and the body—would have been mapped and made available to the function via the event object automatically. This means that you wouldn't have had to create a mapping template as you did in listing 5.9 (the filename would be accessible from `queryStringParameters` on the event object). The reason you didn't do this is because we wanted to show you how to create a custom mapping template and extract only the parameter you need (rather than passing the entire HTTP request to the function). In many cases, proxy integration is very useful and you'll certainly use it as you progress through the chapters. See chapter 7 for a more in-depth discussion on proxy integration versus manual mapping.

Finally, you need to deploy the API and get a URL to invoke from the website:

1 In the API Gateway, make sure your API is selected.
2 Click Actions.
3 Select Deploy API.
4 In the pop-up, select [New Stage].
5 Type dev as the Stage Name.
6 Click Deploy to provision the API (figure 5.20).

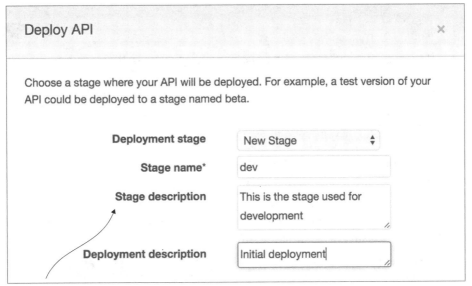

Create different stages such as dev,
test, and production for your API.

Figure 5.20 Every time you make changes to your API, remember to deploy them using the Deploy API button. You can deploy to an existing stage or create a new one.

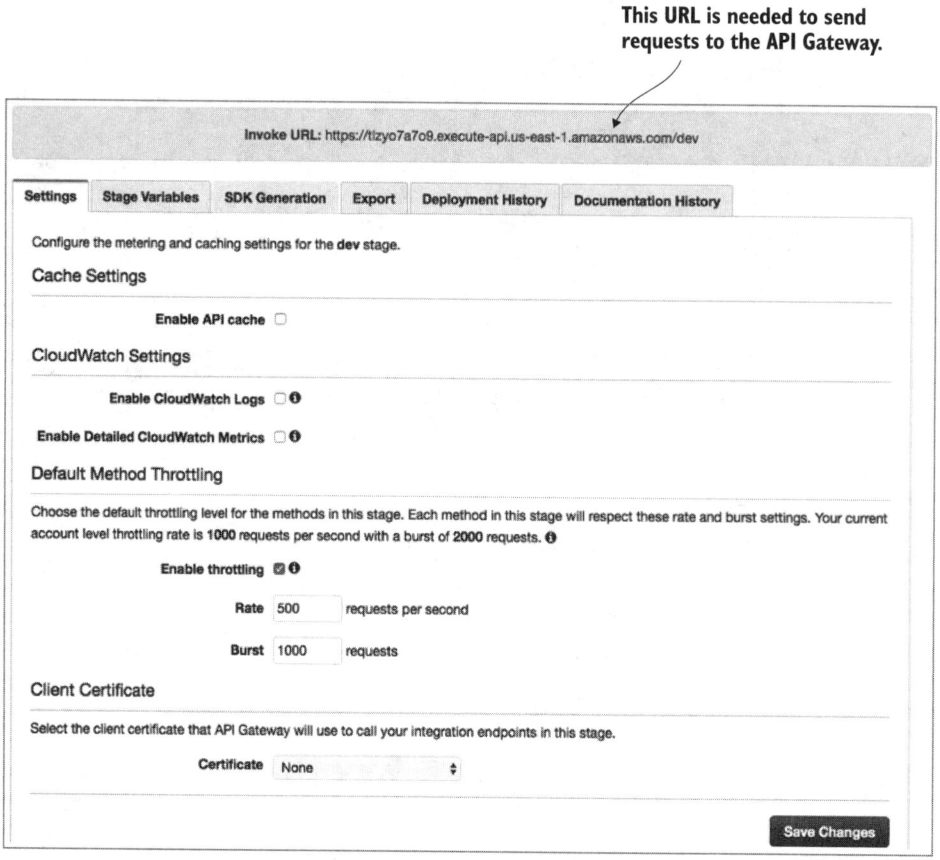

This URL is needed to send requests to the API Gateway.

Figure 5.21 You can use the stage settings page to adjust other settings. We'll cover these in more detail in chapter 7.

The next page you see will show the Invoke URL and a number of options (figure 5.21). Copy the URL, because you'll need it for the User Profile button.

5.3.4   *Invoking Lambda via API Gateway*

The final two steps are to update the Show Profile click handler and config.js to invoke the Show Profile Lambda function via the API Gateway. Open user-controller.js in the js folder of the 24-Hour Video website, and add the code shown in the next listing (right after the logout click-handler definition).

Listing 5.10 The Show Profile click event handler

```
this.uiElements.profileButton.click(function (e) {
    var url = that.data.config.apiBaseUrl + '/user-profile';

    $.get(url, function (data, status) {
```

```
        alert(JSON.stringify(data));
    })
});
```

The retrieved response from the API Gateway must be stringified to be displayed in an alert.

Finally, update the contents of config.js to match the next listing. Once you've done that, you can test the entire system.

Listing 5.11 Updated config.js

```
var configConstants = {
  auth0: {
      domain: 'AUTH0-DOMAIN',
      clientId: 'AUTH0-CLIENTID'
  },
  apiBaseUrl: 'https://API-GATEWAY-URL/dev'
};
```

Update the domain and client ID to match your Auth0 settings (figure 5.7).

Update the apiBaseUrl to match the URL given in the API Gateway.

Check that the 24-Hour Video website is running. If it isn't, run npm start from the terminal (make sure you're in the website's directory) and sign in via Auth0. Click the User Profile button. You should see an alert with the contents of the user's profile in Auth0.

5.3.5 *Custom authorizer*

API Gateway supports custom request authorizers. These are Lambda functions that the API Gateway can use to authorize requests. A custom authorizer runs at the method request stage—that is, before the request reaches the target back end. A custom authorizer can validate a bearer token and return a valid IAM policy, which authorizes the request. If the returned policy is invalid, the request is not allowed to continue. To prevent constant invocations of custom authorizers, policies along with the incoming token are cached for an hour.

The benefit of using a custom authorizer is that you can write a dedicated Lambda function to validate the JWT (instead of doing it in every function you want to invoke). Figure 5.22 shows what a modified request flow looks like when a custom authorizer is introduced.

You're going to implement a custom authorizer now to see how it works. There are three steps:

1 Create a new Lambda function in AWS.
2 Write a custom authorizer function and deploy it.
3 Change the method request settings in the API Gateway to use a custom authorizer.

The first step is to create a regular Lambda function just as you did before:

1 Create a function in Lambda's console.
2 Name this function custom-authorizer.

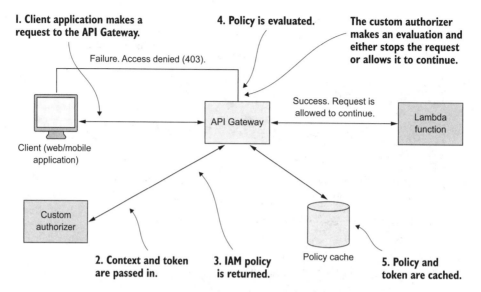

Figure 5.22   The custom authorizer is useful as a means of validating JWT for all Lambda functions that are supposed to be secured.

3   Assign the `api-gateway-lambda-exec-role` to it and save.

4   Make a copy of the `user-profile` Lambda function on your computer and rename it to `custom-authorizer`.

5   Update the function name or the ARN in the deploy script in package.json.

6   Open index.js and replace it with the code in listing 5.12 (this function is referenced from Amazon's documentation at http://amzn.to/24Dli80). As you can see, the code for this Lambda function is similar to that of the `user-profile` function. The main difference is a new function called `generatePolicy`, which returns an IAM policy that allows execution to continue.

Listing 5.12   Custom authorizer

```
'use strict';

var jwt = require('jsonwebtoken');

var generatePolicy = function(principalId, effect, resource) {
    var authResponse = {};
    authResponse.principalId = principalId;
    if (effect && resource) {
        var policyDocument = {};
        policyDocument.Version = '2012-10-17';
        policyDocument.Statement = [];
        var statementOne = {};
        statementOne.Action = 'execute-api:Invoke';
        statementOne.Effect = effect;
        statementOne.Resource = resource;
        policyDocument.Statement[0] = statementOne;
```

The policy stipulates that the API Gateway is allowed to invoke the required resource.

```
        authResponse.policyDocument = policyDocument;
    }
    return authResponse;
}

exports.handler = function(event, context, callback){
    if (!event.authorizationToken) {
        callback('Could not find authToken');
        return;
    }

    var token = event.authorizationToken.split(' ')[1];

    var secretBuffer = new Buffer(process.env.AUTH0_SECRET);
    jwt.verify(token, secretBuffer, function(err, decoded){
        if(err){
            console.log('Failed jwt verification: ', err,
            ➡ 'auth: ', event.authorizationToken);

            callback('Authorization Failed');
        } else {
            callback(null,
            ➡ generatePolicy('user', 'allow', event.methodArn));
        }
    })
};
```

The auth0 secret is accessed through an environment variable that you can set in Lambda's console.

If the token is validated, the function returns a user policy that allows the invocation of the API.

Deploy the function to AWS once you've implemented it. You also need to add the AUTH0_SECRET as an environment variable to the function:

1 In the AWS console, choose Lambda and then choose the custom-authorizer function.
2 In the Code tab, find the Environment Variable section.
3 Add AUTH0_SECRET as the key and your Auth0 secret as the value.
4 Click Save at the top of the page to persist your settings.

The final steps are to create a custom authorizer in the API Gateway and connect it to the GET method you created previously:

1 In the API Gateway, choose the 24-Hour Video API.
2 Select Authorizers from the menu on the left.
3 You should see a New Custom Authorizer form on the right side. If you don't see it, click the Create drop-down and choose Custom authorizer.
4 Fill out the custom authorizer form (figure 5.23).
   – Select your Lambda region (us-east-1).
   – Set the Lambda function name, which is custom-authorizer.
   – Set a name for your authorizer. It can be anything you want, like custom-authorizer or authorization-check.
   – Make sure that the Identity token source is set to method.request.header .Authorization.

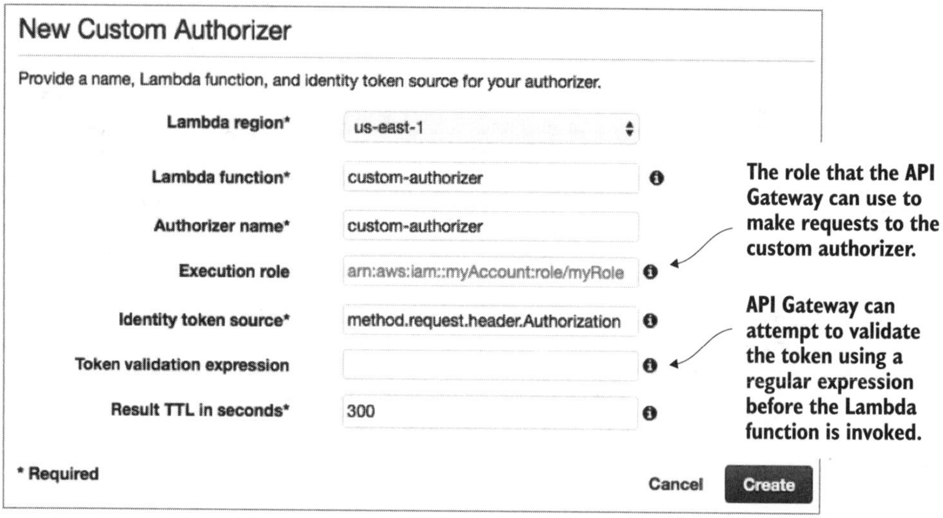

New Custom Authorizer

Provide a name, Lambda function, and identity token source for your authorizer.

Lambda region*	us-east-1
Lambda function*	custom-authorizer
Authorizer name*	custom-authorizer
Execution role	arn:aws:iam::myAccount:role/myRole
Identity token source*	method.request.header.Authorization
Token validation expression	
Result TTL in seconds*	300

The role that the API Gateway can use to make requests to the custom authorizer.

API Gateway can attempt to validate the token using a regular expression before the Lambda function is invoked.

* Required

Cancel   Create

Figure 5.23   You can use the custom authorizer to implement various authorization strategies. You can create multiple authorizers and connect them to methods in the API Gateway.

5   Click Create to create the custom authorizer.

6   Confirm that you want to allow API Gateway to invoke the `custom-authorizer` function.

Now you can set your custom authorizer to invoke automatically whenever a GET request to `/user-profile` is issued:

1   In the API Gateway, click Resources under 24-hour-video (the sidebar on the left).

2   Click GET under `/user-profile`.

3   Click Method Request

4   Click the pencil button next to Authorization.

5   From the drop-down select your custom authorizer and save (figure 5.24).

6   Deploy the API again:
   – Click Actions.
   – Choose Deploy API.
   – Select dev as the Deployment Stage.
   – Choose Deploy.

To test the custom authorizer, make the User Profile button display when the user isn't logged in. To do that, open main.css and remove the style for #user-profile from it. Also, delete your JWT from local storage and refresh the site. Click the User Profile button. Your custom authorizer should reject the request. You can use this custom authorizer for all Lambda functions down the road.

You can create and set a different authorizer for every method, but in most cases a single custom authorizer will do.

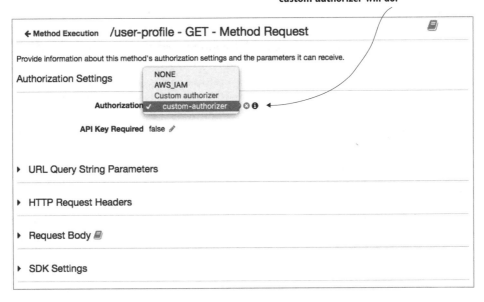

Figure 5.24 Custom authorizers are a good way to authorize requests coming via the API Gateway.

401 Unauthorized

If you've successfully signed in to the 24-Hour Video website and then refreshed after a long period of time, you might see an error message that says, "There was an error getting the profile: 401: Unauthorized." This could be because the JWT cached in your browser has expired. Sign on to your website again and everything should work again (the message will no longer appear). The default JWT expiration is 36,000 seconds (10 hours), but you can override it in Auth0 or you can choose to implement refresh tokens if you're up for a challenge (http://bit.ly/2jxbjPg).

5.4 Delegation tokens

Delegation tokens are designed to make integration between services easier. So far, you've taken a JSON Web Token supplied by Auth0 and sent it across to AWS where it was verified and decoded by a Lambda function. You had to write a little bit of code to do that. Delegation tokens are created for specific services that know how to decode these tokens and extract claims or information. In effect, delegation tokens are tokens created by one service to call another service or API.

5.4.1   *Real-world examples*

Firebase is a real-time streaming database that we'll look at in chapter 9. It supports delegation tokens. If a request from a client comes with a delegation token, Firebase knows how to verify it without you having to do anything (or write any code).

To add support for a Firebase delegation token, you need to generate a secret key in Firebase and add it to Auth0. Then your website can request a delegation token from Auth0, which is signed by the secret key from Firebase. Any subsequent request made to Firebase can be sent with the delegation token, which Firebase knows how to decrypt (because it provided the secret key in the first place). In chapter 9, we'll show you how to provision a delegation token for Firebase in more detail. Similarly, you can set up Auth0 to enable delegated authentication with AWS by setting up a SAML provider and configuring one or more roles.

5.4.2   *Provisioning delegation tokens*

When it comes to Auth0, to get a delegation token you need to configure an add-on for the service you wish to use and then request the token via the /delegation endpoint. If you wish to integrate with a service such as Firebase or use a delegation token with AWS, you'll need to enable the appropriate add-on in Auth0 (figure 5.25).

Every add-on has different configuration requirements, so you'll need to consult relevant Auth0 documentation to find out what's needed. To set up delegated authentication between Auth0 and AWS, refer to https://auth0.com/docs/aws-api-setup. Another great example is described in https://auth0.com/docs/integrations/aws-api-gateway.

5.5   *Exercises*

Try to do the following exercises to confirm your understanding of concepts presented in this chapter:

1 Create a Lambda function (`user-profile-update`) for updating a user's personal profile. Assume that you can access the first name, last name, email address, and userId on the event object. Because you don't have a database yet, this function doesn't need to persist this information, but you can log it to CloudWatch.

2 Create a POST method for the /user-profile resource in the API Gateway. This method should invoke the `user-profile-update` function and pass in the user's information. It should use the custom authorizer developed in section 5.3.5.

3 Create a page in the 24-Hour Video website to allow signed-in users to update their first name, last name, and email address. This information should be submitted to the `user-profile-update` function via the API Gateway.

4 In listing 5.3, you set the token to be included in every request using `$.ajax-Setup`. If your website makes a request to an external party, your token might be stolen. Think of a way to make the system more secure by including the token only when the website issues requests against the API Gateway.

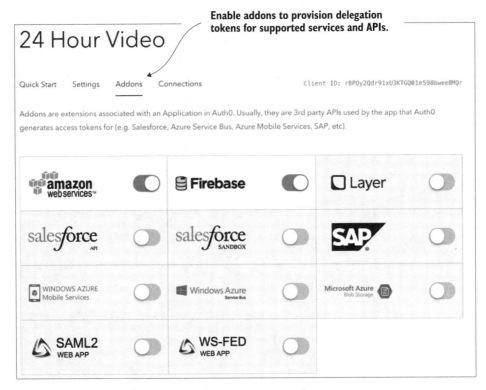

Figure 5.25 Use delegation tokens to reduce the need for more Lambda functions.

5 Modify the `user-profile` Lambda function to no longer validate the JSON Web Token. This validation isn't needed because of the custom authorizer. The function should still request user information from the Auth0 tokeninfo endpoint.

6 Add an additional social identity provider to your Auth0 app such as Yahoo, LinkedIn, or Windows Live.

7 The Auth0 JWT token stored in the browser's local storage will expire after a certain time. This may result in an error message shown to the user when the website is refreshed. Figure out a way to suppress the error message and automatically delete expired tokens.

5.6 *Summary*

In this chapter, we looked at how to enable authentication and authorization in a serverless application. We looked at how services can communicate directly with the client and checked out JSON Web Tokens. We also introduced Auth0, a service that takes care of many authentication and authorization concerns, and we discussed how delegation tokens can be used across different services. Finally, we stepped through an example where you did the following:

- Developed a website for 24-Hour Video
- Created an Auth0 app and added sign-in/out functionality to the website
- Developed a Lambda function to return user profile information
- Implemented an API Gateway and created a custom authorizer that decodes JWT

In the next chapter, we'll look at Lambda functions in much more detail. We'll consider advanced use cases, see how to use patterns to help implement concise functions without a large number of callbacks, and discuss ways to improve the performance of Lambda-based systems.

Lambda the orchestrator

6

This chapter covers

- Invocation types and programming models
- Versioning, aliases, and environment variables
- Usage of the CLI
- Development practices
- Testing of Lambda functions

If there's one thing you take away from this book, it should be an understanding that a compute service such as Lambda is the heart of serverless architecture. You used Lambda in chapters 3 and 5, so you have a feel for it already. This chapter explores Lambda in more detail. It looks at core concepts and investigates design of functions. We explain features such as versioning and aliases and go over important design patterns such as async waterfall. We also continue to add features to 24-Hour Video as we turn it into a full-fledged application.

6.1 Inside Lambda

Serverless compute services like Lambda are as big a shift for cloud computing as S3 was for cloud storage. If you think about it, the two are similar. S3 deals in objects for storage. You provide an object and S3 stores it. You don't know how, you don't know where, and you don't really care. There are no drives to concern yourself with and no such thing as disk space. You can't over-provision or under-provision storage capacity in S3.

Likewise, with Lambda you provide function code; Lambda executes it on demand. You don't know how and you don't know where. There are no virtual machines to concern yourself with, and there are no such things as server farm capacity, too many idling servers, not enough servers to meet demand, or scaling groups. You can't over-provision or under-provision execution capacity in Lambda. It's just what you want it to be and Amazon charges you only for the time it executes. This is why Lambda and similar serverless compute services such as Azure Functions, Google Cloud Functions, and IBM OpenWhisk are as big a shift forward for compute as S3 was for storage (http://bit.ly/2jQnlGB).

> **Function as a service**
>
> Some people prefer to use the acronym *FaaS* (function as a service) to describe technologies like Lambda. In fact, they prefer not to use the term *serverless* at all. They feel that it's not accurate enough and that it needs to be constantly explained. In this book, we've been using the term *serverless* not as a synonym for Lambda but as a descriptor for an approach that encourages you to use a compute service, use third-party services and APIs, and employ powerful patterns and architectures (such as having thick front ends that talk directly to services using delegation tokens). Therefore, we say that *serverless* is an umbrella term that encompasses FaaS and that FaaS is just one aspect (albeit a very important one) of what serverless technologies and architectures have to offer.

6.1.1   Event models and sources

Lambda is a serverless compute service that can execute code in response to the following:

- Events raised in AWS
- HTTP requests arriving through the API Gateway
- API calls made using the AWS SDK
- Manual user invocation via the AWS console

Lambda functions can also run on a schedule, which makes them suitable for repeatable tasks such as backups or system health checks. Lambda supports functions written in four languages: JavaScript (Node.js), Python, C#, and Java. You've been using JavaScript so far, but there's no reason why you couldn't use one of the other languages. They're all first-class citizens.

The two ways to invoke a Lambda function

Lambda supports two invocation types: *Event* and *RequestResponse*.

Event invocation takes place when an event (such as a file being created in S3) triggers a Lambda function. You saw event invocations in chapter 3 when you used S3 and SNS to invoke Lambda. Event invocation is asynchronous. A Lambda function that executes because of an event doesn't send a response back to the event source.

The other model is RequestResponse. It comes into play when Lambda is used with the API Gateway, invoked via the AWS console, or called with the CLI. RequestResponse forces Lambda to execute the function synchronously and return the response to the caller. You used RequestResponse in chapter 5 when you integrated the API Gateway with the `user-profile` Lambda function. Note that if you invoke a function via the SDK/CLI, you can choose whether to use Event or RequestResponse invocation.

6.1.2 *Push and pull event models*

Lambda's event-based invocation is quite interesting. It has two modes: push and pull. In a push model, a service (such as S3) publishes its event to Lambda and directly invokes your function. Figure 6.1 shows what this looks like.

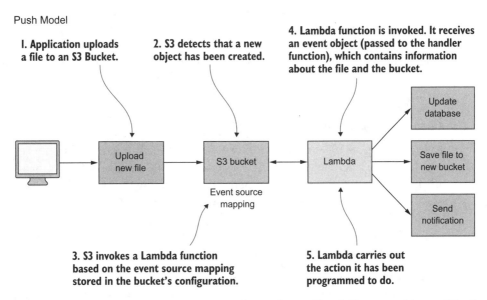

Figure 6.1 Except for stream-based services, which are Amazon Kinesis Streams and DynamoDB, all other AWS services use the push model of operation.

Pull Model

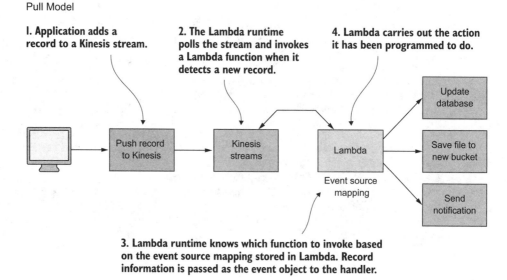

I. Application adds a record to a Kinesis stream.

2. The Lambda runtime polls the stream and invokes a Lambda function when it detects a new record.

4. Lambda carries out the action it has been programmed to do.

3. Lambda runtime knows which function to invoke based on the event source mapping stored in Lambda. Record information is passed as the event object to the handler.

Figure 6.2   The pull model applies to Amazon Kinesis Streams and DynamoDB streams only.

In a *pull* model, Lambda's runtime polls a streaming event source (such as a DynamoDB stream or a Kinesis stream) and invokes your function when needed. Figure 6.2 shows what this looks like.

In both models, an *event source mapping* describes how an event source is associated with a Lambda function. One subtle difference between push and pull is this: "With the pull model, you maintain the mappings in AWS Lambda by creating event source mappings using the relevant AWS Lambda API. With the push model, the event sources maintain the mapping and you use the APIs provided by the event sources to maintain the mapping" (http://amzn.to/1Xb78FV).

6.1.3   *Concurrent executions*

AWS has a cap of 100 concurrent executions across all functions within a region (per account). This cap, however, can be lifted by asking Amazon. The company says that the limit is there to protect developers "from costs due to potential runaway or recursive functions during initial development and testing" (http://amzn.to/29nORER). The number of concurrent executions is calculated differently depending on whether the event source is stream-based (that is, if the event source is Kinesis Streams or a DynamoDB stream) or not.

STREAM-BASED EVENT SOURCE

In a stream-based event source, function invocation concurrency is equal to the number of active shards. If, for example, there are 10 shards, there will be 10 Lambda functions executing concurrently. Lambda functions process records off shards in the order in which they arrive. If a function encounters an error processing a record, it retries until it succeeds or the record expires, before going on to the next one.

NON-STREAM-BASED EVENT SOURCE

Amazon proposes a simple formula for estimating the number of concurrent invocations for non-stream event sources:

```
events (or requests) per second x function duration
```

A simple example is an S3 bucket that publishes 10 events per second with the function taking an average of three seconds to run, which equates to 30 concurrent executions (http://amzn.to/29nORER). If a Lambda function is throttled and continues to be invoked synchronously, Lambda will respond with a 429 error. It's then up to the event source (for example, your application) to try invoking the function again. If a function was invoked asynchronously, AWS will automatically retry the throttled event for up to six hours with delays in between every invocation (http://amzn.to/29c7Bar).

6.1.4   *Container reuse*

Lambda functions execute in a container (sandbox), which provides isolation from other functions and an allocation of resources such as memory, disk space, and CPU. Container reuse is important to understand for more advanced uses of Lambda. When a function is instantiated for the first time, a new container is initialized and the code for the function is loaded (we say that the function is *cold* when this is done for the first time). If a function is rerun (within a certain period), Lambda may reuse the same container and skip the initialization process (we say that the function is now *warm*), thus making it available to execute code quicker.

Tim Wagner, the general manager of Lambda at AWS (http://amzn.to/237CWCk), makes an important point: "Remember, you can't depend on a container being reused, since it's Lambda's prerogative to create a new one instead." This means that every time you run a function, you should assume that you have a new container. But if you use the /tmp folder or touch the filesystem in other ways, your files or changes from the previous invocation may still be there. We've experienced this many times. If it happens to you, you'll have to clean the /tmp directory manually.

Another important detail is what Wagner calls the freeze/thaw cycle. You can run a function and launch a background thread or a process. When the function finishes executing, the background process will become frozen. Lambda may reuse the container the next time you invoke the function and thaw the background process, thus resuming its execution. The background process will continue to run as though nothing happened. Keep this in mind if you decide to run background processes.

6.1.5   *Cold and warm Lambda*

Here's an experiment. Create any simple Hello World function in the AWS console and run it. You can easily do this by using the hello-world blueprint and then clicking the Test button in the console. Have a look at the duration in the summary in the bottom-left corner (figure 6.3).

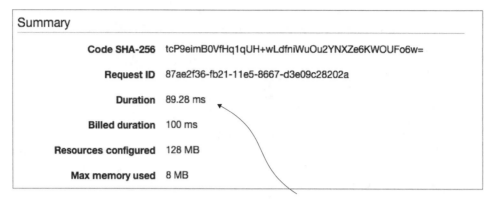

The duration when the function is cold.

Figure 6.3   The time it takes to run a cold function is nearly 90 ms.

Then run the test again and look at the duration in the summary (figure 6.4).

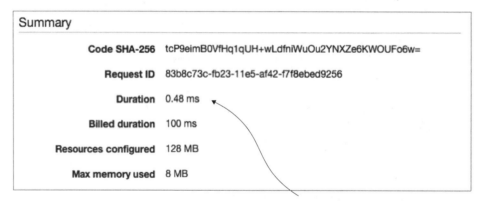

The duration when the function is warm.

Figure 6.4   A warm function runs much quicker than a cold one.

If you compare the duration of both executions, you'll see that the time it takes to run a function for the first time is a lot longer than running it a second time. This is the result of the container reuse we described in the previous section. The first time the function is run (when it's cold), the container needs to be created and the environment needs to be initialized. A lengthy initialization time may be especially noticeable in complex functions that have multiple dependencies. Reusing a container and running a function again is almost always much quicker.

You should try to reduce cold starts (when a function hasn't been run for a long time and needs to fully initialize) to make the application appear more responsive. If you experience many cold starts, you can try a few steps to increase performance:

1 Schedule the function (using scheduled events) to run periodically to keep it warm (http://amzn.to/29AZsuX).

2 Move initialization and setup code out of the event handler. If the container is warm, this code won't run.

3 Increase the amount of memory allocated to the Lambda function. The CPU share is (proportionally) based on the amount of memory allocated to the function. AWS gives an example: "If you allocate 256 MB to your Lambda function, it will receive twice the CPU share than if you allocated 128 MB" (http://amzn.to/23aFKif). The more memory and CPU share the function has, the quicker it will initialize.

4 Reduce as much of your code as possible. Remove unnecessary modules and `requires()` import statements. Fewer modules to include and initialize will help startup performance.

5 Experiment with other languages. Java has the longest cold start. This may change in the future, but if you notice long cold starts using Java, try one of the other languages.

6.2 Programming model

We touched on Lambda's programming model back in chapter 3. Let's look at it now in more detail from the perspective of the Node.js 4.3 runtime you've been using. These are the important elements to consider:

- Function handler
- Callback function
- Context object
- Event object
- Logging

6.2.1 Function handler

You've seen that the function handler is what the Lambda runtime calls to run your function. It's the entry point. Lambda passes in the event data to the handler function as the first parameter, a context object as the second parameter, and a callback object as the third. The syntax for the function handler is as follows:

```
exports.handler = function(event, context, callback) { //code }
```

The callback object is optional and is used if you want to return information to the caller of the function or log an error. Over the next three sections we'll describe event, context, and callback parameters in more detail.

6.2.2 Event object

You already saw the event object in action when you invoked Lambda functions in previous chapters. The event object contains information about the event and the source that triggered the Lambda function. It's just a JSON object with an arbitrary number of properties that are specified by the event source.

You can look at sample event objects in Lambda's console by following this process:

1 Click into a Lambda function.
2 Click Actions.
3 Select Configure Test Event.
4 Select a template from the Sample Event Template drop-down (figure 6.5).

If you invoke a Lambda function via the AWS console, via the CLI, or through an API Gateway, you can create your own event object and customize the way it is structured.

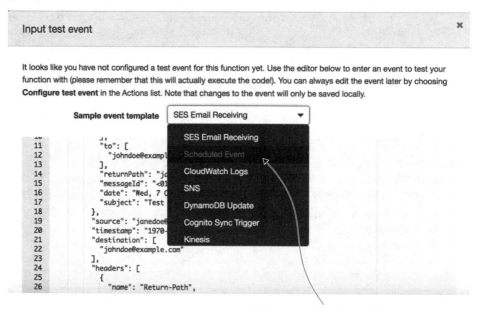

Select from a list of available event templates to see what the event object will look like when Lambda is invoked by different AWS services.

Figure 6.5   The available event templates provided through the AWS console. You can customize a template or create your own from scratch.

6.2.3 Context object

The context object provides a number of useful properties for getting information about Lambda's runtime. You can call a number of methods on the context object, such as done(), succeed(), and fail(). These methods were important in the Node.js 0.1 version of the Lambda runtime but aren't needed in the Node.js 4.3 version. You can review appendix D if you want to know what these are. The other method on the context object that you might find useful is getRemainingTimeInMillis(). Calling this method returns the approximate remaining execution time. This function is valuable if you need to check how much time is left before a timeout (a Lambda function can run for a maximum of five minutes).

The context object also has these useful properties:

- `functionName`—Returns the name of the Lambda function currently executing.
- `functionVersion`—The function version that is executing.
- `invokedFunctionArn`—The ARN used to invoke the function.
- `memoryLimitInMB`—The configured memory limit of the function.
- `awsRequestId`—The AWS request ID.
- `logGroupName`—The CloudWatch log group to which the function will write.
- `logStreamName`—The CloudWatch log stream to which the function will write.
- `identity`—The Amazon Cognito identity if available.
- `clientContext`—Information about client application and device when invoked via the AWS Mobile SDK. It can contain additional information such as platform version, make, model, and locale.

See http://amzn.to/1UK9eib for more information about the methods and properties available via the context object.

6.2.4 *Callback function*

The callback function is an optional third parameter in the handler function. It's used to return information to the caller in the RequestResponse invocation type, such as when a function is invoked via the API Gateway. The syntax for using the callback object is as follows:

```
callback(Error error, Object result)
```

The `Error` parameter is optional and is used when you want to specify information about a failed execution. The second parameter, also optional, is used to provide information to the caller when the function succeeds. Note that you need to pass `null` as the first parameter if you're going to specify the second parameter and there's no error. The following are examples of valid uses of callback:

- `callback(null, "Success");`
- `callback("Error");`
- `callback(); //This is the same as callback(null);`

You don't need to specify any parameters in the callback if you don't want to return information to the caller. You don't even need to add `callback()` to your code if you don't want to return a response or log an error. Lambda will call it for you implicitly if you don't include it in your code. For more information on using the callback function, see the section titled "Using the Callback Parameter" at http://amzn.to/1NeqXM5.

6.2.5   Logging

Logging to CloudWatch can be done using `console.log("message")`. The other supported ways of logging are `console.error()`, `console.warn()`, and `console.info()`, but there's no real distinction between them in terms of CloudWatch. If you invoke a Lambda function programmatically (see section 6.4 for more on this), you can add a `LogType` parameter to receive the last 4 KB of log data (it's returned in the `x-amz-log-results` header of the response). The callback function will also log to a CloudWatch log stream if you provide a non-`null` value as the first parameter. At the end of the day, we highly recommend that you adopt a proper logging framework that will manage alert levels and log objects (for example, have a look at log at http://bit.ly/1VHIxuA).

6.3   *Versioning, aliases, and environment variables*

When Lambda was originally released, it didn't have support for versioning, aliases, or environment variables. But it's now hard to imagine building and running a real production system without these features.

6.3.1   *Versioning*

Versioning allows developers to create new versions of functions without overwriting previous ones. Once a new version of a function is published, the old version can still be accessed but it can't be changed. Importantly, each version of a function has its own unique ARN, and each version can be invoked. To create a new version of a function, follow these steps:

1 Open the Lambda console in AWS and click a function.
2 Choose Actions and choose Publish New Version.
3 Type a description in the dialog box. This description will be added to the version you're about to create.
4 Choose Publish to close the dialog box.

If you click the Qualifiers drop-down and then select the Versions tab, you'll see all current versions of the function (figure 6.6). The most recent version is always identified as $LATEST. If you don't specify a version number when invoking a function, this is the function that's invoked.

Your next question might be how to invoke a specific version of a function. That depends on where you're trying to invoke the function from. If it's the API Gateway, you can specify the function name and version with a colon in between, as you can see in figure 6.7 (for example, `my-special-function:3`).

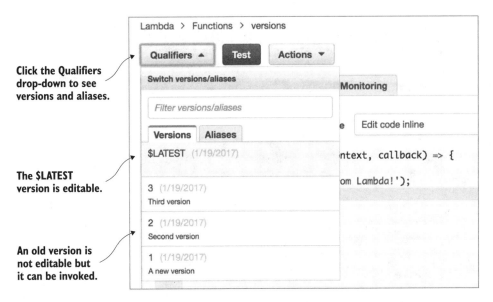

Click the Qualifiers drop-down to see versions and aliases.

The $LATEST version is editable.

An old version is not editable but it can be invoked.

Figure 6.6   Versions are easy to create and invoke through the console and the CLI.

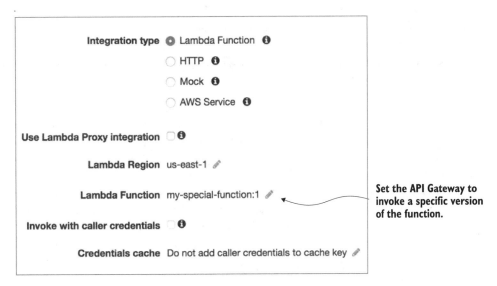

Set the API Gateway to invoke a specific version of the function.

Figure 6.7   Setting the right version of the Lambda function to invoke is trivial in the API Gateway. If you don't specify a version, the API Gateway will invoke the $LATEST version.

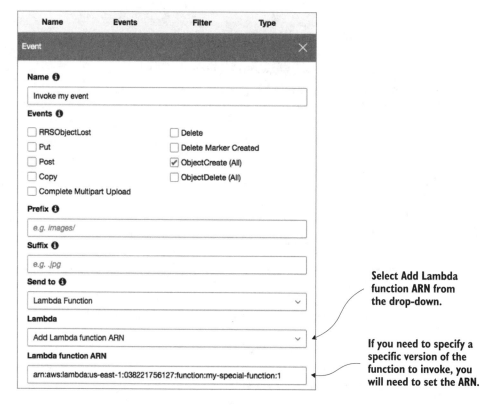

Figure 6.8   S3 uses the ARN to invoke the right version of the function. You can look up the ARN in Lambda's console.

If it's S3, you can specify the function ARN, which, as we mentioned before, is unique for every version of the function (figure 6.8).

6.3.2   *Aliases*

An alias is a pointer or a shortcut to a specific version of a Lambda function. It has an ARN just like a function, and it can be mapped to point to any function (or version) but not to another alias. Having an alias makes things easier when you need to switch from one version of a function to another. Imagine the following scenario:

- You have three versions of a function:
- Version 1 is in production.
- Version 2 is being tested in a staging/UAT environment.
- $LATEST is the current development version.
- You've finished testing function version 2 and want to promote it to production.

- You'd have to update every event source that references function 1 (the current production) to reference function 2. This isn't ideal because it may mean a redeployment of your code and multiple updates throughout your system.

With an alias, this scenario becomes into easier to manage:

1 Create three aliases called dev, staging, and production.
2 Assign the right alias to the right version of the function:
   - The production alias points to version 1.
   - The staging alias points to version 2.
   - The dev alias points to $LATEST.
3 Configure event sources to point to an alias instead of a specific version of a function.

Whenever you need to update the system to use a new version of a function, change the alias to point to that new version instead (figure 6.9). Event sources remain ignorant of the fact that an alias now points to a new version of a function and continue to operate as normal.

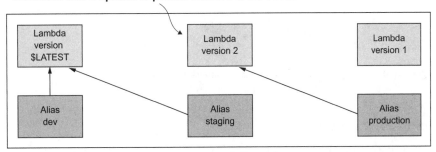

Figure 6.9 Initially an alias called production points to version 1 of a Lambda function. After an update, it's remapped to point to version 2. The staging alias is also remapped to point to the $LATEST version of the function.

To create an alias for a function, follow these steps:

1 Choose Lambda in the AWS console and choose any function.
2 Choose Actions.
3 Choose Create alias.
4 In the dialog box enter a name for the alias, such as *dev* or *production*, a description, and select the version that the alias should point to.
5 Choose Submit to create the alias and close the dialog box.

To view aliases for a function, use the Qualifiers drop-down, just as you did with versions (figure 6.10). A tab in the drop-down allows you to switch the view between versions and aliases. To delete an alias, choose Actions and select Delete Alias. Doing this deletes the alias and any related event source mappings that point to it. Everything else, including function versions, is left intact.

Figure 6.10   You can switch between aliases and versions in the sidebar.

6.3.3   *Environment variables*

You already saw environment variables in chapter 5 when you created the user-profile Lambda function. Environment variables are key-value pairs, which can be set using the Lambda console, CLI, or the SDK. They can be referenced by the function's source code and accessed during function execution.

By using environment variables for settings and secrets, you'll avoid having to bake this information into the function's code. And you'll be able to change variables without having to modify and redeploy the function. Environment variables work with function versioning, which we've discussed in this section. A development version of a function can use a variable that points to the connection string of a development database. The same environment variable can point to the production version of a database for the production version of the function.

BASIC USAGE

Figure 6.11 shows a part of the Lambda console (the Code tab) where you can set environment variables. You may notice that in this book we uppercase the names (keys) of environment variables (for example, UPLOAD_BUCKET). We chose to follow this convention. You don't have to uppercase environment variable names if you don't like that.

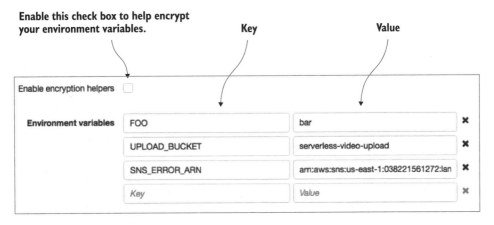

Enable this check box to help encrypt your environment variables.

Key

Value

Enable encryption helpers	☐	
Environment variables	FOO	bar	✖
	UPLOAD_BUCKET	serverless-video-upload	✖
	SNS_ERROR_ARN	arn:aws:sns:us-east-1:038221561272:lan	✖
	Key	Value	✖

Figure 6.11   The key must start with a letter and contain only letters, numbers, and underscores. Values don't have such restrictions, but at the time of this writing you shouldn't use commas in them. You'd have to either use a different delimiter or encrypt the value.

You can set environment variables using the AWS CLI. The CreateFunction and UpdateFunctionConfiguration APIs allow you to do that (more on these APIs in the next section).

> **NOTE**   Some environment variable key names are reserved. You can't, for example, set a key called AWS_REGION or AWS_ACCESS_KEY. To see a full list of reserved variables, have a look at this page: http://amzn.to/2jDCgBa.

Environment variables can be accessed through process.env (for Node.js functions). If you wanted to print the value of the UPLOAD_BUCKET variable shown in figure 6.11, you'd add the following line to your function:

```
console.log(process.env.UPLOAD_BUCKET);
```

ENCRYPTION

For sensitive data, you can choose to encrypt environment variables. You can do it in the console by enabling the Enable Encryption Helpers check box (figure 6.12). The first time you enable it, you'll get a chance to create an encryption key using the AWS Key Management Service (KMS). You'll then have this key available for encryption across all Lambda functions (in each region). You can, of course, create multiple keys too.

Having created a key, you'll be able to encrypt all or some of the variables. In the console, you'll see a button labeled Encrypt next to each environment variable. Use this button to encrypt the variable. The value will be immediately replaced with an encrypted string. You'll also see a button called Code. You can click this button to get a snippet of code that shows how to decrypt the variable within the function.

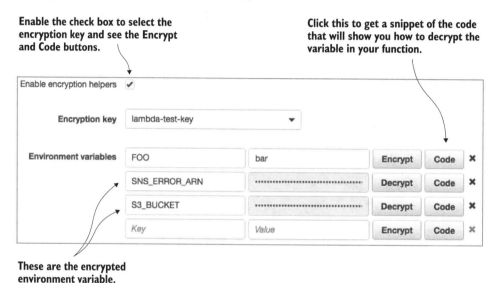

Figure 6.12   Use encryption whenever you're handling sensitive data.

Our advice is to use environment variables for settings and secrets whenever you can. Don't bake these into your function. Use what the platform offers you and you'll find life to be a lot easier.

6.4   Using the CLI

So far, you've primarily used the AWS console to create and configure Lambda functions. It's likely, though, that you'll have to use the CLI at some point to create, update, configure, and delete functions, especially if you start thinking about automation.

6.4.1   Invoking commands

If you followed chapter 3, you installed the AWS CLI (http://amzn.to/1XCoTOC). The CLI allows you to issue commands in the following form:

```
aws lambda <function-name> <command-options>
```

The page at https://docs.aws.amazon.com/cli/latest/reference/lambda/index.html describes available CLI commands. Let's take delete alias (delete-alias) as an example. It has a few optional parameters, but at its core it's as simple as running the following (where the --name flag is the name of the alias):

```
aws lambda delete-alias --function-name return-response --name production
```

Remember that if you invoke CLI commands, you must also have the right IAM security configured. If you were to try running the delete alias command right now, you'd receive an error message, such as "Client error (AccessDeniedException) occurred when calling the DeleteAlias operation." To make it work you'd need to add the DeleteAlias permission to the user's list of permissions.

6.4.2 *Creating and deploying functions*

In chapters 3 and 5 you deployed functions to AWS using the UpdateFunctionCode API. You did it by adding the following script to package.json:

```
aws lambda update-function-code --function-name arn:aws:lambda:
    ➥us-east-1:038221756127:function:transcode-video --zip-file
    ➥fileb://Lambda-Deployment.zip
```

But you had to create the function initially in the AWS console before you could use update-function-code. That's a manual step and doesn't fit with your ethos of complete automation. How would you go about creating and deploying a function entirely from the command line? Let's step through an exercise to see how it's done.

First, you need to update the lambda-upload user to IAM user to allow you to create functions. Back in chapter 4, you created a group called Lambda-DevOps and assigned the user lambda-upload to it. Now you need to edit the group's policy and add a new permission:

1. In the IAM console, open Groups.
2. Click the Lambda-Upload-Policy group.
3. Select the Permissions tab if it's not already selected.
4. In the Inline Policies section, click Edit Policy on the right of the policy name.
5. Add lambda:CreateFunction to the Action array (figure 6.13).
6. Click Apply Policy to save.

You should also double-check that the user lambda-upload is in the Lambda-Upload-Policy group:

1. Click the Users tab in the Lambda-Upload-Policy group.
2. Check to see if the lambda-upload user is listed in the table.
3. If the user isn't listed, click the Add Users to Group button, find lambda-upload in the list, put a checkmark next to the user, and then click the Add Users button.

Policy Document

```
 1 ▾ {
 2        "Version": "2012-10-17",
 3 ▾      "Statement": [
 4 ▾          {
 5                "Sid": "Stmt1451465505000",
 6                "Effect": "Allow",
 7 ▾              "Action": [
 8                    "lambda:GetFunction",
 9                    "lambda:UpdateFunctionCode",
10                    "lambda:UpdateFunctionConfiguration",
11                    "lambda:CreateFunction"
12                ],
13 ▾              "Resource": [
14                    "arn:aws:lambda:*"
15                ]
```

Add CreateFunction to the Action
array. The user will be allowed to
create a new function.

Figure 6.13 A simple update to the policy will allow the user to create functions.

To create a function using the CLI, you need to provide a zip file with the source of the function or point to an S3 bucket that has the source. It's easy to create a function locally and zip it up:

1 Create a file named index.js.
2 Copy the contents of the following listing to the file.
3 Zip the file to create index.zip.

Listing 6.1   Basic function

```
'use strict';

exports.handler = function(event, context, callback) {
  callback(null, 'Serverless Architectures on AWS');
};
```

This function doesn't do anything useful or interesting, but it's enough to test whether you can create functions from the command line.

In the same directory as the zip file of the function, run the command given in the next listing (remember to update the role ARN; it should be the ARN of your own `lambda-s3-execution-role`). Take a look in the Lambda's console to make sure it's there.

Listing 6.2   Working example of the `create-function` command

```
aws lambda create-function --function-name cli-function --handler
    index.handler --memory-size 128 --runtime nodejs4.3 --role
    arn:aws:iam::038221756127:role/lambda-s3-execution-role --timeout 3 --
    zip-file fileb://index.zip --publish
```

This next listing shows a subset of the syntax you used with the `create-function` command, together with an explanation of each of the options. (Lambda supports many more settings and flags than shown in listing 6.3; refer to http://amzn.to/2jeCOfR if you want to see all of the options.)

Listing 6.3 Syntax for the `create-function` command

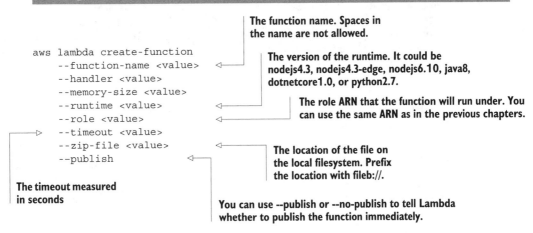

```
aws lambda create-function
    --function-name <value>
    --handler <value>
    --memory-size <value>
    --runtime <value>
    --role <value>
    --timeout <value>
    --zip-file <value>
    --publish
```

The function name. Spaces in the name are not allowed.

The version of the runtime. It could be nodejs4.3, nodejs4.3-edge, nodejs6.10, java8, dotnetcore1.0, or python2.7.

The role ARN that the function will run under. You can use the same ARN as in the previous chapters.

The location of the file on the local filesystem. Prefix the location with fileb://.

The timeout measured in seconds

You can use --publish or --no-publish to tell Lambda whether to publish the function immediately.

Naturally, there are many other useful functions to invoke, including these:

- `delete-function` to delete a function (http://amzn.to/2jdefz4)
- `create-alias` to create an alias (http://amzn.to/2jde9rh)
- `invoke` to invoke a function using the RequestResponse or Event invocation type (http://amzn.to/2jYhui7)
- `publish-version` to publish a new version of a function (http://amzn.to/2jdsCDm)
- `list-functions`, `list-aliases`, `list-versions-by-function` to list functions, aliases, and versions, respectively

6.5 Lambda patterns

If you're using JavaScript (Node.js) to write your Lambda functions, you'll have to deal with asynchronous callbacks. You've already seen these in action in chapter 3 and especially in the third Lambda function that you created in that chapter. Having multiple callbacks is frustrating and complex because following the logic of the program becomes difficult. If your function naturally leads to a series of sequential steps, you can adopt an async waterfall pattern and reduce the complexity of managing multiple asynchronous callbacks.

Not the only game in town

Async waterfall is a good pattern, but it's by no means the only way you can deal with callback hell. ES6 supports promises, generators, and yields (http://bit.ly/2k7OZge), which you can use with Node.js 4.3 and Lambda. You could even try using ES7 features—like async/await and transpiling your code down to promise chains—but that could make debugging harder. In other words, read the next section and think about whether the async waterfall pattern is right for you. In many cases, especially if you're dealing with legacy code that hasn't been ported to Node.js 4+, knowing and applying a pattern like this is a good idea.

6.5.1   *Async waterfall*

Async (http://bit.ly/23RfWVe) is a JavaScript library that can be installed as an npm module. It has several powerful features, one of them being support for the waterfall pattern. This pattern allows you to run a set of functions one after another, passing the result of one function into the next one using a callback function. If one of the functions passes an error into the callback, the execution of the waterfall is stopped, and the next task is not invoked (figure 6.14).

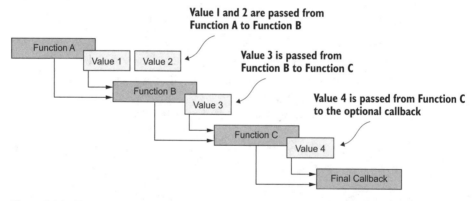

Figure 6.14   The async waterfall pattern allows you to invoke and pass results from one function to another. It makes handling of asynchronous methods easier than using callbacks.

The following listing shows a general example of an async waterfall pattern (this listing is adopted from an example given in http://bit.ly/1WaSNui).

Listing 6.4   Async waterfall example

```
async.waterfall([
  function(callback) {
    callback(null, 'Peter', 'Sam');
  },
  function(arg1, arg2, callback) {      ⟵    arg1 equals 'Peter' and arg2 equals 'Sam'.
    callback(null, 'Serverless');
```

```
  },
  function(arg1, callback) {                    ⟵——— arg1 equals 'Serverless'.
    callback(null, 'Done');
  }
], function (err, result) {          ⟵┐   This is the optional and
    if (err) {                        │   final callback function. In
        console.log(err);             │   here, result is 'Done'.
    } else {
        console.log(result);
    }
});
```

In listing 6.4, take note of the callback function, which is used often. This function must be called on the completion of each task. The first parameter in the callback represents an error. If there's no error, use a `null`. The other parameters can be whatever you want. They're passed on to the next task.

This callback function is similar to the callback you've already seen in Lambda. You must not confuse the two callback functions, however, so we recommend naming the callback used in async waterfall to something else (such as *next*).

24-HOUR VIDEO LIST

As a clone of YouTube, 24-Hour Video needs to list videos that users can click and view. You don't have a database at the moment to store URLs to your videos, but you can create a Lambda function to make a list of files in the S3 bucket. This function can be invoked via the API Gateway, and it can return a list of URLs to your videos. You can use async waterfall for this example because you need to take a few steps in series.

BASICS SETUP

Create a new function on your system and name it `get-video-list`. Here's how to do this:

1 Copy one of the previous functions (such as `transcode-video`) to a new folder and name it `get-video-list`.

2 Remove all contents in index.js.

3 Update package.json to resemble the next listing. The bolded text is what you need to add or modify from your existing file.

Listing 6.5   Package.json for the `get-video-list` function

```
{
  "name": "get-video-list",
  "version": "1.0.0",
  "description": "This Lambda function will list
➥ videos available in an S3 bucket",
  "main": "index.js",
  "scripts": {
      "create": "aws lambda create-function --function-name get-video-list
➥ --handler index.handler --memory-size 128 --runtime nodejs4.3
➥ --role arn:aws:iam::038221756127:role/lambda-s3-execution-role
➥ --timeout 3 --publish --zip-file fileb://Lambda-Deployment.zip",    ⟵
```

You've added a create script to create the function straight from the command line. Remember to update the ARN to match the ARN of your role.

```
  "deploy": "aws lambda update-function-code --function-name get-video-list
⮕  --zip-file fileb://Lambda-Deployment.zip",
    "precreate": "zip -r Lambda-Deployment.zip * -x *.zip *.json *.log",    ◁─┐
    "predeploy": "zip -r Lambda-Deployment.zip * -x *.zip *.json *.log"       │
  },                                                                          │
  "dependencies": {                                                           │
   "aws-sdk": "^2.3.2"                                                        │
  },
  "author": "Peter Sbarski",
  "license": "BSD-2-Clause",
  "devDependencies": {
   "run-local-lambda": "^1.1.0"
  }
}
```

> **You added a precreate script too. It runs right before the create function to generate the zip file.**

Add the async module using npm. In the terminal, change to the directory of the function and run the following:

```
npm install async --save
```

You should also run `npm install` to make sure that the AWS SDK is installed. If you look at package.json, there should be two dependencies: async and aws-sdk.

Now (if you followed section 6.4.2) you can create the required Lambda function in AWS using the command `npm run create`. If you skipped over section 6.4.2, you'll have to create the `get-video-list` function in the AWS console yourself.

IMPLEMENTATION

This function has a fairly simple implementation, as shown in listing 6.6. Notably, it doesn't take into account some scenarios, such as what happens when there are many files in the S3 bucket (the S3 listObjects operation returns up to 1000 objects in the bucket). The function is also not very efficient. But it's a good temporary measure until we introduce a proper database, and it's a good way to show how the waterfall pattern is used.

Listing 6.6   The `get-video-list` function

```
'use strict';

var AWS = require('aws-sdk');
var async = require('async');

var s3 = new AWS.S3();

function createBucketParams(next) {
  var params = {
    Bucket: process.env.BUCKET,
    EncodingType: 'url'
  };

  next(null, params);
}

function getVideosFromBucket(params, next) {
  s3.listObjects(params, function(err, data){
```

> **The createBucketParams function creates configuration for the S3 listObjects function.**

> **The getVideosFromBucket function uses the S3 SDK to get a list of objects from the specified bucket.**

```
      if (err) {
        next(err);
      } else {
        next(null, data);
      }
  });
}
function createList(data, next) {
  var urls = [];
  for (var i = 0; i < data.Contents.length; i++) {
    var file = data.Contents[i];

    if (file.Key && file.Key.substr(-3, 3) === 'mp4') {
      urls.push(file);
    }
  }

  var result = {
    baseUrl: process.env.BASE_URL,
    bucket: process.env.BUCKET,
    urls: urls
  }

  next(null, result);
}
exports.handler = function(event, context, callback){
  async.waterfall([createBucketParams, getVideosFromBucket, createList],
    function (err, result) {
      if (err) {
        callback(err);
      } else {
        callback(null, result);
      }
  });
};
```

> ◁─┐ **The createList function loops through the data and creates an array of objects that are suitable for watching.**

> ◁─ **Objects that have an extension of mp4 are the only ones added to the url array (objects with a .json, .webm, or .hls extension are ignored).**

> ◁─ **The Lambda callback returns the list of URLs together with the baseUrl and the bucket name.**

Deploy the function by executing npm run deploy from the directory of the function.

ENVIRONMENT VARIABLES

The code in listing 6.6 uses two environment variables: BUCKET and BASE_URL. The BUCKET variable is the name of the second S3 bucket with transcoded files. BASE_URL is a base address for S3 buckets, which is https://s3.amazonaws.com. You must add these two variables for the function to work. In the Lambda console, click the get-video-list function, and add these two environment variables at the bottom of the Code tab (figure 6.15).

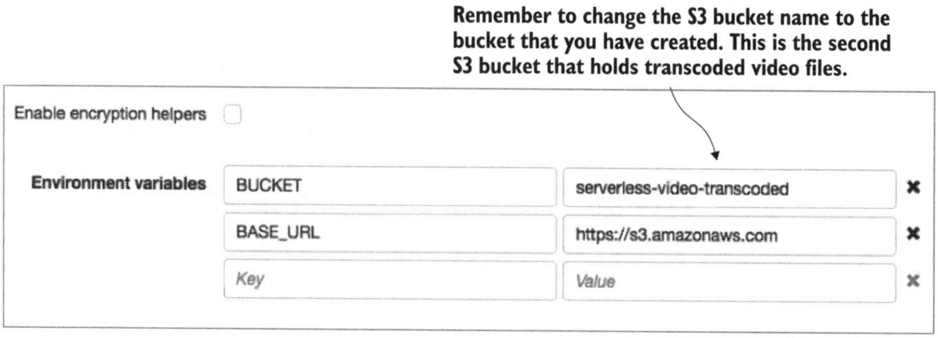

> Remember to change the S3 bucket name to the bucket that you have created. This is the second S3 bucket that holds transcoded video files.

Enable encryption helpers	☐		
Environment variables	BUCKET	serverless-video-transcoded	✖
	BASE_URL	https://s3.amazonaws.com	✖
	Key	Value	✖

Figure 6.15   You must add the BUCKET and BASE_URL environment variables for the function to run.

TESTING

The simplest way to test this function is to jump into the AWS console, click Lambda, and then click `get-video-list`. From there click the Test button. If you get the Input Test Event dialog, click Save And Test to proceed. You should see a list of URLs (if you have mp4s in the bucket) under the Execution Result heading toward the bottom of the page (figure 6.16).

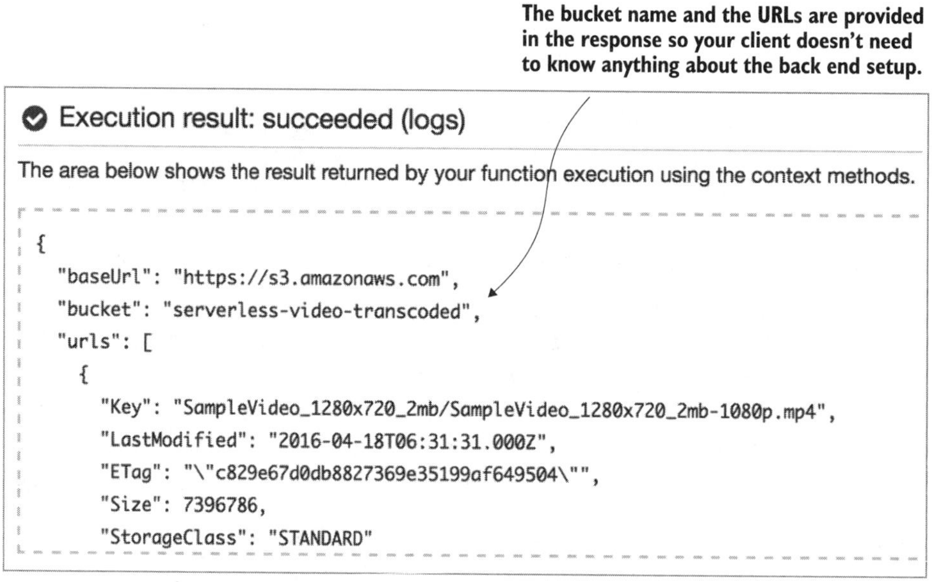

> The bucket name and the URLs are provided in the response so your client doesn't need to know anything about the back end setup.

✔ Execution result: succeeded (logs)

The area below shows the result returned by your function execution using the context methods.

```
{
  "baseUrl": "https://s3.amazonaws.com",
  "bucket": "serverless-video-transcoded",
  "urls": [
    {
      "Key": "SampleVideo_1280x720_2mb/SampleVideo_1280x720_2mb-1080p.mp4",
      "LastModified": "2016-04-18T06:31:31.000Z",
      "ETag": "\"c829e67d0db8827369e35199af649504\"",
      "Size": 7396786,
      "StorageClass": "STANDARD"
```

Figure 6.16   You can preview the response in the AWS console, making it easy to test your Lambda function.

Invoking functions from the command line

The AWS CLI can invoke Lambda functions from the command line. It supports both invocation types, RequestResponse and Event. The syntax for the command can be found in http://amzn.to/269Z2U2. If you decide to try a synchronous Request-Response invocation, you need to provide at least two parameters: the function name and the output file that will contain the response from the function.

To invoke the `get-video-list` function, you need to run the following from your terminal:

```
aws lambda invoke --function-name get-video-list output.txt
```

Remember to grant the right permission (lambda:InvokeFunction) to your IAM user if you decide to use this.

6.5.2 Series and parallel

In addition to waterfall, the async library supports series and parallel patterns of execution. The series pattern is similar to waterfall; it invokes a series of functions one by one. Values (results) are passed into the optional callback function at the very end once the series has finished (figure 6.17).

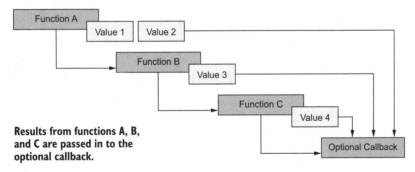

Figure 6.17 The async series pattern can help if you have a series of independent calculations and then get all the results at the end.

The parallel pattern is used to run functions in parallel without waiting for other functions to finish. Once all functions have completed, the results are passed into the optional (final) callback (figure 6.18).

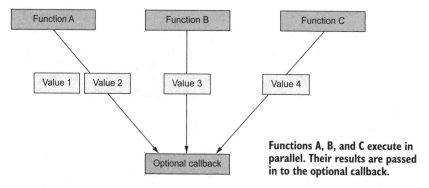

Functions A, B, and C execute in parallel. Their results are passed in to the optional callback.

Figure 6.18 The parallel pattern allows functions to execute at the same time and pass their results to the optional callback function at the end.

6.5.3 *Using libraries*

This advice is a given for most developers. Identify code that's repeated in multiple Lambda functions and move it to another file so that this code is written only once (the Don't Repeat Yourself principle). You can import your libraries using node's `require()`.

Let's see how to practice what we preach and build a library for sending emails using Amazon's Simple Email Service (SES). You can use it to send email when a user uploads a new video or as a way to enable messaging between users. There are two ways you can include this library with the rest of your code:

- You can build a module, deploy it to npm, and then use `npm install --save` to add it. It may take a little more overhead, but it's a good way to manage dependencies and libraries. If having your code publicly available isn't what you want, there's a way to set up and use a private npm repository (see http://bit.ly/1MOsyIF).
- Another approach is to create a lib directory and place your libraries there. Every function can reference the lib directory and import what's needed. This approach may work perfectly well for small applications but it has major disadvantages. Maintaining, sharing, and using different versions of the library will become difficult once you begin to grow. Having two or more versions of the library can become problematic as you try to remember which version goes where. So use this approach sparingly, for experiments or for very simple systems. Go with a proper package management system such as npm if you decide to build anything substantial.

We'll go with the second method in this example, but as part of an exercise later on, we'll ask you to create an npm module for your library, deploy it to the npm repository, and then install it using `npm install`.

GET THE CODE

Create a directory called lib for your library. In this directory make a file called email.js and copy the following listing into it.

Listing 6.7 Adding email support

```
'use strict';

var AWS = require('aws-sdk');
var async = require('async');
var SES = new AWS.SES();

function createMessage(toList, fromEmail, subject, message, next) {
  var params = ({
    Source: fromEmail,
    Destination: { ToAddresses: toList },
    Message: {
      Subject: {
        Data: subject
      },
      Body: {
        Text: {
          Data: message
        }
      }
    }
  });

  next(null, params);
}

function dispatch(params, next) {
  SES.sendEmail(params, function(err, data){
    if (err) {
      next(err);
    } else {
      next(null, data);
    }
  })
}

function send(toList, fromEmail, subject, message) {
  async.waterfall([createMessage.bind(this, toList,
    fromEmail, subject, message), dispatch],
    function (err, result) {
      if (err) {
        console.log('Error sending email', err);
      } else {
        console.log('Email Sent Successfully', result);
      }
  });
};

module.exports = {
  send: send
};
```

You're using the SES service to send email so you need to include it in your library.

Now that you're familiar with the async waterfall pattern, you should try using it where it fits. The bind method call allows you to pass arguments into the createMessage function and run it in the correct context (so that async passes in the callback function).

module.exports is the object returned when you use require(). This makes the send function available to other functions to invoke.

The code in listing 6.7 has a function called send, which can be invoked by external code. It takes four parameters: an array of receiver emails, the sender's own email, a subject, and a message. To use this library in your Lambda functions, follow these steps:

1 Copy the file (email.js) over to the directory of the function.
2 Use require() to load the library in the function:

```
var email = require('email');
```

3 Invoke send and pass the required parameters to it:

```
email.send(['receiver@example.com'], 'sender@example.com', 'Subject',
'Body');
```

You will have noticed that in this library you imported async but didn't bother to run npm install. This is because the library you created will be shipped with a Lambda function that will hopefully have the right npm modules, including async, installed. To be on the safe side, however, you could write a package.json for this library and npm install needed dependencies. In fact, you should do this if you decide to build libraries properly.

Here are a few notes about sending email using SES:

- The role used to execute the function and send email needs to have the ses:SendEmail permission to execute correctly:
- Create a new role or modify an existing one that you wish to use for the function.
- Add a new inline policy and select Policy Generator.
- From the AWS Service drop-down, select Amazon SES.
- From the Action drop-down, select SendEmail and SendRawEmail.
- Click the Add Statement button.
- Then proceed to apply the policy and exit.
- The from email address needs to be verified in the SES console before email can be sent (figure 6.19). To do it, click SES in the AWS console, click Email Addresses, and click Verify a New Email Address. Follow the wizard to verify your email.

You must verify the sender email
address before you can use it.

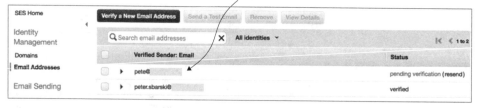

**Figure 6.19 Basic email sending is easy via SES. Try to move code and features that are used often
(such as email sending) into libraries.**

6.5.4   *Move logic to another file*

Building on advice in the previous section, we recommend moving all of your domain/business logic to a different file/library. Your Lambda handler should be a thin wrapper that executes code stored in another file. Having the bulk of your logic in a separate file will lead to an implementation that's more testable and is much more decoupled from Lambda. If one day you decide to move away from Lambda, you'll find it easier to port your code to a new serverless compute service.

6.6   *Testing Lambda functions*

There are two main ways you can test a Lambda function. You can run tests locally (or during continuous integration/deployment) and you can test the function once it's deployed to AWS.

Back in chapter 3, you installed an npm module called run-local-lambda. That package allowed you to invoke a Lambda function locally on the computer and pass in an event, a context, and a callback function. Going forward, however, you need to set up a much more rigorous and robust system for executing tests. You need to have a way to mock dependencies, spy on variables and functions, and manage setup and teardown procedures. This section looks at how to put together a good approach to testing.

6.6.1   *Testing locally*

Let's look at how to test Lambda functions on your computer (later, you'll make these tests run as part of your continuous integration/deployment pipeline). To make this more interesting, you'll write tests for the `get-video-list` function you created in section 6.5.3. You'll use Mocha, Chai, Sinon, and rewire to help you write and run your tests.

In your terminal, change to the directory of the function you created in section 6.5.3 and run the following `npm install` commands to download the required components:

- `npm install mocha -g`
  Mocha (http://bit.ly/1VKV1lY) is a JavaScript test framework.
- `npm install chai --save-dev`
  Chai (http://bit.ly/1pu2xmq) is a test-driven development/behavior-driven development assertion library.
- `npm install sinon --save-dev`
  Sinon (http://bit.ly/1NIhN5q) is a mocking framework. It provides spies, stubs, and mocks.
- `npm install rewire --save-dev`
  Rewire (http://bit.ly/1YNPj05) is a framework for monkey-patching and overriding dependencies for Node.js unit tests.

We should note that Lambda functions are no different from any other regular Node.js application. You can use a different JavaScript framework or assertion library if you prefer.

6.6.2 Writing tests

Having installed the modules, create a new subdirectory called test. In this subdirectory create a file called test.js and open it in your favorite text editor. Copy the next listing into this file.

Listing 6.8 Tests for the `get-video-list` function

```
var chai = require('chai');
var sinon = require('sinon');
var rewire = require('rewire');
var expect = chai.expect;
var assert = chai.assert;

var sampleData = {                       ⟵  This data is provided to the
 Contents: [                                caller when the S3 listObjects()
   {                                         function is invoked.
    Key: 'file1.mp4',
    bucket: 'my-bucket'
   },
   {
    Key: 'file2.mp4',
    bucket: 'my-bucket'
   }
 ]
}

describe('LambdaFunction', function(){
 var listObjectsStub, callbackSpy, module;

 describe('#execute', function() {
  before(function(done){
   listObjectsStub = sinon.stub().yields(null, sampleData);
   callbackSpy = sinon.spy();                        ⟵

   var callback = function(error, result) {      ⟵
     callbackSpy.apply(null, arguments);
    done();
   }

   module = getModule(listObjectsStub);
   module.handler(null, null, callback);    ⟵

  })

   it('should run our function once', function(){
    expect(callbackSpy).has.been.calledOnce;   ⟵
   })0
```

A spy watches a function or a variable and reports on what it does.

This is the callback function that the Lambda function will invoke at the end of its run.

Invoke the handler to run the Lambda function.

This test looks at the spy to check that it has been invoked only once (hence, the callback function was invoked once).

The getModule() call gets a monkey-patched version of your Lambda function.

done() needs to be invoked to tell Mocha that the test has finished.

```
it('should have correct results', function(){
  var result = {
    "baseUrl": "https://s3.amazonaws.com",
    "bucket": "serverless-video-transcoded",
    "urls": [
      {
        "Key": sampleData.Contents[0].Key,
        "bucket": "my-bucket"
      },
      {
        "Key": sampleData.Contents[1].Key,
        "bucket": "my-bucket"
      }
    ]
  }

  assert.deepEqual(callbackSpy.args, [[null, result]]);
  })
 })
})

function getModule(listObjects) {
 var rewired = rewire('../index.js');

 rewired.__set__({
  's3': { listObjects: listObjects }
 });

 return rewired;
}
```

This is additional test data that we think the output from the Lambda function will match.

Compare the output from the Lambda function to the test data to make sure they match.

Rewire is used to patch your Lambda function so that when S3 listObjects() is called, you return your stub and the data prepared earlier instead.

Having implemented listing 6.8, run `mocha` from the directory of the function. You should see output similar to figure 6.20.

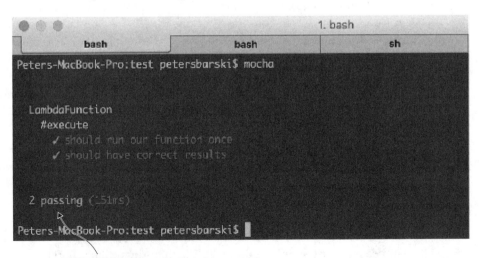

You will see how many tests have passed and failed after running mocha.

Figure 6.20   You can run tests locally and as part of your continuous deployment pipeline.

Let's do a quick review of what happens in your test file:

- You import Chai, Sinon, and rewire and create a sampleData data object that has test data.
- The `before` hook creates stubs and spies and calls the `getModule` function to get a copy of your Lambda function. You use rewire to monkey-patch your Lambda function so that when a request to S3 is made (`s3.listObjects()`) you return a list of objects defined previously in your test file.
- You declare two tests. Both tests check your spy. The first test checks that Lambda's callback function was invoked only once. The second test checks that the arguments passed into Lambda's callback function are what you expect. The second test is a great way to check that a response from a Lambda function is valid in a RequestResponse invocation.

Testing is a broad and complex subject that will take time to master and get right. Thankfully, testing Lambda functions is straightforward compared to more complex Node.js applications. If you want another example, similar to the one you just completed, have a look at http://bit.ly/1MQc4zO.

Our recommendation is to write tests for each Lambda function you create. Once you have a template for wiring up and mocking dependencies (and you can begin by taking listing 6.8 and repurposing it for your needs), creating new tests should become relatively easy.

6.6.3 *Testing in AWS*

You've written a number of wonderful tests on your system and deployed a function to AWS. It's a good idea to test your function in AWS to make sure that it works as you expect. An obvious way to do it is to click the Test button in the console and provide an event for your function to consume. Luckily, there's an even better way to do testing using the unit and load test harness blueprint provided by AWS. This blueprint creates a Lambda function for you that can invoke a Lambda function you wish to test and record the results in a DynamoDB table.

Tim Wagner originally wrote about this in a blog post (http://amzn.to/1Nq37Nx) titled "A Simple Serverless Test Harness using AWS Lambda." You can configure this test harness as follows:

1 Create a new role called `lambda-dynamo` and add an inline policy to it. Add lambda:InvokeFunction and dynamodb:PutItem actions to that policy. For the lambda:InvokeFunction action, set the ARN as `arn:aws:lambda:*:*:*`.
2 Create a new table in DynamoDB and name it unit-test-results. Set the Partition Key to `testId`. Accept all other default settings.
3 In the Lambda's console, click Create a Lambda Function and search for lambda-test-harness among the available blueprints (figure 6.21).
4 Create a new function from the lambda-test-harness blueprint.
5 Set lambda-dynamo as the role for the function and leave the timeout on one minute.

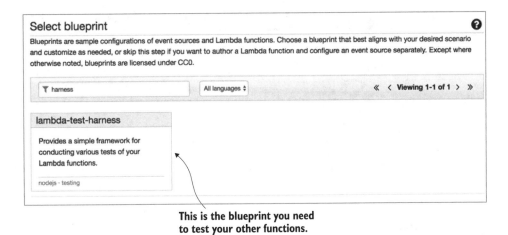

This is the blueprint you need
to test your other functions.

Figure 6.21 Look through the various blueprints on offer. Some of them will give you ideas, and others might save you time.

To correctly run the `lambda-test-harness` function, you need to create an event object that describes a test configuration and pass it to the test harness function. The next listing shows an example test configuration for the `get-video-list` function you developed earlier in this chapter. Note that the event is empty because `get-video-list` doesn't use it during execution.

Listing 6.9 Example unit test configuration

```
{
    "operation": "unit",              ⟵——— The type of test you want to run: unit or load
    "function": "get-video-list",     ⟵——— The function you wish to test
    "resultsTable": "unit-test-results",  ⟵——— The table to store results
    "testId": "MyTestRun",            ⟵——— The ID of the test that will be saved to the database
    "event":{}
}
```

To run the test harness function, click the Test button in the AWS console (assuming you have the function open) and type the configuration from listing 6.9 into the input test event dialog. Then click Save and Test.

Look at the unit-test-results table in DynamoDB for information after executing the function to see the results. To perform a load test, modify the configuration slightly by changing the operation from `unit` to `load` and setting a desired number of iterations. The next listing shows a configuration you can use to execute the function 50 times.

Listing 6.10   Example load test configuration

```
{
    "operation": "load",        ⟵——— In this case you want to run load tests.
    "iterations": 50,           ⟵——— The number of times you want to run your function
    "function": "get-video-list",
    "resultsTable": "unit-test-results",
    "testId": "MyTestRun",
    "event":{}
}
```

Having a mix of tests to run in your local environment and in AWS will give you confidence to make changes and improvements. Don't neglect testing, and do it from the very start.

6.7   *Exercises*

You learned a lot about Lambda in this chapter, but there's no better way to test your knowledge than trying a few exercises. See if you can do the following:

1 Create a Lambda function to check if a given string is a palindrome. Your function should get the string via an environment variable.

2 Implement the email-sending library given in section 6.5.3 and include it in the transcode-video Lambda function. Modify the transcode-video function to send you an email whenever a new transcoding job is created.

3 Package the email-sending library as an npm module and deploy it to the npm repository (see http://bit.ly/1r6heOf for more information on how to do this). When it's deployed, install it into a Lambda function of your choice using npm install <your-module> --save. Update the Lambda function so that it sends email and test it.

4 Create a new Lambda function to send yourself an email every 24 hours. Can you automate it?

5 Add a breaking test to the tests you implemented in section 6.6.2 and run mocha to see what it looks like. Either fix this test or remove it before you proceed to the next question.

6 Write a test for each of the Lambda functions you created in chapters 3 and 5.

7 Create a unit and load-test harness in AWS to test existing Lambda functions. Create a new Lambda function that triggers when new DynamoDB records are inserted and sends you an email with the results of those records.

6.8   *Summary*

A compute service such as Lambda is the heart of serverless architecture. It's the glue that holds everything together. It can serve as a back end for your application or act as a coordinator between other services in your system. In this chapter, we looked at the following:

- Lambda's core principles including invocation types and event models
- Programming model
- Versioning, aliases, and environment variables
- Usage of the CLI
- Patterns such as async waterfall and creation of libraries
- Testing of Lambda functions locally and in AWS

In the next chapter, we'll look at the API Gateway and discuss how to create robust back ends for web and mobile applications.

API Gateway

7

This chapter covers

- Creation and management of API Gateway resources and methods
- Lambda Proxy integration
- API Gateway caching, throttling, and logging

Serverless architectures are versatile. You can use them to build an entire back end or glue a few services together to solve a specific task. Building a proper back end requires the development of an application programming interface (API) that sits between the client and back-end services. In AWS, the API Gateway is this key AWS service that allows developers to create a RESTful API.

This chapter takes a look at the API Gateway. We examine the fundamental activities that go into building an API and discuss features such as staging and versioning, as well as caching, logging, and throttling of requests. You'll also continue to add new functionality to 24-Hour Video such as the ability to list videos facilitated by the API Gateway. Note that API Gateway is a service with many features that can't all be addressed in a single chapter of a book. We recommend reading this chapter and then building a sample API, playing with different features, and reading through the official documentation. Like most of AWS, API Gateway is a rapidly developing service, so don't be surprised if you see one or two new features not discussed here.

7.1 *API Gateway as the interface*

Think of the API Gateway as an interface (figure 7.1) between back-end services (including Lambda) and client applications (web, mobile, or desktop).

We've mentioned before that your front-end application should communicate with services directly. But there are many cases where this isn't possible or desirable in terms of security or privacy. You should perform some actions only from a back-end service. For example, sending an email to all users should be done via a Lambda function. You shouldn't do it from the front end because it would involve loading every user's email address into another user's browser. That's a serious security and privacy issue and a quick way to lose your customers. So don't trust the user's browser and don't perform any sensitive operations in it. The browser is also a bad environment for performing operations that may leave your system in a bad state. Have you seen those websites that say "Do not close this window until the operation has finished"? Avoid building systems like that. They're too brittle. Instead, run operations from a back-end Lambda function, and flag the UI when the operation is completed.

An API Gateway is an example of technology that makes serverless applications easier to build and maintain than their traditional server-based counterparts. In a more traditional system you might need to provision EC2 instances, configure load balancing using Elastic Load Balancer (ELB), and maintain software on each server. The API Gateway removes the need to do all that. You can use it to define an API and connect it

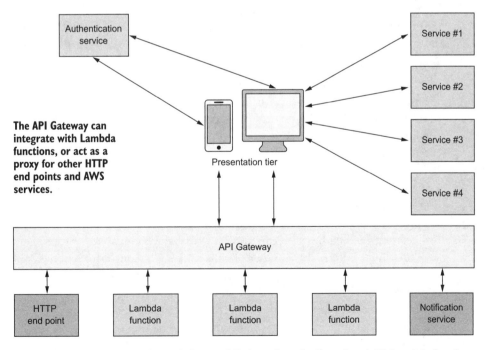

Figure 7.1 The API Gateway is needed, especially for web applications, to establish an interface for back-end services.

to services in minutes. In us-east-1, the API Gateway cost is $3.50 per million API calls received, which makes it affordable for many applications. Let's look now at a few important features of the API Gateway in more detail.

7.1.1 Integration with AWS services

Back in chapter 5, you connected an API Gateway to a `user-profile` Lambda function. You did this so that your website could request information about the user from a Lambda function. Those with keen eyesight would have noticed that Lambda was one of four options. The other three were HTTP Proxy, AWS Service Proxy, and Mock Integration, which are briefly described here.

HTTP PROXY

The HTTP Proxy can forward requests to other HTTP endpoints. Standard HTTP methods (HEAD, POST, PUT, GET, PATCH, DELETE, and OPTIONS) are supported. The HTTP Proxy is particularly useful if you have to build an interface in front of a legacy API or transform/modify the request before it reaches the desired endpoint.

AWS SERVICE PROXY

The AWS Service Proxy can call through to AWS services directly rather than through a Lambda function. Each method (for example, GET) is mapped to a specific action in a desired AWS service, such as adding an item to a DynamoDB table directly. It's much quicker to proxy straight to DynamoDB than to create a Lambda function that can write to a table. Service Proxy is a great option for basic use cases (such as list, add, and remove) and it works across a wide range of AWS services. But in more advanced use cases (especially those that need logic), you'll still have to write a function.

MOCK INTEGRATION

The Mock Integration option is used to generate a response from the API Gateway without having to integrate with another service. It's used in cases such as when a preflight cross-origin resource sharing (CORS) request is issued and the response is predefined in the API Gateway.

7.1.2 Caching, throttling, and logging

It wouldn't be a useful service if the API Gateway didn't have facilities for caching, throttling, encryption, and logging. Section 7.3 deals with these concerns in more detail. Caching can help to reduce latency and alleviate the load on the back end by returning results computed earlier. But caching isn't easy, so you must take care to get it right.

Throttling reduces the number of calls to the API using a token bucket algorithm. You can use it to restrict the number of invocations per second to prevent your back end from being hammered with requests. Finally, logging allows CloudWatch to capture what's happening to the API. It can capture the full incoming request and outgoing response and track information such as cache hits and misses.

7.1.3 Staging and versioning

Staging and versioning are features that you've already used. A *stage* is an environment for your API. You can have up to 10 stages per API (and 60 APIs per account), and it's entirely up to you how to set them up. We prefer to create stages for development, user acceptance testing, and production environments. Sometimes we create stages for individual developers. Each stage can be configured separately and use stage *variables* to invoke different endpoints (that is, you can configure different stages to invoke different Lambda functions or HTTP endpoints).

Each time an API is deployed it creates a version. You can go back to previous versions if you make a mistake, making rollbacks rather easy. Different stages can reference different versions of the API, making it flexible enough to support different versions of your application.

7.1.4 Scripting

Configuring the API Gateway manually (using the AWS console) is fine while you're learning how to use it. But it isn't a sustainable or robust way to work in the long term. Luckily, you can script an entire API using Swagger, which is a popular format for defining APIs (http://swagger.io). Your existing API can be exported to Swagger, and Swagger definitions can be imported as new APIs.

7.2 Working with the API Gateway

In chapter 5, you provisioned a new API for 24-Hour Video. You might recall that an API is made out of resources (which are entities like *user*) that can be accessed through a resource path (for example, /api/user). Each resource can have one or more operations defined against it, represented by HTTP verbs such as GET, DELETE, or POST (figure 7.2).

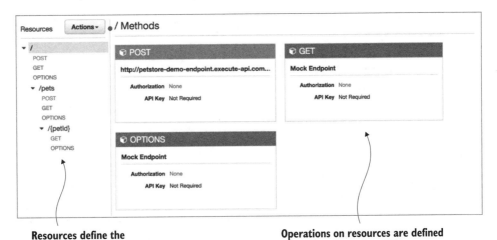

Resources define the structure of the API.

Operations on resources are defined by HTTP verbs such as GET.

Figure 7.2 Resources and methods make up the API. You can see the API at a glance in the API Gateway console.

Create an API in the AWS cloud and authenticate calls.
Web application
Authentication
Video upload
Video transcoder
Media storage
Video list database
Custom API

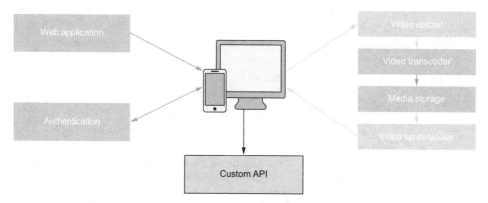

Figure 7.3 In this chapter you're going to build the bulk of your API and explore the features API Gateway has to offer.

In this section, you're going to add a new resource and method to the API Gateway, connect it to a Lambda function, and learn how to use Lambda proxy integration. Figure 7.3 shows which component of the 24-Hour Video system you'll be working on in this chapter.

CREATING A NEW API

If you didn't create an API in chapter 5, you'll have to do it now. To create an API, choose the API Gateway in the AWS console and then click the Create API button. Leave the New API radio button selected, and enter an API name (such as `24-hour-video`) and an optional description. Click Create API to finalize your choice (figure 7.4).

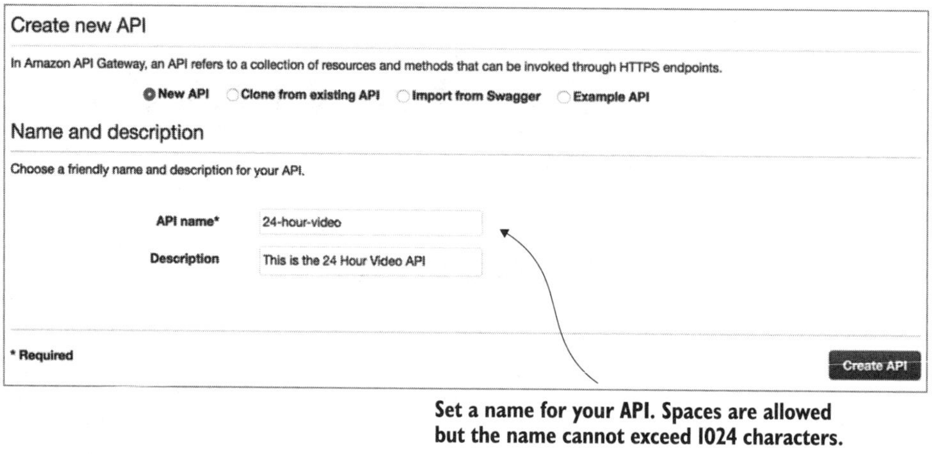

Create new API
In Amazon API Gateway, an API refers to a collection of resources and methods that can be invoked through HTTPS endpoints.
New API
Clone from existing API
Import from Swagger
Example API
Name and description
Choose a friendly name and description for your API.
API name*
24-hour-video
Description
This is the 24 Hour Video API
* Required
Create API
Set a name for your API. Spaces are allowed but the name cannot exceed 1024 characters.

Figure 7.4 Creating a new API takes less than 30 seconds. There is a limit of 60 APIs per AWS account.

7.2.1   The plan

In chapter 6, you created a Lambda function to return a list of videos in your S3 bucket. It would be good to show these videos on your website. You want the user to open the site and see a list of videos they can play—just as they would on YouTube. For this to work, your website needs to issue a request to the `get-video-list` Lambda function via the API Gateway.

You're going to create a resource called *Videos* and add a GET method to it, which you'll use to request and receive the list of videos. When you finish working through this chapter, your implementation of 24-Hour Video will look similar to figure 7.5. To make things a little more interesting, you'll add an optional URL query parameter called `encoding`. You'll use this parameter to return videos of a specific encoding (for example, 720p or 1080p).

Be forewarned: having a Lambda function and an API Gateway to return a list of videos is what you have to do for now because you don't have a database. In chapter 9, we'll show you an alternative way of retrieving video URLs straight from the database without having to use the API Gateway or Lambda.

HTML5 Video tag is used to render videos and display controls. All modern browsers support the HTML5 Video tag and the MPEG-4/H.264 video format so you shouldn't have problems playing video.

Figure 7.5   Your 24-Hour Video website will play videos once you've completed this section.

7.2.2   *Creating the resource and method*

In the API Gateway, choose the 24-hour-video API you created earlier. Then follow these steps to create a resource called *Videos* (figure 7.6):

1 Choose the Actions drop-down menu.
2 Select Create Resource.
3 Set the Resource Name to Videos. The Resource Path should be /videos. Note that your resource paths must not conflict. In the future, you won't be able to create another resource called /videos unless you delete this one.
4 Do not select Configure as Proxy Resource or Enable API Gateway CORS at this stage.
5 Click Create Resource.

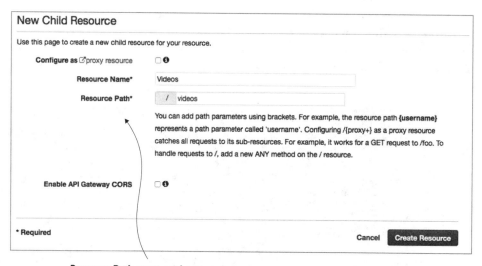

Resource Path must not have any spaces.

Figure 7.6   Create a resource through the Actions drop-down menu. Resource Paths must not clash.

> **Proxy resource and CORS**
>
> When you create a resource in the API Gateway, there's an option called Configure as Proxy Resource (figure 7.6). Enabling this option creates a proxy resource with a "greedy" path variable that looks like {proxy+}. A greedy path variable represents any child resource under a parent resource. For example, if you had a path /video/{proxy+} you could issue requests to /video/abc, /video/xyz, or any other endpoint starting with /video/. All of those requests would be routed to the {proxy+} resource automatically (it's essentially a wildcard for paths). The + symbol tells the API Gateway to capture all requests on the matched resource (https://docs.aws.amazon.com/apigateway/latest/developerguide/api-gateway-set-up-simple-proxy.html#api-gateway-proxy-resource).

Enabling the Configure as Proxy Resource option also creates an ANY method under the resource. The ANY method allows the client to use any HTTP method (GET, POST, and so on) to access the resource. But you don't have to use the ANY resource if you don't want to. You can still create individual methods like GET and POST.

Finally, you can choose a Lambda function proxy or an HTTP proxy as the integration type. We'll discuss Lambda proxy and HTTP proxy integration shortly. When should you enable the Configure as Proxy Resource option? The answer is only if you have a specific reason or a use case for it. Our suggestion is to try to build mature RESTful APIs whenever possible (https://martinfowler.com/articles/richardsonMaturityModel .html) and to resort to Configure as Proxy Resource only when you have to. One final note: the greedy path variable, the ANY method, and proxy integrations are separate features and can be used independently from each other. We'll show how to use Lambda proxy integration in this chapter but leave greedy path variables and the ANY method for you to experiment with.

Yet another option you can turn on when creating a resource is Enable API Gateway CORS. It's safe to enable it during the creation of the resource. It creates an OPTIONS method that's needed for CORS. If you use Lambda or HTTP proxy integration (as you will in this chapter), then everything is set up for you automatically. The option generates the OPTIONS method, and any additional CORS headers can be set in the Lambda function (as you'll shortly see).

But if you end up mapping requests/responses individually, then you need to run Enable CORS from the Actions drop-down every time you create a new method. Running Enable CORS adds a necessary CORS header to Method Response, which you need in this case. We've also noticed that using Enable API Gateway CORS during resource creation generates a slightly more permissive OPTIONS method (but you can tweak it after the fact). Feel free to enable that check box, but don't forget about the Enable CORS option from the Actions drop-down menu.

ADDING A METHOD

Having created the resource, you can create a method for it:

1 Choose the Videos resource in the Resources sidebar.
2 Choose Actions and choose Create Method.
3 A small drop-down box should appear under Videos. Choose it and select GET. Choose the round check mark button to confirm.

INTEGRATING WITH LAMBDA

You should now see integration setup for the GET method. You're going to configure it to invoke your Lambda function:

1 Select the Lambda Function radio button.
2 Check Use Lambda Proxy Integration. We'll discuss what this option does in the next section.
3 Pick us-east-1 from the Lambda Region drop-down.

4 Type `get-video-list` in the Lambda Function text box. As we said in chapter 6, we highly recommend that you use an alias when integrating with a function. An alias will help to switch between different versions of your function without having to reconfigure the event sources. Your alias should point to the $LATEST version of the `get-video-list` Lambda function. To use an alias, type `get-video-list:dev` into the Lambda Function text box, where `dev` is the name of the alias (figure 7.7).

5 Click Save.

6 Click OK in the popup window, and click OK again to confirm.

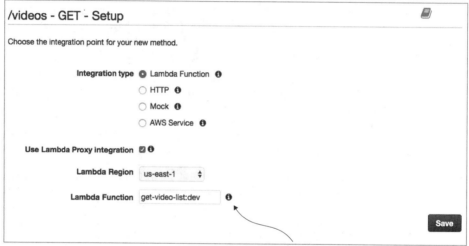

You should always use an alias with an API Gateway.
It will make changes easier to manage.

Figure 7.7 The API Gateway was designed to easily integrate with a Lambda function. It doesn't take long to do.

Lambda Proxy Integration

Lambda Proxy Integration is an option that will make life easier when using API Gateway and Lambda together. If you enable it, API Gateway will map every request to JSON and pass it to Lambda as the event object. In the Lambda function you'll be able to retrieve query string parameters, headers, stage variables, path parameters, request context, and the body from it.

Without enabling Lambda Proxy Integration, you'll have to create a mapping template in the Integration Request section of API Gateway and decide how to map the HTTP request to JSON yourself. And you'd likely have to create an Integration Response mapping if you were to pass information back to the client. Before Lambda Proxy Integration was added, users were forced to map requests and responses manually, which was a source of consternation, especially with more complex mappings.

Lambda Proxy Integration makes things simpler, and in most cases you'll find it's the preferred option. There are cases, however, where you might want to create a specific mapping template (as you did in chapter 5). A mapping can help to produce a succinct and targeted integration payload as needed by the function (as opposed to passing the full request with proxy integration).

If you choose HTTP Request Integration, you'll get an option similar to Lambda Proxy Integration called Use Http Proxy Integration. If you enable this option, your request will be proxied in its entirety to the specified HTTP endpoint. If you don't enable the option, you'll be able to specify a mapping and create a new request payload yourself.

ADDING CORS

You now have a resource and a GET method. You need to enable CORS to allow your clients to access the API. For the moment, you're going to allow any client from any origin to issue GET requests against /videos. As you move to create staging and production versions of the site, you're going to lock down the origin, so that only your website can access the API. To enable CORS, do the following:

1. Choose the Videos resource in the Resources sidebar.
2. Choose Actions.
3. Choose Enable CORS.
4. Leave all settings as they are and click Enable CORS and Replace Existing CORS Headers.
5. You will see a pop-up confirming changes. Click Yes, Replace Existing Value to finish.

CORS security

Security is important to get right. Nothing will take the shine off your newly designed serverless system than someone compromising your security. Remember that in a real-world setting you'll need to restrict CORS to your domain rather than leave it wide open. If you use Lambda proxy integration, then CORS settings must be set in the response created by the Lambda function. If you manually map requests and responses, then you can set CORS settings in the integration response of the method.

7.2.3 Configuring method execution

If you select the GET method of your videos resource, you'll see a page similar to figure 7.8. This page has the following configuration sections that can be accessed:

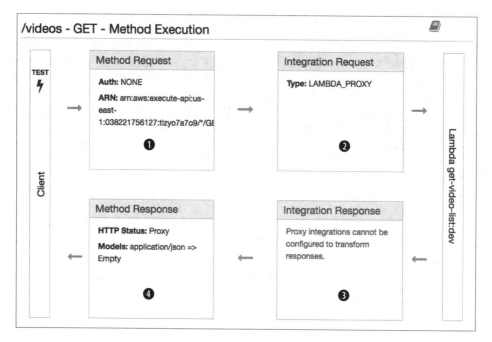

Figure 7.8   The Method Execution screen for the GET method. From here, you can define what goes into the method/integration request and response.

❶ Method Request defines the public interface (header and body) for this combination of resource and method.

❷ Integration Request defines the back end integration (for example, which Lambda function to invoke). We've enabled Lambda proxy integration, which automatically maps and passes HTTP request elements to the Lambda function (via the event object). Lambda proxy integration is convenient, but you could have defined a mapping yourself if you wanted to (see appendix E).

❸ Integration Response defines how data is mapped into a format expected by the caller of the API. Because you're using Lambda proxy integration, there's nothing that needs to be done here.

❹ Method Response defines the public interface that includes headers and the body of the request. Because you're using Lambda proxy integration, you don't need to do anything here. But if you look at appendix E, you'll see how Method Response could come in useful.

METHOD REQUEST

Click Method Request to access its configuration. You can do a number of things here, but they aren't relevant right now because you're using Lambda proxy integration. If you wish to find out what some of these settings do, refer to appendix E. The only option that's applicable at this stage is the custom authorizer. You must set it to

> **Proxy integration vs. manual mapping**
>
> Here's where things get interesting. In this chapter we'll show you how to create an API using Lambda proxy integration. But what if you want to do the same thing without using Lambda proxy integration? What if you want to write a mapping and have granular control over what's available to the Lambda function via the event object? Understanding mappings and models is useful, so we've added appendix E, which explains how to implement an API without Lambda proxy integration. In the appendix we show how to configure integration request and response. We also introduce you to the Velocity Template Language (VTL) and show how to use regular expressions to create HTTP status codes in the API Gateway. We think you'll end up using Lambda proxy integration most of the time, but appendix E serves as a great guide if you wish to understand mappings or want more precise control over the payloads produced by the API Gateway.

authenticate requests to this GET method. To do this, click the pen icon next to Authorization and select your custom authorizer from the list (remember, you created this authorizer in chapter 5). Figure 7.9 shows what this screen looks like.

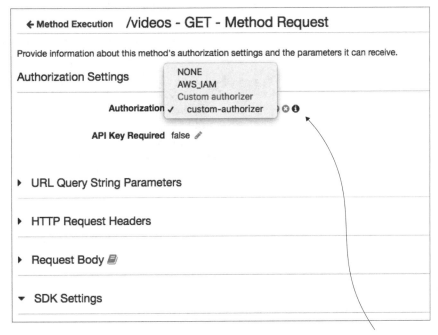

Set a custom authorizer to secure your API.

Figure 7.9   The Method Request page defines the interface and settings that the caller of the API must respect and provide.

Anytime you make a change to the API Gateway, it must be redeployed. If you forget to do this, you won't see any of your modifications. To perform a deployment, do the following:

1 Make sure that the Resources section of your API is selected.
2 Click the Actions drop-down button.
3 Select Deploy API and select a deployment stage (dev) from the drop-down.
4 If you don't yet have a deployment stage, create a new one, and make sure to call it dev.
5 Click Deploy to finish.

7.2.4 *The Lambda function*

The API Gateway side of things is mostly done. The Gateway proxies the HTTP request to the Lambda function, which becomes available to it via the event object. The function can extract useful information like the body of the request, the headers, and query string parameters. At the end, the function must create a specially formed response that the API Gateway can pass back to the client. If this response doesn't follow the prescribed format, API Gateway will return a `502 Bad Gateway` error to the client.

INPUT FORMAT

The following listing shows what an event parameter looks like when API Gateway invokes a Lambda function. The example given here is a basic GET request with a query string parameter called `encoding`. Note that some parts of this listing have been condensed or slightly modified for brevity.

Listing 7.1   The input event parameter

```
{
    resource: '/videos',        <———  Resource path
    path: '/videos',            <———  Path parameters
    httpMethod: 'GET',          <———  The incoming request's method name
    headers: {                  <———  The incoming request's headers
        Accept: '*/*',
        'Accept-Encoding': 'gzip, deflate, sdch, br',
        'Accept-Language': 'en-US,en;q=0.8',
        Authorization: 'Bearer eyJ0eXK...',
        'Cache-Control': 'no-cache',
        'CloudFront-Forwarded-Proto': 'https',
        'CloudFront-Is-Desktop-Viewer': 'true',
        'CloudFront-Is-Mobile-Viewer': 'false',
        'CloudFront-Is-SmartTV-Viewer': 'false',
        'CloudFront-Is-Tablet-Viewer': 'false',
        'CloudFront-Viewer-Country': 'AU',
        DNT: '1',
        Host: 'bl5mn437o0.execute-api.us-east-1.amazonaws.com',
        Origin: 'http://127.0.0.1:8100',
        Pragma: 'no-cache',
        Referer: 'http://127.0.0.1:8100/',
```

```
        'User-Agent': 'Mozilla/5.0 (Macintosh; Intel Mac OS X 10_12_2)
        ⇒AppleWebKit/537.36 (KHTML, like Gecko) Chrome/55.0.2883.95
        ⇒Safari/537.36',
        Via: '1.1 2d7b0cb3d.cloudfront.net (CloudFront)',
        'X-Amz-Cf-Id': 'nbCkMUXzJFGVwkCGg7om97rzrS6n',
        'X-Forwarded-For': '1.128.0.0, 120.147.162.170, 54.239.202.81',
        'X-Forwarded-Port': '443',
        'X-Forwarded-Proto': 'https'
    },
    queryStringParameters: {                ⟵   Any available query
        encoding: '720p'                         string parameters
    },
    pathParameters: null,
    stageVariables: {                       ⟵   Any relevant API Gateway
        function: 'get-video-list-dev'           stage variables
    },
    requestContext: {                       ⟵   Request context including
        accountId: '038221756127',               available identity information
        resourceId: 'e3r6ou',
        stage: 'dev',
        requestId: '534bcd23-e536-11e6-805c-b1e540fbf5c7',
        identity: {
            cognitoIdentityPoolId: null,
            accountId: null,
            cognitoIdentityId: null,
            caller: null,
            apiKey: null,
            sourceIp: '121.147.161.171',
            accessKey: null,
            cognitoAuthenticationType: null,
            cognitoAuthenticationProvider: null,
            userArn: null,
            userAgent: 'Mozilla/5.0 (Macintosh; Intel Mac OS X 10_12_2)
            ⇒]AppleWebKit/537.36 (KHTML, like Gecko) Chrome/55.0.2883.95
            ⇒Safari/537.36',
            user: null
        },
        resourcePath: '/videos',
        httpMethod: 'GET',
        apiId: 'tlzyo7a7o9'
    },                                   ⟵   The body of the
    body: null,                              request as JSON
    isBase64Encoded: false
```

OUTPUT FORMAT

A Lambda function must return a response, via the callback function, that matches the JSON format given in the next listing. If the format isn't followed, the API Gateway will return a 502 Bad Gateway response (https://docs.aws.amazon.com/apigateway/latest/developerguide/api-gateway-set-up-simple-proxy.html).

Listing 7.2   Lambda output format

```
{
    "statusCode": httpStatusCode,
    "headers": { "headerName": "headerValue", ... },
    "body": "..."
}
```

LAMBDA IMPLEMENTATION

You implemented the `get-video-list` Lambda function in chapter 6. Now you need to update this function to work with the API Gateway. The next listing shows an updated implementation that accounts for the API Gateway and Lambda proxy integration. Replace the implementation of the existing function with the code given in the listing and deploy the function to AWS.

Listing 7.3   Get video list Lambda function

This function creates a response with an HTTP status code of 404 or 500 if no videos have been found or another error occurred.

The Access-Control-Allow-Origin header must be included in the response. Remember that in a production version of this code you'd need to restrict this header to your domain.

```
'use strict';

var AWS = require('aws-sdk');
var async = require('async');

var s3 = new AWS.S3();

function createErrorResponse(code, message, encoding) {
    var response = {
        'statusCode': code,
        'headers' : {'Access-Control-Allow-Origin' : '*'},
        'body' : JSON.stringify({'code': code, 'messsage' : message, 'encoding' :
        encoding})
    }

    return response;
}

function createSuccessResponse(result) {
    var response = {
        'statusCode': 200,
        'headers' : {'Access-Control-Allow-Origin' : '*'},
        'body' : JSON.stringify(result)
    }

    return response;
}

function createBucketParams(next) {
    var params = {
        Bucket: process.env.BUCKET
    };

    next(null, params);
}
```

This function creates a response if videos were found. It also sets an HTTP status code of 200 (OK).

```
function getVideosFromBucket(params, next) {
  s3.listObjects(params, function(err, data){
    if (err) {
      next(err);
    } else {
      next(null, data);
    }
  });
}

function createList(encoding, data, next) {
  var files = [];
  for (var i = 0; i < data.Contents.length; i++) {
    var file = data.Contents[i];

    if (encoding) {
      var type = file.Key.substr(file.Key.lastIndexOf('-') + 1);
      if (type !== encoding + '.mp4') {
        continue;
      }
    } else {
      if (file.Key.slice(-4) !== '.mp4') {
        continue;
      }
    }

    files.push({
      'filename': file.Key,
      'eTag': file.ETag.replace(/"/g,""),
      'size': file.Size
    });
  }

  var result = {
    domain: process.env.BASE_URL,
    bucket: process.env.BUCKET,
    files: files
  }

  next(null, result)
}

exports.handler = function(event, context, callback){
  var encoding = null;

  if (event.queryStringParameters && event.queryStringParameters.encoding) {
    encoding = decodeURIComponent(event.queryStringParameters.encoding);
  }

  async.waterfall([createBucketParams, getVideosFromBucket,
    async.apply(createList, encoding)],
    function (err, result) {
      if (err) {
        callback(null, createErrorResponse(500, err, encoding));
      } else {
        if (result.files.length > 0) {
          callback(null, createSuccessResponse(result));
```

You're allowing an optional encoding parameter to help retrieve specific files (such as 720p versions of your videos). If the encoding parameter isn't provided, all (mp4) files in the transcoded video bucket are returned in the response. The way files are selected here is brittle because the filename has to have a specific structure. An exercise at the end will ask you to come up with a better way to do this.

The replace function removes an extra set of double quotes from ETag.

```
      } else {
        callback(null, createErrorResponse(404, 'No files were found',
    ➥encoding));
      }
    }
  });
};
```

You'll notice in listing 7.3 that you always invoke `callback(null, response)` even when you want to return an error to the client. The first parameter to the callback function is `null` although you're dealing with an error state from the user's perspective. Why is that? This is because from Lambda's perspective everything is correct. The function itself didn't fail. The second parameter is the response and whether it needs to inform the client if there's an issue. Luckily you can also set an HTTP status code that the API Gateway will send with the response. If you need to send back a 400 or 500 HTTP status code, that's easy to do by tweaking the payload and changing the `status-Code` parameter to whatever you want. If you forget to put a `null` as the first parameter in the callback, your client will get a 502 response. Having updated the implementation of the `get-video-list` Lambda function, deploy it to AWS.

TESTING IN THE API GATEWAY

You can do a quick test in the API Gateway to check that everything is right. In the Method Execution window for the GET method (figure 7.8), click Test in the client rectangle. In the Query Strings text box enter `encoding=720p` and click Test. If you have any transcoded files ending with -720p.mp4, you should see them listed under Response Body (figure 7.10). If you don't have any 720p files, you should see a response body that states that "No files were found" with an HTTP status code of 404. If you leave the Query String text box empty, then the response body will contain a list of all mp4 files in your transcoded videos bucket.

7.2.5 *Updating the website*

You've done all this work with the API Gateway and Lambda, but there's one last thing to do. You need to update your 24-Hour Video website, which you began in chapter 5, to show videos. You're going to change the front page to show videos that users have uploaded when the page loads. Also, you're going to use the HTML5 video tag to play videos. All the latest versions of major browsers support it.

Set your query string.

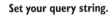

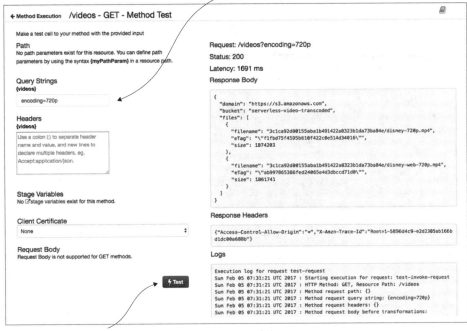

Click Test to see output
on the right-hand side.

Figure 7.10 A successful test of the Lambda function and the API Gateway

To update the site, open index.html in your favorite text editor and remove the entire
section of the code (near the bottom) that begins with <div class="container"> and
ends with </div>. In the place of that div, copy the contents of the following listing.

Listing 7.4 The website index.html

You'll clone this div for
every video that you
have to display.

The copies of the div that
contains the video will be
prepended to the container.

```
<div class="container" id="video-list-container">
  <div id="video-template" class="col-md-6 col">
    <div class="video-card">
      <video width="100%" height="100%" controls>
        <source type="video/mp4"> Your browser does not support the video
        ➥tag.
      </video>
    </div>
  </div>
  <div id="video-list" class="row">
  </div>
</div>
```

Next, you need to implement code that will issue a GET request against your API Gateway and populate the front page with the videos. To do this, create a file called video-controller.js in the js directory of the website and copy the contents of the next listing to it.

Listing 7.5   The website video controller

```
var videoController = {
    data: {
        config: null
    },
    uiElements: {
            videoCardTemplate: null,
            videoList: null,
            loadingIndicator: null
    },
    init: function(config) {
        this.uiElements.videoCardTemplate = $('#video-template');
        this.uiElements.videoList = $('#video-list');

        this.data.config = config;

        this.getVideoList();
    },
    getVideoList: function() {
        var that = this;
        var url = this.data.config.apiBaseUrl + '/videos';

        $.get(url, function(data, status){
            that.updateVideoFrontpage(data);
        });
    },
    updateVideoFrontpage: function(data) {
        var baseUrl = data.domain;
        var bucket = data.bucket;

        for (var i = 0; i < data.files.length; i++){
         var video = data.files[i];

         var clone = this.uiElements.videoCardTemplate.clone().attr('id',
    'video-' + i);

        clone.find('source')
            .attr('src', baseUrl + '/' + bucket + '/' + video.filename);

        this.uiElements.videoList.prepend(clone);
        }
    }
}
```

The apiBaseUrl should be set in your config.js. Check that it is correct and matches what you have in the API Gateway.

For each video returned from the API Gateway, you'll clone the video card template, set the video source, and add it to the video list on the front page.

You're only handling the *happy* case, which won't work in case of an error. You should also be checking for different response codes, especially now that you can control response codes yourself. One of the questions at the end of this chapter will ask you to handle error conditions.

Another file that needs to be changed is main.js in the js directory. Replace the contents of this file with the following code.

Listing 7.6 The website video controller

```
(function(){
    $(document).ready(function(){
        userController.init(configConstants);
        videoController.init(configConstants);
    });
}());
```

> videoController.init(configConstants) will run the getVideoList function and load your videos.

Finally, add `<script src="js/video-controller.js"></script>` above `<script src="js/user-controller.js"></script>` in index.html and save the file. You're finally in a position to see what the website looks like. From the command line, run `npm run start` to launch the website. If you've uploaded any videos, they should appear after a short wait. If you haven't uploaded any videos, you can do it now and then refresh. If you're not seeing any videos after a short wait, look at your browser's console to investigate what's going on.

7.3 *Optimizing the gateway*

In section 7.1, we briefly listed some of the features of the API Gateway, including caching and throttling. Let's look at these in more detail because they'll come in handy as you build your serverless architecture. You can find all of the options we mention in this section in the Settings tab of the Stage Editor. To get to the Settings tab, take these steps:

1. Choose Stages under the 24-Hour Video API.
2. Select dev from the list of stages.

7.3.1 *Throttling*

Let's talk about throttling first, and specifically about rate and burst limit. The *rate* is the average number of times the API Gateway will allow a method to be called per second. The *burst limit* is the maximum number of times the gateway will allow the method to be called. API Gateway sets the "steady-state request rate to 1000 requests per second (rps) and allows bursts of up to 2000 rps across all APIs, stages, and methods within an AWS account" (https://docs.aws.amazon.com/apigateway/latest/developerguide/api-gateway-request-throttling.html).

These defaults can be increased if you ask Amazon. The throttling feature prevents denial-of-service attacks by disallowing additional HTTP requests above the set threshold. You can see how it works by lowering the request rate and putting together a quick Lambda function that will fire off a few hundred requests in rapid succession.

To see how it works for yourself, do the following:

1. Click the Enable Throttling check box.
2. Change the Rate and Burst limits to 5.
3. Click Save (figure 7.11).

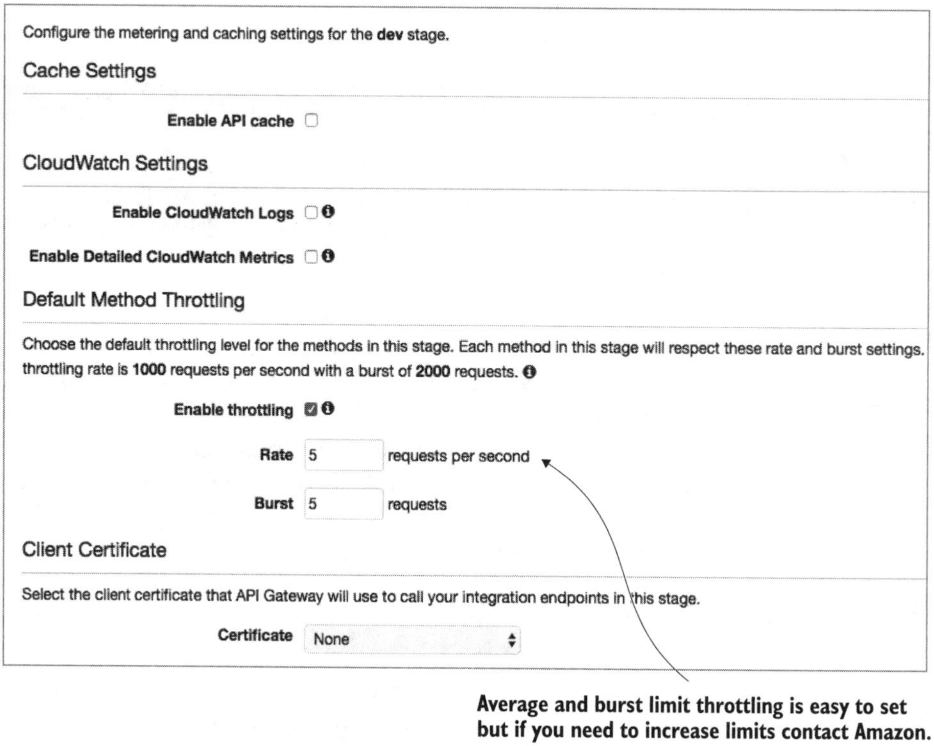

Configure the metering and caching settings for the **dev** stage.

Cache Settings

Enable API cache ☐

CloudWatch Settings

Enable CloudWatch Logs ☐ ❶

Enable Detailed CloudWatch Metrics ☐ ❶

Default Method Throttling

Choose the default throttling level for the methods in this stage. Each method in this stage will respect these rate and burst settings. throttling rate is **1000** requests per second with a burst of **2000** requests. ❶

Enable throttling ☑ ❶

Rate 5   requests per second ▾

Burst 5   requests

Client Certificate

Select the client certificate that API Gateway will use to call your integration endpoints in this stage.

Certificate None   ⬍

Average and burst limit throttling is easy to set but if you need to increase limits contact Amazon.

Figure 7.11   Set the throttling limits and click Save. You can rest assured that if you get a denial-of-service attack, it won't cost you much.

Having set a limit, create a new Lambda function and paste the contents of the next listing into it. This function is based on the https-request blueprint you can select when creating a new function.

Listing 7.7   The denial-of-service Lambda function

```
'use strict';

let https = require('https');

function makeRequests(event, iteration, callback){

    const req = https.request(event.options, (res) => {       ◁──
        let body = '';
        console.log('Status:', res.statusCode);
        res.setEncoding('utf8');
        res.on('data', (chunk) => body += chunk);
        res.on('end', () => {
            console.log('Successfully processed HTTPS response, iteration: ',
          ➥iteration);

            if (res.headers['content-type'] === 'application/json') {
                console.log(JSON.parse(body));
            }
```

Execute a common request and log the status code as well as the body of the response.

```
        });
    });

    return req;
}
exports.handler = (event, context, callback) => {
    for (var i = 0; i < 200; i++) {
        var req = makeRequests(event, i, callback);
        req.end();
    }
};
```

200 requests will be made against your API in a rapid succession. This is enough to test whether throttling works.

> **Disable your custom authorizer**
>
> If you've enabled a custom authorizer for the /videos GET method, you should temporarily disable it to run this test. In Resources, click GET under /videos, select Method Execution, and then set the Authorization drop-down to NONE. Deploy the API for the change to take effect. Don't forget to set your custom authorizer back once you've finished the throttle test.

To run the function, click Test and paste the contents of the next listing as the event. Change the hostname to the hostname of your API and click Save and Test.

Listing 7.8 The denial-of-service Lambda function

```
{
  "options": {
    "hostname":"bd54gbf734.execute-api.us-east-1.amazonaws.com",
    "path":"/dev/videos",
    "method": "GET"
  },
  "data": ""
}
```

Change the hostname to point to your API Gateway.

The test may take a few seconds to run, but you can scroll down the page to see the results under Log Output. Not all of the results will be captured there, so you can choose the logs link next to the Execution Result heading. If you scroll through the log, you'll see that most requests did not succeed. After you've finished testing, don't forget to set the Rate and Burst limits back to more sensible numbers or uncheck Enable Throttling.

7.3.2 Logging

We strongly recommend that you enable CloudWatch Logs and CloudWatch Metrics for your API. To do this, you need to have an IAM role that has permissions to write to Cloud-Watch and you need to specify the ARN of this role in the API Gateway. Create a new role, call it `api-gateway-log` in the IAM console, and attach a policy called `AmazonAPIGateway-PushToCloudWatchLogs` to it (figure 7.12). Write down the ARN of the role.

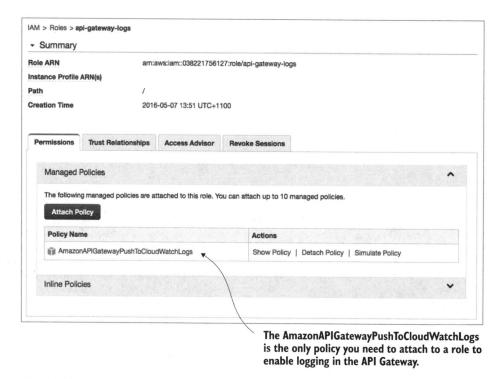

The **AmazonAPIGatewayPushToCloudWatchLogs**
is the only policy you need to attach to a role to
enable logging in the API Gateway.

Figure 7.12   The API Gateway requires you to create and manually assign a role.

To finish, you need to configure the API Gateway:

1 Choose Settings at the bottom left of the API Gateway screen.
2 Copy the role ARN into the CloudWatch log role ARN text box and click Save.
3 Go back to the Stage Editor and enable logging by choosing the check boxes
   next to Enable CloudWatch Logs and Enable Detailed CloudWatch Metrics (figure 7.13).
4 Optionally, you can also turn on full logging of request/response data, but for
   now leave it disabled. Don't forget to click Save Changes.

To check that everything has been correctly set up, follow these steps:

1 Open CloudWatch in the AWS console.
2 Choose Logs and look for a log group called /aws/apigateway/welcome.
3 Choose that log group and click the first log stream.
4 You should see a message similar to "Cloudwatch logs enabled for API Gateway."

As you begin using your API Gateway, logs will begin to appear in CloudWatch. In fact,
these logs will help you in the next section.

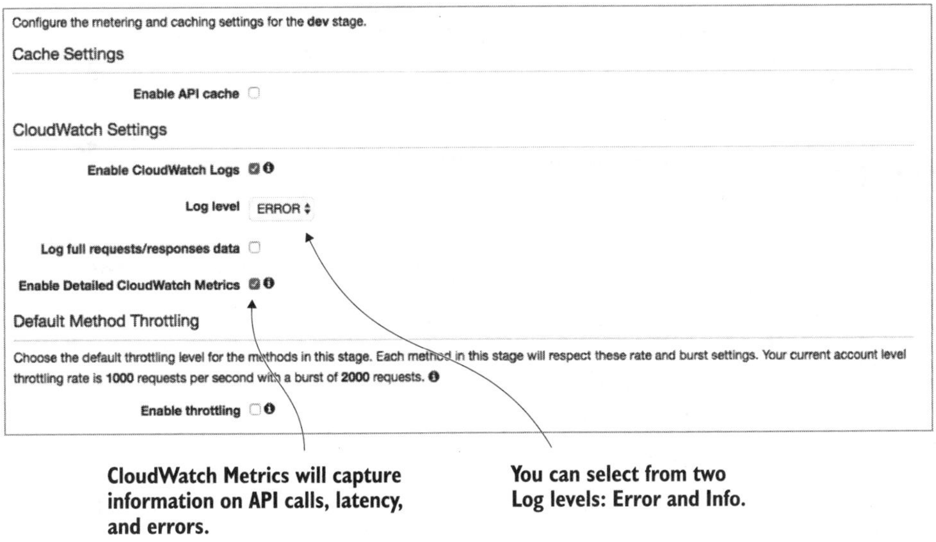

Configure the metering and caching settings for the **dev** stage.

Cache Settings

        Enable API cache ☐

CloudWatch Settings

    Enable CloudWatch Logs ☑ ❶

        Log level   ERROR ⬍

  Log full requests/responses data ☐

Enable Detailed CloudWatch Metrics ☑ ❶

Default Method Throttling

Choose the default throttling level for the methods in this stage. Each method in this stage will respect these rate and burst settings. Your current account level throttling rate is **1000** requests per second with a burst of **2000** requests. ❶

        Enable throttling ☐ ❶

CloudWatch Metrics will capture information on API calls, latency, and errors.

You can select from two Log levels: Error and Info.

Figure 7.13   Always turn on logging for your API Gateway. You never know when you'll need it.

7.3.3   Caching

The AWS documentation (https://docs.aws.amazon.com/apigateway/latest/developerguide/api-gateway-caching.html) has a great section on caching. Caching can increase the performance of your API by returning a result without calling your back-end service. Enabling cache is easy, but you also have to know when to invalidate the cache so that your clients are not served stale results. It also costs money.

An API Gateway cache can be as small as 0.5 GB and as large as 237 GB. Amazon charges per hour for a cache and the price depends on the size of the cache. As an example, 0.5 GB is $0.020 per hour, whereas 237GB is $3.800 per hour. You can find the pricing table at https://aws.amazon.com/api-gateway/pricing/.

> **Caching is a hard problem**
>
> There's a common saying that there are two hard things in computer science: cache invalidation, naming things, and off-by-one errors. Caching is hard to get right regardless of the system, so it will always take a bit of tweaking and experimenting the first time you do it.

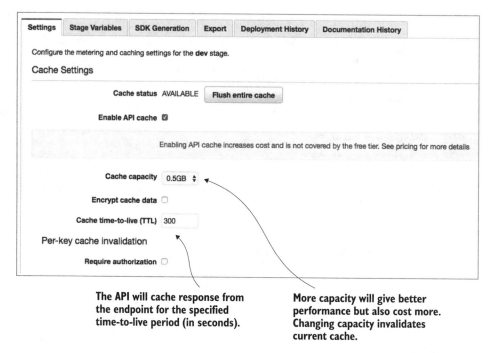

Figure 7.14   Enabling an API cache is easy, but don't forget that it isn't free. The default TTL for a cache is 300 seconds, and the maximum is 3600 seconds.

To enable caching for your API, choose Enable API Cache in the Stage Editor (figure 7.14).

What difference does caching make? It all depends on how long the endpoint (such as your Lambda function) normally takes to run. As a quick and dirty test, we ran 500 requests against our `get-video-list` API with and without caching. Without caching, the overall execution time was around 30,000 to 31,000 ms. With caching, the duration was around 15,000 ms. Your mileage will vary, but for heavy-duty systems, caching will make a difference. You can see the results for yourself, including duration and memory consumption, in figure 7.15.

There are some helpful things you should know about caching (if you want to know the details refer to https://docs.aws.amazon.com/apigateway/latest/developerguide/api-gateway-caching.html):

- To verify that caching is functioning you can look at the CacheHitCount and CacheHitMiss in CloudWatch.
- You can override caching for individual methods. In fact, you can override throttling and CloudWatch settings for each individual method (figure 7.16):
  - Choose Stages in the API Gateway and expand your API.
  - Choose the desired method and then select Override This Method.
  - Change the settings for CloudWatch, caching, and throttling for this specific method.

Summary		Log output
Code SHA-256	V3ZGxyUfTFtjyfRr78JeOUpVdW+O1zHR 4Nw7Xzel8IY=	The area below shows the logging calls in your code. These correspond to a single row within the CloudWatch log group corresponding to this Lambda function. Click here to view the CloudWatch log group.
Request ID	6788e4f8-142c-11e6-8e84- 79a279dedbcd	
Duration	14675.70 ms	
Billed duration	14700 ms	
Resources configured	128 MB	
Max memory used	85 MB	

```
 files:
  [ { filename: '518763837_2/518763837_2-web-720p.mp4',
      eTag: '8a07e00dbb7818bf123916334636767a-8',
      size: '37011014' },
    { filename: 'badmoms-tlr1_h480p/badmoms-tlr1_h480p-web-720p.mp4',
      eTag: '0f52ac4c819c5f644596f804a3540e92-9',
      size: '43452962' },
    { filename: 'barbershopthenexctcut-tlr2_h480p/barbershopthenexctcut-tlr2_h480p-web-720p.mp4',
      eTag: 'b80aa8348c98a3e41d6cca72c3e03bf7-9',
      size: '42965247' },
```

Duration without caching. Max memory used is higher at 97 MB.

Summary		Log output
Code SHA-256	V3ZGxyUfTFtjyfRr78JeOUpVdW+O1zHR 4Nw7Xzel8IY=	The area below shows the logging calls in your code. These correspond to a single row within the CloudWatch log group corresponding to this Lambda function. Click here to view the CloudWatch log group.
Request ID	6788e4f8-142c-11e6-8e84- 79a279dedbcd	
Duration	14675.70 ms	
Billed duration	14700 ms	
Resources configured	128 MB	
Max memory used	85 MB	

```
 files:
  [ { filename: '518763837_2/518763837_2-web-720p.mp4',
      eTag: '8a07e00dbb7818bf123916334636767a-8',
      size: '37011014' },
    { filename: 'badmoms-tlr1_h480p/badmoms-tlr1_h480p-web-720p.mp4',
      eTag: '0f52ac4c819c5f644596f804a3540e92-9',
      size: '43452962' },
    { filename: 'barbershopthenexctcut-tlr2_h480p/barbershopthenexctcut-tlr2_h480p-web-720p.mp4',
      eTag: 'b80aa8348c98a3e41d6cca72c3e03bf7-9',
      size: '42965247' },
```

Duration with caching. Max memory used is lower at 85 MB.

Figure 7.15 In this scenario, caching makes a big difference in terms of performance and cost (the Lambda function executing requests runs for half the time, which is cheaper).

Enable this radio button to override CloudWatch, caching, and throttling settings for a specific resource and method.

Stages [Create]

- ▾ 🔒 dev
  - ▾ /
    - ▾ /user-profile
      - GET
      - OPTIONS
    - ▾ /videos
      - GET
      - OPTIONS

dev - GET - /videos

Invoke URL: https://oyseckx1rh.execute-api.us-east-1.amazonaws.com/dev/videos

Use this page to override the dev stage settings for the GET to /videos method.

Settings ○ Inherit from stage
          ● Override for this method

CloudWatch Settings

Enable CloudWatch Logs ☑ ❶

Log level [INFO ↕]

Log full requests/responses data ○

Enable Detailed CloudWatch Metrics ☑ ❶

Method Throttling

Choose the throttling level for this method. Your current account level throttling rate is **1000** requests per second with a burst of **2000** requests. ❶

Enable throttling ☑ ❶

Rate [1000] requests per second

Burst [2000] requests

Figure 7.16 Having more granular control over methods can be helpful.

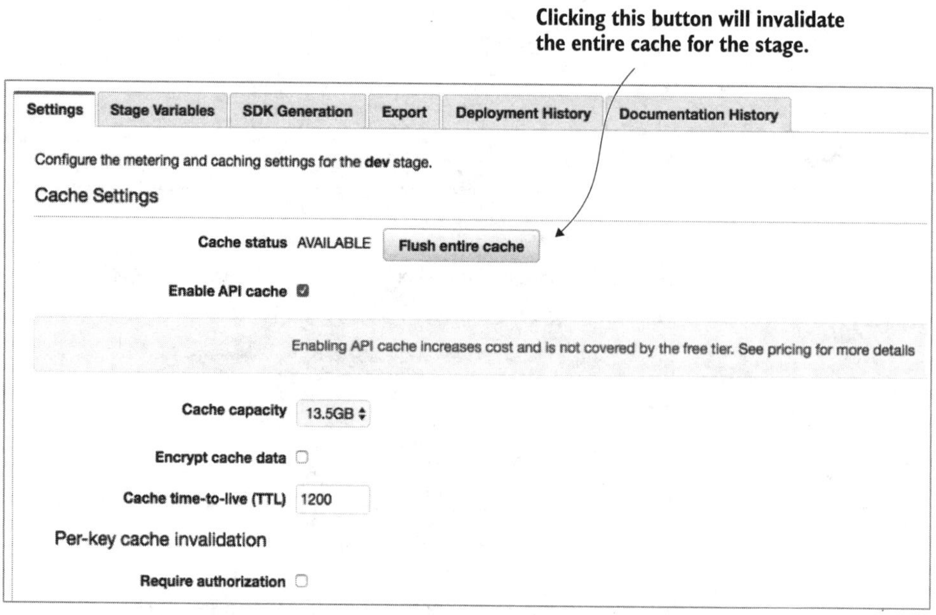

Clicking this button will invalidate
the entire cache for the stage.

| Settings | Stage Variables | SDK Generation | Export | Deployment History | Documentation History |

Configure the metering and caching settings for the **dev** stage.

Cache Settings

Cache status   AVAILABLE   **Flush entire cache**

Enable API cache ☑

Enabling API cache increases cost and is not covered by the free tier. See pricing for more details

Cache capacity   13.5GB ↕

Encrypt cache data ☐

Cache time-to-live (TTL)   1200

Per-key cache invalidation

Require authorization ☐

Figure 7.17   The entire cache can be invalidated with a click of a button if you need to do so.

- When a cache has been created, it can be flushed/invalidated in the Stage Editor by clicking the Flush Entire Cache button (figure 7.17).
- It's possible to cache a response based on custom headers, URL paths, and query strings. For example, a request with a query string /videos?userId= peter can have a different cached response to /videos?userId=sam.
- A client can also be configured to invalidate specific cache entries by sending a request with the Cache-Control: max-age=0 header. You'll have to set an InvalidateCache policy to prevent just any client from invalidating your cache.
- You can control how unauthorized requests to invalidate a cache are handled ranging from a 403 (unauthorized) response to a warning.

7.4   *Stages and versions*

We've briefly mentioned stages with regard to the API Gateway but haven't explored what they are. To refresh your memory, a stage is an environment for your API. You can have stages to represent development, UAT, production, and anything else you want. You can have a stage for each developer if you need to. APIs can be deployed to different stages and each can have its own unique URL.

One of the nice things about stages is that they support stage variables, which are key/value pairs. These act as environment variables. They can be used in mapping templates and passed to Lambda functions, HTTP and AWS integration URIs, or in

AWS integration credentials. You can configure different stages of the same API to invoke different Lambda functions or pass the value of a stage variable to another HTTP endpoint.

7.4.1 Creating a stage variable

To create a stage variable (figure 7.18), do this:

1 Choose the Stage Variables tab in the Stage Editor.
2 Choose Add Stage. Type in a name and a value, and click the check mark button to save.

Each stage maintains its individual variables. If you need to have a variable called `function` available in three stages, you must create it individually three times.

You can create up to 10 stages for each API.

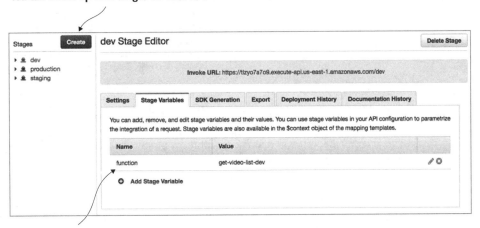

Add a variable specific to each stage.

Figure 7.18   Remember to add variables to each stage that references them.

7.4.2 Using stage variables

A stage variable can be referenced in a mapping template or in place of a Lambda function name or an HTTP integration URI. It takes the form of `stageVariables .<variable_name>`. Often you'll have to surround the stage variable with $ and {} as per the shorthand notation for references in the Velocity Template Language (see appendix E for more information). The following is an example that works in our case because we created a stage variable called `function` in the previous section:

```
${stageVariables.function}
```

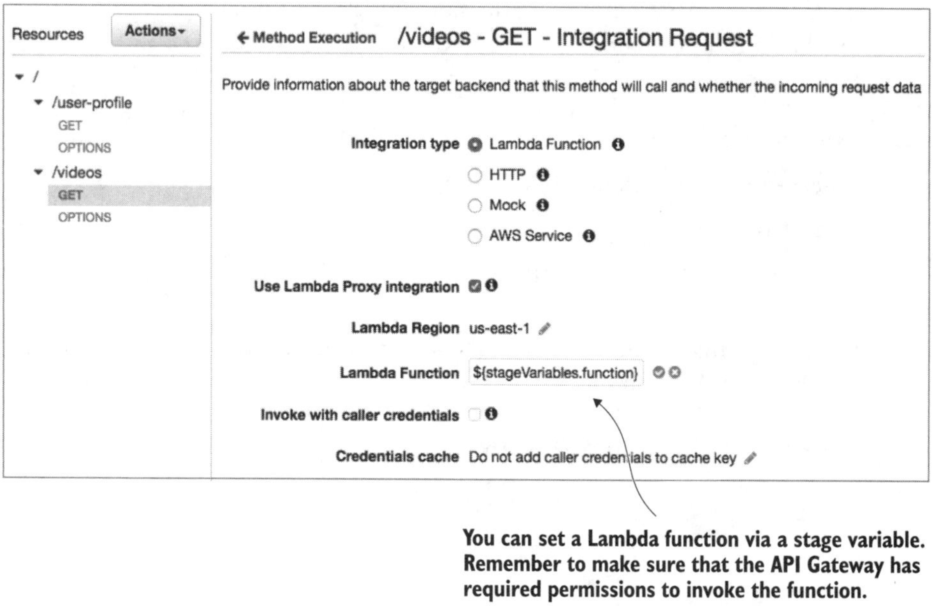

You can set a Lambda function via a stage variable.
Remember to make sure that the API Gateway has
required permissions to invoke the function.

Figure 7.19   Stage variables can be set manually in the AWS console, created using the CLI, or
specified in a Swagger definition.

If you wanted to reference this stage variable in place of a Lambda function name in
the integration request, you could do it directly (figure 7.19).

Figure 7.20 shows a real example from the production system we discussed in
chapter 2 (A Cloud Guru). This system has API Gateway stages such as production, uat
(user acceptance test), and development. Lambda functions have aliases such as
`serverless-join:production` and `serverless-join:uat`. Using a stage variable in
the API Gateway allows it to invoke the right Lambda function when the appropriate
URI is invoked (for example, `myapi/staging` and `myapi/production`).

7.4.3   *Versions*

If you want to roll back to a previous deployment of your API, you can do it via the
Deployment History tab in the Stage Editor. Every deployment you make has a
date/time stamp (and a description if you entered one) to help you identify earlier
revisions. You can select a different version (figure 7.21) and click the Change Deployment button at the bottom of the page to go to a different version. This is a useful feature if you make a mistake and need to go back a version while you figure out what
went wrong.

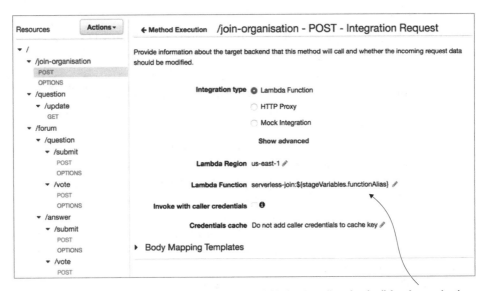

This stage variable is set to "production" for the production stage; "UAT" for the UAT stage, and so on. It is used to invoke the right Lambda function for the given stage.

Figure 7.20 Stage variables are indispensable if your API Gateway has multiple stages that need to integrate with different Lambda functions or endpoints.

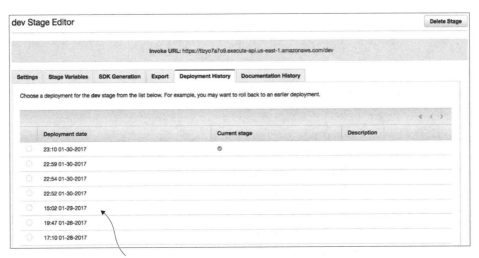

Select a different version and scroll down the page to click Change Deployment button for the change to take effect.

Figure 7.21 Reverting to an earlier version of the API is easy and is one of the excellent features of the API Gateway.

7.5   *Exercises*

In this chapter, we covered a lot of the functionality that the API Gateway offers. Try to complete the following exercises to reinforce your knowledge:

1 In section 7.2 you implemented the `get-video-list` function using Lambda proxy integration. Read appendix E and implement it again using manual mapping. Create a new resource (such as /videos-manual) so that you don't have to get rid of the existing /videos resource.

2 In listing 7.5 you created and populated video-controller.js. At the moment the logic in the controller will load every video. But the code also supports the `encoding` parameter, which can return specific encodings. Modify the GET request in listing 7.5 to return only 720p videos.

3 The `get-video-list` function can be brittle if you want to return videos with a particular encoding. Objects have to have the encoding (for example, 720p) specified as part of the filename to work. This can break if you rename the file in the S3 bucket. Think of a different, more robust way to implement this. You should be able to rename objects in S3 and still retrieve files based on their encoding.

4 Create a new Lambda function to allow the user to change the name of a file in an S3 bucket. The user should be able to supply the existing path to the file and a new key (filename). Create a resource and a POST method and connect it to the Lambda function. Modify the 24-Hour Video user interface to allow the user to rename any video.

5 Create and configure two new stages: staging and production. Deploy your API to these new stages.

6 Perform a rollback of one of your deployments to get a feel for what it's like.

7.6   *Summary*

In this chapter we looked at the API Gateway, including how to

- Create a resource and configure a GET method
- Use Lambda proxy integration
- Return a response from a Lambda function via the API Gateway
- Use throttling and caching and turn on logging
- Create and use stage variables

In the next chapter you'll look at storage in more detail. You'll see how to upload files directly to an S3 bucket and use a Lambda function to grant the uploader the permissions to do so. You'll also take a look at securing access to files and generating pre-signed URLs.

Part 3

Growing your Architecture

Y ou've smashed through parts 1 and 2 but you're still hungry for more. I understand. Thankfully, this part is designed to give you a lot to chew on. File and data storage are critical, so you need to understand how those work in a serverless application. Then you also need to revisit important concepts such as microservices, think about error handling in a distributed architecture, and investigate other AWS services like step functions. Finally, it's important to read the appendixes that follow the last chapter. Check out appendix G especially, because you'll need that information to learn how to script and deploy your serverless applications.

This final part is about combining and coalescing everything you've learned and moving even further. You'll learn how to grow your serverless architecture and firmly establish yourself on the path to serverless mastery.

Storage

Many applications and systems that you create need to store files. These may be profile images, documents uploaded by a user, or artifacts generated by the system. Some files are temporary and transient, whereas other files must be kept for a long time. A reliable service for storing files is Amazon's Simple Storage Service (S3). It was Amazon's first available web service, launched in March 2006, and it has been a cornerstone AWS service ever since. In this chapter, we'll explore S3 in more detail. We'll look at features such as versioning, storage classes, and transfer acceleration. And you'll continue to work on 24-Hour Video by adding new storage-related features.

8.1 Smarter storage

You've been working with S3 since chapter 3 but haven't had a proper, in-depth look at it. Apart from basic file storage, S3 has many great features. These include versioning, hosting of static websites, storage classes, cross-region replication, and requester-pays buckets. Let's explore some of the more compelling features of S3 and see how they're useful.

> **MORE INFORMATION ON S3** If you ever need a thorough guide to S3, Amazon's documentation is a great reference. Check out https://docs.aws.amazon .com/AmazonS3/latest/dev/Welcome.html for good walkthroughs and examples of how S3 works.

8.1.1 *Versioning*

Up until now you've been using S3 as a basic storage mechanism for files (or objects, as S3 refers to them). Back in chapter 3 you created two S3 buckets to store videos. One of the buckets was for users uploading files. The other bucket was for transcoded files. This was simple and practical, but it also meant that you could overwrite and lose existing files. Luckily, S3 has an optional feature that allows it to keep copies of all versions of every object. This means that you can overwrite an object and then go back to previous versions of that object at any time. It's powerful and completely automatic. We've been thankful for versioning when we've accidentally deleted files and had to restore them.

Buckets don't have versioning enabled by default, so it must be turned on. And once versioning is enabled, it can't be turned off in that bucket, only suspended. Thus, a bucket can be in only one of the following three possible states:

- Unversioned (default)
- Versioning enabled
- Versioning suspended

As expected, the cost of using S3 goes up when versioning is used. But you can remove versions you no longer need so that you're not billed for the files you don't want to keep. S3 Object Lifecycle Rules (see section 8.1.4) and versioning can help to automate removal and archival of old versions. For example, you can set up an S3 bucket to work like an operating system trash can (that is, you can set up a rule to delete old files from the bucket after a period of time, such as 30 days).

USING VERSIONING

To enable versioning, follow these steps:

1 In the AWS console, click into a bucket in S3 and then click Properties.
2 Click Versioning.
3 Choose Enable Versioning, and then click *Save*.

You can now overwrite, delete, and then recover older versions of an object yourself:

1 Upload a few files to your bucket and then replace a file that you already have in the bucket.

2 At the time of writing, versioning was best managed using the old S3 console. To access the old S3 console, click the S3 service in AWS, and then choose the Switch to the Old Console button.

3 In the old S3 console click a bucket that has versioning enabled.

4 Click the Show button next to Versions and review the available files you can download.

5 Right-click next to the version of the file you want to download (figure 8.1).

6 You can also delete a file. You will see it marked with a delete marker. If you click the Hide button next to Versions, deleted files and markers will disappear.

Every versioned object in S3 has a unique version ID. As you can see from figure 8.1, you can have many objects with the same key but different IDs (see the second-to-last column in the diagram). If you decide to retrieve a version programmatically, you need to know its ID. The version ID isn't hard to get using the AWS SDK or the REST

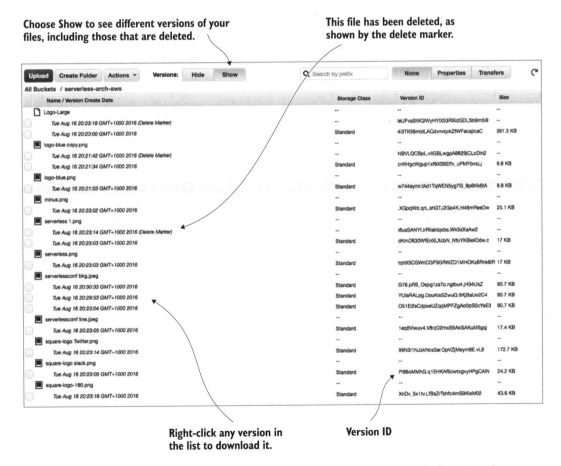

Figure 8.1 All versions of a file in a versioned S3 bucket can be accessed programmatically or through the console.

API. You can retrieve all objects and their version IDs or retrieve the version ID for a given key. You'll also get other useful metadata such as the object's LastModified date. Once you know the version ID, it's easy to download the file. If, for example, you were retrieving an image using the REST API, you could issue a GET request to /my-image .jpg?versionId=L4kqtJlcpXroDTDmpUMLUo HTTP/1.1 to get it.

8.1.2   *Hosting a static website*

Static website hosting is a popular use case for S3 buckets. S3 doesn't support server-side code (that is, code that needs to execute on a server), but it can serve static website content like HTML, CSS, images, and JavaScript files. S3 is an effective way to host static websites because it's quick and cheap to set up. After static website hosting is enabled, content in the bucket becomes accessible to web browsers via an endpoint provided by S3.

> ### Why A Cloud Guru moved away from S3
>
> A Cloud Guru (https://acloud.guru) initially hosted its static website on S3. The website built on AngularJS worked well except in cases of certain web crawlers. The team discovered that rendering of rich-media snippets of the website on Facebook, Slack, and other platforms didn't work. This was because crawlers used by those platforms couldn't run JavaScript. A Cloud Guru needed to serve a rendered, static HTML version of the website that those crawlers could parse. Unfortunately, with S3 and Cloud-Front that couldn't be done. There was no way to prerender and serve an HTML version of the site to Facebook and then another (JavaScript-driven) version to everyone else. In the end, A Cloud Guru chose to move to Netlify (a static website-hosting service) to solve its problem.
>
> Netlify integrates with a service called prerender.io. Prerender.io can execute JavaScript and create a static HTML page. This HTML page can then be served to crawlers while normal users continue to use the regular SPA website. Netlify (https://www .netlify.com) is a great little service that's worth checking out.

ENABLING STATIC WEBSITE HOSTING

Let's walk through the process to see how to enable static website hosting and allow you to serve HTML from the bucket:

1 Click into a bucket in S3 and then select Properties.
2 Click Static Website Hosting.
3 Choose Use This Bucket to Host a Website.
4 In the Index Document text box, type the name of your index file (for example, index.html).
5 Note the endpoint (this is how you will access your website) and choose Save (figure 8.2).

This is the endpoint you will
use to access your website.

You must enter the name of your
index document to be able to save.

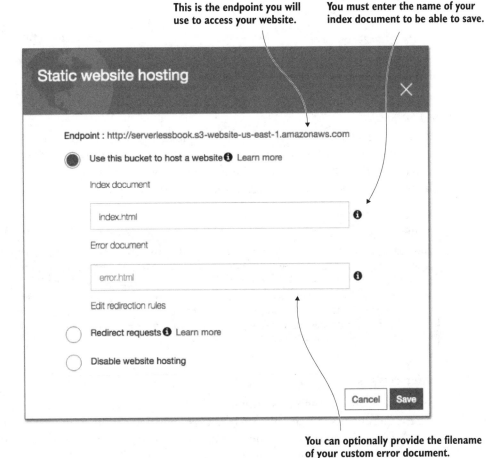

You can optionally provide the filename
of your custom error document.

Figure 8.2 S3 static website hosting is a cheap and easy way to run your website.

Next, you need to set up a bucket policy to grant everyone access to the objects in the bucket:

1 In the bucket click Permissions.
2 Click the drop-down that says Access Control List and select Bucket Policy.
3 Copy the following listing into the text box and click Save.

Listing 8.1 Permission policy

```
{
    "Version": "2012-10-17",
    "Statement": [
        {
            "Sid": "PublicRead",
            "Effect": "Allow",
            "Principal": "*",
```

```
            "Action": [
                "s3:GetObject"
            ],
            "Resource": [
                "arn:aws:s3:::BUCKET-NAME/*"          Change BUCKET-NAME to
            ]                                          the name of your bucket.
        }
    ]
}
```

To test whether static website hosting works, upload an HTML file to the bucket (make sure it's named index.html) and open the bucket's endpoint in a web browser. You can go one step further: copy the 24-Hour Video website to the bucket and try to open it (in fact, this is one of the exercises at the end of this chapter).

> **Domains**
>
> You can buy a domain name and use Amazon's Route 53 as the DNS provider for the domain. If you do this, be aware of a few gotchas. For example, the name of your bucket must match the name of your domain. So if your domain is www.google.com, the bucket must also be called www.google.com. Consult the following step-by-step guide if you want to set up a custom domain with your S3 bucket: https://docs.aws .amazon.com/AmazonS3/latest/dev/website-hosting-custom-domain-walkthrough.html.

8.1.3   Storage classes

Moving away from versioning, we think it's fair to say that different data has different storage requirements. Some data, such as logs, may need to be kept for a long time but accessed infrequently. Other kinds of data may need to be accessed frequently but may not need the same kind of storage reliability. Luckily, S3 has something for everyone because it supports four kinds of storage classes with different levels of redundancy, access characteristics, and pricing (https://docs.aws.amazon.com/AmazonS3/latest/dev/storage-class-intro.html):

- Standard
- Standard_IA (infrequent access)
- Glacier
- Reduced Redundancy

We'll discuss these in more detail, but first a note about pricing. Pricing is a combination of factors such as the storage class, location (region) of the files, and the quantity of data stored. For this example, we'll simplify our requirements and assume the following:

- The free usage tier is ignored altogether.
- Files are stored in the US East region.
- You're not storing more than 1 TB.

If your requirements are different, you can always check the S3 pricing page for more detail (https://aws.amazon.com/s3/pricing/). Also, note that apart from storage, S3 charges for requests and data transfers.

STANDARD

This is the default storage class in S3. It's set automatically on any object you create or upload (if you don't specify a different class yourself). This class is designed for frequent access to data. The cost is $0.0300 per GB for the first TB of data (per month). This class, as well as Standard_IA and Glacier classes, has a durability rating of 99.999999999%.

STANDARD_IA

This class is designed for less frequently accessed data. Amazon recommends using this class for backups and older data that requires quick retrieval when needed. The request pricing is higher for Standard_IA than for Standard ($0.01 per 10,000 requests for Standard_IA versus $0.004 per 10,000 requests for Standard). The storage cost, however, is less at $0.0125 per GB for the first TB of data (per month).

GLACIER

The Glacier storage class is designed for infrequent access to data and where retrieval can take three to five hours. It's the best option for data such as backups that don't require real-time access. The Glacier storage class uses the Amazon Glacier service, but objects are still managed from the S3 console. It's important to note that objects can't be created with the Glacier class from the get-go. They can only be transitioned to Glacier using lifecycle management rules (see section 8.1.4). Glacier storage is charged at $0.007 per GB for the first TB of data (per month).

REDUCED REDUNDANCY

The fourth class is Reduced Redundancy storage (RRS), which is designed to be cheaper and with less redundancy than other classes. This class has a durability rating of 99.99% (as opposed to all other classes that are designed for a durability rating of 99.999999999%). Amazon recommends using this storage class for data that can be easily re-created (for example, use the Standard storage class for original images uploaded by users and use RRS for autogenerated thumbnails). Naturally, RRS costs are lower. The price for storage is $0.0240 per GB for the first TB (per month).

8.1.4 Object lifecycle management

Lifecycle management is a great feature of S3 that can be used to define what happens to an object over its lifetime. In essence, you can set up rules to do the following:

- Move an object to a cheaper, less frequently accessed storage class (Standard_IA).
- Archive objects using the Glacier storage class (which will reduce storage costs even further but prevent you from having real-time access to your files).
- Permanently delete an object.
- End and clean up incomplete multipart uploads.

Every rule requires you to enter a time period (in days from the creation of the file) after which it takes an effect. You can, for example, set up a rule to archive an object to Glacier class storage 20 days after it has been created.

Configure lifecycle management

To set up lifecyle management for your objects, follow these steps:

1 Open a bucket and choose Lifecycle.
2 Click the Add Lifecycle Rule button.
3 Enter a rule name such as `file archival` and click Next.
4 Click the Current Version check box.
5 From the drop-down box select Transition to Amazon Glacier After and in the Days after Object Creation text box enter `30` (figure 8.3).

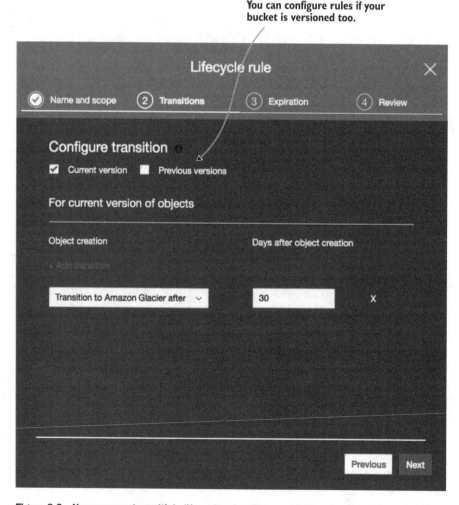

Figure 8.3   You can create multiple lifecycle rules if you need to support complex scenarios.

6 Click Next and again select the Current Version check box.

7 Enter 60 in to the Expire Current Version of Object text box.

8 Check Clean Up Incomplete Multipart Upload and leave it on 7 days.

9 Click Next and then click Save.

If you ever want to disable or edit a rule at a later stage, you can do it later in the Life-cycle section of the bucket.

8.1.5 *Transfer acceleration*

Transfer acceleration is a feature of S3 that allows it to upload and transfer files more quickly than normal using Amazon's CloudFront distributed edge locations. Amazon recommends using transfer acceleration in cases where users from all over the world need to upload data to a centralized bucket (this could be a use case for 24-Hour Video) or transfer gigabytes (or terabytes) of data across continents (https://docs.aws .amazon.com/AmazonS3/latest/dev/transfer-acceleration.html). You can use the speed comparison tool (figure 8.4) to see what effect enabling transfer acceleration would have for you (http://s3-accelerate-speedtest.s3-accelerate.amazonaws.com/en/accelerate-speed-comparsion.html). The pricing for data transfer (in and out) ranges from $0.04/GB to $0.08/GB, depending on which CloudFront edge location is used to accelerate the transfer.

ENABLING TRANSFER ACCELERATION

To enable S3 bucket transfer acceleration using the AWS console, follow these steps:

1 Open a bucket and choose Properties.

2 Click Transfer Acceleration under Advanced Settings.

3 Click Enable and then choose Save. You should immediately see a new end-point created for you to use. If you want to get the performance benefits, you must use this URL.

You can suspend transfer acceleration by choosing the Suspend option at any time. You can also enable transfer acceleration using the AWS SDK or the CLI. Refer to https:// docs.aws.amazon.com/AmazonS3/latest/dev/transfer-acceleration-examples.html for more information.

8.1.6 *Event notifications*

We first used S3 event notifications all the way back in chapter 3 when we connected Lambda and then SNS to a bucket. The purpose of event notifications is to receive notifications when the following events take place in a bucket:

- A new object is created using PUT, POST, COPY, or on CompleteMultiPartUpload
- An object is deleted or (in case of versioning) a delete marker is created
- A Reduced Redundancy Storage (RRS) object is lost

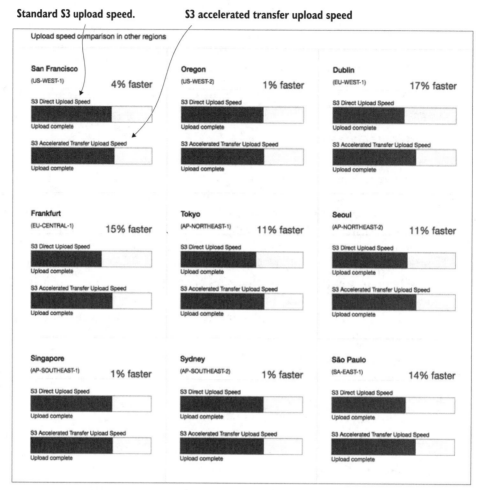

Figure 8.4   **Transfer acceleration can help if your users are uploading files from all over the world.**

S3 can publish events to the following destinations (the bucket and the target must be in the same region):

- Simple Notification Service
- Simple Queue Service
- Lambda

You might remember to grant S3 permissions to post messages to SNS topics and SQS queues. You worked on an IAM policy for SNS and S3 permissions in chapter 3, but we haven't looked at how to do it with SQS. The following listing shows an example policy that you'd need to attach to an SQS queue if you decided to use it as a destination for

S3 events. Naturally, S3 must also be given permission to invoke Lambda functions, but if you use the S3 console, it will be done for you automatically.

Listing 8.2 SQS policy

```
{
 "Version": "2008-10-17",
 "Id": "MyID",
 "Statement": [
  {
   "Sid": "ExampleID",
   "Effect": "Allow",
   "Principal": {
     "AWS": "*"
   },
   "Action": [                          Explicitly allow the
    "SQS:SendMessage"            ◁──    SendMessage SQS action.
   ],
   "Resource": "SQS-ARN",
   "Condition": {
      "ArnLike": {                      Change YOUR_BUCKET_NAME
      "aws:SourceArn":                  to the name of your bucket as
      "arn:aws:s3:*:*:YOUR_BUCKET_NAME" ◁── appropriate.
    }
   }
  }
 ]
}
```

You can find more information on S3 events, including examples and IAM policies, at https://docs.aws.amazon.com/AmazonS3/latest/dev/NotificationHowTo.html.

Event message structure

S3 events are important to understand if you use S3 and Lambda (or SNS or SQS) together. S3 events are a JSON message with a specific format that describes the bucket and the object. We briefly looked at the S3 event message structure in chapter 3 (section 3.1.4) when you tested the `transcode-video` function locally. Appendix F provides a more detailed overview of the event message structure, which you might find useful going forward.

8.2   Secure upload

So far, you've been uploading your videos directly to a bucket using the S3 console when you wanted to test 24-Hour Video. But that's not going to work for your end users. They need an interface to be able to upload their files to the 24-Hour Video website. You also don't want just anyone (that is, anonymous users) to upload files. Only registered, authenticated users should be allowed to do this. In this section, you're going to work on adding secure upload functionality to 24-Hour Video. Your

Enable browser-based uploads of video files to S3

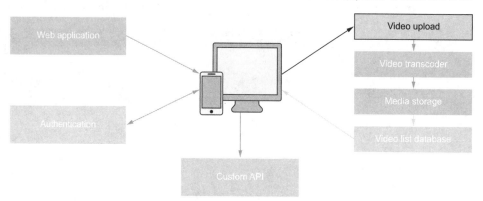

Figure 8.5   Video uploading is a core feature of 24-Hour Video. Without it, your users wouldn't be able to upload their videos.

end users will be able to click a button on the website, select a file, and upload it to an S3 bucket. Figure 8.5 shows which component of your architecture you'll be working on in this section.

8.2.1   *Architecture*

To upload a file from a user's browser to a bucket in a secure, authenticated fashion, you need the following:

- A security policy that contains relevant information and conditions about the upload (such as the name of the upload bucket)
- An HMAC signature constructed using a secret access key of the resource owner (that is, an IAM user) who has permissions to create new files
- The access key ID of the IAM user whose secret key was used to generate the signature
- The file you want to upload

To get started, you're going to create a Lambda function. This function will validate the user and generate a policy and a signature needed to upload the file to S3. This information will be sent back to the browser. Upon receiving this information, the user's browser will begin an upload to a bucket using HTTP POST. All this will be invisible to the end user because they'll just select a file and upload. Figure 8.6 shows this flow in full.

You could do it differently and use Auth0 to provide you with temporary AWS credentials and then use the AWS JavaScript SDK to upload the file. It's a viable way of doing things (https://github.com/auth0-samples/auth0-s3-sample) but we wanted to write a Lambda function to show you how to generate a policy and upload using a simple POST request. Having a Lambda function will also give you more opportunities to

This process is seamless to the user. From their perspective, the file begins to upload after a short wait at the start (while the policy and the signature are retrieved).

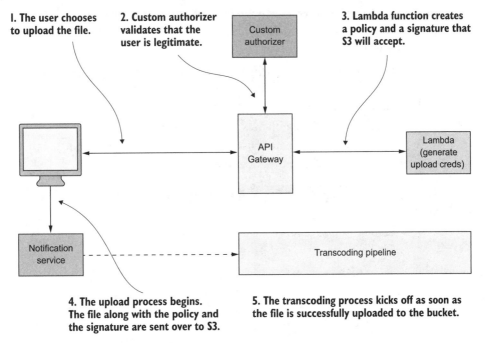

I. The user chooses to upload the file.

2. Custom authorizer validates that the user is legitimate.

3. Lambda function creates a policy and a signature that S3 will accept.

4. The upload process begins. The file along with the policy and the signature are sent over to S3.

5. The transcoding process kicks off as soon as the file is successfully uploaded to the bucket.

Figure 8.6 The upload process is transparent to the end user, but behind the scenes a small amount of orchestration takes place.

do interesting things later on (such as logging attempts to request credentials, updating a database, and sending a notification to an administrator).

8.2.2 Upload policy Lambda

Here are the steps you need to carry out to get everything working:

1 Create an IAM user whose credentials you'll use to generate a signature. This signature (and the accompanying security policy) will be needed to successfully upload a file to S3.
2 Implement and deploy a Lambda function. This function will generate the signature and the security policy.
3 Connect your Lambda function to the API Gateway.
4 Update the S3 Cross-Origin Resource Sharing (CORS) configuration. This needs to be done in order to upload files from a browser to a bucket.
5 Update the 24-Hour Video website to allow users to select and upload files.

IAM USER

The IAM user you're going to create will have the permissions needed to upload files to S3. If you don't give this user the right permissions, uploads will fail. Create a new IAM user in the IAM console as per normal (refer back to chapter 4 for more information on creating IAM users if you need help) and name the user `upload-s3`. Make sure to save the user's access and secret keys in a secure place. You'll need them later. From here follow these steps:

1 Make sure the `upload-s3` user is opened in the IAM console.
2 Choose Add Inline Policy at the bottom of the Permissions tab.
3 Choose Custom Policy and click Select.
4 Set the name of the policy as `upload-policy`.
5 Copy the code in the next listing to the policy document body.
6 Choose Apply Policy to save and exit.

Listing 8.3 Upload policy

```
{
    "Version": "2012-10-17",
    "Statement": [
        {
            "Effect": "Allow",
            "Action": [
                "s3:ListBucket"
            ],
            "Resource": [
                "arn:aws:s3:::YOUR_UPLOAD_BUCKET_NAME"      ◁─────┐
            ]
        },
        {                                                          Set the name of
            "Effect": "Allow",                                     your upload
            "Action": [                                            bucket instead of
                "s3:PutObject"                                     YOUR_UPLOAD_
            ],                                                     BUCKET_NAME.
            "Resource": [
                "arn:aws:s3:::YOUR_UPLOAD_BUCKET_NAME/*"    ◁─────┘
            ]
        }
    ]
}
```

LAMBDA FUNCTION

The only parameter that this Lambda function takes is the name of the file the user wants to upload. The output from this function is the following:

- The policy document.
- A keyed-hash message authentication code (HMAC) signature.
- A new key for the object (you'll add a prefix to the filename to avoid potential clashes from other users uploading files with the same name).

- The IAM user's access key ID. (This key needs to be included when the policy document is uploaded to S3; the key is public so it can be shared without adversely affecting security.)
- Upload URL.

All of this information is needed to upload a file to S3.

Clone one of the other Lambda functions you've written previously on your computer and rename it to get-upload-policy. Update package.json as you see fit (you'll have to update the ARN or the function name in the deployment script if you want to deploy the function from the terminal). Also, update dependencies to match the following listing. Remember to run npm install from the terminal to install these dependencies.

Listing 8.4 Lambda dependencies

```
"dependencies": {
  "async": "^2.0.0",
  "aws-sdk": "^2.3.2",
  "crypto": "0.0.3",
}
```

This dependency will allow you to use async waterfall in the Lambda function.

The AWS-SDK is needed only for local testing. Lambda's runtime provides it automatically.

Crypto is used to create the signature from the policy document.

Having updated package.json, copy the next listing to index.js.

Listing 8.5 Get upload policy Lambda

```
'use strict';

var AWS = require('aws-sdk');
var async = require('async');
var crypto = require('crypto');

var s3 = new AWS.S3();

function createErrorResponse(code, message) {
  var response = {
    'statusCode': code,
    'headers' : {'Access-Control-Allow-Origin' : '*'},
    'body' : JSON.stringify({'message' : message})
  }

  return response;
}

function createSuccessResponse(message) {
  var response = {
    'statusCode': 200,
    'headers' : {'Access-Control-Allow-Origin' : '*'},
    'body' : JSON.stringify(message)
  }
```

The base64encode function converts a given buffer (which is a stringified policy document) to its base64 representation.

The generateExpirationDate function creates a date that's one day into the future. This is when the policy will expire. Uploads after this date won't work. Expiration date policy must be set in the ISO 8601 UTC date format.

```
    return response;
}

function base64encode (value) {
    return new Buffer(value).toString('base64');
}

function generateExpirationDate() {
    var currentDate = new Date();
    currentDate = currentDate.setDate(currentDate.getDate() + 1);
    return new Date(currentDate).toISOString();
}

function generatePolicyDocument(filename, next) {
    var directory = crypto.randomBytes(20).toString('hex');
    var key = directory + '/' + filename;
    var expiration = generateExpirationDate();

    var policy = {
        'expiration' : expiration,
        'conditions': [
            {key: key},
            {bucket: process.env.UPLOAD_BUCKET},
            {acl: 'private'},
            ['starts-with', '$Content-Type', '']
        ]
    };

    next(null, key, policy);
}

function encode(key, policy, next) {
    var encoding = base64encode(JSON.stringify(policy))
    .replace('\n','');
    next(null, key, policy, encoding);
}

function sign(key, policy, encoding, next) {
    var signature = crypto.createHmac('sha1',
    process.env.SECRET_ACCESS_KEY)
    .update(encoding).digest('base64');
    next(null, key, policy, encoding, signature);
}

exports.handler = function(event, context, callback){
    var filename = null;

    if (event.queryStringParameters &&
    event.queryStringParameters.filename) {
        filename = decodeURIComponent(event.queryStringParameters.filename);
    } else {
        callback(null, createErrorResponse(500,
        'Filename must be provided'));
        return;
```

The generatePolicyDocument function creates the policy document, which is effectively a JSON structure with conditions as key/value pairs.

Note something interesting here: you're adding a prefix (a random hex string) to the filename to create a new key to avoid clashes between files with the same filename in the bucket.

Specify the condition the S3 access control list must meet.

The encode function converts the policy to its base64 representation.

The sign function creates an HMAC signature out of the policy using the IAM user's secret key.

The filename of the file the user wants to upload will be passed in from the client, via the API Gateway, to the function.

```
  }
async.waterfall([async.apply(generatePolicyDocument, filename),
⇨ encode, sign],
   function (err, key, policy, encoding, signature) {
     if (err) {
        callback(null, createErrorResponse(500, err));
     } else {
        var result =
        {
          signature: signature,
          encoded_policy: encoding,
          access_key: process.env.ACCESS_KEY,
          upload_url: process.env.UPLOAD_URI + '/'
          ⇨ + process.env.UPLOAD_BUCKET,
          key: key
        }

        callback(null, createSuccessResponse(result));
     }
   }
 )
};
```

> Async waterfall is the pattern that's applied in the handler function. You saw this function in chapter 6 (it allows each function to pass the results in to the next function). At the end, the function returns the policy, the signature, and a few other properties to the caller.

Create a new blank function in the AWS console (you can always refer to appendix B for information on how to create a Lambda function) and name it `get-upload-policy`. Assign the `lambda-s3-execution-role` role to the function. You should have that role from chapter 3. Deploy the function from your computer to AWS (you can run `npm run deploy` from the terminal, but make sure to set the right ARN in package.json).

Finally, you need to set the right environment variables for the `get-upload-policy` to work. In the AWS console, open the `get-upload-policy` Lambda function and add four environment variables at the bottom. These variables should be your upload bucket (`UPLOAD_BUCKET`), the access key of the upload-s3 user you created (`ACCESS_KEY`), the secret access key of that user (`SECRET_ACCESS_KEY`), and the S3 upload URL (`UPLOAD_URI`). Figure 8.7 shows what this looks like.

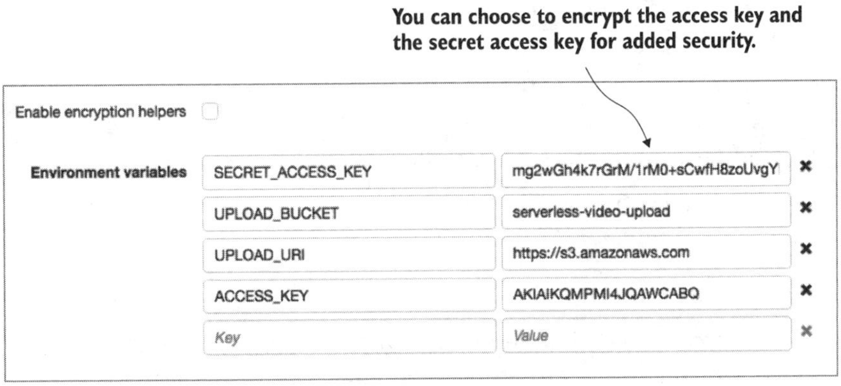

You can choose to encrypt the access key and the secret access key for added security.

Enable encryption helpers	☐	
Environment variables	SECRET_ACCESS_KEY	mg2wGh4k7rGrM/1rM0+sCwfH8zoUvgY ✖
	UPLOAD_BUCKET	serverless-video-upload ✖
	UPLOAD_URI	https://s3.amazonaws.com ✖
	ACCESS_KEY	AKIAIKQMPMI4JQAWCABQ ✖
	Key	Value ✖

Figure 8.7 Remember to update environment variables to your specific settings.

API GATEWAY

It's time to turn to the API Gateway. You need to create an endpoint that will invoke the Lambda function you just created:

1 Choose API Gateway in the console and click 24-hour-video API.

2 Make sure Resources is selected and choose Actions.

3 Select Create Resource from the menu and name it `s3-policy-document`.

4 Choose Create Resource to save.

5 Make sure that `s3-policy-document` is selected under Resources.

6 Choose Actions and select Create Method.

7 From the drop-down box under the resource name, select GET and click the check mark button to save.

8 In the screen that immediately appears
   – Select the Lambda Function radio button.
   – Check Use Lambda Proxy Integration.
   – Set us-east-1 as the Lambda Region.
   – Type `get-upload-policy` into the Lambda function text box.
   – Choose Save and click OK in the dialog box that appears.

9 Finally, you need to enable CORS:
   – Choose Actions and select Enable CORS.
   – Choose Enable CORS and replace existing CORS headers.
   – Click Yes, Replace Existing Values.

You care about security so you should enable your custom authorizer for this method (you might remember that a custom authorizer is a special-function Lambda function that's called by the API Gateway to authorize the incoming request):

- Choose GET under /s3-policy-document in Resources.
- Choose Method Request.
- Click the edit icon next to Authorization.
- Select your custom authorizer.
- Click the check mark icon to save.
- Choose Method Execution to return to the main screen.

Finally, deploy the API Gateway (click Deploy API under Actions) to make your changes live. The AWS Lambda and API Gateway side of things are done, but there's one more thing left do in AWS. You need to update the upload bucket CORS configuration to make sure that POST uploads are allowed.

8.2.3 *S3 CORS configuration*

The default S3 CORS configuration won't allow POST uploads to take place. That's the default set by AWS. It's easy to change, though. Click into your upload bucket and follow these steps:

1 Click Permissions.

2 From the drop-down below, select CORS Configuration.

3 Copy the following code to the configuration text box.

4 Choose Save.

Listing 8.6   S3 CORS configuration

```xml
<?xml version="1.0" encoding="UTF-8"?>
<CORSConfiguration xmlns="http://s3.amazonaws.com/doc/2006-03-01/">
    <CORSRule>
        <AllowedOrigin>*</AllowedOrigin>
        <AllowedHeader>*</AllowedHeader>
        <AllowedMethod>POST</AllowedMethod>
        <MaxAgeSeconds>3000</MaxAgeSeconds>
    </CORSRule>
</CORSConfiguration>
```

POST is the only HTTP method you're allowing. If you had a GET method in your configuration, you can remove it.

The AllowedHeader element specifies which headers are allowed. Every header listed in Access-Control-Request-Headers (during the preflight request) must match an AllowedHeader for the request to succeed.

Now you can move on to your website.

8.2.4 *Uploading from the website*

You're going to add a new file called upload-controller.js to the 24-Hour Video website. Create this file in the js folder and copy listing 8.7 to it. The purpose of this file is to do the following:

- Allow the user to select a file to upload
- Invoke the Lambda function to retrieve the policy and the signature
- Upload the file to S3

Listing 8.7   Upload controller implementation

```javascript
var uploadController = {
    data: {
        config: null
    },
    uiElements: {
        uploadButton: null
    },
    init: function (configConstants) {
        this.data.config = configConstants;
        this.uiElements.uploadButton = $('#upload');
        this.uiElements.uploadButtonContainer = $('#upload-video-button');
        this.uiElements.uploadProgressBar = $('#upload-progress');

        this.wireEvents();
    },
    wireEvents: function () {
        var that = this;
```

The requestDocumentUrl contains the URL to the API Gateway endpoint you've created. Remember to apply encodeURI to any query string parameters.

```
this.uiElements.uploadButton.on('change', function (result) {
    var file = $('#upload').get(0).files[0];
    var requestDocumentUrl =
➡ that.data.config.apiBaseUrl +
➡ '/s3-policy-document?filename=' +
➡ encodeURI(file.name);

    $.get(requestDocumentUrl, function (data, status) {
        that.upload(file, data, that)
    });
});
},
upload: function (file, data, that) {

    this.uiElements.uploadButtonContainer.hide();
    this.uiElements.uploadProgressBar.show();
    this.uiElements.uploadProgressBar.
➡ find('.progress-bar').css('width', '0');

    var fd = new FormData();
    fd.append('key', data.key)
    fd.append('acl', 'private');
    fd.append('Content-Type', file.type);
    fd.append('AWSAccessKeyId', data.access_key);
    fd.append('policy', data.encoded_policy);
    fd.append('signature', data.signature);
    fd.append('file', file, file.name);

    $.ajax({
        url: data.upload_url,
        type: 'POST',
        data: fd,
        processData: false,
        contentType: false,
        xhr: this.progress,
        beforeSend: function (req) {
            req.setRequestHeader('Authorization', '');
        }
    }).done(function (response) {
        that.uiElements.uploadButtonContainer.show();
        that.uiElements.uploadProgressBar.hide();
        alert('Uploaded Finished');
    }).fail(function (response) {
        that.uiElements.uploadButtonContainer.show();
        that.uiElements.uploadProgressBar.hide();
        alert('Failed to upload');
    })
},
progress: function () {
    var xhr = $.ajaxSettings.xhr();
    xhr.upload.onprogress = function (evt) {
        var percentage = evt.loaded / evt.total * 100;
```

You first issue a request to a Lambda function to get the policy, signature, and other properties. When the response comes back, you invoke the upload function to upload the actual file.

This creates a FormData object to which you can easily append key/value pairs with the data you need to supply. The end result of using this FormData object will be an HTML form with the multipart/form-data encoding type.

jQuery is used to perform an Ajax POST request and upload the file. You need to set the URL and form data.

There's no need to supply the Authorization bearer token in this request, so remove it.

There is a progress bar on the main page which will gradually update as the file upload takes place.

```
        $('#upload-progress').find('.progress-bar')
    ➥.css('width', percentage + '%');
    };
    return xhr;
  }
}
```

Open index.html and add the line `<script src="js/upload-controller.js"></script>` above `<script src="js/config.js"></script>` to include the new file in the web-site. Finally, below the line that says `<div class="container" id="video-list-container">`, copy the contents of the next listing, which contains HTML for an upload button and an upload progress bar.

Listing 8.8 Index.html

```
<span id="upload-video-button" class="btn btn-info btn-file">
  <span class="glyphicon glyphicon-plus"></span>
    <input id="upload" type="file" name="file">    ⬦──── The file upload button
</span>

<div class="progress" id="upload-progress">
  <div class="progress-bar progress-bar-info progress-bar-striped"
    ➥role="progressbar" aria-valuemin="0" aria-valuemax="100">  ⬦─┐ File upload
  </div>                                                          │ progress bar
</div>
```

Edit main.js to include `uploadController.init(configConstants);` under `video-Controller.init(configConstants);` and modify main.css in the css directory and include the contents of the following listing at the bottom of the file.

Listing 8.9 Website CSS

```
#upload-video-button {            ⬦─────┐ If the user isn't authenticated, the upload
    display: none;                      │ button and the progress bar are hidden.
    margin-bottom: 30px;                │ They're shown only when the user logs in
}                                       │ to the system.
.btn-file {
    position: relative;
    overflow: hidden;
}

.btn-file input[type=file] {
    position: absolute;
    top: 0;
    right: 0;
    min-width: 100%;
    min-height: 100%;
    font-size: 100px;
    text-align: right;
    filter: alpha(opacity=0);
    opacity: 0;
    outline: none;
    background: white;
```

```
        cursor: inherit;
        display: block;
}
#upload-progress {
        display: none;
}
#video-list-container {
        text-align: center;
        padding: 30px 0 30px;
}
.progress {
        background: #1a1a1a;
        margin-top: 6px;
        margin-bottom: 36px;
}
```

If the user isn't authenticated, the upload button and the progress bar are hidden. They're shown only when the user logs in to the system.

There's one more step. You need to modify user-controller.js to do the following:

- Show an upload button only after the user has logged in
- Hide the upload button and the progress bar when the user logs out
- Hide the upload button while a file is uploading and the progress bar is shown

In user-controller.js make the following edits:

- Add `uploadButton: null` under `profileImage: null`.
- Add `this.uiElements.uploadButton = $('#upload-video-button');` under `this.uiElements.profileImage = $('#profilepicture');`.
- Add `this.uiElements.uploadButton.css('display', 'inline-block');` under `this.uiElements.profileImage.attr('src', profile.picture);`.
- Add `that.uiElements.uploadButton.hide();` under `that.uiElements.profile-Button.hide();`.

TAKING IT FOR A SPIN

Start the web server by running npm `start` from the terminal (in the website's directory). Open the website in a browser and log in. You should see a blue button appear in the middle of the page. Click this button and upload the file. If you have the web browser's developer tools opened, you can inspect requests. You'll see that first there is a request to /s3-policy-document followed by a multipart POST upload to S3 (figure 8.8).

You might notice something odd if you inspect the transcoded bucket at this time. The key of newly uploaded files will look like this: <guid>/file/<guid>/file.mp4 instead of <guid>/file.mp4. That's a little bit puzzling until you look at the transcode-video Lambda function you implemented in chapter 3. This function sets an OutputPrefix, which prepends a prefix and is the cause of your problem. You needed an output prefix originally when you uploaded files directly to S3. Now you're creating a prefix manually in the upload-policy Lambda function, so you don't need to do it twice. Remove the line OutputKeyPrefix: outputKey + '/', from the transcode-video Lambda function and redeploy it. That will fix the annoyance.

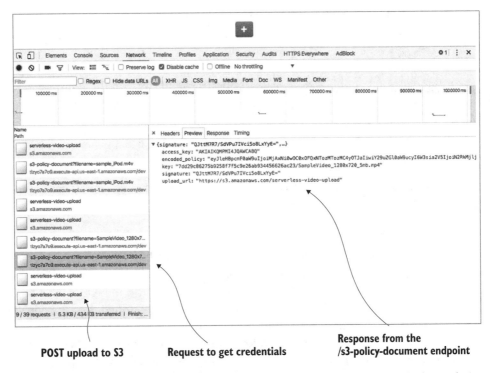

POST upload to S3   Request to get credentials

Response from the
/s3-policy-document endpoint

Figure 8.8   The upload to S3 is quick, but you can enable transfer acceleration to make it even faster.

8.3 *Restricting access to files*

So far you've made your transcoded video files public. But what if you want to secure these videos and make them available only to authenticated users? You might decide to charge for videos (bandwidth isn't free!) where only users who have registered and paid have access to files. To implement such a system, you need to do two things:

- Disable anonymous/public access to video files in the transcoded bucket.
- Generate presigned, time-limited URLs for authorized users that they can use to access videos.

8.3.1 *Removing public access*

To restrict public access to files, you need to remove the bucket policy you already have. In the transcoded bucket, do the following:

1 Click Permissions.
2 From the drop-down below, select Bucket Policy.
3 Click Delete to remove the policy.

You may also remember that you have a `set-permissions` Lambda function that changes permissions on the video (you created that function in chapter 3). You can remove that Lambda function or, better yet, disconnect it from SNS (it's invoked from the `transcoded-video-notifications` SNS topic). Remove the subscription from SNS now.

Furthermore, you'll need to change the permission for each video to make sure that it can't be publicly accessed. To do this you need to do the following:

1 Click each video in the S3 bucket.
2 Select Permissions.
3 If there is an AllUsers grantee, click it and deselect all check box options.
4 Click Save. The AllUsers grantee should disappear from the list.

If you try refreshing 24-Hour Video now, you'll see that every request for a video will come back as Forbidden, with a 403 status code.

8.3.2 *Generating presigned URLs*

The second step is to generate presigned URLs to allow users to access videos without hitting the 403 status code. You're going to modify the `get-video-list` function to generate these presigned URLs and then return them to the client. Having this capability allows you to add additional functionality to 24-Hour Video. For example, you can put the `get-video-list` function behind a custom authorizer and force users to log in before they can retrieve videos. And once you have a database, you can implement features like private videos, subscriptions, and lists. With presigned URLs, you can control who gets access to which videos and for how long.

VIDEO LISTING

Let's first update the video-listing Lambda function to generate presigned URLs and return them. Replace the line `urls.push(file);` in the `createList` function with the code in the next listing.

Listing 8.10 Video listing Lambda

```
var params = {Bucket: process.env.BUCKET, Key: file.Key};
var url = s3.getSignedUrl('getObject', params);       ⟵──┐ Generate a presigned URL
                                                          │ using the AWS S3 SDK.
files.push({
  'filename': url,
  'eTag': file.ETag.replace(/"/g,""),
  'size': file.Size
});
```

WEBSITE

Modify video-controller.js in 24-Hour Video and replace the line

```
clone.find('source').attr('src',baseUrl + '/' + bucket + '/' + video.filename);
```

with

```
clone.find('source').attr('src', video.filename);
```

Refresh the website (make sure the web server is running) to see the videos again. You may have noticed that now you're passing back the full URL rather than an S3 key as before. It's also important to keep in mind that the default expiration for presigned URLs is 15 minutes. After 15 minutes your users would have to refresh to get new URLs. You can control the expiration by adding an `Expires` property to `params` (it's specified as an integer in seconds). The following would make the URL valid for 30 minutes:

```
var params = {Bucket: config.BUCKET, Key: file.Key, Expires: 18000}
```

8.4 Exercises

In this chapter we covered useful S3 features and implemented video uploads for 24-Hour Video. Try to complete the following exercises to reinforce your knowledge:

1 Enable transfer acceleration for the upload bucket and modify the rest of the implementation to work with the new endpoint.

2 Implement object lifecycle management to clean up the upload bucket. Set up a rule to remove files that are five days old.

3 The upload credentials are valid for a day. That's probably way too long. Change credentials to be valid for two hours instead.

4 Create a new bucket in S3 and enable static website hosting. Copy the 24-Hour Video website to it and make it accessible over the internet. You'll have to make changes to Auth0 and to config.js to make everything work.

5 At the moment, presigned URLs will expire after 15 minutes (which is the default). Change the expiry to 24 hours instead.

6 Modify the implementation of 24-Hour Video website so that the `get-video` Lambda function is called when the user logs in. Unauthenticated users should see the main site with a message prompting them to register to view videos.

7 In listing 8.6 you used a wildcard for `AllowedHeader` in the bucket's CORS configuration. Instead of using a wildcard, specify the headers your system requires for the upload to work.

8 Think of a way to have public and private videos. The next chapter will have a few clues for you.

9 In section 8.3.1 you had to manually go through each video and change permission settings. Write a new Lambda function to enumerate the bucket, find all videos, and update their permissions.

8.5 Summary

In this chapter, we explored S3 and you added a new feature to 24-Hour Video. The S3 features we covered in section 8.1 are useful for managing files. You learned about the following:

- Different types of storage classes
- Versioning

- Transfer acceleration
- Hosting of static websites
- Object lifecycle rules
- Event notifications

You can use this knowledge to effectively manage your storage service. We also showed how to upload files directly from a user's web browser and how to generate presigned URLs. In the next chapter, we'll introduce Firebase. This real-time streaming database can be a powerful addition to your serverless application. You'll also work to complete 24-Hour Video by adding this last piece of the puzzle.

Database

Most applications need to store data and, in most cases, a database is a common-sense solution. In this chapter we introduce Firebase as our database of choice. Firebase is a NoSQL database that has great features such as real-time streaming using WebSockets, offline capabilities, and a declarative security model. Firebase is great for quickly getting started, it scales well, and it's immediately familiar to anyone who understands JSON.

As with most things in software development, the choice of a database should depend on your requirements. If your application is going to work with relational data, use a relational database. In a scenario where a NoSQL approach is appropriate but some structure is needed, a document database such as MongoDB or CouchDB might be more useful. If a scalable key/value store and fast lookups are important, then Firebase is a good option. And for some applications, a graph database might suit better than anything else. The best advice we can give is to look at your requirements, assess available options, and decide based on what's a good fit for your domain and application. There's no best database or even database type for serverless architectures. Everything depends on your goals and requirements.

9.1 *Introduction to Firebase*

Firebase is a platform developed by Google that's a collection of products such as a database and services for authentication, messaging, storage, and hosting. The products that make up the overall Firebase platform are interesting and useful, but we focus on the database in this chapter. The Firebase database is a real-time, schemaless, cloud-hosted NoSQL solution (from here on, when we refer to Firebase, we mean the database and not the entire platform). Firebase can sync data to clients over HTTP (using WebSockets), which is where the real-time aspect comes in, and synchronize data if a client goes offline and then back online. Firebase stores data as JSON, which makes it simple to understand and edit. Nevertheless, simplicity introduces limitations. Firebase isn't flexible when it comes to structuring and querying data. There can be a lot of redundancy, which is a natural side effect of a database that's essentially denormalized by default.

9.1.1 *Data structure*

Let's discuss how data is stored in Firebase. As we've mentioned, Firebase stores data as JSON objects. Data is stored as nodes with associated keys that can be specified by you or generated by the database (you're always working with key/value pairs). The main advice that we can give you is to flatten and denormalize your data as much as possible. Figure 9.1 shows an example of a Firebase database and what the data structure looks like.

The Firebase guide to structuring the database (https://firebase.google .com/docs/database/web/structure-data) gives a few helpful hints that include the following:

- *Avoid nesting data.* The database supports the nesting of data that's 32 levels deep. But retrieving data from a location in the database retrieves all of its child nodes too. Furthermore, if your security rules grant read/write access to a particular location, all of the children get the same rights automatically.
- *Flatten and denormalize data as much as possible.* This will introduce repetition and redundancy into your data but will make retrieval simpler and faster.
- *In scenarios where many-to-many relationships are required, it's better to store the relationship of the entities on both ends.* This duplicates data and requires two updates if the relationship changes. Firebase gives an example, which we've slightly modified in the following listing, to illustrate this concept.

> **Listing 9.1 Many-to-many relationship**

```
{
  "users": {
    "psbarski" : {
      "name" : "Peter Sbarski",
      "groups" : {
```

```
          "serverlessheroes": true,
          "acloudguru" : true
        }
      }
    }
  },
  "groups" : {
    "serverlessheroes" : {
        "name" : "Serverless Heroes",
        "members" : {
          "psbarski" : true,
          "acollins" : true,
          "skroonenburg" : true
        }
      }
    }
  }
}
```

Users belong to groups and groups have multiple users. This many-to-many relationship is specified explicitly in Firebase. If the relationship changes, two writes/updates to the database are needed. See https://firebase.google.com/docs/database/web/structure-data for more information and examples.

The root of the tree   Data is stored in nodes that have a key

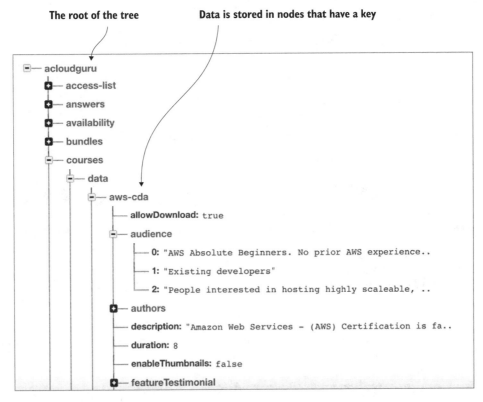

Figure 9.1   This is an example database structure from the A Cloud Guru database, which is a large online learning management system.

9.1.2   *Security rules*

The Firebase Database Rules define when, and by whom, data can be read and written, how data is structured, and what indexes should exist. We'll start with security and describe the four main types of rules (you can find much more information at https://firebase.google.com/docs/database/security/):

- `.read` & `.write`—Describes if and when data is allowed to be read and/or written by users. These rules cascade, which means that read access granted to /abc/ will automatically extend to /abc/123/ and /abc/123/xyz/ unless they're specifically overridden.
- `.validate`—Describes what a correctly formatted value looks like. Unlike `.read` and `.write` rules, `.validate` rules do not cascade and must evaluate to `true` to succeed.
- `.indexOn`—Specifies an index to support ordering and querying.

There are predefined variables that can be used in rules. These include the following:

- `now`—The current time in milliseconds since Linux epoch
- `root`—The root of the database
- `newData`—New data being written
- `data`—Current data (before a new operation takes place)
- `auth`—Content of an authenticated user's token
- `$` (variables)—A wildcard used to represent IDs and dynamic keys

An example of a Firebase validation rule is as follows.

Listing 9.2   Firebase validation rule

```
"$answer_id": {
    ".validate": "newData.isNumber() && (newData.val() == -1 || newData.val() == 1)"
}
```

This rule validates that the new data being written is a number and is either -1 or 1.

The rule in listing 9.2 is fairly simple, but it's indicative of the types of rules you can write to read, write, and validate data. A more detailed guide on security rules is available at https://firebase.google.com/docs/database/security/securing-data.

9.2   *Adding Firebase to 24-Hour Video*

You're going to integrate Firebase into 24-Hour Video and use it to store information about videos uploaded by users. We chose Firebase because you don't need a relational database for your application. Real-time streaming updates also make for a great user experience. You can bind Firebase to your user interface and have your UI update automatically whenever data in Firebase changes.

24-Hour Video will interact with the database in the following ways:

- Your website will read names of video files from Firebase. This will allow you to create a full URL to the video by prepending the S3 domain. The `get-video-list` function will no longer be needed.
- Whenever a user uploads a video, the existing `transcode-video` Lambda function will write to Firebase to indicate that a new video is being processed. That will allow you to show a nice spinner animation on your website to indicate that a video is coming.
- After a video is transcoded, you'll run a new Lambda function to update Firebase with the necessary information, such as the S3 key of the transcoded file. This will close the loop and allow the website to show and play the new video.

Figure 9.2 shows how the component you're about to implement fits into the greater feature.

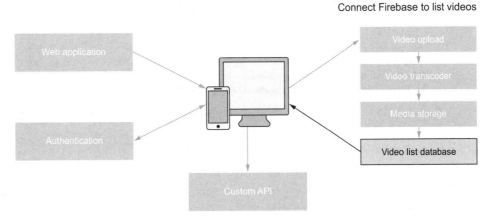

Figure 9.2 You're going to implement the last major component of your system by adding Firebase.

9.2.1   Architecture

Let's discuss the architecture you're about to build. At the end of this chapter you'll have finished the event-driven pipeline that you began building all the way back in chapter 3. The user will be able to upload a video, get a visual indication that a video is being processed, and then see the new video after it has been transcoded. Firebase will be used to push updates to the website, which will enable you to build a nice user experience. Figure 9.3 shows this flow.

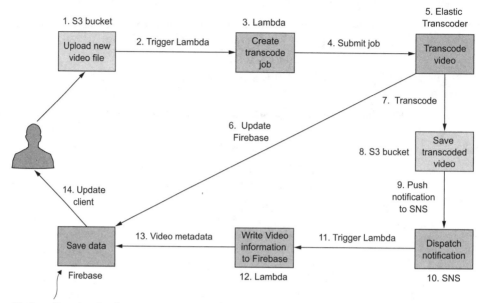

Firebase is updated twice:
I. When a video is about to be transcoded.
2. When transcoding has finished and there is a new video users can watch.

Figure 9.3   This is a modification of the architecture you began in chapter 3.

The plan for this chapter will then be as follows:

1 Create a Firebase account and a database.
2 Create a new Lambda function to save video metadata to Firebase (you'll also need to modify the SNS topic you created in chapter 3 to invoke this function).
3 Update the `transcode-video` function to save placeholder information to Firebase (so that you can show the user that a video is transcoding).
4 Update the website to access Firebase. If you implemented presigned URLs in chapter 9, you'll need to invoke this function to get the URLs for your videos after getting the relevant data (that is, the S3 key) out of the database. If you didn't implement secure URLs in the previous chapter, then you can store direct URLs to your videos in Firebase.

In chapter 8 we discussed ways of securing access to files, and at the end of that chapter you implemented a way to generate signed URLs. We're going to ignore signed URLs for a moment to get the database going. Later in this chapter we'll look at signed URLs and how to make everything work with Firebase. If you have existing videos that you've been testing with, make sure that they're publicly accessible/viewable in S3 (you basically need to undo what you did in section 8.3.1). That will be enough to complete this section.

9.2.2 Setting up Firebase

Go ahead and set up a Firebase account and a Firebase database now:

1 Open https://firebase.google.com and create a new account.
2 Having registered your account, go into the main console and choose Create New Project.
3 In the pop-up window, specify a name for your project (such as 24-hour-video) and select your region. Then choose Create Project.
4 Firebase has numerous interesting products apart from its database (figure 9.4). But for now, choose Database from the menu on the left.
5 You'll see that you have an empty database. That's okay; you'll add some data later. For now, take note of the database URL (figure 9.5). You'll need it.

A database is just one of the products offered by Firebase. There is also storage, hosting of web apps, crash reporting, notifications, analytics and other services. A lot of the services are aimed at mobile (iOS & Android) development.

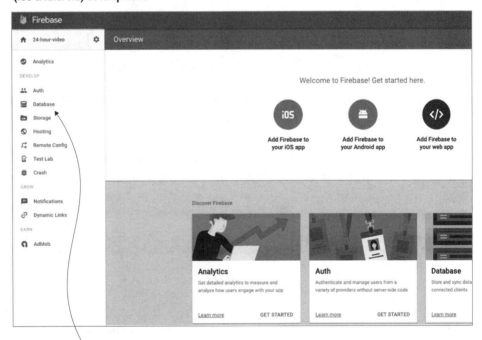

Choose Database to set up your Firebase database.

Figure 9.4 Firebase is not just a database service. It offers many other services to choose from.

The database URL you need to need to remember.

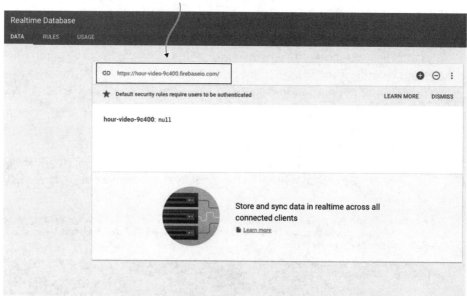

Figure 9.5   You'll access the database from the 24-Hour Video website via this URL.

The 24-Hour Video website will access Firebase directly to read from it. For now, to make things easier, you'll allow your website to do it without authenticating with Firebase. Later in the chapter you'll secure read access:

1   In the same Database console as before, select Rules from the top menu.
2   Copy the security rules given in the following listing into the Security Rules text box.
3   Choose Publish when you've finished.

Listing 9.3   Firebase rules

```
{
  "rules": {
    ".read": "true",              Anyone will be able to read
                                  data from the database.
    ".write": "auth != null"
  }                               Any entity writing to the database
}                                 still needs to be authenticated.
```

9.2.3   *Modifying Transcode Video Lambda*

Imagine yourself as a user uploading a video through your 24-Hour Video website. As a user, you'd want to know if your video uploaded successfully and if or when it was available for playback. If, for whatever reason, the video wasn't ready for playback (because of transcoding), you'd want an indication (such as a message or a loading animation) to tell you so. You can achieve these requirements by showing a progress bar while the file is being uploaded to S3 and then showing an animated placeholder image to indicate that the upload is being processed or transcoded. As soon as the video has finished processing, you can take off the placeholder and show the video.

The progress bar is easy; you can write a small amount of code to monitor the upload and gradually fill it in. The placeholder image is also straightforward. You'll modify the transcode-video Lambda function to write to Firebase and insert a placeholder record whenever a new video is sent to the Elastic Transcoder. Your website will respond to this placeholder record and show a shiny animation. Finally, you'll create a new function to remove the placeholder record from the database and insert the S3 key of the transcoded video (when it's ready). Right now, however, let's look at the transcode-video Lambda function and the changes you need to make to it.

FIREBASE SECURITY

To insert a placeholder record, the transcode-video function will write to Firebase, so it needs to be able to authenticate with it. To do this you're going to create and use a *service account*. A service account belongs to the application rather than any individual user (https://developers.google.com/identity/protocols/OAuth2ServiceAccount), which makes it perfect for use in Lambda:

1 In the Firebase console, click the Settings button, which looks like a cogwheel.
2 Select Permissions from the popup.
3 Choose Service Accounts from the menu on the left.
4 Choose Create Service Account.
5 In the Create Service Account popup, set the service name to be lambda and select Editor as the project role from the Roles drop-down.
6 You should also check Furnish a New Private Key. Leave the Key Type set to JSON (figure 9.6).
7 Click Create, and save the generated private key somewhere safe on your computer.

TRANSCODE VIDEO FUNCTION

You have the private key for the service account in Firebase, so now you can update the transcode-video function. First, prepare the function to work with Firebase:

1 Copy the private key (that is, the generated JSON file) to the directory of your transcode-video function. This private key will be referenced by your code.
2 The Firebase npm package must be added to the function. To do this, in your terminal navigate to the transcode-video function directory and run npm install firebase --save.
3 Open package.json and modify the predeploy line to be "predeploy": "zip -r Lambda-Deployment.zip * -x *.zip *.log". You've removed the *.json extension because you now need JSON files to be included in the zip. Previously, the predeploy script would skip over all JSON files.

This private key will need to be deployed together with the Lambda function.

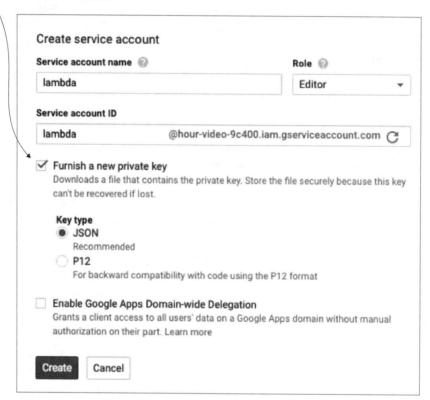

Create service account

Service account name ⓘ   Role ⓘ

lambda   Editor   ▼

Service account ID

lambda   @hour-video-9c400.iam.gserviceaccount.com ⟳

☑ **Furnish a new private key**
Downloads a file that contains the private key. Store the file securely because this key can't be recovered if lost.

Key type
◉ JSON
  Recommended
○ P12
  For backward compatibility with code using the P12 format

☐ **Enable Google Apps Domain-wide Delegation**
Grants a client access to all users' data on a Google Apps domain without manual authorization on their part. Learn more

[Create] [Cancel]

Figure 9.6   The service account will be used by the Lambda function to write to Firebase.

4 Jump into the AWS console, open Lambda, and click your function. You need to set four environment variables for the function to work: Elastic Transcoder region (ELASTIC_TRANSCODER_REGION), Elastic Transcoder pipeline ID (ELASTIC_TRANSCODER_PIPELINE_ID), the filename of the private key (SERVICE_ACCOUNT), and the database URL (DATABASE_URL). Previously the Elastic Transcoder region and pipeline ID were specified directly in the transcode-video function, but now that you've learned about environment variables, it's better to use them instead (figure 9.7).

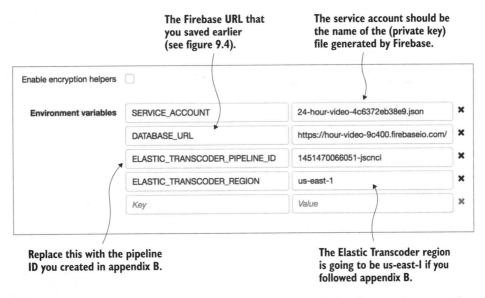

The Firebase URL that you saved earlier (see figure 9.4).

The service account should be the name of the (private key) file generated by Firebase.

Replace this with the pipeline ID you created in appendix B.

The Elastic Transcoder region is going to be us-east-I if you followed appendix B.

Figure 9.7 You must set and save the environment variables for the function to perform correctly.

Now it's finally time to update index.js with the new implementation of your function. Overwrite your existing implementation of the transcode-video function with what's shown in the next listing.

Listing 9.4 Updated `transcode-video` function

```
'use strict';

var AWS = require('aws-sdk');
var firebase = require('firebase');

var elasticTranscoder = new AWS.ElasticTranscoder({
    region: process.env.ELASTIC_TRANSCODER_REGION
});

firebase.initializeApp({
  serviceAccount: process.env.SERVICE_ACCOUNT,
  databaseURL: process.env.DATABASE_URL
});

function pushVideoEntryToFirebase(key, callback) {
    console.log('Adding video entry to firebase at key:', key);

    var database = firebase.database().ref();

    database.child('videos').child(key)
        .set({
            transcoding: true
        })
        .then(function () {
            callback(null, 'Video record saved to firebase');
        })
```

The firebase.initializeApp needs to be run to correctly initialize and authenticate with Firebase.

The pushVideoEntryToFirebase function will only run if the Elastic Transcoder job was submitted successfully. This function will create an entry in the database with a key called transcoding set to true.

This returns the root of the JSON tree in Firebase.

```
        .catch(function (err) {
            callback(err);
        });
    }

exports.handler = function (event, context, callback) {
    context.callbackWaitsForEmptyEventLoop = false;

    var key = event.Records[0].s3.object.key;

    var sourceKey = decodeURIComponent(key.replace(/\+/g, ' '));

    var outputKey = sourceKey.split('.')[0];

    var uniqueVideoKey = outputKey.split('/')[0];

    var params = {
        PipelineId: process.env.ELASTIC_TRANSCODER_PIPELINE_ID,
        Input: {
            Key: sourceKey
        },
        Outputs: [
            {
                Key: outputKey + '-720p' + '.mp4',
                PresetId: '1351620000001-000010'
            }
        ]
    };

    elasticTranscoder.createJob(params, function (error, data) {
        if (error) {
            console.log('Error creating elastic transcoder job.');
            callback(error);
            return;
        }

        console.log('Elastic transcoder job created successfully');
        pushVideoEntryToFirebase(uniqueVideoKey, callback);
    });
};
```

It's important to set this flag to false because you want to suspend the function as soon as you invoke a callback.

You'll produce only one output for now to keep things a bit easier.

This Elastic Transcoder preset produces a generic 720p. As an exercise, move this preset to an environment variable.

The transcoding job started, so make a record in Firebase that the UI can show right away.

Note the following interesting details about the code in listing 9.4:

- At the top of the `handler` function is the following line: `context.callback-WaitsForEmptyEventLoop = false;`. This property needs to be set to `false` to immediately suspend the Lambda function as soon as your callback is invoked. Normally you don't need to do this, but you have a special case here because you're using Firebase. After you write to Firebase, it will open a connection, which may keep the Lambda function alive until its timeout. This is bad not only because it'll cost more to run this function but also because the Lambda runtime will see this timeout as an error and try to invoke the function again. It will rinse and repeat three times, sowing more confusion. So don't forget to set this property to `false` when you use Firebase.

- The function `pushVideoEntryToFirebase` will create a key called `processing` with a value set to `true`. This function takes a parameter called `key`, which is a GUID isolated from the key name of the S3 object. This is the GUID that was generated by the `get-upload-policy` function you created in chapter 9.

Having implemented the function, deploy it to AWS (remember to run `npm run deploy` from the terminal), run the website, and upload a video file. You should be able to inspect the Firebase console and see a new entry added to it, as shown in figure 9.8.

This node represents a collection of objects (videos).

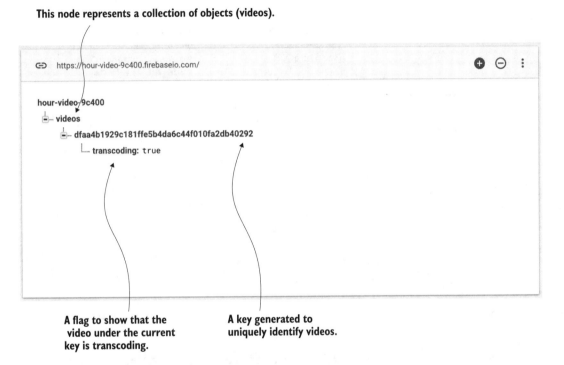

A flag to show that the video under the current key is transcoding.

A key generated to uniquely identify videos.

Figure 9.8   Your database has a simple hierarchical structure.

9.2.4   *Transcode Video Firebase Update*

Having updated the `transcode-video` function, you need to create a new Lambda function to run after the transcoding process has finished. This Lambda function will write information about the newly transcoded file to Firebase:

1 Make a copy of the Transcode Video function and rename it to Transcode Video Firebase Update.
2 Create a new Lambda function in AWS and name it `transcode-video-firebase-update`. Set its timeout for 10 seconds.
3 Update package.json in Transcode Video Firebase Update to account for the new Lambda function created in AWS and run `npm install`.

4   Remember to update the ARN in package.json to reflect the ARN of your new
    function in AWS.

5   In the Lambda console, click the `transcode-video-firebase-update` function
    and add the following environment variables: your database URL, the filename
    of the private key generated by Firebase, the full path to the `transcoded videos`
    S3 bucket, and the bucket's region (figure 9.9).

6   Make sure that the Firebase private key is also in the directory of the function.

7   Overwrite index.js with the contents of listing 9.5.

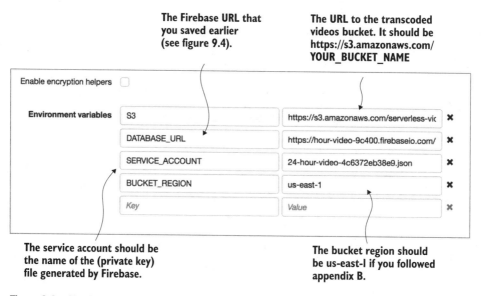

The Firebase URL that you saved earlier (see figure 9.4).

The URL to the transcoded videos bucket. It should be https://s3.amazonaws.com/ YOUR_BUCKET_NAME

The service account should be the name of the (private key) file generated by Firebase.

The bucket region should be us-east-I if you followed appendix B.

Figure 9.9   Check that your environment variables are copied across correctly and saved.

Listing 9.5   Transcode video Firebase update

```
'use strict';

var AWS = require('aws-sdk');
var firebase = require('firebase');

firebase.initializeApp({
    serviceAccount: process.env.SERVICE_ACCOUNT,
    databaseURL: process.env.DATABASE_URL
});

exports.handler = function(event, context, callback){
    context.callbackWaitsForEmptyEventLoop = false;

    var message = JSON.parse(event.Records[0].Sns.Message);

    var key = message.Records[0].s3.object.key;
    var bucket = message.Records[0].s3.bucket.name;
```

This Lambda function will be invoked using SNS; hence you need to unpack it.

```
var sourceKey = decodeURIComponent(key.replace(/\+/g, ' '));

var uniqueVideoKey = sourceKey.split('/')[0];

var database = firebase.database().ref();

database.child('videos').child(uniqueVideoKey).set({
    transcoding: false,
    key: key,
    bucket: process.env.S3
}).catch(function(err) {
    callback(err);
});
};
```

> The transcoding flag needs to be set to false to indicate that the transcoding process has finished and the user can now view the file.

The Transcode Video Update function is similar to the function you implemented in the previous section. Its purpose is only to update Firebase to set the `transcoding` key to `false` and set the S3 key of the video that was newly created. You can now deploy the function to AWS.

9.2.5 Connecting Lambda

The Transcode Video Firebase Update function is implemented, but you need a way to invoke it when a video lands in the transcoded S3 bucket. If you completed chapter 3, you have an SNS topic called `transcoded-video-notification`. Add the Transcode Video Firebase Update function as a subscriber to the topic (figure 9.10).

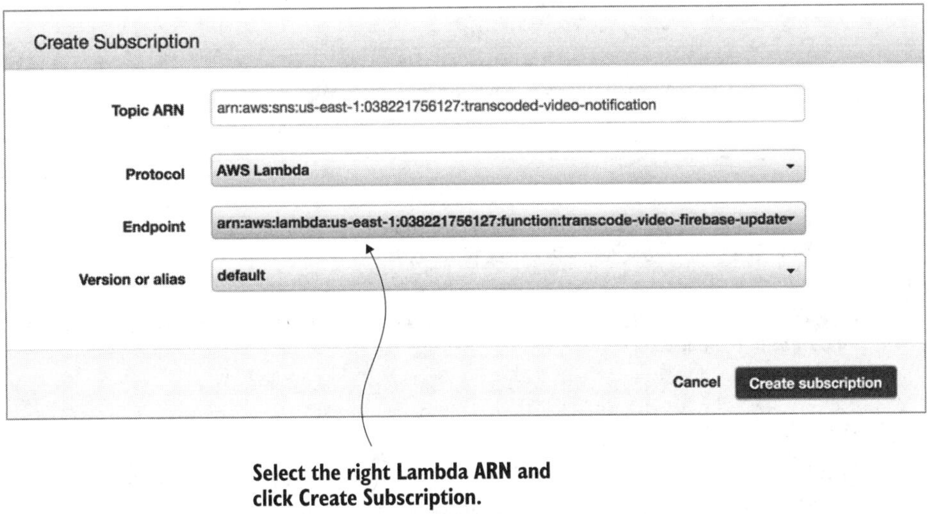

Select the right Lambda ARN and click Create Subscription.

Figure 9.10 Create a subscription for the `transcoded-video-notification` topic and set the Lambda function.

If you didn't implement that SNS topic, you'll need to wire up the bucket to invoke the function directly. You'll also have to modify the implementation of the function to parse an S3 event rather than an event coming from SNS.

RUNNING A TEST

You can now run a simple test to see if your workflow is working. Upload a new video file via the 24-Hour Video website and then take a peek at the Firebase console. At first you should see an entry similar to figure 9.8. But after a while (the time will depend on the size of your video), you should see an entry resembling one of the records in figure 9.11. (That is, your entry will have a bucket, a key, and a `transcoding` flag set to `false`.)

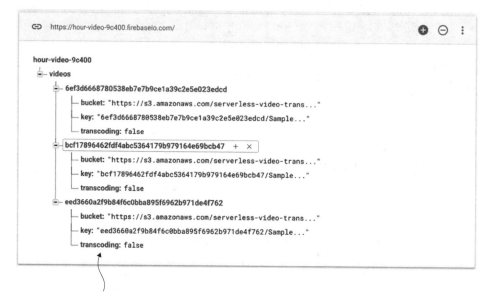

The key and the bucket will be set by the new Lambda function. The transcoding key will be set to false.

Figure 9.11   If everything has been implemented correctly, you'll see Firebase update records in real time right in the console.

9.2.6   *Website*

Finally, you need to update the 24-Hour Video website. You'll make sure that the website binds to your database and is always up to date through the magic of WebSockets. To make the user experience a bit nicer, once a user uploads a file, you'll show a spinner to indicate that the file is being processed. As soon as transcoding is done, you'll hide the spinner and show the actual video. As you're binding to Firebase, it might take a second or two to establish a connection, load data, and display everything onscreen. Instead of having the user look at a blank screen, you'll show another spinner image to indicate that the bulk of the data is loading.

SPINNERS

You need to create two spinner images. One spinner image will be used the first time a user hits the website to show that data is loading. The other spinner image will be used in place of a video while it's being transcoded. Let's get these spinners sorted first:

1   In the main website directory find a folder called img. Create this folder if it doesn't exist.

2   Go to http://loading.io and download any spinner or loading image you like to the img folder. Grab the SVG version and name the file loading-indicator.svg. This will be the spinner image that appears when the user first loads the website.

3   Repeat the previous step, but this time grab a different image. Save it to the img folder and name it transcoding-indicator.svg. This is the spinner image that will appear each time the user uploads a new video.

4   To add the website-loading image, open index.html and add the contents of the following listing above this line: `<div id="video-template" class="col-md-6 col">`.

Listing 9.6   Loading placeholder image in index.html

```
<object id="loading-indicator" type="image/svg+xml" data="img/loading-
    ⇒indicator.svg">
   Your browser does not support SVG
</object>
```

5   To add the transcoding spinner image, open index.html and replace the `<div id="video-template" class="col-sm-4 col">` block with the code in the next listing.

Listing 9.7   Transcoder placeholder image in index.html

```
<div id="video-template" class="col-sm-4 col">
    <div class="video-card">
        <div class="transcoding-indicator">          ⟵   If you upload multiple
            <object type="image/svg+xml" data="img/transcoding-indicator.svg">     videos, you'll see multiple
                Your browser does not support SVG                                   loader images at the same
            </object>                                                               time. It looks quite nice.
        </div>
        <video width="100%" height="100%">
            <source type="video/mp4">
            Your browser does not support the video tag.
        </video>
    </div>
</div>
```

You need to add a touch of CSS magic to make things look nice. Open main.css and copy the contents of the next listing to the very end of the file.

Listing 9.8   Updated CSS

```css
#loading-indicator {
    margin: 90px auto;
    display: block;
}

.transcoding-indicator object {
    margin-top: 30px;
}

body {
    background: #1e1e1e;
}
```

CONFIG

To connect to Firebase you'll need the API key and the database URL. The easiest way to get them is to log into the Firebase console, click your project, and then click the button labeled Add Firebase to Your Web App. You should see a pop-up that looks similar to figure 9.12.

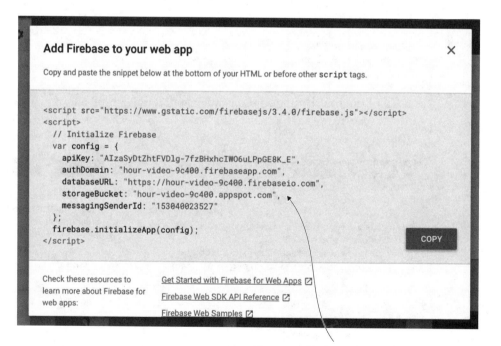

The storageBucket and messagingSenderId aren't needed for 24-Hour Video.

Figure 9.12   Firebase helpfully gives you the required configuration information. You can get similar config information if you're building an iOS or Android app.

Open config.js in your website, create a new object called firebase within config-
Constants, and copy the apiKey and databaseURL from the pop-up. Your config
should look similar to the following.

Listing 9.9   Updated config.js

```
var configConstants = {
    auth0: {
        domain: 'serverless.auth0.com',
        clientId: 'r8PQy2Qdr91xU3KTGQ01e598bwee8LQr'
    },
    firebase: {
        apiKey: 'AIzaS4df5hnFVDlg-5g5gbxhcIWO6uLPpsE8K2E',
        databaseURL: 'https://hour-video-d500.firebaseio.com'
    },
    apiBaseUrl: 'https://t1zyo7a719.execute-api.us-east-1.amazonaws.com/dev'
};
```

> apiKey and databaseURL are the only two new properties added from Firebase. Make sure to update these to what was provided by Firebase.

> The apiBaseUrl should point to your API Gateway API.

It would also be useful to add the Firebase library to your website. In the pop-up that
you opened earlier, there should be a line similar to <script src="https://www
.gstatic.com/firebasejs/3.4.0/firebase.js"></script>. Copy that line into
index.html just above <script src="js/user-controller.js"></script>.

VIDEO CONTROLLER

You need to replace your video controller because you're now going to be binding to
Firebase. You'll implement the following functions in the new video controller:

- init—Function to initialize the controller as usual
- addVideoToScreen—Function to add an HTML5 video element to the UI
- updateVideoOnScreen—Function responsible for showing and hiding the
  placeholder image
- getElementForVideo—Helper function to get the video ID
- connectToFirebase—Function that will initialize a connection to Firebase and
  update the UI when data in Firebase changes

Copy the contents of the next listing to video-controller.js, completely replacing
what's already there.

Listing 9.10   Update video controller

```
var videoController = {
    data: {
        config: null
    },
    uiElements: {
        videoCardTemplate: null,
        videoList: null,
        loadingIndicator: null
    },
```

```
        init: function (config) {
            this.uiElements.videoCardTemplate = $('#video-template');
            this.uiElements.videoList = $('#video-list');
            this.uiElements.loadingIndicator = $('#loading-indicator');

            this.data.config = config;

            this.connectToFirebase();
        },
        addVideoToScreen: function (videoId, videoObj) {
            var newVideoElement = this.uiElements.videoCardTemplate.
            ⇒clone().attr('id', videoId);

            newVideoElement.click(function() {                    ◁─────────────┐
                var video = newVideoElement.find('video').get(0);               │
                                                                                │
                if (newVideoElement.is('.video-playing')) {       If the user has
                    video.pause();                                clicked the video,
                    $(video).removeAttr('controls');              play it or pause it
                }                                                 depending on state.
                else {
                    $(video).attr('controls', '');
                    video.play();
                }

                newVideoElement.toggleClass('video-playing');
            });

            this.updateVideoOnScreen(newVideoElement, videoObj);

            this.uiElements.videoList.prepend(newVideoElement);
        },
        updateVideoOnScreen: function(videoElement, videoObj) {
            if (!videoObj)
            {
                return;                                           If the video is currently
            }                                                     transcoding, hide the video and
            if (videoObj.transcoding) {              ◁─────────── show the placeholder image.
                videoElement.find('video').hide();
                videoElement.find('.transcoding-indicator').show();
            } else {
                videoElement.find('video').show();
                videoElement.find('.transcoding-indicator').hide();
            }
 Set the video
   URL on the   videoElement.find('video').attr('src',
 video HTML5    ⇒ videoObj.bucket + '/' + videoObj.key);
   element. ┗▷ },
        getElementForVideo: function(videoId) {
            return $('#' + videoId);
        },
        connectToFirebase: function () {
            var that = this;                                     Initialize a
                                                                 connection to
            firebase.initializeApp(this.data.config.firebase);   ◁──── Firebase.
```

The /.info/connected is a special location that can tell you whether you're connected to Firebase.

Get the reference to the videos node in your database.

```
var isConnectedRef = firebase.database().ref('.info/connected');

var nodeRef = firebase.database().ref('videos');

   isConnectedRef.on('value', function(snap) {
   if (snap.val() === true) {
     that.uiElements.loadingIndicator.hide();
   }
});
```

This block of code hides the loading spinner once you detect that a connection to Firebase exists.

This closure is run each time a new child (movie) is added to the database.

```
   nodeRef
     .on('child_added', function (childSnapshot) {
       that.uiElements.loadingIndicator.hide();

       that.addVideoToScreen(childSnapshot.key,
       ➥childSnapshot.val());
     });


   nodeRef
     .on('child_changed', function (childSnapshot) {

       that.updateVideoOnScreen(that.getElementForVideo
       ➥(childSnapshot.key), childSnapshot.val());
     });
   }
};
```

Update the video object on screen with the new video details from Firebase.

This closure is run when a change is made to an existing record (for example, a video has finished going through the transcoding process and is now available).

The videoController function updates the UI whenever a record (child) is added or updated in Firebase. The code that you've added responds to events from Firebase and makes changes. Because it uses WebSockets, you don't need to poll for changes. They're pushed to your website as they happen. One thing that's missing from the implementation is a way to handle deletions in Firebase. When a record is deleted from Firebase, you should immediately update the UI to remove the video. This can be done using the child_removed event and implemented in the similar fashion as child_added and child_changed. One of the exercises at the end of this chapter asks you to implement it.

Another interesting bit of code in listing 9.10 has to do with detecting the connection state of your application. The /.info/connected is a special Boolean flag provided by Firebase that you can inspect to see if you have a connection to the database or not. It's a useful flag that can allow you to detect if your client goes offline (or comes back online) and carry out compensating actions. In this example, if the client goes offline, you might want to show a message in the UI to say that the connection has been lost and it's likely that the client won't be able to access any videos.

9.2.7   *End-to-end testing*

You're now in a good position to test 24-Hour Video end to end. The first thing you should see when running the website is a spinner that disappears a few moments after a connection to Firebase is established. Then you can begin uploading videos (if you don't have any already). You should see a placeholder image for each video uploaded with an associated spinner until the transcoding process is completed and the video is available for viewing (figure 9.13).

This placeholder image pulsates while we wait for the video to become available.

Figure 9.13   The 24-Hour Video website is finally starting to come together. Nearly all the major features have been implemented.

9.3   *Securing access to files*

In chapter 8, we discussed how to secure access to files and create presigned URLs. In order to get Firebase working, we ignored that aspect of the system. It's now time to have a look at it. You're going to add one more step to your process. You'll issue an HTTP request to retrieve presigned URLs once data from Firebase has been read. This will introduce a bit of latency, but that's a tradeoff you have to have. Figure 9.14 shows what you're going to do.

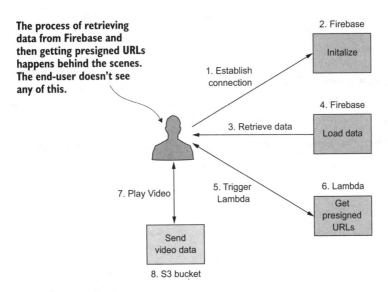

Figure 9.14 We've introduced one additional step to get presigned URLs after data from Firebase has been loaded.

Note that you could architect this differently. The 24-Hour Video website could issue a request to an HTTP endpoint that could query Firebase and return a list of signed URLs. There's nothing wrong with that approach and it could work just as well. But we wanted to illustrate the real-time nature of the database and show how the interface could respond in near real time to data changes made within it.

One other thing that you might want to do (if you didn't do it in chapter 8) is stop the set-permissions Lambda function from being run. This Lambda function, which you created in chapter 3, sets permissions on video files to make them publicly accessible. It gets invoked by an SNS message that's created when a new function is added to the second (transcoded files) bucket. To disable this function, do the following:

1 Find it in the Lambda console.
2 Select Triggers from the tab menu.
3 Click Disable next to the SNS configuration and then click Disable in the popup menu.

If you now happen to upload a new video file via the 24-Hour Video website, it won't be playable. If you open your browser's developer tools, you'll see HTTP requests for video files return with a 403 (Forbidden) status request code.

9.3.1 Signed URL Lambda

In chapter 8 you modified the get-video-list function to return a list of presigned URLs. This function used to enumerate the S3 bucket and then return a list of URLs. You don't need to enumerate the bucket anymore because you have Firebase, so you'll create a new function called `get-signed-url` just to generate and return signed URLs for your videos. This function will take a parameter, which is the S3 key of the file, and return a signed URL.

To implement this function, make a copy of the `get-video-list` Lambda function from chapter 8 and name it `get-signed-url`. Then erase the existing index.js and copy the contents of the following listing into it. Remember to update package.json to reflect the name of the new function and its ARN.

Listing 9.11 The `get-signed-url` Lambda function

```
'use strict';

var AWS = require('aws-sdk');
var s3 = new AWS.S3();

exports.handler = function(event, context, callback){
    s3.getSignedUrl('getObject', {Bucket: process.env.BUCKET, Key:
 ➥event.queryStringParameters.key, Expires: 900},
        ➥function(err, url) {
        if (err) {
          callback(err);
        } else {

          var response = {
            'statusCode': 200,
            'headers' : {'Access-Control-Allow-Origin':'*'},
            'body' : JSON.stringify({'url': url})
          }

          callback(null, response);
        }
    });
}
```

The getSignedUrl is an asynchronous function that will generate a signed URL. You previously used it in chapter 8.

Remember to update CORS and not leave it open for everyone once you move past this example. You can store the allowed origin as an environment variable.

This function doesn't need any specific settings apart from one environment variable. Create a variable called BUCKET and set it to the name of your S3 bucket with transcoded files. Deploy the function from your computer to AWS. The Lambda function that you just created is fairly simple. It accepts a key, which is the filename of the file in the bucket, and generates a signed URL that it returns. Because you're using Lambda proxy integration with API Gateway, you need to create a response message that includes the HTTP status code, required HTTP headers, and the body of the response.

9.3.2 *API Gateway settings*

Your 24-Hour Video website will invoke an endpoint that will pass the key of the S3 object to the Lambda function and return a signed URL in the response. To do this in the API Gateway, follow these steps:

1 Select your 24-Hour Video API.
2 Create a new resource and name it `signed-url`.

   3 Select Enable API Gateways CORS.

   4 Click Create Resource.

Having created the resource, make sure it's selected and create a GET method under it. Check that Lambda Function is selected and that Use Lambda Proxy Integration is checked. Choose your Lambda region from the drop-down and, finally, set the get-signed-url Lambda function. Deploy the function once everything is ready.

9.3.3 Updating the website again

Now you have to update your website yet again. As your website loads data from Firebase and you get information about each video, you need to invoke the get-signed-url Lambda function to get the signed URL. Replace the updateVideoOnScreen function with the implementation given in the next listing.

Listing 9.12 Getting secure URLs

```
updateVideoOnScreen: function(videoElement, videoObj) {
    if (!videoObj){
      return;
    }

    if (videoObj.transcoding) {
        videoElement.find('video').hide();
        videoElement.find('.transcoding-indicator').show();
    } else {
        videoElement.find('video').show();
        videoElement.find('.transcoding-indicator').hide();

        var getSignedUrl = this.data.config.apiBaseUrl          The URL you need
        + '/signed-url?key=' + encodeURI(videoObj.key);          to invoke to get
                                                                 the signed URL for
                                                                 the video
        $.get(getSignedUrl, function(data, result) {
          if (result === 'success' && data.url) {
            videoElement.find('video').attr('src', data.url);
          }
        })                    If the result is success, assign the
    }                         signed URL to the video element.
}
```

If you run the website and refresh the page, you should see the videos appear on the page. You can play them again by clicking each one.

9.3.4 Improving performance

The code in the listing works, but it's terribly inefficient because your website has to issue a request to get a signed URL for every video. It might be okay if you have five videos, but it won't scale if you have thousands of videos and thousands of clients. They will cause a denial-of-service (DoS) attack on your API Gateway until it starts refusing connections (your clients will see a 429 Too many requests response).

   How would you solve this problem? One way would be to make the system get a signed URL only when a user clicks a video. This may result in a slight delay, but it's not a bad option. If the user isn't allowed to get the video, they could be redirected to a login or signup page. Still, this may not be very efficient if the user is clicking many videos. Another option is to request a whole batch of signed URLs once when the main page loads and then request additional signed URLs on demand.

Listing 9.13 shows a modified get-signed-url function that takes an array of keys (passed into the function in the body of the request) and generates an array of objects that contain signed URLs. This function iterates through an array of keys using async.forEachOf, which encapsulates the asynchronous invocation of the get-signed-url function. When all signed URLs are generated, they're returned in the response to the call. The async.forEachOf function is part of the async framework that we discussed at length in chapter 6.

> **Listing 9.13 Updated `get-signed-url` function**

The body of the request object contains keys that you need to sign. JSON.parse() parses a JSON string and produces a JSON object that you can work with.

Asynchronously iterate through all keys in the body. The third parameter of the forEachOf function is invoked when all iterated functions have finished or an error occurred.

```javascript
'use strict';

var AWS = require('aws-sdk');
var async = require('async');

var s3 = new AWS.S3();

exports.handler = function(event, context, callback){
    var body = JSON.parse(event.body);
    var urls = [];

    async.forEachOf(body, function(video, index, next) {
        s3.getSignedUrl('getObject', {Bucket: process.env.BUCKET,
        Key: video.key, Expires: 9000}, function(err, url) {
            if (err) {
                console.log('Error generating signed URL for', video.key);
                next(err);
            } else {
                urls.push({firebaseId: video.firebaseId, url: url});
                next();
            }
        });

    }, function (err) {
        if (err) {
            console.log('Could not generate signed URLs');
            callback(err);
        } else {
            console.log('Successfully generated URLs');

            var response = {
                'statusCode': 200,
                'headers' : {'Access-Control-Allow-Origin':'*'},
                'body' : JSON.stringify({'urls': urls})
            }
```

```
        callback(null, response);
    }
  });
}
```

The function given in listing 9.13 is designed to be invoked via an API Gateway using Lambda proxy integration. It also expects that the necessary keys are passed in to the function in the body of the request. The body would need to look like the example given in the next listing. You're passing in the Firebase ID and the key of the file in S3. The Firebase ID is needed so that you can later match the returned signed URL to its entry in Firebase if you need to.

Listing 9.14 The body of the batch `get-signed-urls` request

```
[{"firebaseId":"0b18db4cbb4eca1a","key":"0b18db4cbb4eca1a/video-720p.mp4"},
{"firebaseId":"38b8c18c85ec686f","key":"38b8c18c85ec686f/video2-720p.mp4"},
{"firebaseId":"6ef3d6668780538e","key":"6ef3d6668780538e/video3_2mb-720p.mp4"},
{"firebaseId":"7b58d16bf1a1af6aa1","key":"7b58d16bf1a1af6aa1/video4-720p.mp4"}]
```

To generate the required request and its body, refer to the following listing, which shows the kind of function you can implement in the 24-Hour Video website.

Listing 9.15 24-Hour Video `get-Signed-Urls`

> Using jQuery map you can translate an array of objects coming from Firebase to a new array of items that you can send to the Lambda function.

> A regular POST request is made with the help of jQuery. The body of the request is a stringified map of keys you just created.

```
nodeRef
  .on('child_added', function (childSnapshot) {
     that.getSignedUrls(childSnapshot.val());
});

getSignedUrls: function(videoObjs) {
  if (videoObjs) {
    var objectMap = $.map(videoObjs, function (video, firebaseId) {
      return {firebaseId: firebaseId, key: video.key};
    })

    var getSignedUrl = this.data.config.apiBaseUrl + '/signed-url';

    $.post(getSignedUrl, JSON.stringify(objectMap),
    function(data, status){
        if (status === 'success') {
        //iterate through the response and add videos to the page
      }
      else {
        //handle error
      }
    });
  }
}
```

> If the POST request returns with an error, it needs to be handled.

> The response should contain an array of Firebase IDs and signed URLs. You can iterate through these and add videos to the page.

An exercise at the end of this chapter will ask you to finish the implementation of the batched retrieval of presigned URLs. You'll need to finish the implementation in listing 9.15 to get everything working.

9.3.5 *Improving Firebase security*

If you've been following along and implementing everything we've been discussing—including presigned URLs—you should have a reasonably robust and secure system. There's one problem. If you look back at listing 9.3, you'll see that your Firebase security rule allows any authenticated user to read from Firebase. In some instances, that might be a reasonable thing to do, especially if you're building a public system. But you want to force your users to log in before they can view videos (and generate presigned URLs), which is why you should lock down Firebase so that only authenticated users can read from it.

First, lock down the rules:

1 In Firebase's console find and open your database.
2 Select Rules from the top menu.
3 Copy the security rules given in the next listing into the Security Rules text box.
4 Choose Publish once you've finished.

Listing 9.16   Firebase rules

```
{
  "rules": {
    ".read": "auth != null",     ⊲——  Now you're going to secure reads
    ".write": "auth != null"            so that your users have to log in
  }                                      before they can use the website.
}
```

Having implemented the new rule, refresh your website. Nothing should come up, because you're not allowed to read without authenticating. Next, you'll use Auth0 to issue a custom delegation token whenever a user signs in. This token will be sent to Firebase and used to authenticate the user there.

HELLO AUTH0

Open Auth0 and click Clients. Then, next to your app (that is, 24 Hour Video), click Addon. Click the big Firebase button. You should see a popup that explains how to configure the integration between Firebase and Auth0. We're using SDK Version 3, so you should follow those instructions. The first thing you need to do is configure a JSON service in Firebase:

1 Open Firebase and select your project.
2 Click the settings cog and select Permissions.
3 Choose Service Accounts from the sidebar.
4 Click Create Service Account.

5   In the Service Account Name type autho.

6   From the Role drop-down select Project and then Viewer.

7   Click Furnish a New Private Key.

8   Make sure JSON is selected as the key type.

9   Choose Create and save the resulting file to your computer as auth0-key.json.

You may have already noticed that you did something similar in section 9.2.3, so it should be relatively easy. Remember that Auth0 pop-up you saw when you clicked the big Firebase button? Go back to that pop-up and follow these steps:

1   Choose the Settings tab.

2   Select Use SDK v3+ Tokens.

3   Copy the `private_key`, `private_key_id`, and `client_email` from auth0-key.json into the appropriate text boxes in the pop-up (figure 9.15).

4   Click Save when finished, close the pop-up, and remember to enable Firebase in the main Addons page (if you haven't done so already—figure 9.16).

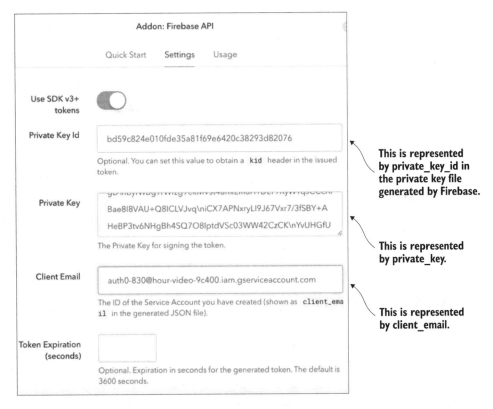

Figure 9.15   The values for this settings page can be obtained from the auth0-key.json file you generated earlier.

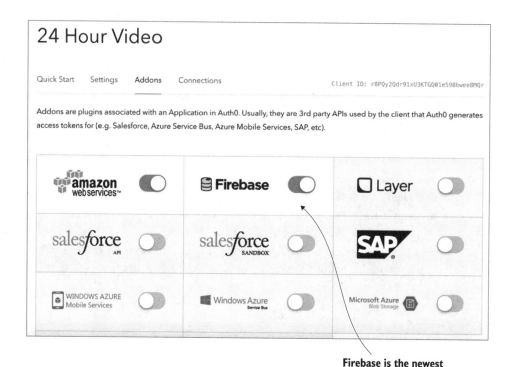

Firebase is the newest
addition to the family.

Figure 9.16   Don't forget to enable Firebase on the main Addons configuration page.

DELEGATION TOKEN

Auth0 provides a delegation token endpoint, which you can use to retrieve a delegation token for Firebase. The process involves your user logging in first and then requesting a Firebase token. Then, using this Firebase token, you can authenticate with Firebase and get the required data. Remember that JavaScript is asynchronous, so you should use either promises or, better yet, a finite-state machine library to make sure things are done in the correct order. Make sure you do the following:

1 Perform user authentication with Auth0 first.
2 Retrieve the Firebase delegation token from Auth0.
3 Authenticate with Firebase using the delegation token.
4 Retrieve data from Firebase and display it to the user.

The full implementation and the changes that you need to make to the 24-Hour Video website are too numerous to be published on these pages. Nevertheless, the most important code listings are given next. These should show you how to implement everything. If you want to see a complete implementation, please look at the source code provided with this book.

MAKING WEBSITE CHANGES

To get the delegation token for Firebase, you need to request it from Auth0 after logging in. Listing 9.17 shows source code for a function that retrieves and saves the Firebase delegation token after a user successfully logs in to Auth0. This function should go into user-controller.js. To help find the right parameters and values for your system, log in to Auth0 and go to https://auth0.com/docs/api/authentication. Scroll down to Delegated Authentication and expand the section that describes how to obtain a delegation token. This section will help you find the right parameters and even perform a test by issuing a request to the /delegation endpoint.

Listing 9.17 Get Firebase token

The JWT token that identifies the user. This token
is retrieved when the user logs in to Auth0.

The scope parameter
specifies what attributes to
include in the issued token.
You can set it to openid.

The api_type
should be set to
firebase.

The grant_type should be set to
urn:ietf:params:oauth:grant-type:jwt-bearer.

```
getFirebaseToken: function(token){
    var that = this;
    var config = this.data.config.auth0;

    var url = 'https://' + config.domain + '/delegation';

    var data = {
        id_token: token,
        scope: config.scope,
        api_type: config.api_type,
        grant_type: config.grant_type,
        target: config.target,
        client_id: config.clientId
    }

    $.post(url, data, function(data, status) {
        if (status === 'success') {
            localStorage.setItem('firebaseToken', data.id_token);
            that.authentication.resolve();
        } else {
            console.log('Could not get retrieve firebase delegation token',
            ➥data, status);
            that.authentication.fail();
        }
    }, 'json');
}
```

The client_id identifies the requesting app. It looks
something like r8PQy2Qdr9IxU3KTGQ0Ie598bwee8MQr.
You can grab it from the clients page after logging in to
Auth0.com.

You're using deferred objects to
allow you to return and resolve
promises at a later stage.

The target parameter identifies the
API endpoint in Auth0. This is
usually the same as the client_id.

Save the firebase token to
local storage for later use.

To make listing 9.17 work, you'd need to make other changes to user-controller.js, video-controller.js, and config.js. You may have also gleaned from listing 9.17 that you're using deferred objects (see this line, for example: `that.authentication .resolve()`). The reason for using deferred objects is that you want to run code that only other code successfully resolves. The next listing shows the new implementation of main.js, which waits for `userController.init` to successfully resolve before it runs the init functions for `videoController` and `uploadController`.

Listing 9.18 The main.js file

```
(function(){
  $(document).ready(function(){
    userController.init(configConstants)
      .then(function() {
          videoController.init(configConstants);
          uploadController.init(configConstants);
      }
    );
  });
}());
```

> The init function of userController resolves a deferred object. When that resolves successfully, the other init functions can run.

The user-controller.js file also now has a `deferredAuthentication` function whose purpose is to check whether the right user tokens are stored in local storage and then react accordingly (that is, resolving successfully or trying to get the right token from Auth0 and Firebase). The init function invokes the `deferredAuthentication` function when it finishes its own execution (see the following listing).

Listing 9.19 The `deferredAuthentication` function

```
deferredAuthentication: function() {
  var that = this;
  this.authentication = $.Deferred();

  var idToken = localStorage.getItem('userToken');

  if (idToken) {
    this.configureAuthenticatedRequests();
    this.data.auth0Lock.getProfile(idToken, function(err, profile) {
      if (err) {
        return alert('There was an error getting the profile: ' +
        err.message);
      }
      that.showUserAuthenticationDetails(profile);
    });

    var firebaseToken = localStorage.getItem('firebaseToken');

    if (firebaseToken) {
      this.authentication.resolve();
    } else {
      this.getFirebaseToken(idToken);
```

> Check if the Auth0 and Firebase JWT tokens are in local storage and try to load them.

> If the Firebase token isn't found but the Auth0 authentication token exists, invoke the getFirebaseToken function implemented in listing 9.17.

```
    }
  }
  return this.authentication;
}
```

This function returns a deferred object, which is, in turn, returned by the init function to the code executing in main.js.

Refer to the code provided with this book (or look at https://github.com/sbarski/serverless-architectures-aws) for other miscellaneous code changes you need to implement to make everything work. Or, better yet, treat it as an exercise and figure out the remaining code changes yourself. At the end, you should have a working website that requires you to log in before all videos are loaded and displayed. On log out, all videos should be removed from the interface.

9.4 *Exercises*

Try the following exercises to further cement your understanding of Firebase and serverless architectures:

1 The `connectToFirebase` function in the video controller reacts to `child_added` and `child_changed` events. Add support for `child_removed` to automatically remove a video from the user interface when a related record is deleted from Firebase.

2 You can currently detect when the client makes a connection to Firebase. The bit of code that's responsible for it is in the video controller. Update the video controller to display a message on the UI if the client goes offline or loses connection. The message should say that the client is offline.

3 Finish the implementation you began in section 9.3.4 so that you have pre-signed URLs working with Firebase.

4 Explore the products that the Firebase platform has to offer. How do these differ from similar AWS services?

5 Explore security rules and indexes in more detail. In which cases can you use indexes, and what kind of security rules can you introduce to make your 24-Hour Video database even more secure?

9.5 *Summary*

In this chapter, you learned about Firebase. You implemented Firebase with 24-Hour Video and saw how to read/write to it from a website and from a Lambda function. Firebase is a great database for driving a user interface, and it works well if your information storage and reporting needs aren't complex. Firebase is fast, and its real-time streaming and offline capabilities are very useful. Its support for delegation tokens makes it straightforward to use in a serverless architecture. In the next chapter, we'll wrap up our book and look at what you've been able to achieve and how you can take your architecture further.

Going the last mile

This chapter covers

- Deployment and frameworks
- Microservices with Lambda
- State machines and AWS Step Functions
- Monetizing APIs on AWS Marketplace

Serverless is an approach to development of software that encourages developers to use a compute service to execute code, make use of third-party services, and apply certain patterns and practices. A serverless approach to the design of software allows developers to move more quickly and focus on solving their core problem instead of managing infrastructure or worrying about issues such as autoscaling groups. We've been discussing serverless throughout the book, but there are a few points we didn't touch on. In this last chapter we're going to discuss microservices, construction of state machines, and monetization opportunities for serverless APIs on AWS.

10.1 Deployment and frameworks

Two important subjects that we haven't yet covered are deployment and frameworks. In chapter 6, you implemented a way to deploy Lambda functions using npm, and in chapter 7 we discussed using Swagger to create your API Gateway. But we know you can do better and that you need a framework for organizing and deploying everything in concert. Going forward, you should be able serverless application and deploy it from a continuous integration (CI) from a developer's machine, at the push of a button. If you can't do that and you of deployment is manual, you're not going to enjoy building serverless applications. Go for automation every time you can, and your future self will thank you for it.

Appendix G introduces the Serverless Framework and the Serverless Application Model (SAM). Serverless Framework is a CLI tool written in node.js that can help you script and deploy serverless applications to AWS. It is developed by an independent startup called Serverless, Inc. and supported by an ever-growing community of open source contributors. One of the best features of the Serverless Framework is its plugin system that allows anyone to add new features.

SAM is an extension (a transform) to CloudFormation that provides a way to easily define Lambda functions, API Gateway APIs, and DynamoDB tables and then deploy them using CloudFormation. It's developed by AWS as a means of making organization and deployment of serverless apps easier.

The only note we might add here is that if your serverless application is contained within AWS, you can use Serverless Framework or SAM to automate nearly everything. But if you use external services such as Firebase or Auth0, your frameworks aren't likely to support them. So you may have to think about additional ways of automating and scripting your system if you end up using non-AWS services.

10.2 *Toward better microservices*

You created the sample application, 24-Hour Video, with a set of services built on Lambda. Your application can scale thanks to Lambda, Firebase, Auth0, and other services. It can be argued, however, that what you built isn't a true microservices architecture. This is because all of your services share the same database. In a pure microservices architecture, each service would have its own data storage mechanism and be entirely decoupled and independent of other microservices.

Software engineering is often a game of trade-offs. What you've implemented in this book also has its pros and cons. The advantage is that for an application of its size, there's one database to manage. You don't need to think about synchronizing data and eventual consistency. The architecture is easy to understand and relatively easy to debug. But if you were building a truly large, distributed application, you might consider implementing a traditional microservices approach.

As we've mentioned, in a pure microservices architecture each service has its own data store. There's an advantage to doing this. A change in the database schema of one microservice won't affect another service. Development teams can own individual microservices, implement, deploy, and move more quickly. Another benefit is that developers can choose the right database and storage mechanism for each microservice depending on its requirements. One service might use a NoSQL database whereas another might use a relational data store. Being able to choose the right tool for the job and the right database to fit the data model can be a big benefit.

It goes without saying that moving to a true microservices architecture introduces its own challenges. There needs to be a way to synchronize data and roll back from errors. Eventual consistency needs to be handled and concurrent updates reconciled. You may want to consider implementing event sourcing (https://martinfowler.com/eaaDev/EventSourcing.html) too. But these challenges need to be solved if teams wish to benefit from microservices. Our recommendation is to think deeply about whether a microservices approach is right for your application. If you're building a large, distributed application, then it may very well be. But if you're building a small, constrained application, then it may not be worth the trouble.

What is eventual consistency?

You might be familiar with the Domain Name System (DNS). DNS resolves human-readable hostnames such as www.google.com to IP addresses. When a change needs to be made to DNS, it may take time to propagate because authoritative name servers need to be updated and caching DNS servers need to be refreshed. Some clients may get the most recent data more quickly than others, but in the end, all clients will get the same result (the system will have *converged*). DNS is an example of an eventually consistent system. Eventually all requests will get the same data.

DynamoDB is another example. AWS states that "an eventually consistent read might not reflect the results of a recently completed write. Consistency across all copies of data is usually reached within a second. Repeating a read after a short time should return the updated data." It is, however, possible to turn on strong read consistency in DynamoDB if the application needs it. There's a difference between DNS and DynamoDB in that DNS as a caching system provides no guarantees for monotonic reads, whereas DynamoDB does (a monotonic read guarantees that once a new value has been returned, the old value will never be read again).

Understanding eventual consistency is key to understanding distributed systems and how to build microservices architecture. If you're building a distributed application with multiple microservices and data stores, you'll end up dealing with a situation where some services have more recent data than others. But if the system has been architected correctly, everything should ultimately converge and all services should have the same, consistent data after a time.

Figures 10.1 and 10.2 show two different examples of microservices architectures where each service has its own data store.

Note that in figure 10.1 services are coupled to each other. The Checkout service must be aware of other services to invoke them. It must also wait for their responses before it can terminate. If you're building microservices and have a tight coupling between them (that is, if a service has to issue synchronous API calls and wait for responses), you might want to rethink your approach. A tight coupling between microservices may put restrictions on how quickly they can be developed and deployed.

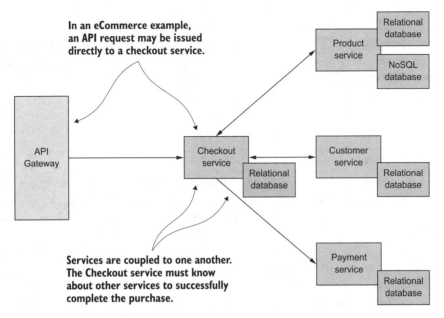

In an eCommerce example, an API request may be issued directly to a checkout service.

Services are coupled to one another. The Checkout service must know about other services to successfully complete the purchase.

Figure 10.1 Microservices have their own databases. But in this example, services have a coupling via synchronous API calls.

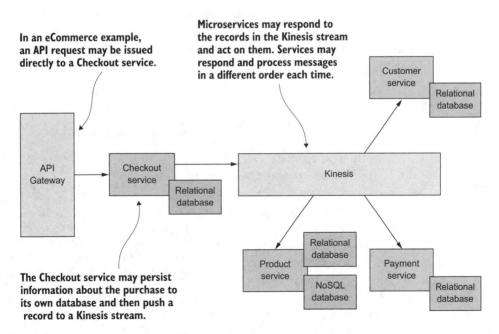

In an eCommerce example, an API request may be issued directly to a Checkout service.

Microservices may respond to the records in the Kinesis stream and act on them. Services may respond and process messages in a different order each time.

The Checkout service may persist information about the purchase to its own database and then push a record to a Kinesis stream.

Figure 10.2 Microservices have their own data stores. Three of the microservices subscribe to a Kinesis stream and consume messages off it. They don't need to have direct knowledge of each other.

Figure 10.2 shows a more decoupled approach where a Kinesis stream is used as a message-delivery mechanism. In this example, services don't need to know about each other, but they must subscribe to a messaging system like Kinesis Streams to receive events or messages. Working on services in this scenario becomes easier because teams can develop and release microservices independently. On the other hand, in this scenario fault recovery and error handling may be trickier. If one message successfully updates the database in one service but fails at another, how do you roll back? How do you handle a situation if data goes out of sync between services?

10.2.1 Handling errors

Look back at figures 10.1 and 10.2 and imagine a situation where a customer bought a product. A transaction is carried out, but unfortunately the customer microservice experiences a catastrophic failure (it goes down). The transaction must be aborted and changes to any other services and databases rolled back. The system must be able to automatically recover, especially if other services have already updated their data in an assumption that the overall transaction will succeed. In figure 10.1, the overarching Checkout service may be able to handle the issue. It could invoke services it talks to and get them to roll back. But what about in figure 10.2? There's no overarching service in charge of the transaction. Everything is distributed.

One way you could try to solve this problem is by creating an *error-handling* microservice. This service could notify or roll back other services in case of an issue. Every service in your architecture would need a way to notify the error-handling service and have a way to pass in the right contextual information (about what has happened) to it. Figure 10.3 shows a sample architecture that includes an error-handling service.

As figure 10.3 shows, the error-handling service can read messages from an SNS topic and then force other services to roll back or carry out compensating actions. The exact behavior of the error-handling service is up to you.

DEAD LETTER QUEUE

Lambda supports the concept of dead letter queues (DLQ), which can help you recover from failures. Lambda can automatically push a message to a DLQ, which can be an SNS topic or an SQS queue, whenever it fails to successfully process an event (and the default number of retries has been carried out). You can write another Lambda function to read messages from this SNS topic/SQS queue and carry out the relevant compensating actions, send alerts, and so on. If you refer back to figure 10.3, you'll see that the SNS error topic can be replaced by the DLQ managed

> **DLQ at work**
>
> So you've enabled DLQ; you should know the following: DLQ is not supported when the event source is a DynamoDB table, a Kinesis stream, or an API Gateway resource request integration. It works, however, when a function is asynchronously invoked (as can be done with S3 or SNS). If you wanted to make it work with an architecture similar to the one in figure 10.3, you'd have to use an SNS topic instead of a Kinesis stream as the main messaging transport system.

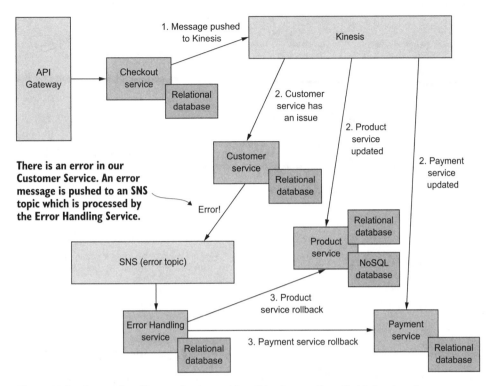

Figure 10.3 An error-handling service is used to roll back operations that take place in services if something fails.

by AWS. You'll then only need to write the error-handling service to process messages from a DLQ.

The combination of a DLQ and Lambda offers a robust approach for handling errors. This is because a function can fail in a number of ways. It can crash because of a programming bug or a timeout or because the callback function was invoked with an error. Any of these outcomes would push a message to the DLQ without the developer having to do anything. DLQ can be enabled in the Advanced Settings section of the Lambda console (figure 10.4) or when a Lambda function is created.

Our advice is to make use of DLQ as much as possible because it's natively supported by Lambda and doesn't require additional programming effort. Before DLQ was supported by Lambda, developers had to write their own implementation, which was much more brittle and unreliable, especially when functions crashed. If you use DLQ, remember to write a function to process messages from the DLQ topic/queue and, at the very least, send a notification to the administrator that something has failed.

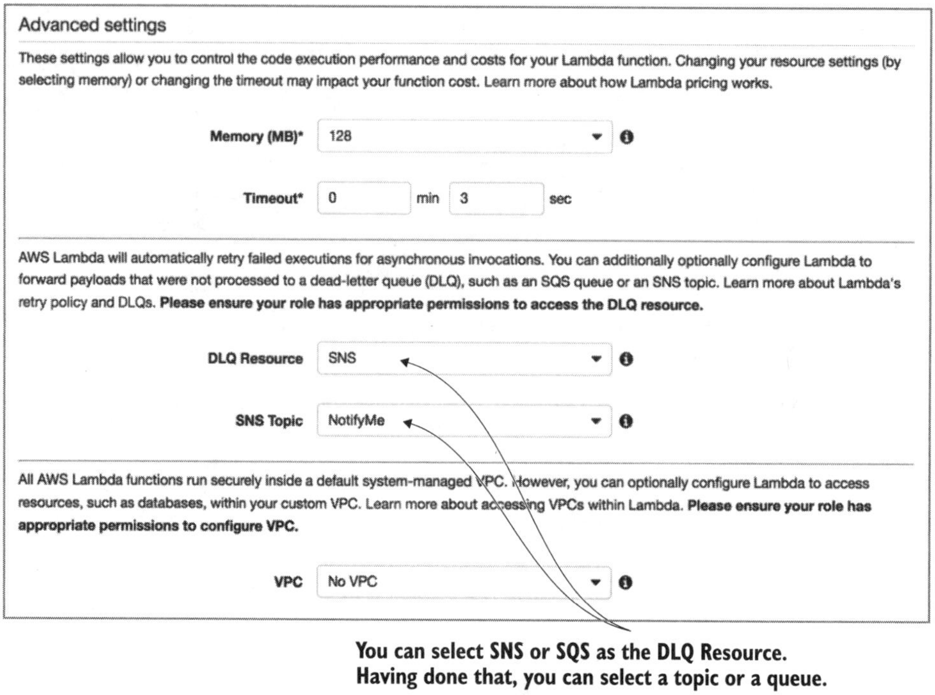

You can select SNS or SQS as the DLQ Resource.
Having done that, you can select a topic or a queue.

Figure 10.4   DLQ is straightforward to enable. You'll need to create an SNS topic or an SQS queue for it.

ACTIVE MONITORING

An active monitor or a watchdog service is a supervisor in a system. It can detect and proactively address problems. Your microservices can periodically send data to your active monitor with information about their state (or your watchdog can ping and monitor services itself).

A watchdog can carry out compensating actions if it determines that something has gone wrong. One example of this is data synchronization. It may be worth checking from time to time that data across different services is consistent. We recommend this if you end up dealing with numerous databases in a microservices architecture. If your watchdog determines that one database is out of sync with another, it can carry out corrective action by synchronizing across databases or alerting the administrator. Obviously, you don't want to end up in this type of situation, but you need to think of and prepare for these kinds of things in large, distributed systems.

10.3 *Step Functions*

Step Functions is an AWS service for creating and coordinating workflows. Step Functions can be thought of as a state machine with a set of states and transitions. Each step (or state) can be a Lambda function, code running on an EC2, or even something executing in your own infrastructure. The Step Functions service triggers each step and retries if there's an error. It can activate steps sequentially or in parallel, have choice states, catch failures, and pause between executions of steps. Step Functions is a great way to define workflows and have a system that manages it for you, including state and error handling. It's far easier to use it and to debug than if you had to define complex workflows with Lambda yourself. The pricing for Step Functions is based on the number of state transitions. The first 4,000 state transitions are free each month, with the next 1,000 state transitions priced at $0.025. It goes without saying that if you end up using services (such as Lambda) with Steps Functions, you'll have to pay for those services as well.

10.3.1 *Image-processing example*

A basic example is an image-processing system. Let's say you need to take an image, make a bunch of copies, and then manipulate those copies in interesting ways. Imagine you want to do the following:

- Add a border to one copy.
- Make another one black and white.
- Create a thumbnail out of the third copy.

Finally, you'd want to receive a notification, such as an email, when all the operations were successfully carried out. Think about it: how you would do it with Lambda alone? You could write one giant function that would do the image-manipulation work and then send an email at the end. That works, but goes against the single-responsibility principle we mentioned in chapter 1. Furthermore, combining so many actions would make the function run longer. And if you had to add more features later, the function would become more difficult to manage. Another approach would be to write an individual function for each transformation and then send a notification at the end. You'd need a database or some other data storage mechanism to keep track of which transformations were done. Otherwise, you wouldn't know when all the functions were finished to send an email. The point here is that this problem is solvable with Lambda (and possibly other services), but Step Functions makes this sort of task easier to implement and maintain.

LAMBDA FUNCTIONS FIRST

Let's look at how you'd design a basic Step Functions system that would satisfy the requirements of the example:

1 First, you'd need to create a Lambda function to execute your Step Functions state machine. You'd need to configure an S3 event to trigger this function, which would, in turn, run the state machine.

2 Next, you'd need to create the three Lambda functions to do image transformations. Each function would download the file from S3 to its local temporary storage, make needed changes, and then upload the new version back to S3. Each image-transformation function would also execute the callback function and pass in the name of the new file as the second parameter.

3 You'd also need to create an end state (Send Notification) function. This function would be invoked after the other three functions successfully completed their work. It would send an email using the Simple Email Service.

Figure 10.5 shows how these functions should be composed. The Start and the End labels in the diagram define where the Step Functions state machine begins and ends. The interesting part about it is the last Lambda function (Send Notification function). This function should execute only if the other three functions finish and terminate successfully. The fact that the Send Notification function will be invoked only if the other three functions succeed is important because it means that you don't need to maintain state. You don't need a database and don't need to manually keep track of successful/failed executions.

Before moving on to the next step, go into the AWS console and create the necessary functions we just described. You don't need to implement them immediately, but you need to create them so that you can reference their ARNs in your state machine.

CREATING STEP FUNCTIONS

To create a Step Functions state machine, find the Step Functions icon in the AWS console and click it. You can create your first state machine by clicking the blue Get Started button in the middle of the screen. In the Create State Machine screen, give

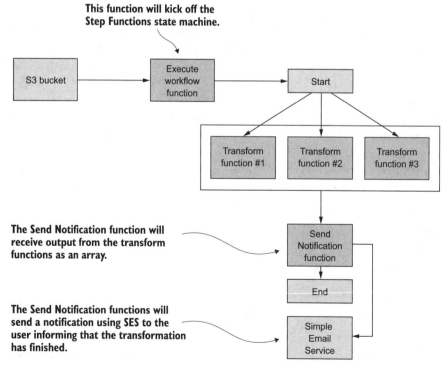

Figure 10.5   This is the design of the system in the AWS console, where you'll see a diagram representing your state machine.

your state machine a name. You'll also see blueprints designed to start you off. You can choose one and then continue to modify it in the code window.

Listing 10.1 shows an example of a state machine that matches your requirements. Copy and paste the listing to the code window in the console and then click the refresh button in the preview window to see an updated graph. This graph shows your state machine. If you make a mistake in your code (which is called the Amazon States Language), the graph will appear broken. Once you're satisfied with the state machine, click Create State Machine. You'll see a pop-up that will allow you to select or create an IAM role. Click the drop-down, select the role automatically provided for you, and then click OK.

Listing 10.1 Amazon States Language

```
{
  "Comment": "Using Amazon States Language using a
➥ parallel state to execute three branches at the same time",
  "StartAt": "Parallel",
  "States": {
    "Parallel": {
      "Type": "Parallel",
      "Next": "Final State",
      "Branches": [
        {
          "StartAt": "Transform 1",
          "States": {
            "Transform 1": {
              "Type": "Task",
              "Resource": "<TRANSFORM FUNCTION 1 ARN>",    ◁───┐
              "End": true
            }
          }
        },
        {
          "StartAt": "Transform 2",
          "States": {
            "Transform 2": {                                      Substitute with
              "Type": "Task",                                     the ARN of the
              "Resource": "<TRANSFORM FUNCTION 2 ARN>",   ◁───    tree transform
              "End": true                                         functions you
            }                                                     created earlier.
          }
        },
        {
          "StartAt": "Transform 3",
          "States": {
            "Transform 3": {
              "Type": "Task",
              "Resource": "<TRANSFORM FUNCTION 3 ARN>",   ◁───┘
              "End": true
            }
          }
        }
      ]
```

```
      ]
    },
    "Final State": {
      "Type": "Task",
      "Resource": "<SEND NOTIFICATION FUNCTION ARN>",
      "End": true
    }
  }
}
```

Substitute with the ARN of the Send Notification function.

RUNNING STEP FUNCTIONS

If you completed the steps outlined in the previous section, you'll end up on a screen from which you can run the state machine. You can choose the New Execution button to trigger an execution immediately. If you run an execution and it succeeds, it will look something like figure 10.6.

The graph is a useful visualization of the system (especially as it becomes more complex).

Review the input and the output of the state machine using tabs.

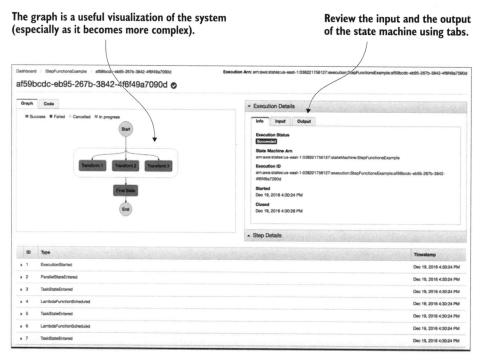

Figure 10.6   A successful execution of Step Functions. There's a bit of detail to explore for both successes and failures.

CONNECTING EVERYTHING ELSE

Having created a state machine in Step Functions, you still have a bit left to do. You need to create an S3 bucket, configure Simple Email Service, and write the actual Lambda functions. These are left for you as an exercise, but it's worth having a discussion about the Execute Workflow function. This is the function that executes your state machine after being triggered by an S3 event (it's also the only function in your system that's outside your state machine; see figure 10.5). The following code snippet does most of what you want. Note the params object in the listing. It specifies the ARN of the state machine you've created and the input parameters. These input parameters should be the bucket name and the object key.

Listing 10.2 Executing the Step Functions state machine

```
var AWS = require('aws-sdk');
var stepFunctions = new AWS.StepFunctions();

var params = {
    stateMachineArn: '<STATE MACHINE ARN>',
    input: "{'bucket':'serverless-image-transform', 'key':'image.png'}",
    name: 'MyTest'
};

stepFunctions.startExecution(params, function(err, data) {
    if (err) {
        callback(err);
    }
    else {
        callback(null, 'Step Functions executionARN: ' + data.executionArn);
    }
});
```

The ARN of the state machine created in the previous step

The input to the state machine: the bucket and the key

A label (or name) for the execution

The executionArn parameter can be used to check on ongoing or finished executions.

The startExecution function call in listing 10.2 is asynchronous. Your state machine could run for a long time, so the Lambda function can't wait for a result. You could, however, periodically enquire about the state of execution using executionArn returned by startExecution. The next listing shows the snippet of code that you could use to do it.

Listing 10.3 Describing execution with Step Functions

```
var AWS = require('aws-sdk');
var stepFunctions = new AWS.StepFunctions();

var params = {
    executionArn: '<STATE MACHINE EXECUTION ARN>'
};

stepFunctions.describeExecution(params, function(err, data) {
    if (err) console.log(err, err.stack);
    else     console.log(data);
}
```

Replace with the state machine execution ARN given by the startExecution function in listing 10.2.

Describes the state of the execution, including if it's finished and what the final output might be

As we noted earlier, the Send Notification function will run only when the three transformation functions have finished. The event object for the Send Notification function will contain an array of values. These values are whatever the other three functions pass to their callbacks. You could, for example, pass the key and the bucket of the transformed file in to the callback of each of the functions: `callback(null, {'bucket': 'my-bucket', 'key': 'thumbnail.png'})`. In the Send Notification function, you could extract the bucket names and object keys from the array and send them via SES.

WHAT'S NEXT WITH STEP FUNCTIONS

We've covered only the bare minimum when it comes to Step Functions. We've described how to build a simple parallel state machine, but you can do more with retry failure and catch failure, choice states, and wait states. We haven't discussed activities and how to connect Step Functions to code running on your own machine. If you're interested in learning more, look at the AWS documentation on Step Functions (https://aws.amazon.com/documentation/step-functions/) and check out the Amazon States Language, which will help you understand and quickly put together awesome state machines (https://states-language.net/spec.html).

10.4   *AWS Marketplace*

Among many interesting announcements made by AWS at the end of 2016 were the announcements about the integration of the API Gateway with the AWS Marketplace (https://aws.amazon.com/marketplace). Namely, AWS made a decision to allow people to monetize and sell their APIs on its online Marketplace. The idea is simple: build an API using the API Gateway, submit it to the Marketplace, and, if approved, earn money from it. AWS handles bill calculation and collection and then pays you on a regular basis. The API you build with the API Gateway can be anything you want, but AWS needs to approve it before it can be sold on the Marketplace. You can also make your API entirely serverless by combining API Gateway with Lambda (or other AWS services), or you can combine the API with your on-premises infrastructure or code running on EC2. The design and implementation are entirely up to you.

If you want to sell your API on the Marketplace, here are the high-level steps you'll need to carry out:

1 Create your API using API Gateway and any other products or services. You're not restricted to using AWS only. If you want to use Google's Vision API or IBM's Document Conversion Service, go ahead and use it.

2 Deploy the API and create usage plans. Usage plans allow you to set different limits and quotas. You can use this to create different subscription plans for your users.

3 Create and configure a developer portal for your users. This portal will list usage plans and allow your users to sign up for your service. When users sign up, your platform should create an API key for them.

4 Create an SaaS product in the AWS Marketplace and get it approved.

5 Integrate your AWS Marketplace product with the developer portal. The SaaS Seller Integration Guide (https://s3.amazonaws.com/awsmp-loadforms/SaaS+ Seller+Integration+Guide.pdf) details how to do it.

6 Launch your API and start earning a profit.

To make things easier to set up, AWS has published a sample developer portal on GitHub (https://github.com/awslabs/aws-api-gateway-developer-portal). You can clone this repository and use it to spin up the required Lambda functions, API Gateway, Cognito user pools, S3 buckets, and the website. This is easy to do because everything is automated and the instructions are provided in the repository. These instructions also describe how to configure the AWS Marketplace to work with the developer portal. Figure 10.7 shows what the sample developer portal looks like after your user has registered and logged in. You can, of course, customize the developer portal or come up with your own.

Another useful and in-depth guide to selling an API on the AWS Marketplace can be found in the official AWS documentation (https://docs.aws.amazon.com/apigateway/latest/developerguide/sell-api-as-saas-on-aws-marketplace.html). We're excited about the AWS Marketplace because everyone has an equal opportunity to build fantastic serverless SaaS products and make them available to the entire world. Let us know if you end up building a product and putting it on the AWS Marketplace.

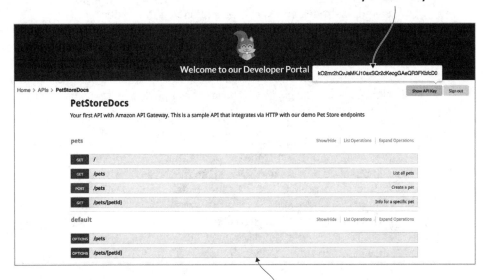

The API key created for your user.

Users can review and learn more about the API your product provides.

Figure 10.7 The sample developer portal provided by AWS is awesome for getting started quickly.

10.5   *Where from here*

We have good news for you! You've made it to the very end. We hope that you're proud of the journey you've made. You learned about serverless architectures and patterns; discovered services such as AWS Lambda, API Gateway, Auth0, and Firebase; and put together a fully working video-sharing website with security and a transcoding pipeline. You've had to read up on many different technologies, practices, and patterns. There's a lot to absorb and learn in this book, especially if this is your first exposure to serverless technologies and architectures. We find that the best way to learn is by doing, so take the 24-Hour Video system you've built and add new features to it. And if you do build something, reach out to us and tell us what you've done.

Advanced 24-Hour Video exercises

If you've completed the 24-Hour Video video-sharing website discussed in this book, here are some additional exercises you can try:

- Style the website to make it attractive for your users. Make sure that messages and warnings make sense and that users have a clear idea of what to do.
- Add a form to allow your users to edit and save their public information. This information may include a nickname and a picture. Put a link to the user's public profile next to the videos they've uploaded.
- Allow users to publish and unpublish videos they have uploaded, and allow them to set titles and short descriptions on their videos.
- Add an email notification system so that users know when their videos have been uploaded and published/unpublished (if you've implemented the previous exercise).
- Implement a view tracker to record how many views each video has had.
- Allow the user to specify which videos are private and which are public. Public videos can be viewed by anyone. Private videos require other users to log in before they can watch.
- Modify the Elastic Transcoder to create thumbnails of each video. Allow users to select one of the thumbnails and then use it to represent a video.
- Add an internal messaging system so that users can talk to each other. Users should get a notification from the system that they've received a message from another user and log in to the website to view messages.
- Add a tagging system so that users can tag videos with related keywords (for example, adventure, action, comedy, drama, and so on).
- Allow users to delete videos entirely.
- Add a search system to allow users to search for videos. It should search across titles, descriptions, and tags if these have been implemented.
- Create SAM templates for the functions you developed while reading this book.

Technology changes quickly, so it's great to have a few sites to go to for recent news and information. The website https://serverless.zone features a great collection of blogs regarding serverless architectures that you might find interesting. The same goes for the blog on A Cloud Guru (https://read.acloud.guru/serverless/) and the blog on the Serverless Framework website (https://serverless.com/blog). We also suggest keeping an eye on Serverlessconf (https://serverlessconf.io), which is the world's only conference dedicated exclusively to serverless technologies and architectures. Serverlessconf takes place all over the world and is a great place to meet organizations and individuals interested in advancing serverless architectures.

We hope you've enjoyed the book and learned something from it. Serverless architectures and technologies are still new, but awareness is growing rapidly. Over the next few years, you'll see many organizations, small and large, embrace serverless technologies to move quickly and reduce costs. And you'll see millions of startups built entirely on serverless technologies and architectures. This space is still new, so this is your opportunity to get in and to make a difference. You can become the next thought leader, the next big serverless innovator. We're excited by the opportunities and the potential, and we'll continue to observe how serverless technology matures and evolves over the coming years. This is the end of this book, but the beginning of an exciting serverless journey for all of us. Thank you for reading *Serverless Architectures on AWS*.

appendix A
Services for your
serverless architecture

This appendix covers

- Useful services for serverless architecture
- Products and services appropriate for source control and DevOps

AWS has an array of services that you can use for building serverless architectures. Lambda is a key service, but other services can be very useful, if not essential, for solving certain problems. There are many excellent non-AWS services too, which you should consider when putting together your architecture. The following is a sample of services that we've found useful, but it's not an exhaustive list. This book describes and shows how to use these services, and many others, to create robust serverless architectures. You can use this list as a quick reference if you find that we refer to a service somewhere in the book and you need a quick refresher on what it's all about.

A.1   API Gateway

The Amazon API Gateway is a service that you can use to create an API layer between the front-end and back-end services. The lifecycle management of the API Gateway allows multiple versions of the API to be run at the same time, and it supports multiple release stages such as development, staging, and production. API Gateway also comes with useful features like caching and throttling of requests.

The API is defined around resources and methods. A resource is a logical entity such as a user or product. A method is a combination of an HTTP verb, such as GET, POST, PUT, or DELETE, and the resource path. The API Gateway integrates with Lambda and, as you'll see in chapter 7, makes moving data in and out of Lambda straightforward. API Gateway can also connect to various AWS services via an AWS service proxy and forward requests to regular HTTP endpoints.

A.2   Simple Notification Service

Amazon Simple Notification Service (SNS) is a scalable pub-sub service designed to deliver messages. Producers or publishers create and send messages to a topic. Subscribers or consumers subscribe to a topic and receive messages over one of the supported protocols. SNS stores messages across multiple servers and data centers for redundancy and guarantees at-least-once delivery. At-least-once delivery stipulates that a message will be delivered at least once to a subscriber but, on rare occasions due to the distributed nature of SNS, it may be delivered multiple times.

In cases when a message can't be delivered by SNS to HTTP endpoints, it can be configured to retry deliveries at a later time. SNS can also retry failed deliveries to Lambda in cases where throttling is applied. SNS supports message payloads of up to 256 KB.

A.3   Simple Storage Service

Simple Storage Service (S3) is Amazon's scalable storage solution. Data in S3 is stored redundantly across multiple facilities and servers. The event notifications system allows S3 to send events to SNS, SQS, or Lambda when objects are created or deleted. S3 is secure by default, with only owners having access to the resources they create, but it's possible to set more granular and flexible access permissions using access control lists and bucket policies.

S3 uses the concept of buckets and objects. *Buckets* are high-level directories or containers for objects. *Objects* are a combination of data, metadata, and a key. A *key* is a unique identifier for an object in a bucket. S3 also supports the concept of a *folder* as a means of grouping objects in the S3 console. Folders work by using key name prefixes. A forward slash character "/" in the key name delineates a folder. For example, an object with the key name documents/personal/myfile.txt is represented as a folder called documents, containing a folder called personal, containing the file myfile.txt in the S3 console.

A.4   Simple Queue Service

Simple Queue Service (SQS) is Amazon's distributed and fault-tolerant queuing service. It ensures at-least-once delivery of messages similar to SNS and supports message payloads of up to 256 KB. SQS allows multiple publishers and consumers to interact with the same queue, and it has a built-in message lifecycle that automatically expires and deletes messages after a preset retention period. As with most AWS products, there are access controls to help control access to the queue. SQS integrates with SNS to automatically receive and queue messages.

A.5   Simple Email Service

Simple Email Service (SES) is a service designed to send and receive email. SES handles email-receiving operations such as scanning for spam and viruses and rejection of email from untrusted sources. Incoming email can be delivered to an S3 bucket, or used to invoke a Lambda notification or create an SNS notification. These actions can be configured as part of the receipt rule, which tells SES what to do with the email once it arrives.

Sending emails with SES is straightforward but there are limits, which are in place to regulate the rate and the number of messages being sent out. SES will automatically increase the quota as long as high-quality email, and not spam, is being sent.

A.6   Relational Database Service and DynamoDB

Amazon Relational Database Service (RDS) is a web service that helps with the setup and operation of a relational database in the AWS infrastructure. RDS supports the Amazon Aurora, MySQL, MariaDB, Oracle, MS-SQL, and PostgreSQL database engines. It takes care of routine tasks such as provisioning, backup, patching, recovery, repair, and failure detection. Monitoring and metrics, database snapshots, and multiple availability zone (AZ) support are provided out of the box. RDS uses SNS to deliver notifications when an event occurs. This makes it easy to respond to database events such as creation, deletion, failover, recovery, and restoration when they happen.

DynamoDB is Amazon's NoSQL solution. Tables, items, and attributes are Dynamo's main concepts. A table stores a collection of items. An item is made up of a collection of attributes. Each attribute is a simple piece of data such as a person's name or phone number. Every item is uniquely identifiable. Lambda integrates with DynamoDB tables and can be triggered by a table update.

A.7   CloudSearch

CloudSearch is a search solution from AWS that supports structured data and plain text. CloudSearch takes snippets of data as JSON or XML and generates an index that can be queried. This service supports Boolean, prefix, range, and full-text search, as well as faceting, highlighting, and autocomplete. Every document provided to Cloud-Search is supplied with an ID, generated by the user, that makes the document uniquely identifiable. Search requests can be carried out using GET requests. Results can be returned as JSON or XML, and they can be sorted and paginated and include useful metadata such as a relevance score.

A.8   Elastic Transcoder

Elastic Transcoder is an AWS service for transcoding media to other formats, resolutions, and bitrates. This service is useful if you need to have versions of your media playable on different devices. Elastic Transcoder comes with a number of presets, or templates, that define how a video should be transcoded. And, if needed, you can create your own.

Elastic Transcoder integrates with S3 and SNS, which it uses for notifications when a job is completed or an error condition is raised. Elastic Transcoder has additional features such as watermarking, transcoding of captions, and digital rights management support.

A.9   Kinesis Streams

Kinesis Streams is a service for real-time processing of streaming big data. It's typically used for quick log and data intake, metrics, analytics, and reporting. It's different from SQS in that Amazon recommends that Kinesis Streams be used primarily for streaming big data, whereas SQS is used as a reliable hosted queue, especially if more fine-grained control over messages, such as visibility timeouts or individual delays, is required.

In Kinesis Streams, shards specify the throughput capacity of a stream. The number of shards needs to be stipulated when the stream is created, but resharding is possible if throughput needs to be increased or reduced. In comparison, SQS makes scaling much more transparent. Lambda can integrate with Kinesis to read batches of records from a stream as soon as they're detected.

A.10   Cognito

Amazon Cognito is an identity management service. It integrates with public identity providers such as Google, Facebook, Twitter, and Amazon or with your own system. Cognito supports user pools, which allow you to create your own user directory. This allows you to register and authenticate users without having to run a separate user database and authentication service. Cognito supports synchronization of user application data across different devices and has offline support that allows mobile devices to function even when there's no internet access.

A.11   Auth0

Auth0 is a non-AWS identity management product that has a few features that Cognito doesn't. Auth0 integrates with more than 30 identity providers, including Google, Facebook, Twitter, Amazon, LinkedIn, and Windows Live. It provides a way to register new users through the use of its own user database, without having to integrate with an identity provider. In addition, it has a facility to import users from other databases.

As expected, Auth0 supports standard industry protocols including SAML, OpenID Connect, OAuth 2.0, OAuth 1.0, and JSON Web Token. It's dead simple to integrate with AWS Identity and Access Management and with Cognito.

A.12 *Firebase*

Firebase (owned by Google) is a company and also a suite of interesting products. One of the products that we particularly like is its NoSQL real-time database. Data in Firebase is stored as JSON. One of the nice things about Firebase is its real-time synchronization. It allows all connected users to receive updates as soon as they happen. Firebase can be accessed through a REST API and through client libraries, which are available for different languages and platforms. Firebase also has services for static hosting of files and authentication of users.

A.13 *Other services*

The list of services provided in this section is a short sample of the different products you can use to build your application. There are many more services, including those provided by large cloud-focused companies such as Google and Microsoft and smaller, independent companies like Auth0.

There are also auxiliary services that you need to be aware of. These can help you be more efficient and build software faster, improve performance, or achieve other goals. When building software, consider the following products and services:

- Content delivery networks (CDN) such as CloudFront
- DNS management (Route 53)
- Caching (ElastiCache)
- Source control (GitHub)
- Continuous integration and deployment (Travis CI)

For every service suggestion, you can find alternatives that may be just as good or even better, depending on your circumstances. We urge you to do more research and explore the various services that are currently available.

appendix B
Installation and setup

This appendix covers

- Identity and Access Management setup in AWS
- Creation of S3 buckets, Lambda functions, and Elastic Transcoder in AWS
- Local system setup and installation of the Node package manager
- Creation of package.json for a Lambda function

The purpose of this appendix is to help you set up your machine, environment, and AWS for the 24-Hour Video example that begins in chapter 3. 24-Hour Video will be referred to and improved throughout the book, so we highly recommend that you try to implement it to get a better understanding of serverless architecture.

Before you begin, there are two main prerequisites: a computer running Mac OSX, Linux, or Windows and a working internet connection. We'll take care of everything else as we journey through the book.

B.1   *Preparing your system*

In this appendix you're going to set up services in AWS and install software on your computer. Here's what you'll install on your machine:

- Node.js and its package manager (npm) to help manage Lambda functions and keep track of dependencies.
- AWS Command Line Interface (CLI) to help perform deployments.
- If you're a Windows user, you may also have to install a utility (such as Gnu-Win32) to create zip files out of Lambda functions to help with deployment.

In AWS you'll create the following:

- Identity and Access Management user and role
- S3 buckets to store video files
- The first Lambda function
- Elastic Transcoder pipeline to help encode videos

In chapter 3 and beyond you'll add additional Lambda functions and AWS services and install other npm modules to help with testing and development. This appendix may seem lengthy, but it explains a number of things that will help you throughout the book. If you've already used AWS, you'll be able to whiz through it quickly.

B.2   *Setting up an IAM user and CLI*

To begin, you need to have an AWS account, which you can create at https://aws.amazon .com. After your account is created, download and install the appropriate version of the AWS CLI for your system from http://docs.aws.amazon.com/cli/latest/userguide /installing.html. There are different ways to install the CLI, including an MSI installer if you're on Windows, via Pip (a Python-based tool), or via a bundled installer if you're on Mac or Linux. You'll also need to install Node.js. You can download it from https://nodejs.org/en/download/. The Node Package Manager (npm) comes bundled with Node.js.

The first action you need to do in AWS is create an Identity and Access Management (IAM) user. This user's security policy and credentials will be used to authorize deployment of Lambda functions from your computer straight to AWS. To create the user and set up correct permissions, follow these steps:

1 In the AWS console, click IAM (Identity and Access Management), click Users, and then click Add user.
2 Give your new IAM user a name such as `lambda-upload` and select the Programmatic access check box (figure B.1). Selecting this check box will allow you to generate the access key ID and the secret access key (you'll need these keys for `aws configure` in a few steps).
3 Click Next: Permissions to proceed.
4 Don't select anything in the Set Permissions for lambda-upload screen and click Next: Review to proceed.

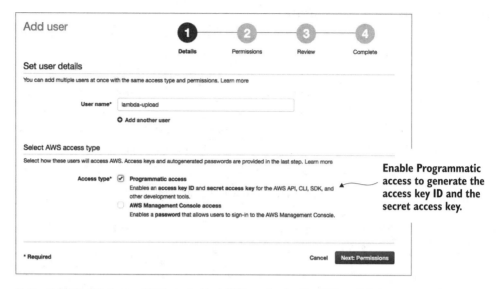

Figure B.1   Creating a new IAM user is straightforward using the IAM console.

5   On the final screen you'll see a message saying that the user has no permissions. That's okay for now. You'll address this later. Click Create User to finish the setup.

6   You should now see a table with the username, the access key ID, and the secret access key. You can also download a CSV file with these keys. Download it now to retain a copy of the keys on your computer, and click Close to exit (figure B.2).

7   Run `aws configure` from a terminal on your system. The AWS CLI will prompt for user credentials. Enter the access and secret keys generated for `lambda-upload` in the previous step.

8   You'll also be prompted to enter a region. Lambda may not be available in all regions, so choose a region where it is offered, such as us-east-1. We recommend that you use the same region for all services in your system (you'll find that it's cheaper). We recommend N. Virginia (us-east-1), and we'll assume for the duration of this appendix that you're using that region too.

9   There will be one more prompt asking you to select the default output format. Set it as `json` and finish the configuration.

B.3   *Setting user permissions*

You need to grant user `lambda-upload` permission to deploy Lambda functions. This includes creating a new inline policy, specifying permissions to allow function deployments, and attaching this policy to the IAM user:

1   In the IAM console, click Users, and click `lambda-upload`. You should land on the Permissions tab.

2   Click Add Inline Policy to create the first policy for your user (figure B.3).

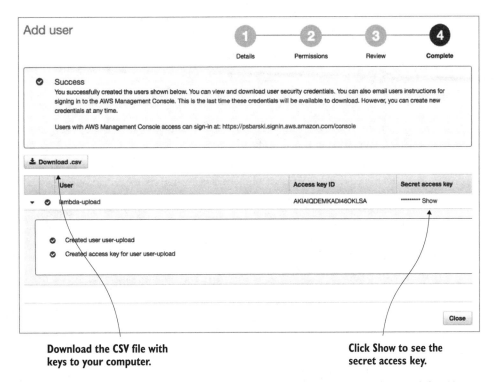

Download the CSV file with
keys to your computer.

Click Show to see the
secret access key.

Figure B.2 Remember to save the access key ID and the secret access key. You won't be able to
get the secret access key again once you close this window.

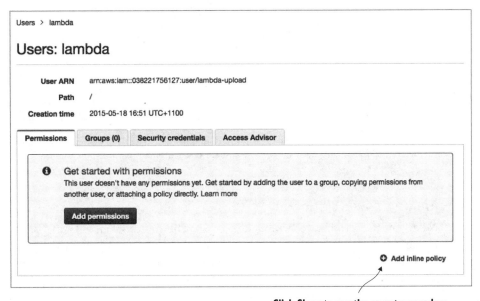

Click Show to see the secret access key.

Figure B.3 You'll begin by adding a new inline policy.

3 From the Inline Policy Options screen, select Policy Generator and then select AWS Lambda from the AWS Service drop-down.

4 From the Action drop-down choose the following three actions:
   – GetFunction
   – UpdateFunctionCode
   – UpdateFunctionConfiguration

5 In the Amazon Resource Name (ARN) text box enter `arn:aws:lambda:*` and then click Add Statement (figure B.4).

6 The Next Step button should become enabled, so click it to proceed to the Review Policy screen. Click Apply Policy to save and go back to the Summary screen.

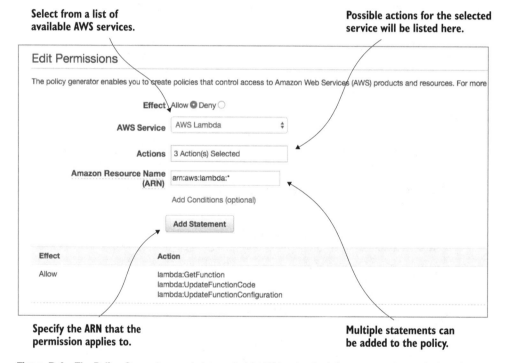

Select from a list of available AWS services.

Possible actions for the selected service will be listed here.

Specify the ARN that the permission applies to.

Multiple statements can be added to the policy.

Figure B.4   The Policy Generator can help you to identify and select the necessary permissions for your users and roles. The policy must have at least one statement before you can save it.

B.4   *Making new S3 buckets*

Next, you need to create two buckets in S3. The first bucket will serve as the upload bucket for new videos. The second bucket will contain transcoded videos put there by the Elastic Transcoder. All users of S3 share the same bucket namespace, which means that you have to come up with bucket names that are not in use. For this example, we'll assume that the first bucket is named `serverless-video-upload` and the second bucket is named `serverless-video-transcoded`.

Bucket names

Bucket names must be unique throughout the S3 global resource space. We've already taken `serverless-video-upload` and `serverless-video-transcoded`, so you'll need to come up with different names. We suggest adding your initials (or a random string of characters) to these bucket names to help identify them throughout the book (for example, `serverless-video-upload-ps` and `serverless-video-transcoded-ps`).

To create a bucket, in the AWS console click S3 and then click Create Bucket. Type in a name for the bucket and choose US East (N. Virginia) as the region (figure B.5). Continue clicking through the wizard (you don't need to specify any additional options) until you get to the end. Your bucket should immediately appear in the console.

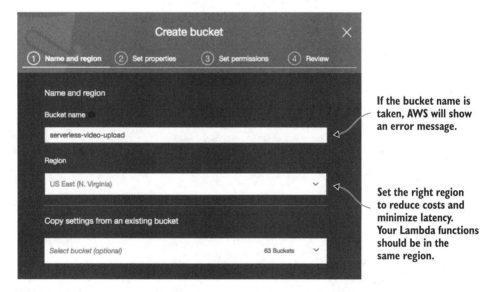

Figure B.5 Create two buckets from the S3 console. One must be for uploads. The other one will store transcoded videos. Bucket names are globally unique, so you'll have to come up with your own, new names.

New console vs. old console

There's a chance that when you click on S3 you'll see the old console, which doesn't look as nice as figure B.5. You can switch to the new console by clicking the Opt In link on the right side. This book assumes that you're using the new console unless we explicitly mention or ask you to switch to the old one.

B.5   *Creating an IAM role*

Now you need to create an IAM role for your future Lambda functions. This role will allow functions to interact with S3 and the Elastic Transcoder. You'll add two policies to this role: AWSLambdaExecute and AmazonElasticTranscoderJobsSubmitter. The AWSLambdaExecute policy allows Lambda to interact with S3 and CloudWatch. Cloud-Watch is an AWS service used for collecting log files, tracking metrics, and setting alarms. The AmazonElasticTranscoderJobsSubmitter policy allows Lambda to submit a new transcoding job to the Elastic Transcoder:

1   In the AWS console, click IAM, and then click Roles.
2   Click Create New Role and name it lambda-s3-execution-role. Click Next Step to proceed to Role Type selection.
3   Under the AWS Service Roles click AWS Lambda and then select the following two policies:
    – AWSLambdaExecute
    – AmazonElasticTranscoderJobsSubmitter
4   Click Next Step to attach both policies to the role, and then click Create Role to save.
5   You'll be taken back to the role summary page. Click lambda-s3-execution-role again to see the two attached policies (figure B.6).

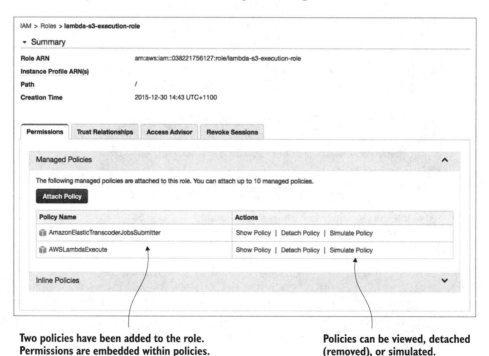

Two policies have been added to the role. Permissions are embedded within policies.

Policies can be viewed, detached (removed), or simulated.

Figure B.6   Two managed policies are needed for the lambda-s3-execution-role to access S3 and create Elastic Transcoder jobs.

B.6   *Preparing for Lambda*

It's finally time to create the first Lambda function, although we're not going to provide an implementation for it just yet. We'll provide the implementation in chapter 3. The plan, however, is for this function to be responsible for kicking off an Elastic Transcoder job when a new file is added to the upload (`serverless-video-upload`) bucket:

1   In the AWS console, click Lambda, and then click Create a Lambda Function.
2   Select the Blank Function blueprint.
3   On the Configure Triggers screen click Next. You'll configure a trigger at a later time.
4   Name the function `transcode-video` and make sure that Node.js 4.3 is selected in the Runtime drop-down.
5   Leave the Lambda function code as it is. If you delete this code, you won't be able to save (figure B.7).
6   Under Role select Choose an Existing Role and then in Existing Role select `lambda-s3-execution-role`.
7   Leave all Advanced settings as they are. Click Next to go the Review screen, and from there choose Create Function to finish.

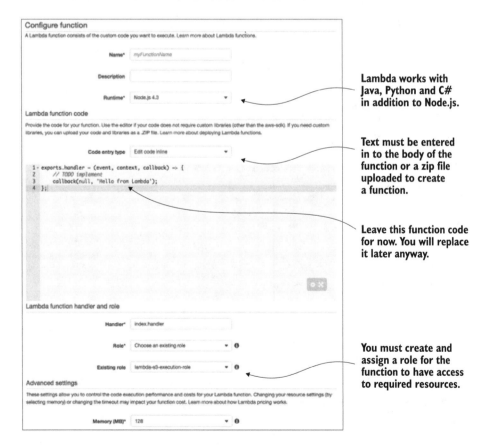

Figure B.7   A Lambda function can be created without specifying the implementation. You can deploy the completed function at a later stage.

B.7   *Configuring Elastic Transcoder*

Finally, you need to set up an Elastic Transcoder pipeline to perform video transcoding to different formats and bitrates:

1   In the AWS console click Elastic Transcoder and then click Create a New Pipeline.
2   Give your pipeline a name, such as 24 Hour Video, and specify the input bucket, which in our case is the upload bucket (`serverless-video-upload`).
3   Leave the IAM role as it is. Elastic Transcoder creates a default IAM role automatically.
4   Under Configuration for Amazon S3 Bucket for Transcoded Files and Playlists, specify the transcoded videos bucket, which in our case is `serverless-video-transcoded`. The Storage Class can be set to Standard.
5   You're not generating thumbnails but you should still select a bucket and a storage class. Use the second, transcoded videos bucket for it again (figure B.8).
6   Click Create Pipeline to save.

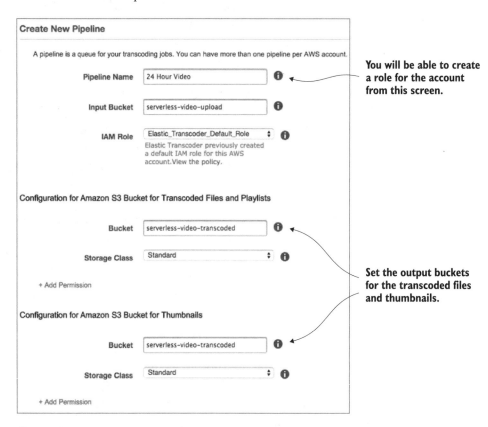

Figure B.8   Elastic Transcoder requires you to enter S3 bucket names for input, output, and thumbnails.

B.8   *Setting up npm*

Lambda functions can be written and then copied to AWS by hand, but that's not a sustainable way of managing development and performing deployments. You'll use npm to help test, package, and deploy functions to AWS automatically. If you prefer to use a task runner such as Grunt or Gulp in lieu of working with npm directly, you can, of course, instrument your environment to use one of those tools instead. But you'll use npm because it's capable of doing everything you need it to do and you won't need to worry about another utility.

Create a directory, such as transcode-video, for the first Lambda function. Open it in a terminal window, and run `npm init transcode-video`. You can accept defaults for all of the questions from `npm init` as long as you modify the package.json file to look like listing B.1. Open package.json in your favorite text editor and make sure to pay special attention to the dependencies section. If you're using Windows, read the information about zipping in the sidebar titled "Zip and Windows."

Zip and Windows

One important point to note is that in chapter 3 (and beyond) you're going to create zip files. You'll need to zip up Lambda functions (and their dependencies) to deploy them to AWS. In package.json you'll write a special predeploy script that will use the `zip` command to do this.

If you're using Linux or Mac, you should have zip preinstalled so you don't need to do anything. Windows users, however, may need to install zip, or a similar tool, themselves. One option is to download and install GnuWin32 zip from http://gnuwin32 .sourceforge.net/packages/zip.htm. You'll need to add the path for zip.exe to the Path system variable. See http://www.computerhope.com/issues/ch000549.htm for more information on how to set path and environment variables in Windows.

If you happen to have another file archiver, such as 7zip, you can try to use it instead. Make sure that it runs from the command line and change any zip parameter values in package.json that might be different for the tool you're using.

Another option is to find a zip archiver package in the npm registry, install it as a *dev dependency*, and use it instead. If you're on Windows this is your challenge!

After you've updated package.json to look like listing B.1, run `npm install` from the terminal to download and install the required dependency, which is the AWS SDK. The Lambda execution environment provides the AWS SDK (as well as ImageMagick) so you don't need to include it with the function when it's deployed. But you'll add it now because in chapter 3 you'll run and test the function locally and that will require the use of the SDK.

Listing B.1   Transcode video package.json

```
{
    "name": "transcode-video",
    "version": "1.0.0",
    "description": "Transcode Video Function",
    "main": "index.js",
    "scripts": {
      "test": "echo \"Error: no test specified\" && exit 1"
    },
    "dependencies": {                        There is one main dependency,
        "aws-sdk": "latest"           ◁───   which is the AWS SDK.
    },
    "author": "Peter Sbarski",
    "license": "BSD-2-Clause"
}
```

This is it for installation and configuration in appendix B. You can jump back to chapter 3 to begin putting together 24-Hour Video.

appendix C
More about authentication and authorization

This appendix covers

- Basics of authentication and authorization
- OAuth 2.0 flow
- JSON Web Tokens

This appendix serves as a short refresher on authentication and authorization. It describes the OAuth 2.0 flow process, the OpenID Connect protocol, and the inner workings of JSON Web Tokens.

C.1 Basics of authentication and authorization

In simple web and mobile applications, the back-end server is usually responsible for the authentication and authorization of users. A password authentication scheme may work as follows (figure C.1):

1 A user enters a username and password in a mobile application or a website.

2 The user's credentials are sent to the server. The application looks up the user in a database and validates the submitted password.

3 If validation succeeds, the server returns a cookie or a token with, optionally, embedded claims about the user. Claims are assertions about a user, which may include the user's unique identifier, role, email address, or any other useful or relevant information. If validation fails, the user is notified and prompted to reenter credentials.

4 Subsequent requests to the server are sent with the cookie or token provided by the server earlier. The system may inspect the cookie or the token for embedded claims, which can include the user's role or arbitrary information needed to decide whether the user can perform an action. Alternatively, the system can look up the user's role in a database to grant authorization to perform an action.

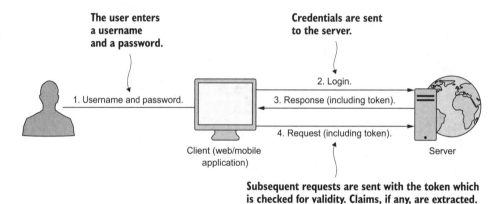

Figure C.1 This simple cookie/token forms authentication flow is familiar to all developers.

In more complex scenarios additional systems or steps may be involved. OpenID, for example, is an open standard authentication protocol designed to allow users to authenticate via a third-party service (an OpenID identity provider) instead of having to develop a custom sign-in system. OpenID Connect adds an authentication layer on top of OAuth 2.0. A protocol like OpenID Connect is needed to enforce security and bridge the gap between authentication and authorization. Although it might seem that OAuth 2.0 could be used for authorization as well as authentication, it would be a mistake to assume that. Having an authorization system without an authentication component could lead to attackers gaining improper access to resources. Figure C.2 shows what an OpenID Connect flow looks like.

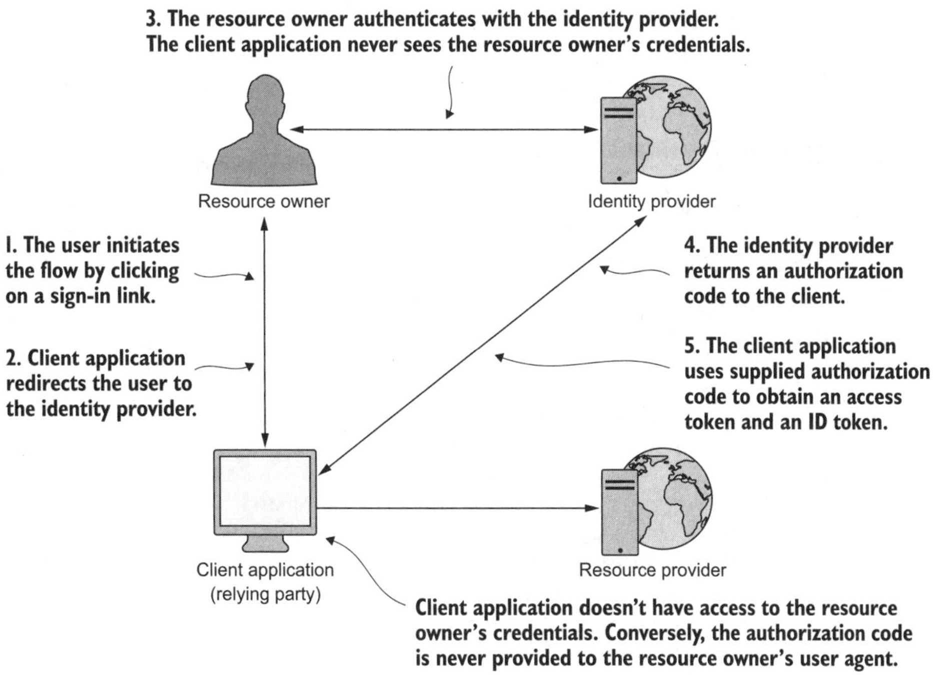

**3. The resource owner authenticates with the identity provider.
The client application never sees the resource owner's credentials.**

Resource owner

Identity provider

I. The user initiates the flow by clicking on a sign-in link.

4. The identity provider returns an authorization code to the client.

2. Client application redirects the user to the identity provider.

5. The client application uses supplied authorization code to obtain an access token and an ID token.

Client application
(relying party)

Resource provider

Client application doesn't have access to the resource owner's credentials. Conversely, the authorization code is never provided to the resource owner's user agent.

Figure C.2   OpenID Connect is an authentication protocol based on OAuth 2.0. It's widely supported in the industry and is used by services such as Auth0.

Authentication vs. authorization

What's the difference between authentication and authorization? Authentication is the process of verifying who the user is; for example, confirming that user Bob is who he represents himself to be. Authorization is about verifying what the user is allowed to do. Is Bob allowed to view this page? Is Bob allowed to delete a database record? Authentication and authorization are independent concepts (authenticated and non-authenticated users can be authorized to do different things) but are often linked in discussions about security.

OpenID is mainly concerned with authentication. OAuth is mainly about authorization. OpenID Connect is an extension of OAuth 2.0 designed to bring authentication and authorization together. For a more detailed explanation, see https://oauth.net/articles/authentication/.

OAuth 2.0 grant types

The OAuth 2.0 specification (https://tools.ietf.org/html/rfc6749), which is used by OpenID Connect, defines four different grant types for different authorization scenarios:

- *Authorization* code for applications running on a web server including server-side rendered web apps: This is a common grant type that implements three-legged OAuth. If you've used GitHub, Google, Facebook, or another identity provider to sign in to a website or application, then you've experienced it.

  In an authorization code grant, an authorization server—or the IdP—acts as an intermediary between the client (that is, the website or application that the user wants to log on to) and the resource owner (that is, the user). When the user signs in to the authorization server, they're redirected to the client with an authorization code, which the client captures and exchanges with the authorization server for an access token. A client can then access a resource server with the access token and retrieve protected resources.

- *Implicit* for mobile or browser-based JavaScript-only apps that can't be trusted with maintaining client secrets: The implicit grant type is a simplified variation of the authorization code flow. As before, the user is redirected to the authorization server to sign in, but instead of the server returning an authentication code, the client is immediately sent an access token. The implicit grant type is needed for the class of applications where the client is unable to store secrets. But there are security implications to using the implicit grant type. It should be used as a second choice when the authorization code grant type is unavailable.

- *Resource owner credentials* for directly logging in to a client with a username and password: This is similar to the type of authentication shown in figure C.1. A resource owner provides credentials directly to the client, which exchanges them for an access token.

- *Client credentials* for accessing resources outside any user's specific context: This grant type is useful for machine-to-machine authorization where the client uses its own credentials as an authorization grant.

C.2   JSON Web Token

JSON Web Token (https://tools.ietf.org/html/rfc7519) is an open standard used to transport claims between parties. These tokens have properties that make them useful in serverless systems:

- JWT is URL-safe by design. Tokens can be passed in the body of the request or in the URL query.
- JWT is compact and self-contained.
- JWT can be digitally signed to guarantee integrity and encrypted to guarantee confidentiality.
- JWT is an open standard and the tokens are easy to create and parse. Libraries are available for JavaScript and other languages.

Claims are encoded in JWT as a JSON object and are sent as a JSON Web Signature (JWS) or JSON Web Encryption (JWE) structure. The JWS payload is digitally signed by the entity creating the token to prevent tampering. The JWT spec defines support for symmetric and asymmetric signing algorithms. Tokens created with an asymmetric signing algorithm can be verified using a public key on a client. Naturally, JWT signed with a symmetric algorithm requires the secret signing key to validate the signature. These can't be exposed to clients, but you can use them in a Lambda function to validate the token.

It's also important to note that in JWS the claims (payload) portion is not encrypted in any way. It's only Base64-encoded so it can be trivially inspected and read. Do not send any sensitive information in it. JWE, on the other hand, encrypts the content of the message instead of digitally signing it. It's possible to encrypt the JWT claims and then embed them in a JWS if you want to enforce confidentiality and integrity at the same time.

JWT consists of three segments: header, body, and signature. Figure C.3 shows what a JWT token looks like and points out how to identify each segment.

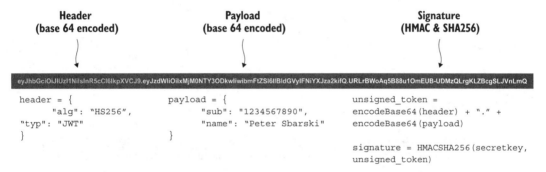

Figure C.3   The JWT structure is composed of three segments separated by a period.

The header of JWT is composed of two parts: the declaring type (JWT) and the hashing algorithm. The payload consists of JWT claims. There's a set of reserved claims that, although not mandatory, is useful to have. Auth0, for example, includes the following minimum subset of claims in every token:

- *iss*—Issuer of the token
- *sub*—Subject of the token
- *aud*—Audience expected to consume the token
- *exp*—Expiration time
- *iat*—Issued-at timestamp

Finally, the signature is used to verify the integrity of the token. Typical JWT implementations support signature computation using HMAC with the SHA-256 cryptographic hash function (HS256) or RSA with SHA-256 (RS256).

The website jwt.io has an interactive debugger (figure C.4) for testing whether you have correctly generated your symmetric or asymmetric JWT. It also lists available libraries for token signing/verification for different languages and platforms.

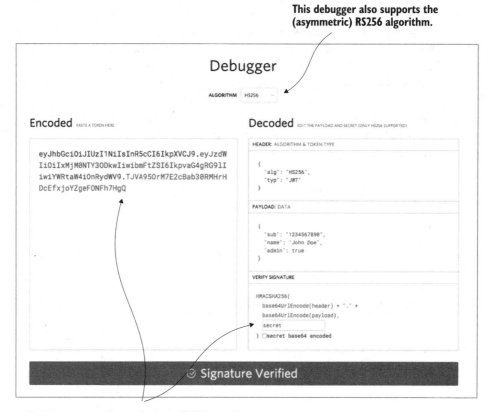

This debugger also supports the (asymmetric) RS256 algorithm.

Test if you properly encoded your JWT by pasting in the token and setting the secret key.

Figure C.4   The jwt.io debugger allows you to test your JSON Web Tokens. You can change the payload and the header to see how the token changes.

appendix D
Lambda insider

This appendix covers

- Execution environment
- Lambda's limitations
- Older runtimes

Chapter 6 focuses on AWS Lambda, but it's a rather vast topic, so we had to omit some things. This appendix covers information not included in chapter 6, such as information about Lambda's execution environment, inherent limitations, and older runtimes.

D.1 Execution environment

At the time we wrote this appendix, Lambda ran on Amazon Linux with kernel version 4.1.17-22.30.amzn1.x86-24. If you're like us, you might be interested in peeking under the hood and exploring the environment that Lambda has to offer. Luckily, we can get a bit of understanding of what's under the covers by running shell commands. To try this yourself, do the following:

1 Open the Lambda console, and click Create a Lambda Function.
2 In the Blueprint Selection screen, type node-exec. That should filter the available blueprint functions to just one function named node-exec.
3 Click the node-exec function.
4 Click Next on the Configure Triggers screen.
5 Give your new function a name (for example, run-command).
6 In the Role section, select an existing role or create a new one. Your function will not interact with other AWS resources, so it can take on a basic role.
7 Click the Next button and then click Create Function.

You can now run this function and pass in commands you want the function to execute:

1 Make sure you're looking at the run-command function in the console, click Actions, and click Configure Test Event.
2 The event object needs to have a key called cmd and the command to execute. The following listing shows an example of an event object that will execute ls -al. You can replace ls -al with any shell command you wish to execute.

Listing D.1   Event object to run the ls command

```
{
    "cmd" : "ls -al"
}
```

Table D.1 shows the output if you run a few common commands.

Table D.1   System and environmental information for your container

Command	Purpose	Abbreviated output
uname -a	Prints system information.	Linux ip-10-0-95-167 4.1.17-22.30.amzn1.x86_64 #1 SMP Fri Feb 5 23:44:22 UTC 2016 x86_64 x86_64 x86_64 GNU/Linux
pwd	Prints the current working directory.	/var/task
ls -al	Lists the contents of current directory.	drwxr-xr-x 2 slicer 497 4096 Apr 4 10:10 . drwxr-xr-x 20 root root 4096 Apr 4 09:04 .. -rw-rw-r-- 1 slicer 497 478 Apr 4 10:09 index.js
env	Prints shell and environmental variables.	AWS_SESSION_TOKEN=FQoDYXd... AWS_LAMBDA_LOG_GROUP_NAME=/aws/lambda/run2 LAMBDA_TASK_ROOT=/var/task LD_LIBRARY_PATH=/usr/local/lib64/node-v4.3.x/lib:/lib64:/usr/lib64:/var/runtime:/var/runtime/lib:/var/task:/var/task/lib AWS_LAMBDA_LOG_STREAM_NAME=2017/01/23/[$LATEST]a6 5f9e2f349d4e9a8c9e193b0e175e78

Table D.1 System and environmental information for your container *(continued)*

Command	Purpose	Abbreviated output

env
(continued)
		`AWS_LAMBDA_FUNCTION_NAME=run_command`
		
		`PATH=/usr/local/lib64/node-`
		`v4.3.x/bin:/usr/local/bin:/usr/bin/:/bin`
		
		`AWS_DEFAULT_REGION=us-east-1`
		
		`PWD=/var/task`
		
		`AWS_SECRET_ACCESS_KEY=G9zLllGtxmL4...`
		
		`LAMBDA_RUNTIME_DIR=/var/runtime`
		
		`LANG=en_US.UTF-8`
		
		`NODE_PATH=/var/runtime:/var/task:/var/runtime/`
		`node_modules`
		
		`AWS_REGION=us-east-1`
		
		`AWS_ACCESS_KEY_ID=ASIAIKGQE5YIXTNE54JQ`
		
		`SHLVL=1`
		
		`AWS_LAMBDA_FUNCTION_MEMORY_SIZE=128`
		
		`_=/usr/bin/env`

cat
/proc/cpuinfo
	Prints the type of processor used by the system.	`processor        : 0`
		`vendor_id        : GenuineIntel`
		`cpu family       : 6`
		`model            : 63`
		`model name       : Intel(R) Xeon(R) CPU E5-2666`
		`v3 @ 2.90GHz`
		`stepping         : 2`
		`microcode        : 0x36`
		`cpu MHz          : 2900.074`
		`cache size       : 25600 KB`
		`physical id      : 0`
		`siblings         : 2`
		`core id          : 0`
		`cpu cores        : 1`
		`apicid           : 0`
		`initial apicid   : 0`
		`fpu              : yes`
		`fpu_exception    : yes`
		`cpuid level      : 13`
		`wp               : yes`
		`flags            : fpu vme de pse tsc msr pae`
		`mce cx8 apic sep mtrr pge mca cmov pat pse36`
		`clflush mmx fxsr sse sse2 ht syscall nx pdpe1gb`
		`rdtscp lm constant_tsc rep_good nopl xtopology`
		`eagerfpu pni pclmulqdq ssse3 fma cx16 pcid sse4_1`
		`sse4_2 x2apic movbe popcnt tsc_deadline_timer aes`
		`xsave avx f16c rdrand hypervisor lahf_lm abm`
		`fsgsbase bmi1 avx2 smep bmi2 erms invpcid xsaveopt`
		`bogomips         : 5800.14`
		`clflush size     : 64`

Table D.1 System and environmental information for your container *(continued)*

Command	Purpose	Abbreviated output
cat /proc/cpuinfo *(continued)*		cache_alignment : 64 address sizes : 46 bits physical, 48 bits virtual
		processor : 1 vendor_id : GenuineIntel cpu family : 6 model : 63 model name : Intel(R) Xeon(R) CPU E5-2666 v3 @ 2.90GHz stepping : 2 microcode : 0x36 cpu MHz : 2900.074 cache size : 25600 KB physical id : 0 siblings : 2 core id : 0 cpu cores : 1 apicid : 1 initial apicid : 1 fpu : yes fpu_exception : yes cpuid level : 13 wp : yes flags : fpu vme de pse tsc msr pae mce cx8 apic sep mtrr pge mca cmov pat pse36 clflush mmx fxsr sse sse2 ht syscall nx pdpe1gb rdtscp lm constant_tsc rep_good nopl xtopology eagerfpu pni pclmulqdq ssse3 fma cx16 pcid sse4_1 sse4_2 x2apic movbe popcnt tsc_deadline_timer aes xsave avx f16c rdrand hypervisor lahf_lm abm fsgsbase bmi1 avx2 smep bmi2 erms invpcid xsaveopt bogomips : 5800.14 clflush size : 64 cache_alignment : 64 address sizes : 46 bits physical, 48 bits virtual
ls /var/runtime/ node_modules	Lists included NodeJS modules. You do not need to provide these modules with your function.	awslambda aws-sdk dynamodb-doc imagemagick

D.2 Limitations

Lambda executes code and scales automatically. It can handle thousands of requests per second. As with any system, however, there are limitations to think about. Table D.2 summarizes these. You can find the original AWS documentation related to Lambda's limits at https://docs.aws.amazon.com/lambda/latest/dg/limits.html.

Table D.2 Lambda limits

What is it?	Default limit	Explanation
Ephemeral disk capacity (/tmp space)	512 MB	The total disk capacity you can use for temporary files
Number of file descriptors	1024	Maximum number of files that can be opened by the function
Number of processes and threads (combined total)	1024	Maximum number of threads and processes that can be spawned by the function
Maximum execution duration per request	300 seconds	The maximum number of seconds the function can execute for before it's killed by the runtime
Invoke request body payload size (RequestResponse)	6 MB	The maximum size of the request when the function is invoked using the AWS SDK, the API Gateway, or the console
Invoke request body payload size (Event)	128 K	The maximum size of the request when the function is invoked by an event in AWS
Invoke response body payload size (RequestResponse)	6 MB	The maximum size of the response when the function is invoked using the AWS SDK, API Gateway, or the console

D.3 Working with older runtimes

AWS initially released Lambda, which used Node.js 0.10.42. That version of Lambda didn't support the `callback` function. Instead, methods (`succeed`, `fail`, and `done`) available via the context object allowed the developer to cleanly terminate the function and return data to the caller. If you happen to come across a version of a Lambda function that uses the old Node.js 0.10.42 runtime, here's what you need to know to use it correctly.

To properly terminate a Lambda function, you need to invoke one of the following three methods (this is different from the Node.js 4.3 or 6.10 versions where you can use `callback`):

- `context.succeed(Object result)`
- `context.fail(Error error)`
- `context.done(Error error, Object result)`

You must always terminate the function using a succeed, fail, or done function. If you don't do that, your function may continue to run even after you think it's finished.

D.3.1 *Succeed*

The context.succeed(Object result) method is called to indicate that the function has successfully finished execution. The result parameter is optional (you can use context.succeed() or context.succeed(null)), but it must be compatible with JSON.stringify if you decide to include it.

In case of a RequestResponse invocation type, calling this method will return an HTTP status 200 (OK). The body of the response will be set to the stringified version of result.

D.3.2 *Fail*

The context.fail(Error error) method is called to indicate that the function failed. Calling this function raises a handled exception. The error parameter is optional (you can leave it out or use a null). In the case of RequestResponse, if this parameter is provided, Lambda will try to stringify it and include it as the response body. It will set the HTTP status code to 400 (Bad Request) and also log the first 256 KB of the error object to CloudWatch.

D.3.3 *Done*

Finally, there's the context.done(Error error, Object result) method. This method can be used in lieu of the succeed and fail methods. The error and result parameters are optional. If a non-null value is provided for the error parameter, this function is treated the same way as context.fail(error). If the error parameter is null, then the function is treated as a context.succeed(result) method.

appendix E
Models and mapping

This appendix covers

- API Gateway models and mapping

Chapter 7 gives you a thorough look at the API Gateway. In that chapter you get to create a resource and a GET method, connect it to a Lambda function, and use Lambda proxy integration. Lambda proxy integration makes it straightforward to invoke a Lambda function via the API Gateway and to return a response. Most of the logic takes place in the function, with the Gateway proxying the request to the function and the response to the client.

The API Gateway doesn't force you to use Lambda proxy integration, however. You can decide how to transform requests and responses within the Gateway and have more control over what goes out of the Gateway. This appendix gives you information about how to implement models and mappings and teaches you other tips and tricks not covered in chapter 7.

E.1   Get video list

If you implemented the `get-video-list` function in chapter 7, this is an alternative way of showing how to do the same thing without proxy integration. To get started, we'll assume that you've created the /videos resource and a GET method. You can begin following this appendix instead of section 7.2.3. There's one important point to mention here, though: if you enabled Lambda proxy integration when creating the GET method, you must now turn it off. To do this, click the GET method under the /videos resource, and then click Integration Request. Make sure to unselect Use HTTP Proxy Integration if it's selected.

E.1.1   GET method

We're going to take things step by step, because there are more elements to configure in the API Gateway than if you were using proxy integration. Right now, click the GET method under /videos to see the Method Execution view.

METHOD REQUEST

The first step is to update the settings in your method request. Choose Method Request from the Method Execution view to access its configuration. You can do a number of things here:

- Set authorization settings, including the custom authorizer as you did in chapter 5.
- Add support for a URL query string parameter.
- Add support for a custom HTTP request header.
- Add support for a request model. This is used for non-GET method types, so you can ignore it for now.

Your `get-video-list` function doesn't take any parameters at the moment, but let's imagine that it can take an optional `encoding`. It needs to return a list of videos specific for that encoding (for example, just 720p videos if `encoding` is set to `720p`). If `encoding` is not specified, then the function will return all videos just as it does now. Let's also say that the `encoding` is supplied via the URL. Here's how you'd set it up:

1 Expand URL Query String Parameters.
2 Choose Add Query String.
3 Type `encoding` and click the round checkmark button to save.
4 Don't enable caching yet because you need to think through your cache-invalidation strategy first. Enabling this Caching check box will create a specific cache key when caching is enabled for the stage (figure E.1).

INTEGRATION REQUEST

Integration Request is the next page you need to step through. You've already configured the Lambda function to invoke. All that's left to do is configure the body mapping template. This mapping template tells the API Gateway how to transform the request, including elements such as headers and query strings, into a format the consuming service can understand. Our example has a URL query string called `encoding`.

Set whether an API key needs to be included in the request to allow it to continue. API keys can be added in the API Gateway console.

Caching can be enabled for a set of different parameters including URL paths and query strings. Cache invalidation needs to be thought through if you enable it.

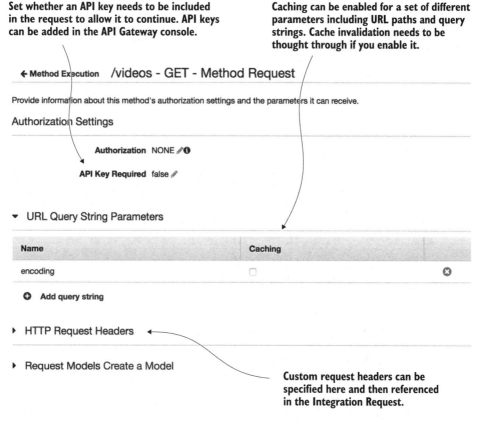

Figure E.1 The Method Request page defines the interface and settings that the caller of the API must respect and provide.

You might want to map it to a property called encoding on the event object that your Lambda function can access:

1 Access Integration Request from the Method Execution window.
2 Expand Body Mapping Templates.
3 Choose Add Mapping Template.
4 Type application/json into the Content-Type text box and click the checkmark button to save.
5 Click Yes, Secure This Integration if a dialog presents asking to change passthrough behavior.
6 On the right side, you should see an edit box in which you can specify the mapping. To map encoding to be available via the event object, copy the contents of listing E.1 to the text box and choose Save. The "Payload mapping" sidebar

and AWS documentation (https://docs.aws.amazon.com/apigateway/latest/developerguide/api-gateway-mapping-template-reference.html) describe mapping in greater detail.

Listing E.1   Mapping URL query string

```
{
    "encoding" :
    "$input.params('encoding')"          ◁──┐
}
```
| The $input.params('encoding') method looks
at the path, the query string, and the header
value for a property called encoding.

Payload mapping

The API Gateway API Request and Response Payload-Mapping Template Reference (https://docs.aws.amazon.com/apigateway/latest/developerguide/api-gateway-mapping-template-reference.html) is full of interesting tidbits. Not only can you extract values from the request (including those from the path, query string, or header), but you can also do quite a bit more; for example:

- `$input.body` returns the raw payload as a string.
- `$input.json(value)` evaluates a JSONPath expression and returns the result as a JSON string.
- `$input.params()` returns a map of all request parameters.

You also have access to the `$context` variable, which has a lot of useful information about the API call. You have information about the identity of the caller (if it's provided), the HTTP method, and the gateway deployment stage from which the API call is originating.

Finally, you have access to the `$util` variable, which contains a few useful utility functions:

- `$util.escapeJavaScript()` escapes characters in a string (using JavaScript string rules).
- `$util.parseJson()` takes a stringified JSON representation and produces a JSON object.
- `$util.urlEncode()` and `$util.urlDecode()` convert a string to and from application/x-www-form-urlencoded format.
- `$util.base64Encode()` and `$util.base64Decode()` encode and decode base64-encoded data.

API Gateway offers a shortcut so you don't need to specify values individually. This might be useful if you have numerous parameters and don't want to maintain a complex mapping.

In the drop-down box next to Generate Template, select Method Request Passthrough. The API Gateway will set a template for you that maps "all parameters including path, querystring, header, stage variables, and context…" (https://docs

.aws.amazon.com/apigateway/latest/developerguide/api-gateway-mapping-template-reference.html; see figure E.2).

In most cases, however, you should craft your own mapping and not pass everything through to the endpoint. We did it in this example to show you the syntax, methods, and parameters that you can apply.

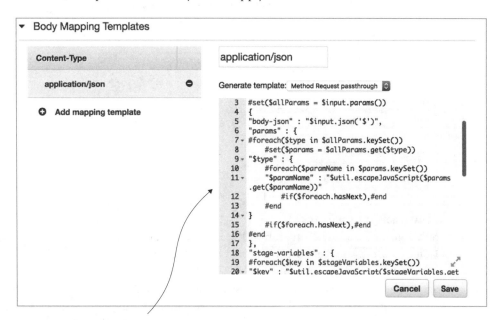

This template will map every parameter but it's also less efficient.

Figure E.2 The easy way is to map everything. It will add extra parameters that you may not necessarily need to the event object. You might notice that this is similar to what you get when using Lambda proxy integration.

If you use Method Request Passthrough to get all parameters passed to the integration point, you can review what it looks like by logging the event object using CloudWatch. The following listing shows some of the properties you can access.

Listing E.2 Method Request Passthrough

```
{
    'body-json': '{}',
    params: {
        path: {},
        querystring: {
            encoding: 'some-encoding'
        },
        header: {}
    },
    'stage-variables': {},
```

Properties such as header, path, and body-json will be populated if they exist and are specified via Method Request.

```
context: {
    'account-id': '038221756127',
    'api-id': 'tlzyo7a7o9',
    'api-key': 'test-invoke-api-key',
    'authorizer-principal-id': '',
    caller: '038221756127',
    'cognito-authentication-provider': '',
    'cognito-authentication-type': '',
    'cognito-identity-id': '',
    'cognito-identity-pool-id': '',
    'http-method': 'GET',
    stage: 'test-invoke-stage',
    'source-ip': 'test-invoke-source-ip',
    user: '038221756127',
    'user-agent': 'Apache-HttpClient/4.3.4 (java 1.5)',
    'user-arn': 'arn:aws:iam::038221756127:root',
    'request-id': 'test-invoke-request',
    'resource-id': 'e3r6ou',
    'resource-path': '/videos'
  }
}
```

> The context reveals much (potentially) useful information, such as the resource-path and http-method.

INTERMISSION—LET'S DO A TEST

You've now configured Integration Request and Method Request. That's enough for you to do a test, so take a breather and check if you're on the right track.

In the Method Execution page, choose Test on the left side. You'll be taken to a page from which you can execute a test against your GET method. If you've defined the encoding query string, you'll see a text box in which you can enter a value to test it. For the moment, it does nothing, so you can leave it alone. Instead, click the Test button at the bottom of the page. You'll see a response body on the right side (figure E.3).

INTEGRATION RESPONSE

It's now time to look at the response that will be sent back to the client. As you begin using the API Gateway more and more, you might come across a scenario where the client expects data in a different format than what the API Gateway receives from its integration point. If you have complete control over the client, then it may be okay. You can modify the client and make it handle the response. But what if you don't have control over the client? Luckily, the API Gateway has the ability to transform one schema to another. You already saw glimpses of this when you configured the Integration Request. But what you did was pretty ad hoc. To build a more-solid system, you can define a model (or a schema) and build a robust mapping template to transform data from one format to another.

If you look at the current response from the API Gateway (figure E.3), you'll see an object with two properties (baseUrl and bucket) and an array of URLs. Each URL has five properties (Key, LastModified, Etag, Size, and StorageClass). Let's come up

Status: 200

Latency: 282 ms

Response Body

The response from the Lambda function is immediately shown.

```
{
  "baseUrl": "https://s3.amazonaws.com",
  "bucket": "serverless-video-transcoded",
  "urls": [
    {
      "Key": "3c1ca92d80155aba1b491422a8323b1da73ba84e/disney-1080p.mp4",
      "LastModified": "2017-01-03T11:16:10.000Z",
      "ETag": "\"66cfbeb5fcf1357117b663c1780ec52c\"",
      "Size": 4095570,
      "StorageClass": "STANDARD"
    },
    {
      "Key": "3c1ca92d80155aba1b491422a8323b1da73ba84e/disney-720p.mp4",
      "LastModified": "2017-01-03T11:16:10.000Z",
      "ETag": "\"f1fbd75f4595b610f422c0e514d34016\"",
      "Size": 1874203,
      "StorageClass": "STANDARD"
    },
    {
      "Key": "3c1ca92d80155aba1b491422a8323b1da73ba84e/disney-web-720p.mp4",
      "LastModified": "2017-01-03T11:16:07.000Z",
      "ETag": "\"ab997865386fed24065e4d3dbccd71d0\"",
      "Size": 1861741,
      "StorageClass": "STANDARD"
    }
  ]
}
```

Figure E.3   The test page is an excellent tool for testing whether your API has been correctly configured.

with a different schema that reduces the amount of data you need to send back to the client and makes things a little more obvious. Here's what you want to do:

- Rename baseUrl to domain.
- Rename URLs as files.
- Rename Key to filename.
- Remove LastModified (you already have an ETag) and StorageClass.

First, you need to create a model in the API Gateway:

1 Choose Models on the right side under 24-Hour Video.
2 Click the Create button.
3 Enter a model name such as GetVideoList.
4 Set Content Type to application/json, and enter a description if you wish (figure E.4).

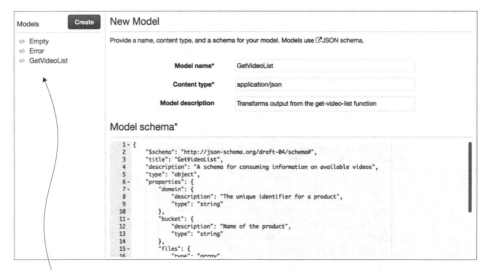

You can create as many models as
you wish to use across your API.

Figure E.4   Models, which use JSON Schema, define the output format for your data.

API Gateway uses JSON Schema (http://json-schema.org/) to define the expected format. If your schema conforms to JSON Schema v4 (http://json-schema.org/latest/
json-schema-core.html), everything should work. You can always check if your schema
is correct by running it through the online JSON Schema Validator (http://www
.jsonschemavalidator.net/). For now, copy the schema from the next listing to the
Model Schema editor and click Create Model.

Listing E.3   GetVideoList JSON Schema

```
{
    "$schema": "http://json-schema.org/draft-04/schema#",
    "title": "GetVideoList",
    "description": "A schema for consuming information on available videos",
    "type": "object",
    "properties": {
        "domain": {
            "description": "The unique identifier for a product",
            "type": "string"
        },
        "bucket": {
            "description": "Name of the product",
            "type": "string"
        },
        "files": {
            "type": "array",
            "items": {
                "type": "object",
                "properties": {
                    "filename": {
```

Most of the
properties
are optional
but are
typically
included by
convention.

Some things are mandatory, and the API Gateway
won't let you save if you don't form your schema
correctly. For example, if you define "type" as an
array, you must also have "items" defined.

```
                "type": "string"
            },
            "eTag": {
                "type": "string"
            },
            "size": {
                "type": "integer",
                "minimum": 0
            }
          }
        }
      }
    },
    "required": ["domain", "bucket"]
}
```

After creating the schema, follow these steps to modify Integration Response:

1 Choose Resources under 24-Hour Video.
2 Choose GET under /videos.
3 Choose Integration Response.
4 Expand the response type (it should be the one with the Method response status of 200) and then expand Body Mapping Templates.
5 Choose application/json and then from the Generate Template drop-down select GetVideoList. The text box below the drop-down should autopopulate with a bit of code. Update this code to make it work with your model (refer to listing E.4 and see figure E.5).
6 Click Save when you've finished.

One thing to be aware of: API Gateway supports JSONPath notation and Velocity Template Language (VTL), so your mapping templates can have loops and logic. See https://velocity.apache.org/engine/devel/vtl-reference.html for more information about VTL and what you can do with it, and see http://goessner.net/articles/JsonPath/ for more information about JSONPath.

Listing E.4 Body Mapping Template

```
#set($inputRoot = $input.path('$'))
{
  "domain" : "$inputRoot.baseUrl",
  "bucket" : "$inputRoot.bucket",
  "files" : [
    #foreach($elem in $inputRoot.urls)
    {
        "filename" : "$elem.Key",
        "eTag" : $elem.ETag,
        "size" : "$elem.Size"
    }
    #if($foreach.hasNext),#end
    #end
    ]
}
```

$inputRoot is the root object of the original data (JSON object).

API Gateway uses the Velocity Template Language, so programming language constructs such as foreach and if are supported.

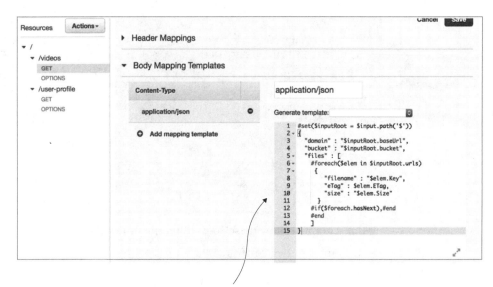

The Body Mapping Template can transform one schema to another. This is useful especially if you have no control over your client.

Figure E.5   Templates can be applied to an Integration Response and to an Integration Request.

Now that the mapping template has been implemented, you can retest your GET method to see if you get a different response from it. Go back to the main Method Execution window and click Test. Click the Test button and look at the response body. It should look similar to figure E.6.

E.1.2   *Handling errors*

So far we've only considered the happy path for your GET method. We've assumed that the GET method will always succeed and return a response with an HTTP status code of 200 and a response body with a list of your videos. But what if this isn't always the case? What if your Lambda function throws an error or encounters an unexpected result? It would be useful to return a different HTTP status code and a different body so that your client could handle it appropriately.

Let's see how you can handle happy and unhappy cases by extending your get-video-list Lambda function further. Remember that encoding parameter you included in the previous section? You're now going to use it. Consider the following requirements:

- If encoding is valid but you don't have any videos for that encoding, the GET method will return a 404 (Not Found) HTTP status code.
- If encoding isn't provided, then you'll continue to do what you've done before and return all videos with a 200 (OK) HTTP status code.
- If there is any other kind of error, you'll return a 500 (Internal Server Error) HTTP status code and the error message.

**The response should match the
GetVideoList model we defined earlier.**

```
Status: 200
Latency: 210 ms
Response Body

{
  "domain": "https://s3.amazonaws.com",
  "bucket": "serverless-video-transcoded",
  "files": [
    {
      "filename": "09689a80d3e24b53fc22e7bbbcbeba93742609a2/starwars-1080p.mp4",
      "eTag": "842840e726722a35f94394b277776edd",
      "size": "8099349"
    },
    {
      "filename": "09689a80d3e24b53fc22e7bbbcbeba93742609a2/starwars-720p.mp4",
      "eTag": "cab1e7013dd8954b0e785cde687a2406",
      "size": "3228449"
    },
    {
      "filename": "09689a80d3e24b53fc22e7bbbcbeba93742609a2/starwars-web-720p.mp4",
      "eTag": "384b7fa380b8c62252c6395f6e677a45",
      "size": "3023305"
    },
    {
      "filename": "19b7436f5facc1ae4399cad3588679bab7064f05/avengers-720p.mp4",
      "eTag": "edb72f2c34e4fcff27fed24f3d1cf935",
      "size": "2744412"
    },
```

Figure E.6   The response from the API should be different when the new model is implemented.

You're also going to configure the API Gateway to return the appropriate HTTP code and a response body based on what the Lambda function returns via its callback. You'll configure Method Response and Integration Response to make it happen. This is how it will work:

- In the API Gateway, Method Response will be configured to handle new HTTP status codes, such as 200, 404, and 500.
- Integration Response will extract the response from Lambda and decide which HTTP status code to set.

UPDATING THE LAMBDA FUNCTION

You're going to update the Lambda function to return an appropriate response when things go bad. When things go right, you'll use your callback to return the list of files as per normal. That will generate a 200 HTTP status response code. When things go bad, however, you'll generate and return an object with three properties: status code, message, and the encoding parameter. In the API Gateway, you'll write a regex to match on the status code and assign the right HTTP status to the response. You'll also extract the message and the encoding parameter and add it to the response. To do this, you'll create a new mapping template. It will override the existing mapping template that you use for the happy case.

> **Regex**
>
> The regex in the API Gateway works only if you return an error via a callback. You have to use `callback(result)` if you want your error conditions to work. If you use `callback(null, result)`, the API Gateway will ignore your regex and always choose the default response and template (which is 200 unless you change it).

Open index.js of the `get-video-list` function in your favorite text editor and replace the implementation with the following code.

Listing E.5 `get-video-list` function

```
'use strict';

var AWS = require('aws-sdk');
var async = require('async');

var s3 = new AWS.S3();

function createErrorResponse(code, message, encoding) {
  var result = {
    code: code,
    message: message,
    encoding: encoding
  };

  return JSON.stringify(result);          ◄─── This rather simple function
}                                              returns a stringified version of
                                               your error response object. It
function createBucketParams(next) {            will be used in the API Gateway.
  var params = {
    Bucket: process.env.BUCKET
  };

  next(null, params);
}

function getVideosFromBucket(params, next) {
  s3.listObjects(params, function(err, data){
    if (err) {
      next(err);
    } else {
      next(null, data);
    }
  });
}

function createList(encoding, data, next) {
  var files = [];
  for (var i = 0; i < data.Contents.length; i++) {
    var file = data.Contents[i];

    if (encoding) {
      var type = file.Key.substr(file.Key.lastIndexOf('-') + 1);   ◄───
      if (type !== encoding + '.mp4') {
```

In chapter 3 you appended the type of the encoding to the end of the name (for example, myfile-720p.mp4). Now you can check whether the requested encoding matches the end of the filename.

```
            continue;
          }
        } else {
          if (file.Key.slice(-4) !== '.mp4') {
            continue;
          }
        }
        files.push(file);
      }

      var result = {
        baseUrl: process.env.BASE_URL,
        bucket: process.env.BUCKET,
        urls: files
      }

      next(null, result)
    }

    exports.handler = function(event, context, callback){
      var encoding = null;

      if (event.encoding) {
        encoding = decodeURIComponent(event.encoding);
      }

      async.waterfall([createBucketParams, getVideosFromBucket,
          async.apply(createList, encoding)],
        function (err, result) {
          if (err) {
            callback(createErrorResponse(500, err, event.encoding));
          } else {
            if (result.urls.length > 0) {
              callback(null, result);
            } else {
              callback(createErrorResponse(404, 'no files for the given encoding
          were found', event.encoding));
            }
          }
      });
    };
```

> If the requested encoding doesn't match what's in the filename, you can skip the file and go to the next one.

> If encoding wasn't supplied, then you make a list of all files ending with mp4.

Having implemented the function, deploy it to AWS by running `npm run deploy` from the command line.

CONFIGURING THE METHOD RESPONSE

You're going to configure method response first. Choose Method Response in the Method Execution page and add two new responses:

- 404
- 500

Your page should look like figure E.7.

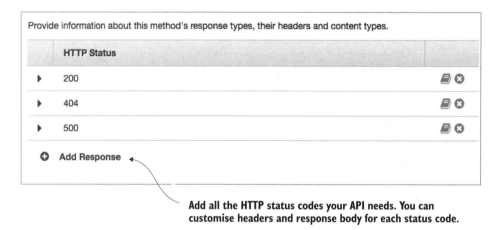

Add all the HTTP status codes your API needs. You can customise headers and response body for each status code.

Figure E.7 Don't rely on a single (200) HTTP status code. Add as many status codes as your system needs.

CONFIGURING THE INTEGRATION RESPONSE

Now you can configure the integration response. In the Method Execution page, choose Integration Response. Here you need to add three responses. You'll write a simple regex to inspect the output from the Lambda function. Then, based on the result, you'll set the right method response status. To do this, follow these steps:

1 Choose Add Integration Response.
2 Type `.*"code":404.*` in the Lambda Error Regex column.
3 Select 400 from the drop-down below and choose Save.
4 Choose Add Integration Response again.
5 Type `.*"code":500.*` in the Lambda Error Regex column.
6 This time select 500 from the drop-down and choose Save.

You should now see a view similar to figure E.8.

You've created the regex to match on the output from the Lambda function. Take `.*"code":404.*`, for example: the string `"code":404` looks for an occurrence of that specific text in the response from the Lambda function. The characters `.*` allow any other text to precede and follow `"code":404`. If you don't include `.*`, your regex will expect only `"code":404` in the response.

Expand each of the new response types you've created and repeat the following for each response:

1 Expand Body Mapping Templates.
2 Choose Add Mapping Template.
3 Type `application/json` and click the checkmark button to save.
4 Copy the mapping template from the next listing to the template edit box.
5 Click Save.

First, declare response types using Method Response. Then, map the possible responses from the backend to this method's response types.

	Lambda Error Regex	Method response status	Output model	Default mapping	
▶	-	200		Yes	✕
▶	.*"code":404.*	404		No	✕
▶	.*"code":500.*	500		No	✕
⊕ Add integration response ◀					

Click **Add integration response** to add a new **HTTP** status code mapping.

Figure E.8 Setting a new integration response requires only a regex and a method response status. You can customize header mapping and body mapping templates for each response.

Listing E.6 Mapping template for the error conditions

```
#set ($message = $util.parseJson($input.path('$.errorMessage')))
{
    "code" : "$message.code",
    "message" : $message.message,
    "encoding" : "$message.encoding"
}
```

The properties from the error response object are now available and accessible. They can be mapped to the response.

Create a JSON object from the errorMessage property. This property is always added by Lambda. It contains the stringified representation of the error object generated by the createErrorResponse function in listing E.5.

You now have a way to control exactly what the API Gateway returns when there's an error. Note that you can modify response header mappings for each response code. You can access them above Body Mapping Templates.

TESTING STATUS CODES

You can test whether the new status codes work straight from the API Gateway. Click back to Method Execution and click Test. Type 2160p in the Encoding Query String text box and click Test. After the test runs, look on the right side of the page. You should see Status set to 404 and a response body based on the mapping template you set up in listing E.6.

E.1.3 Deploying API Gateway

Having configured your GET method, you need to deploy it:

1 In the API Gateway, choose Resources under the 24-hour-video API.
2 Choose Actions.
3 Choose Deploy API.

4   You should see a dialog video with a Deployment Stage label and a drop-down.
5   From the drop-down select Dev:

If you can't choose Dev from the drop-down, it means that you didn't create a stage back in chapter 5. That's not hard to fix. Simply choose [New Stage] and type in dev as the stage name (figure E.9).

6   Click Deploy.

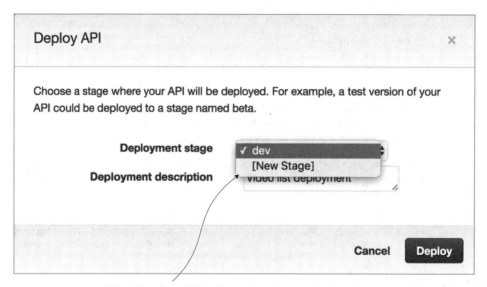

Select [New Stage] if the dev deployment stage
is missing from the list.

Figure E.9   **API Deployment via the console is a quick operation.**

You've now learned how to use models and mapping templates to exercise greater control over the API Gateway. Jump back to chapter 7 and carry on from section 7.2.5.

appendix F
S3 event message structure

This appendix covers

- S3 event message structure

If you use S3 with Lambda, you need to understand the S3 event message structure for the purpose of extracting needed information from the message. This appendix describes the structure of the event message, so that you're aware of the available properties and their expected values.

F.1 S3 structure

The following listing shows an example S3 event message after an object has been added to a bucket. This example is adapted from https://docs.aws.amazon.com/AmazonS3/latest/dev/notification-content-structure.html.

Listing F.1 S3 Event message structure

```
{
    "Records":[          ◁——— Top-level structure is an array of objects.
    {
        "eventVersion":"2.0",
```

```
"eventSource":"aws:s3",
"awsRegion":"us-east-1",
"eventTime":"1970-01-01T00:00:00.000Z",      ◁──┐ Time specified in the
"eventName":"ObjectCreated:Put",                  │ ISO-8601 format
"userIdentity":{

"principalId":"AIDAJDPLRKLG7UEXAMPLE"   ◁────── User who caused the event
},
"requestParameters":{
   "sourceIPAddress":"127.0.0.1"   ◁── IP address where the request originated
},
"responseElements":{
   "x-amz-request-id":"C3D13FE58DE4C810"
},
"s3":{
   "s3SchemaVersion":"1.0",
   "configurationID":"configRule",   ◁── Bucket notification configuration ID
   "bucket":{
      "name":"MY_BUCKET",
      "ownerIdentity":{
         "principalId":"A3NL1KOZZKExample"      ◁────── Owner of the bucket
      },
      "arn":"arn:aws:s3:::MY_BUCKET_ARN"   ◁────── Bucket ARN
   },
   "object":{
      "key":"HappyFace.jpg",               ◁────── Key of the object
      "size":1024,
      "eTag":"d41d8cd98f00b204e9800998ecf8427e",
      "versionId":"096fKKXTRTtl3on89fVO.nfljtsv6qko",  ◁──┐ Object version
      "sequencer":"0055AED6DCD90281E5"    ◁──┐              │ (if versioning
   }                                         │              │ is enabled)
  }                          The sequencer used
 }                           to determine the
]                            order of events
}
```

F.2   A few things to remember

- The key of the object is encoded. For example, the file hello world.jpg is encoded to hello+world.jpg.
- Event notifications are not guaranteed to arrive in order, but you can use the sequencer to determine which event came later (a greater hex value indicates that the sequence came later).

appendix G
Serverless Framework
and SAM

This appendix covers

- An overview of the Serverless Framework 1.x
- An overview of the Serverless Application Model

Automation and continuous delivery are important if you're building anything on a cloud platform such as AWS. If you take a serverless approach, it becomes even more critical because you end up having more services, more functions, and more things to configure. You need to be able to script your entire application, run tests, and deploy it automatically. The only time you should deploy Lambda functions manually or self-configure API Gateway is while you learn. But once you begin working on real serverless applications, you need to be able to script everything and have a repeatable, automated, and robust way of provisioning your system. In this appendix, we introduce Serverless Framework and the Serverless Application Model (SAM) to help you organize and deploy serverless applications.

Serverless Framework is an all-encompassing tool that can help to define, test, and deploy serverless applications to AWS. It's supported by a full-time team at Serverless, Inc., and a number of open source contributors from all over the world. It's a tool that's used with great success by many companies worldwide to manage their serverless applications.

SAM is an extension to CloudFormation, developed by AWS. It allows users to script their Lambda, API Gateway, and DynamoDB tables using a simple syntax and then deploy using CloudFormation commands and know-how that they already have.

G.1   Serverless Framework

The Serverless Framework (https://serverless.com) is an MIT open source framework that's actively developed and maintained by a full-time team. At its essence, it allows users to define a serverless application—including Lambda functions and API Gateway APIs—and then deploy it using a command-line interface (CLI). It helps you organize and structure serverless applications, which is of great benefit as you begin to build larger systems, and it's fully extensible via its plugin system.

G.1.1   Installation

Serverless Framework is a Node.js CLI tool, so the first thing you need to do is to install Node.js on your machine. Refer to appendix B for instructions on installation of Node.js.

> **NOTE** Serverless Framework runs on Node.js v4 or higher, so make sure you pick a recent Node.js version.

You can verify that Node.js is installed successfully by running the command `node --version` in a terminal window. You should see the corresponding Node.js version number printed out. Next, open your terminal and run `npm install -g serverless` to install Serverless Framework. When the installation process completes, you can verify that Serverless Framework is installed successfully by running the command `serverless` from your terminal.

CREDENTIALS

The Serverless Framework needs access to your AWS account so that it can create and manage resources on your behalf. To let the Serverless Framework access your AWS account, you're going to create an IAM user with admin access, which can configure the services in your AWS account. This IAM user will have its own set of AWS access keys.

> **NOTE** Normally in a production environment, we'd recommend reducing the permissions of the IAM user that the Framework uses. Unfortunately, the Framework's functionality is growing so fast that we don't yet have a list or a finite set of permissions it needs. Consider using a separate AWS account in the interim if you can't get permission to your organization's primary AWS accounts.

Follow these steps:

1 Create or log in to your Amazon Web Services account and go to the Identity & Access Management (IAM) page.

2 Click Users, and then on Create New Users, enter a name, like `serverless-admin`, in the first field to remind you that this user is the Framework.

3 Select Programmatic Access and click Next: Permissions.

4 Select Attach Existing Policies Directly and search for "AdministratorAccess." Select the administrator access policy and click Next: Review.

5 Click Create User.

6 On the next page, you'll see the access key ID and the secret access key. Save them to a temporary file. You can also download a CSV file with the keys. Click Close when finished.

You can configure the Serverless Framework to use your AWS API key and secret key using this command from a terminal:

```
serverless config credentials --provider aws --key [ACCESS_KEY] --secret
    ➥ [SECRET_KEY]
```

AWS credentials

Running `serverless config credentials --provider` will store the credentials under a default AWS profile at the following location in your computer: ~/.aws/credentials. If you followed our previous chapters, you might already have keys for the `lambda-upload` user in the credentials file. Running the previous command will overwrite your existing keys.

There are two ways you can deal with this: instead of overwriting your `lambda-upload` keys, you can either add AdministratorAccess permissions to the `lambda-upload` user or add multiple credentials to ~/.aws/credentials, like so:

```
[default]
aws_access_key_id=[ACCESS_KEY]
aws_secret_access_key=[SECRET_KEY]

[serverless]
aws_access_key_id=[ACCESS_KEY]
aws_secret_access_key=[SECRET_KEY]
```

Then add a profile setting to your provider configuration in serverless.yml:

```
service: new-service
provider:
name: aws
 runtime: nodejs4.3
 profile: serverless
```

SERVICES

A service is the Framework's unit of organization. You can think of it as a project (though you can have multiple services for a single project or application). A service is where you define your functions, the events that trigger them, and the resource your functions use, all in a single file called serverless.yml, as shown in the following listing.

Listing G.1   Service—serverless.yml

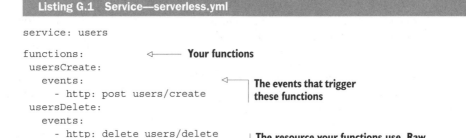

```
service: users

functions:                    ◁──── Your functions
 usersCreate:
   events:                         ◁─┐ The events that trigger
     - http: post users/create       │ these functions
 usersDelete:
   events:
     - http: delete users/delete   ┌ The resource your functions use. Raw
                                    │ AWS CloudFormation syntax goes here.
 resource:                      ◁──┘
```

The point of a service is to keep your functions and all of their dependencies together in one unit. When you deploy with the Framework by running `serverless deploy`, everything in serverless.yml is deployed at once.

PLUGINS

You can overwrite or extend the functionality of the Framework using plugins. Every serverless.yml can contain a `plugins:` property, which features the plugins the service uses (see the following listing).

Listing G.2   Plugins—serverless.yml

```
plugins:           ◁─┐ You can find a list of available plugins at
 - serverless-offline  │ https://github.com/serverless/serverless#vl-plugins.
 - serverless-secrets
```

G.1.2   *Beginning Serverless Framework*

As we've mentioned, in the Serverless Framework, a service is like a project. It's where you define your AWS Lambda functions, the events that trigger them, and any AWS infrastructure resource they require.

ORGANIZATION

In the beginning of an application, many people use a single service to define all of the functions, events, and resource for that project, as shown in the next listing.

Listing G.3   Your application

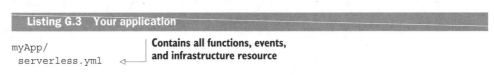

```
myApp/             ┌ Contains all functions, events,
 serverless.yml  ◁─┘ and infrastructure resource
```

But as your application grows, you can break it out into multiple services. Some people organize their services by workflows or data models and group the functions related to those workflows and data models together in the service, as shown here.

Listing G.4 Your application

```
users/
  serverless.yml
posts/
  serverless.yml
comments/
  serverless.yml
```

Contains functions for users, posts, and comments in separate files

This makes sense because related functions usually use common infrastructure resources, and you want to keep those functions and resources together as a single unit of deployment for better organization and separation of concerns.

CREATION

To create a service, use the `create` command. You must also pass in a runtime (for example, node.js or Python) that you want to write the service in. You can also pass in a path to create a directory and autoname your service:

```
serverless create --template aws-nodejs --path myService
```

The following runtimes are available in the Serverless Framework for AWS Lambda:

- aws-nodejs
- aws-python
- aws-java-gradle
- aws-java-maven
- aws-scala-sbt

> **Getting help**
>
> You can run `serverless` to see a list of available commands and then run the command `serverless <command-name> --help` to get more information about each command. Considerable information about the Framework is also available online at https://serverless.com/framework/docs/.

SCAFFOLDING

You'll see the following files in your working directory:

- serverless.yml
- handler.js

Each service configuration is managed in the serverless.yml file. The main responsibilities of this file are as follows:

- Declare a serverless service
- Define one or multiple functions in the service
- Define the provider the service will be deployed to (and the runtime if provided).
- Define custom plugins to be used
- Define events that trigger each function to execute (for example, HTTP requests)
- Define a set of resources (for example, 1 AWS CloudFormation stack) required by the functions in this service
- Allow events listed in the `events` section to automatically create the resource required for the event upon deployment
- Allow flexible configuration using Serverless variables

You can see the name of the service, the provider configuration, and the first function inside the `functions` definition, which points to the handler.js file. Any further service configuration will be done in this file, as shown in the following listing.

Listing G.5   A more complete serverless.yml example

```
service: users

provider:
 name: aws
 runtime: nodejs4.3
 memorySize: 512

functions:
 usersCreate:              ◁──── A function
   handler: index.create
   events:                 ◁──── The events that trigger this function
     - http:
         path: users/create
         method: post
 usersDelete:              ◁──── A function
   handler: index.delete
   events:                 ◁──── The events that trigger this function
     - http:
         path: users/delete
         method: delete

resource:                  ◁──── The resources your functions use.
 Resource:                        Raw AWS CloudFormation goes here.
   usersTable:
     Type: AWS::DynamoDB::Table
     Properties:
       TableName: usersTable
       AttributeDefinitions:
         - AttributeName: email
           AttributeType: S
       KeySchema:
         - AttributeName: email
           KeyType: HASH
       ProvisionedThroughput:
```

```
        ReadCapacityUnits: 1
        WriteCapacityUnits: 1
```

Every serverless.yml translates to a single AWS CloudFormation template, and a Cloud-Formation stack is created from that resulting CloudFormation template. The handler.js file contains your function code. The function definition in serverless.yml will point to this handler.js file and the function will be exported here.

LOCAL AND REMOTE DEVELOPMENT

The Serverless Framework offers a command to run your AWS Lambda functions on AWS Lambda after they've been uploaded. Additionally, the Framework allows you to run your AWS Lambda functions locally via a powerful emulator, so you don't have to re-upload your functions every time you want to run your code. You can do this by running a few commands.

This command runs your functions locally:

```
serverless invoke local --function myFunction
```

This command runs your functions remotely:

```
serverless invoke --function myFunction
```

You can pass data into both commands via the following options:

```
--path lib/data.json
--data "hello world"
--data '{"a":"bar"}'
```

You can also pass data in from standard input:

```
node dataGenerator.js | serverless invoke local --function functionName
```

G.1.3 *Using the Serverless Framework*

The Serverless Framework was designed to provision your AWS Lambda functions, events, and infrastructure resources safely and quickly. It does this via a couple of methods designed for different types of deployments.

DEPLOY ALL

The following command is the main way of doing deployments with the Serverless Framework:

```
serverless deploy
```

Use this command when you've updated your function, event, or resource configuration in serverless.yml and you want to deploy that change (or multiple changes at the same time) to Amazon Web Services. The Serverless Framework translates all syntax in serverless.yml to a single AWS CloudFormation template. By depending on Cloud-Formation for deployments, users of the Serverless Framework get the safety and reliability of CloudFormation. At a high level, these steps take place when the serverless deploy command is run:

1 An AWS CloudFormation template is created from your serverless.yml.
2 If a stack has not yet been created, it's created with no resource except an S3 bucket, which will store zip files of your function code.
3 The code of your functions is then packaged into zip files.
4 Zip files of your functions' code are uploaded to your code S3 bucket.
5 Any IAM roles, functions, events, and resources are added to the AWS Cloud-Formation template.
6 The CloudFormation stack is updated with the new CloudFormation template.

Use `serverless deploy` in your CI/CD systems because it's the safest method of deployment. You can print the progress during the deployment if you use verbose mode, as follows:

```
serverless deploy --verbose
```

This method defaults to dev stage and us-east-1 region. But you can change the default stage and region in your serverless.yml file by setting the `stage` and `region` properties inside a provider object, as the following example shows.

Listing G.6 Regions and stages

```
service: service-name
provider:
  name: aws
  stage: beta          The stage and region for
  region: us-west-2    your configuration
```

You can also deploy to different stages and regions by passing in flags, as shown in the following command:

```
serverless deploy --stage production --region eu-central-1
```

DEPLOY FUNCTION

The `serverless deploy function` method doesn't touch your AWS CloudFormation stack. Instead, it overwrites the zip file of the current function on AWS. This method is much faster than running vanilla `serverless deploy`, because it doesn't rely on CloudFormation:

```
serverless deploy function --function myFunction
```

The Framework packages the targeted AWS Lambda function into a zip file. That zip file is uploaded to your S3 bucket using the same name as the previous function, which the CloudFormation stack is pointing to. Use this when you're developing and want to test on AWS, because it's much faster. During development, people often run this command several times, as opposed to `serverless deploy`, which is run only when larger infrastructure provisioning is required.

G.1.4 Packaging

Sometimes you might like to have more control over your function artifacts and how they're packaged. You can use the `package` and `exclude` configuration for this.

EXCLUDE/INCLUDE

Exclude allows you to define globs that will be excluded from the resulting artifact. If you want to include files, you can use a glob pattern prefixed with `!`, such as `!re-include-me/**`. Serverless will run the glob patterns in order. For example, the next listing shows how to exclude all node_modules but then re-include a specific module (in this case, node-fetch).

Listing G.7 Exclude

```
package:
 exclude:
   - node_modules/**
   - "!node_modules/node-fetch/**"
```
The node-fetch folder is included but all other folders in node_modules are excluded.

ARTIFACT

For complete control over the packaging process, you can specify your own zip file for your service. Serverless won't zip your service if it's configured, so `include` and `exclude` will be ignored. An example of this is shown in the next listing.

Listing G.8 Artifact

```
service: my-service
package:
 include:
   - lib
   - functions
 exclude:
   - tmp
   - .git
 artifact: path/to/my-artifact.zip
```
Specify a path to a zip file on your own system. If your own artifact is specified, include and exclude options are ignored.

PACKAGING FUNCTIONS SEPARATELY

If you want even more control over your functions during deployment, you can configure them to be packaged independently. This allows you to optimize the way they're deployed. To enable individual packaging, set `individually` to `true` in the service-wide packaging settings. Then, for every function, you can use the same `include/exclude/artifact` config options as you can service-wide. The `include/exclude` options will be merged with the service-wide options to create one `include/exclude` config per function during packaging (see the following listing).

Listing G.9 Packaging functions separately

```
service: my-service
package:
 individually: true
```

```
exclude:
  - excluded-by-default.json
functions:
 hello:
   handler: handler.hello
   package:
     include:
        - excluded-by-default.json    ◁
 world:
   handler: handler.hello
   package:
     exclude:
        - event.json
```

> **You're including this file so it will be in the final package of this function only.**

G.1.5   *Testing*

Testing a serverless architecture can be challenging for several reasons, including the following:

- Your architecture is highly dependent on multiple third-party services, which require their own tests.
- Those third-party services are cloud-based services and are inherently tricky to test locally.
- Asynchronous, event-driven workflows are especially complicated to emulate and test.

Because of these issues, we suggest the following testing strategy:

- Write your business logic in a way that separates it from AWS Lambda's API.
- Write unit tests to verify that the business logic is working well.
- Write integration tests to verify integrations with other services (for example, AWS services) are working correctly.

EXAMPLE

Let's take a simple Node.js function as an example. The responsibility of this function is to save a user into a database and send a welcome email. See the following listing for the implementation.

Listing G.10   The mailer function

```
const db = require('db').connect();
const mailer = require('mailer');

module.exports.saveUser = (event, context, callback) => {
 const user = {
   email: event.email,
   created_at: Date.now()
 }
 db.saveUser(user, function (err) {    ◁
   if (err) {
     callback(err);
   } else {
```

> **This is a basic, made-up example in which you save a user to an imaginary database and send a welcome email.**

```
    mailer.sendWelcomeEmail(event.email);
    callback();
  }
});
};
```

There are two main problems with this function:

- The business logic isn't separated from the third-party services it uses, making it hard to test. An example of this is that the business logic is dependent on how AWS Lambda passes in data (the event object).
- Testing this function requires running a DB instance and mail server.

First, the business logic should be separated. A side benefit of this is that it will matter less whether the logic is running in AWS Lambda, Google Cloud Functions, or a traditional HTTP server. You'll separate the business logic first, as shown in the next listing.

Listing G.11 Mailer function business logic

```
class Users {
  constructor(db, mailer) {
    this.db = db;
    this.mailer = mailer;
  }

  save(email, callback) {
    const user = {
      email: email,
      created_at: Date.now()
    }

    this.db.saveUser(user, function (err) {
      if (err) {
        callback(err);
      } else {
        this.mailer.sendWelcomeEmail(email);
        callback();
      }
    });
  }
}
```

> **Note that you're passing in the callback function from the handler. You don't need to pass anything back to the handler, thus making the flow of information simpler.**

The Users class is separate and more easily testable, and it doesn't require running any of the external services. Instead of real DB and mailer objects, you can pass mocks and assert if saveUser and sendWelcomeEmail have been called with proper arguments. You should have as many unit tests as possible and run them on every code change. Of course, passing unit tests doesn't mean your function is working as expected. That's why you also need integration tests. After extracting all of the business logic to a separate module, all that's left is a simple handler function, as shown in the next listing.

Listing G.12 Mailer handler function

```
const db = require('db').connect();
const mailer = require('mailer');
const users = require('users')(db, mailer);

module.exports.saveUser = (event, context, callback) => {
 users.save(event.email, callback);
};
```

> The only responsibility of the handler is to invoke the save function.

The code in listing G.12 is responsible for setting up dependencies, injecting them, and calling business logic functions. This code will be changed less often. To make sure the function is working as expected, integration tests should be run against the deployed function. They should invoke the function (serverless invoke) with the fixture email address, check if the user is actually saved to the DB, and check if email was received.

G.1.6 *Plugins*

A plugin is custom JavaScript code that creates new, or extends existing, commands within the Serverless Framework. The Serverless Framework's architecture is merely a group of plugins that are provided in the core. If you (or your organization) have a specific workflow, you can install a prewritten plugin or write a plugin to customize the Framework to your needs. External plugins are written exactly the same way as the core plugins.

INSTALLING PLUGINS

External plugins are added on a per-service basis and are not applied globally. Make sure you're in your service's root directory; then install the corresponding plugin with the help of npm by running the following command:

```
npm install --save custom-serverless-plugin
```

You need to tell Serverless that you want to use the plugin inside your service. You do this by adding the name of the plugin to the plugins section in the serverless.yml file, as shown in the following listing. The custom section in the serverless.yml file is the place where you can add necessary configurations for your plugins (the plugins author or documentation will tell you if you need to add anything there).

Listing G.13 Adding plugins

```
plugins:
 - custom-serverless-plugin
custom:
 customkey: customvalue
```

LOAD ORDER

Keep in mind that the order in which you define your plugins matters. Serverless first loads all the core plugins and then the custom plugins in the order in which you've defined them, as shown in the following listing.

Listing G.14 Load order

```
# serverless.yml

plugins:
  - plugin1          Plugin 1 is loaded
  - plugin2          before plugin 2
```

WRITING PLUGINS

These are the three concepts you need to know when authoring plugins:

- *Command*—CLI configuration, commands, subcommands, options
- *LifecycleEvent*—An event that happen sequentially when the command is run
- *Hook*—Code that runs when a LifecycleEvent takes place during a command

A command can be called by a user (for example, `serverless deploy`); it has no logic, but simply defines the CLI configuration (for example, command, subcommands, and parameters) and the lifecycle events for the command. Every command defines its own lifecycle events, as shown in the next listing.

Listing G.15 Creating a serverless plugin

```
'use strict';

class MyPlugin {
 constructor() {
  this.commands = {
   deploy: {
    lifecycleEvents: [
     'resource',
     'functions'
    ]
   },
  };
 }
}

module.exports = MyPlugin;
```

Listing G.15 lists two events. But for each event, additional before and after events are created. Therefore, the following six lifecycle events exist in that example:

- before:deploy:resource
- deploy:resource
- after:deploy:resource
- before:deploy:functions

- deploy:functions
- after:deploy:functions

The name of the command in front of a lifecycle event is used for hooks. A hook binds code to any lifecycle event from any command, as the next listing shows.

Listing G.16   Hooks in a serverless plugin

```
'use strict';

class Deploy {
 constructor() {
  this.commands = {
   deploy: {
    lifecycleEvents: [
     'resource',
     'functions'
    ]
   },
  };

  this.hooks = {
   'before:deploy:resource': this.beforeDeployResources,
   'deploy:resource': this.deployResources,
   'after:deploy:functions': this.afterDeployFunctions
  };
 }
 beforeDeployResources() {
  console.log('Before Deploy Resource');
 }

 deployResources() {
  console.log('Deploy Resource');
 }

 afterDeployFunctions() {
  console.log('After Deploy functions');
 }
}
module.exports = Deploy;
```

Each command can have multiple options. Options are passed in with a double dash (--) like this:

```
serverless function deploy --function functionName
```

Option shortcuts are passed in with a single dash (-) like this:

```
serverless function deploy -f functionName
```

The options object will be passed in as the second parameter to the constructor of your plugin. In it, you can optionally add a shortcut property, as well as a required property. The Framework will return an error if a required option is not included, as shown in the following listing.

Listing G.17   Options in a plugin

```
'use strict';

class Deploy {
 constructor(serverless, options) {
   this.serverless = serverless;
   this.options = options;

   this.commands = {
     deploy: {
       lifecycleEvents: [
         'functions'
       ],
       options: {
         function: {
           usage: 'Specify the function you want to deploy
           ➥(for example, "--function myFunction")',
           shortcut: 'f',
           required: true
         }
       }
     },
   };

   this.hooks = {
     'deploy:functions': this.deployFunction.bind(this)
   }
 }

 deployFunction() {
   console.log('Deploying function: ', this.options.function);
 }
}

module.exports = Deploy;
```

The serverless instance that enables access to global service config during runtime is passed in as the first parameter to the plugin constructor, shown in the next listing.

Listing G.18   Accessing the global service config

```
'use strict';

class MyPlugin {
 constructor(serverless, options) {
   this.serverless = serverless;
   this.options = options;

   this.commands = {
     log: {
       lifecycleEvents: [
         'serverless'
```

```
      ],
    },
  };
  this.hooks = {
    'log:serverless': this.logServerless.bind(this)
  }
}
logServerless() {
  console.log('Serverless instance: ', this.serverless);
}
}

module.exports = MyPlugin;
```

Command names need to be unique. If you load two commands and both want to specify the same command (for example, you have an integrated command `deploy` and an external command also wants to use `deploy`), the Serverless CLI will print an error and exit. If you want to have your own `deploy` command, you need to name it something different, like `myCompanyDeploy`, so it doesn't clash with existing plugins.

G.1.7 Examples

Here are a few examples with the Serverless Framework that you can try for yourself.

REST API

In this example, you're going to create a simple REST API with a single HTTP endpoint using the Serverless Framework. The following serverless.yml (listing G.19) will deploy a single AWS Lambda function, create an AWS API Gateway REST API with an HTTP endpoint, and then connect the two. Listing G.20 shows the implementation of the Lambda function. You can deploy this easily with the `serverless deploy` command.

Listing G.19   Simple REST API—serverless.yml

```yaml
service: serverless-simple-http-endpoint

provider:
 name: aws
 runtime: nodejs4.3

functions:
 currentTime:
   handler: handler.endpoint
   events:
     - http:
         path: ping
         method: get
```

Listing G.20   Simple REST API—handler.js

```javascript
'use strict';

module.exports.endpoint = (event, context, callback) => {
```

```
const response = {
  statusCode: 200,
  body: JSON.stringify({
    message: 'Hello,
    ➥the current time is ${new Date().toTimeString()}.'
  }),
};

callback(null, response);
};
```

IoT EVENT

This example demonstrates how to set up an IoT rule on the AWS IoT platform to send events to a Lambda function. You can use this to react to any IoT events with an AWS Lambda function. You can deploy this easily with the `serverless deploy` command. The following listing shows the implementation for serverless.yml, and listing G.22 shows the Lambda function.

Listing G.21   IoT Event—serverless.yml

```
service: aws-node-iot-event

provider:
 name: aws
 runtime: nodejs4.3

functions:
 log:
   handler: handler.log
   events:
     - iot:
         sql: "SELECT * FROM 'mybutton'"
```

Listing G.22   IoT event—handler.js

```
module.exports.log = (event, context, callback) => {
 console.log(event);
 callback(null, {});
};
```

SCHEDULED

Listing G.23 is an example of an AWS Lambda function that runs on a schedule like a cron job. You can deploy this easily with the `serverless deploy` command. This listing shows the implementation of the serverless.yml file, whereas listing G.24 shows the implementation of the function.

Listing G.23   Scheduled—serverless.yml

```
service: scheduled-cron-example

provider:
 name: aws
 runtime: nodejs4.3
```

```
functions:
  cron:
    handler: handler.run
    events:
      - schedule: rate(1 minute)
  secondCron:
    handler: handler.run
    events:
    - schedule: cron(0/2 * ? * MON-FRI *)
```

Invoke Lambda
function every minute.

Invoke Lambda function
every second minute from
Monday through Friday.

Listing G.24   Scheduled—handler.js

```
module.exports.run = (event, context) => {
  const time = new Date();
  console.log(`Your cron function "${context.functionName}" ran at ${time}`);
};
```

AMAZON ALEXA SKILL

The following example demonstrates how to create your own Alexa skill using AWS Lambda. First, you need to register your skill in the Amazon Alexa Developer Portal (https://developer.amazon.com/edw/home.html). To do this, you need to define the available intents and then connect them to a Lambda function (https://developer .amazon.com/public/solutions/alexa/alexa-skills-kit/getting-started-guide). You can define and update this Lambda function with Serverless and deploy with the serverless deploy command. The following listing shows the implementation of serverless.yml, and listing G.26 shows the implementation of the function written in Python.

Listing G.25   Alexa skill—serverless.yml

```
service: aws-python-alexa-skill

provider:
  name: aws
  runtime: python2.7

functions:
  luckyNumber:
    handler: handler.lucky_number
    events:
      - alexaSkill
```

Listing G.26   Alexa skill—handler.py

```
import random

def parseInt(value):
    try:
        return int(value)
    except ValueError:
        return 100
```

```
def lucky_number(event, context):
    print(event)
    upperLimitDict = event['request']['intent']['slots']['UpperLimit']
    upperLimit = None
    if 'value' in upperLimitDict:
        upperLimit = parseInt(upperLimitDict['value'])
    else:
        upperLimit = 100

    number = random.randint(0, upperLimit)
    response = {
        'version': '1.0',
        'response': {
            'outputSpeech': {
                'type': 'PlainText',
                'text': 'Your lucky number is ' + str(number),
            }
        }
    }

    return response
```

> This function chooses a random number between 0 and 100 and then uses speech output to say what it is.

G.2 *Serverless Application Model*

AWS CloudFormation (https://aws.amazon.com/cloudformation) is an AWS service that allows you to create and provision AWS resources and services like EC2, S3, DynamoDB, and Lambda. You define resources in a text file called a *template*, and CloudFormation creates and deploys them for you. CloudFormation helps you deal with dependencies and the order in which resources are provisioned. It's a core tool for automation of infrastructure within AWS and something serious solution architects and infrastructure gurus can't do without. And, frankly, without scripting and automating infrastructure, you're not using AWS to its full potential anyway. CloudFormation, or its third-party alternative tool called Terraform (https://www.terraform.io), is something you should know.

It turns out, however, that defining serverless applications made with Lambda, API Gateway, and DynamoDB can be complex and time-consuming if you do it directly in CloudFormation. It's understandable, too: CloudFormation is older than Lambda and API Gateway and wasn't designed and optimized for serverless applications. Thankfully, the team responsible for Lambda and API Gateway saw this and came up with the Serverless Application Model (SAM).

SAM (https://aws.amazon.com/about-aws/whats-new/2016/11/introducing-the-aws-serverless-application-model/) allows you to use a simpler syntax to define serverless applications. CloudFormation can process a SAM template and transform it to standard CloudFormation syntax (something the Serverless Framework does too). It's amazing to see how elegant and succinct SAM is, compared with regular CloudFormation templates (https://docs.aws.amazon.com/AWSCloudFormation/latest/UserGuide/transform-section-structure.html). We encourage you to take a good look at SAM if you're going to automate your infrastructure and use CloudFormation. Use the simpler model and your future self will thank you for it.

G.2.1   *Getting started*

To begin writing a SAM template, create a new JSON or YAML CloudFormation template with an AWSTemplateFormatVersion at the top. First, you need to include a transform statement at the root of the template (under the template format version). The transform tells CloudFormation which version of SAM is used and how to process the template. The transform section for JSON templates must be `Transform: AWS::Serverless-2016-10-31`, and for YAML it must be `"Transform" : "AWS::Serverless-2016-10-31"`.

If a transform isn't specified, CloudFormation won't know how to process SAM (https://docs.aws.amazon.com/AWSCloudFormation/latest/UserGuide/transform-section-structure.html). The current SAM specification (https://github.com/awslabs/serverless-application-model) defines three overarching resource types that can be used within a SAM template:

- AWS::Serverless::Function (Lambda function)
- AWS::Serverless::Api (API Gateway)
- AWS::Serverless::SimpleTable (DynamoDB table)

The specification also defines a number of event source types for Lambda including S3, SNS, Kinesis, DynamoDB, API Gateway, a CloudWatch event, and more. And it allows you to specify additional properties such as environment variables for a function. Let's get into a quick example right now to see how SAM and CloudFormation can help you script and deploy Lambda functions. It's important to note that SAM may have limitations at this stage. At the time of writing, for example, an existing S3 bucket couldn't be specified as an event source. The bucket would have to be created in the template to be used as an event source for Lambda. By the time you read this book, SAM will have been improved, so take a look at https://github.com/awslabs/serverless-application-model before you begin.

G.2.2   *Example with SAM*

To work through this exercise, you must have the AWS CLI installed on your computer. If you don't have it installed, refer to appendix B for more details. You'll be invoking CLI commands so your IAM user (it's lambda-upload if you've been following the 24-Hour Video application) needs the right permissions for CloudFormation. The user must have permissions to interact with CloudFormation and S3 for artifact uploads and additional permissions to do what CloudFormation is trying to accomplish. The setup of these permissions is outside the scope of this appendix, but we encourage you to go to https://aws.amazon.com/cloudformation/aws-cloudformation-articles-and-tutorials/ for tutorials and examples. If you just want to experiment and learn, you can give lambda-upload full administrator rights (you might have done it while going through the previous section already), but don't forget to revoke them as soon as you've finished.

Assuming you have the CLI installed and lambda-upload has the right permissions, in a new directory create a file called index.js. This will be the Lambda function you're going to deploy using SAM. Copy the following code to this file. The Lambda function itself is trivial. It retrieves an environment variable called HELLO_SAM and then uses it as a parameter to the callback function.

Listing G.27 Basic Lambda function

```
exports.handler = function(event, context, callback) {
    var message = process.env.HELLO_SAM;          ◁──── Retrieves the environment
    callback(null, message);                              variable HELLO_SAM
}
```

In the same folder as index.js, create a new file called sam_template.yaml and copy the next listing to it.

Listing G.28 SAM template

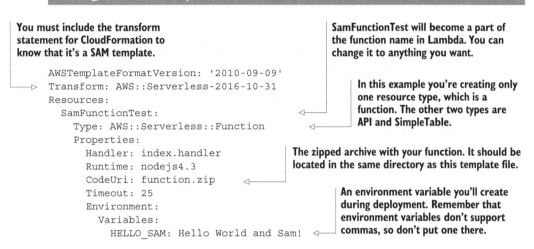

You must include the transform statement for CloudFormation to know that it's a SAM template.

SamFunctionTest will become a part of the function name in Lambda. You can change it to anything you want.

```
AWSTemplateFormatVersion: '2010-09-09'
Transform: AWS::Serverless-2016-10-31
Resources:
  SamFunctionTest:
    Type: AWS::Serverless::Function
    Properties:
      Handler: index.handler
      Runtime: nodejs4.3
      CodeUri: function.zip
      Timeout: 25
      Environment:
        Variables:
          HELLO_SAM: Hello World and Sam!
```

In this example you're creating only one resource type, which is a function. The other two types are API and SimpleTable.

The zipped archive with your function. It should be located in the same directory as this template file.

An environment variable you'll create during deployment. Remember that environment variables don't support commas, so don't put one there.

Open the directory that contains your Lambda function and zip index.js into an archive called function.zip. Make sure you call it function.zip because this is what your SAM template specifies. You also need to create an S3 bucket that will contain artifacts like the Lambda function, which CloudFormation will deploy. Jump into the S3 console and create a new bucket in N. Virginia (us-east-1). Call this bucket something akin to serverless-artifacts (your name will have to be unique). Jump back into the console and run the command given in the next listing.

Listing G.29 CloudFormation package

```
aws cloudformation package
➡ --template-file sam_template.yaml          ◁──── The template file you
➡ --output-template-file sam_processed.yaml         created in listing G.28
➡ --s3-bucket serverless-artefacts           ◁────
```

The package command will generate a new template, sam_processed.yaml, for you and place it in the current directory.

You must specify the S3 bucket you created. The name of your bucket will be different, so don't forget to change it.

The CloudFormation `package` command carries out two important actions. It uploads your zip file with the Lambda function to S3 and creates a new template that points to the uploaded file. Now you can execute the CloudFormation `deploy` command to create your Lambda function. Here's the command you need to run from the terminal.

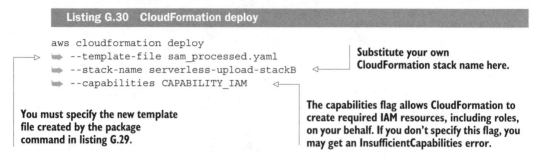

Listing G.30   CloudFormation deploy

```
aws cloudformation deploy
    --template-file sam_processed.yaml
    --stack-name serverless-upload-stackB
    --capabilities CAPABILITY_IAM
```

Substitute your own
CloudFormation stack name here.

You must specify the new template
file created by the package
command in listing G.29.

The capabilities flag allows CloudFormation to
create required IAM resources, including roles,
on your behalf. If you don't specify this flag, you
may get an InsufficientCapabilities error.

If everything goes well you should see a message in the terminal window that your stack was successfully created/updated. You can jump into the Lambda console and take a look at your new function. Don't forget to check that the environment variable was created too. If you want to learn more about SAM, check out https://aws.amazon .com/blogs/compute/introducing-simplified-serverless-application-deplyoment-and-management/ and https://docs.aws.amazon.com/lambda/latest/dg/serverless-deploy-wt.html for further information and examples.

G.3   *Summary*

Serverless Framework and SAM are tools you can use to organize and deploy your serverless applications. At this stage, Serverless Framework is a more fully featured system with many useful plugins and a strong community. If you choose it, you won't go wrong. But that doesn't mean that you shouldn't keep an eye on SAM. The mere fact that it is supported by AWS means a lot, so watch it as it grows and matures.

The one thing you might have noticed is that we haven't addressed non-AWS services. Supporting hybrid environments is difficult, and neither Serverless Framework nor SAM will be of much help (although Serverless Framework is moving quickly to support multiple vendors and compute offerings such as Azure Functions, Open-Whisk, and Google Cloud Functions). For now, however, you'll either have to stay entirely within AWS or do extra work (which may involve additional scripting) if you wish to support non-AWS services.

index